EX LIBRIS

A KELMAN
ENTERPRISES &
INTELLECTUAL
PROPERTY
PREMIER
CLASSIC

LIBERTY'S LIEUTENANTS

THE LIVES AND CAMPAIGNS OF LIBERTY'S GREATEST COMMANDERS

Matthew S. Kelman

A KE&IP Classic.
Midhurst, Ontario

FINAL EDITION XII KE&IP
Alba Gu Brath Edition

Published in Canada by
Kelman Enterprises & Intellectual Property.
Midhurst, Ontario.

DESIGNED BY MATTHEW S KELMAN.

Printed and bound in Columbia, South Carolina

17 16 15 14 13 12
11 10 9 8 7 6 5 4 3 2 1

This book is available at quantity discounts with bulk purchase for any use. For information, please email matthew@keip.ca

ISBN 978-0-9950747-0-5

Cover Design by KE&IP. © 2017
Cover Photograph of the Battle of Stirling Bridge
Courtesy of the Public Domain

Dedicated to all the heroes past, present and future,
who sacrificed their all for the cause of liberty.

The Beattie Family,

Thanks for the support.
Hope you enjoy.

-[illegible signature]

Contents

Renaissance & Revolution

Map Index

Map Legend

Infantry
Cavalry
Elephants
Scottish Schiltron
Infantry Square
Paratrooper Drop
Army Advancing into Position
Assault
Army Retreating
Bridge
Redoubt
Fortified Line
Major City/Battle
Railroad
Swamp
Mountain Range
Open Water

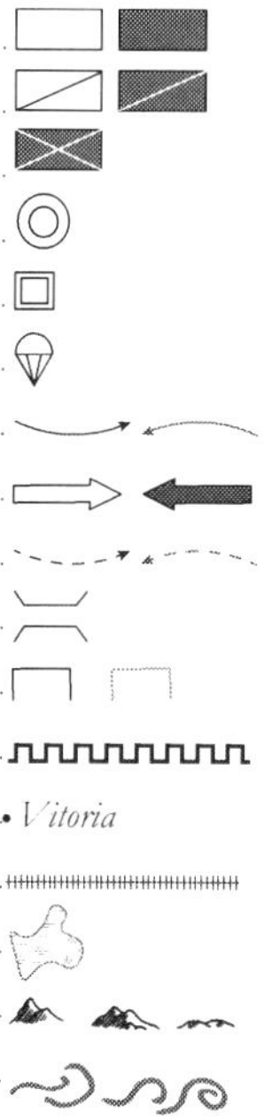

Liberty's Lieutenants

"I hope that history may be the best cure for a sick mind, at least it can remind us of what we once were and show us the depths to which we are now sinking."

-Livy, Roman Poet and Historian

Why Liberty?

Liberty is an elusive political ideal that is difficult to define and capture in its essence. Liberty is often associated with the concept of freedom, but it is not necessarily synonymous with it. Liberty is also associated with the concepts of equality and democracy but it is often at odds with them, especially with modern redefinitions to the concept of equality. This brief introduction shall begin by attempting to define the concept of liberty. It will then proceed to an examination of the philosophical foundations and brickwork of liberty as brought to us by the great thinkers of the ages. We shall wrap it up with a brief explanation of why the various soldiers were chosen with.

The express purpose of this work is two-fold. First, to emphasize to society and the reading public of the primacy that the principle of liberty should hold amongst the other ideas that politics and philosophy have given the human race. And secondly, to re-familiarize the Western and wider world with the great lieutenants of liberty and their campaigns and battles to preserve and advance liberty and civilization.

The Merriam-Webster dictionary defines liberty as "…the quality or state of being free: a. the power to do as one pleases b: freedom from physical constraint c: freedom from arbitrary or despotic control d: the positive enjoyment of various social, political, or economic rights and privileges e: the power of choice."[1] This is a good place to start, but this can be expanded on and made more specific from a purely, rights-based, political perspective. This work shall proceed under the definition of liberty that follows below.

By and large, liberty can be defined by six freedoms. One, the freedom of conscience. Essentially the freedom to think what you like, including, but not limited to, your own beliefs on religion, politics, and science. Two, the freedom of speech. Your freedom to express your (above said) beliefs in a public arena. Three, freedom of association. The right of peoples to assemble into groups, militias, and congresses for the purpose of creating laws to govern and defend themselves. Four, freedom to bear arms. The right of law-abiding, responsible men to create and bear arms for either their own personal defence or for the defence of their country. Five, the freedom of movement, essentially not to be restricted to a confined area, but rather having the freedom to roam the countryside at your pleasure or to pursue your destiny. Last but not least, the freedom to own property and to lay claim to the fruits of your labour. The right to own land and moveable property (chattel) and the right to work or not work where and when you should please. Liberty is not just a political concept, as it encompasses all aspects of human life and society and as stated above it is also defined by economics, culture, and philosophy.

While John Locke postulated that liberty is the natural condition of mankind,[2] throughout the history of civilization it would appear that tyranny and slavery are more the norm. There are very few examples of an organized group of people living and prospering under the aegis of liberty and law. But when this does occur these examples all shine through the shroud of an otherwise dark human history. The ancient Greek poleis of Athens and Thebes, the early Roman Republic, Parliamentary Britain, the American Republic and the greater (contemporary) Western world, are the few examples that stick out.

With so few examples of liberty, outweighed by so many examples of tyranny and despotic regimes it would seem that it is easier and safer, for both rulers, and ruled alike, to organize and run their societies through the ways and means of despotism and tyranny. Largely because it concentrates much of the decision making in the power of one person. However, whenever and wherever liberty did or does exist it not only becomes contagious amongst the oppressed, but it also creates a powerful energy amongst the free population that transforms them into an almost irresistible force, culturally, economically, and especially militarily.

Therefore, in many ways liberty, being the diametric opposite of tyranny and slavery, is inherently threatening to dictators and absolutist regimes and so tyrants make all efforts within their power to snuff liberty out of existence. Liberty is then, of course, not easy to maintain as it is vulnerable on multiple fronts to internal and external forces. In order to maintain it, liberty requires not only constant vigilance, but also an elastic and enduring balance between security, order and the basic freedoms.

The ancient civic values that fostered the great democracies and republics are now seen as old fashioned and requiring too great a personal effort to be given a second thought. This is especially true in today's age, where it would seem that liberty is taking a second place (or worse) to the concept of equality and the much-touted concept of 'social justice'. Through the use of market researched catch phrases and good public relations campaign, the proponents of tyranny have masked the ugly realities that government mandated equality and social justice wreak upon the freedoms, culture and economic livelihood of a people. Liberty is no longer cool, and the values required to preserve it are ridiculed and scorned in today's modern society.

♦ ♦ ♦

The ancient Greek poleis were the first states to construct a workable balance between the freedoms of its citizens and the security of their state. From the classical Greek world also came the first highly developed philosophies and theories on how a government did, could, and should be run. Socrates, the first great philosopher, lived and died with the belief that subservience to the polis and the law of the polis (or state) should be the duty of all citizens. No citizen should be above or beyond the law. While this sounds good in principle, it didn't work out well for Socrates. Democracy in Athens was volatile to say the least. More often than not it degenerated into rule by the mob controlled by demagogues. The law of the land would change with the mood of whatever regime or mob was in charge. Eventually, a regime came to power and prosecuted Socrates for the ambiguous and laughable charge of corrupting the children with his teachings. Socrates committed suicide in accordance with the court's ruling, the law was the law.

Rule by a mob was (and is) just as arbitrary and tyrannical as government by a dictator, and so, some of Socrates pupils tried to construct a more stable method of government that could sidestep the problems of direct democracy. Plato, next in line to Socrates, theorized that government and society should be organized by the best and brightest, in short bureaucrats. While Plato essentially espoused a top-down approach to government, which leaves little room for individual liberty, there is something to be said on behalf of the permanence and stability fostered through the construction of hierarchical institutions. Even if Plato's 'Republic' has similarities with modern day communist/socialist regimes, his theorizing on bureaucracy as a means to curb some of the radical and arbitrary tendencies of direct democracy went a long way towards providing political theory with an alternative to the arbitrary nature of either monarchy or direct democracy.

The best and the brightest would also be in charge of the government if it were left up to Aristotle, the next great philosopher produced by Greek culture. For Aristotle, the best and the brightest would not be made up of bureaucrats, but rather the men of great deeds and great families - the aristocracy. Another product of the destabilizing effects of direct democracy, Aristotle's theory of aristocracy aimed to moderate the will of the common man by entrusting the powers of the state in the great families. By the time of Aristotle's writing the Athenian polis was no longer a dynamic power on the world stage. The monarchs of Macedonia stood ready to unify the Greek peninsula and conquer much of the known world.

While the Macedonian kings were busy in the east, the Romans were occupied with creating the world's first republic. Located to the west of Greece, the Romans were a practical people first and foremost, without the time to philosophize about what they were doing. While they were short on political theory, they were successful in establishing an enduring mixed constitution. The secret to the success of the Roman Republic lay within the elastic balance between the aristocracy and the common man. The greatest danger to the Republic was when one man (usually from the aristocracy) attempted to co-opt the general population into crowning him their king. The Republic never succumbed to foreign aggression. Even when Hannibal and the Carthaginians had stripped Rome of most of its Italian territory, the Republic endured. It was the ambitions of its citizens that racked the state with civil war, and only when Julius Caesar and his heir Octavius had surpassed every other aristocrat did the mixed constitution of the Senate and the People of Rome cease to have any practical meaning.

For over an agonizing thousand years, the histories of mankind endured a dark age where most of the world was ruled by tyranny. There would be no peace. The only refuge for philosophy to find was within the confines of the Christian church. The only hope for mankind lay with an appeal to heaven. It would require an appeal to heaven and to the ancient gods of war for the peoples of the British Isles to assert their rights as English men against the whims of an arbitrary monarch. The Magna Carta was not crafted by political philosophers but rather was greatly influenced by an astute student of theology, Stephen Langton,[3] the power of the document was backed by the resolve of the baron's swords. That all men should be subjects of the law was not a new idea, but, none the less, it carried with it revolutionary consequences for the way men thought.

Even after the introduction of Magna Carta in England, the peoples of Europe who lived through the strife of feudalism and the middle ages had good reason to be concerned for the security of their persons. As Thomas Hobbes would put it, life was 'solitary, poor, nasty, brutish and short.'[4] The preeminent philosopher of unlimited state power, to be wielded by the monarch, Hobbes would need to be answered if the cause of liberty was to progress into the modern age. That rebuttal came to us through the philosopher John Locke.

Locke, a product of turbulent, revolutionary times, postulated that the reason people formed states was for more than just personal and economic security, they were also concerned with the preservation of their natural libertyies. In Locke's Second Treatise of Government he expanded on his social contract theory, which held that there was an unwritten covenant between the sovereign and the people. If the sovereign had overstepped the contract or failed to live up to its details, the people were justified in overthrowing the sovereign and electing a new one. This is exactly what happened during the 'Glorious (English) Revolution' where the British people disposed of their Catholic King (who had absolutist tendencies) and replaced him with the Protestant King of Holland. The new King's power was widely restricted as per the contract that invited him to come rule over Great Britain. While Locke was the preeminent apologist/intellectual for the Glorious Revolution, his influence would continue to be felt down through the ages.

The drafters of the American Declaration of Independence would practically take entire sections out of Locke's treatises. Every political philosopher that came after Locke would have to contend with his ideas about the role of government. Locke's

Chapters

Store# 00907 Chapters Barrie
76 Barrie View Drive
Barrie,ON L4N 8V4
Phone: (705) 735-6735

YOUR FEEDBACK MATTERS
Tell us about your visit today
for a chance to win a $500 giftcard
Complete our survey at.
www.indigofeedback.com

Store# 00907 Term# 002 Trans# 327859
Operator: 535JS 03/10/2018 14:28

SALE

****

CONSIGNMENT 1 $19.95G
9780999307311

****

Items: 1

Subtotal:	$19.95
GST: 5.0%	$1.00
Total:	**$20.95**
CASH:	**$25.00**
Change:	$4.05

****

With our free plum rewards program,
you could have earned 100 plum points
Join today!

****

Store# 00907 Term# 002 Trans# 327859
GST Registration # R897152665

*00907002032785*91*

35,000	$100

Explore the benefits of plum rewards and become a member for free! Visit indigo.ca/plumrewards to learn more.

Chapters Indigo COLES indigo.ca

Refunds or exchanges may be made within 14 days if item is returned in store-bought condition with a receipt. Items with a gift receipt may be exchanged or refunded onto a credit note for the value of the item at the time of purchase We cannot provide an exchange or refund on magazines or newspapers.

plum™ rewards

Points Required	Reward Value
2,500	$5
4,500	$10
8,500	$20
20,000	$50
35,000	$100

Explore the benefits of plum rewards and become a member for free! Visit indigo.ca/plumrewards to learn more.

Chapters Indigo COLES indigo.ca

Refunds or exchanges may be made within 14 days if item is returned in store-bought condition with a receipt. Items with a gift receipt may be exchanged or refunded onto a credit note for the value of the item at the time of purchase. We cannot provide an exchange or refund on magazines or newspapers.

political philosophy would take on a life of its own as the guiding philosophy of the English-speaking world, and later the wider Western world.

However, since the end of the Second World War Locke's hold on the Western world has been somewhat diminished. Even though the state-centric model of government, in which the individual's liberty is subverted to that of the collective, was defeated in the Cold War, there has been a resurgence of neo-socialist ideology amongst 'intellectuals' and the hoi polloi. While the people of Eastern Europe, only recently liberated from the boot heel of socialist tyranny, generally resist this neo-socialist, progressive trend of thinking, a significant portion of the Western population, who have lived a relatively spoiled life, have bought into the failed ideas of the state-centric approach. Only time will tell if the West can awaken itself from this juvenile phase of stupidity and get back to preserving the most fragile and precious aspect of its political heritage, liberty.

While the post-modern age has witnessed a great expansion of the world's population living under the aegis of liberty, it is also degenerating into a culture of excess and materialism very much resembling the last Roman generation at the twilight of the Republic. The younger generation needs to become familiar with the concept of liberty and also the sacrifices made by the great fighting men (and women) of the past to preserve and advance this unique and precious concept. Hopefully, it will not require another appeal to heaven.

♦ ♦ ♦

Onto the question of why were some soldiers chosen while others were not? Believe it or not, there was some method to the madness that is this book. First and foremost, the generals in question had to be fighting in service of a state dedicated to the principle of liberty. This work will make no attempt at social justice moral relativism, it is unabashedly allied to the camp of western civilization. Secondly, the commander in question had to hold the foremost/supreme level of command at some point in his or her career. This rule was somewhat bent in the first and last chapters for Xenophon and Sharon. Xenophon was one of four men who shared supreme command of the Greek ten thousand. Sharon never attained the highest level of command within the Israeli Defense Forces military structure, but later in his civilian career he became the civilian head of the IDF (as defense minister) and the Prime Minister of Israel, so in some ways, he surpassed the rest of his strictly military contemporaries.

Eisenhower's career shared similar problems when it came to meeting the criteria for this book. Technically General George Marshall held the highest level of command of the American forces during the Second World War. However, Eisenhower was the man on the ground in the theatre and was promoted to the rank of Supreme Allied Commander, Marshall was the one directing American forces from Washington. When it comes to comparing who from the Second World War held similar responsibilities to the field marshals of the pre-modern age, Eisenhower is the closest thing the western allies ever produced.

Another subject of this book which will likely create some controversy, and thus require a brief explanation, would be General Robert E. Lee. The predictable objection to Lee will be that he fought for a rebel alliance whose aim was to propagate the existence of African slavery in the southern states of America. This is an outrageously simplistic and distorted view of history for a number of reasons. This work will briefly list a few objections to the detractors of Lee's character and cause here.

The American Civil War began as a dispute over the legality of a state or region to secede from the original American union. While the continuation of slavery was the underlying cause of the secession movement, it was not until half way through the war that the abolition of slavery became a secondary war aim of the Lincoln regime. The secession of the Southern States had the moral and philosophical precedent of the American Revolution, indeed, many of the participants referred to the conflict as the Second American Revolution. If you want to argue that the Confederate secession was all about preserving the institution of slavery, you could just as easily say that about the Thirteen Colonies and their rebellion against Great Britain. If you want to condemn Lee for supposedly fighting to preserve slavery you must also impugn the reputation of George Washington who was also a Virginian slave owner. There may be some legitimate arguments over the morality of the Confederate cause, but it is hard to argue against Lee's character and motivation for fighting against the Lincoln regime. As with most things the morality of both sides in that conflict is not a clear cut black and white, but rather a few shades of gray.

The rest of the subjects of this book should, without controversy or excessive argument (other than from the politically correct-progressive wing), become evident as to their importance in history.

With that I shall leave the reader to continue on to the main portion of the work, I would suggest that you start from the beginning and go to the end, but the book is structured in such a way that you could skip to whichever section or chapters that interests the reader most. Good luck and good reading.

But before I leave you to it I would like to take the time to thank some important people. First off, I have to thank my parents for tolerating me from 2012 to 2015 while I whittled away at this, as well as my extended family and friends who were generous in their encouragement. Iris Maligot of France also deserves credit for her enthusiasm on Fogo Island and her kind donation of a stetched portrait picture of William Wallace she drew before I had barely put pen to paper. James Tuckett of Midhurst provided me with greatly appreciated feedback and suggestions helping me to better convey these stories, as well as editing my work. Of course there was Bailey, and Michelle of

Ottawa who also provided me with editorial services and who have worked tirelessly to ensure I remain both fashionable and down to earth. There are others, I am sure, whom I have neglected to mention, but you know who you are and I remain gratefully and forever,

Yours to be counted upon,

Matthew S. Kelman
Ottawa, Ontario
Spring 2017

The Ancients

"I would not be beholden to a tyrant, for his acts of tyranny. For it is but usurpation in him to save, as their rightful lord, the lives of men over whom he has no title to reign."

-Cato the Younger, Roman Statesman

Xenophon of Athens

Xenophon was born sometime around 430 BC to his father Gyrllus in the deme (neighbourhood) of Erchia in Athens.[1] When Xenophon was born the city state (or polis as they were called), Athens, was at the height of its power and ruled an empire known as the Delian League, which stretched across the Aegean Sea. Xenophon grew up in the midst of the 'Peloponnesian War' that pitted Athens, her empire and her allies against Sparta and her allies.

Very little is known about Xenophon's early life other than that he was born into an aristocratic family and that he was a student and friend of the great philosopher, Socrates. Xenophon first made an appearance on the historical stage when he volunteered as an observer for the Spartan led expeditionary force hired out by Cyrus, a Persian royal family member, against the Persian king, Artaxerxes. Before we delve any further into Xenophon's active career, we shall first examine the context of the Greek wars with the Persian Empire and the subsequent Peloponnesian War amongst the Greek poleis.

♦ ♦ ♦

In any mainstream history, Greek civilization is always the starting point from which the development of Western civilization begins. This is certainly justified when you consider the immense influence the ancient Greeks exerted on all aspects of life for later generations of Europeans. The Greeks occupied the southern portion of the Balkan Peninsula and the western coast of Asia Minor, as well as numerous colonies along the

Mediterranean, and Black Sea coastline. which both have a very mountainous geography.

The Greeks were organized into various poleis. Dramatically reinforced by geography, each polis was self-contained, self-sufficient, completely sovereign onto themselves and independent of one another, unless one was a colony.

The various poleis were constantly at war with one another, or if not currently at war, they were extremely jealous of their sovereignty and their liberties. The mountainous terrain only accentuated their sense of independence and political isolation. However, there were numerous factors that united the poleis, such as a common alphabet, common language (and variations of it), common culture, drama, mathematics, and philosophy. They also worshipped the same pantheon of gods, shared a common history, mythology, and participated in the exclusively Greek Olympic athletic games.[2] Perhaps most importantly the Greeks were united in their, varying but similar, conception of the political concept of liberty. Greece was a land of disordered liberty.

For centuries the Greek poleis and people went about their business without getting militarily involved in international affairs outside their immediate geographic theatre. Likewise, as Greece was considered a cultural backwater, no outside power felt the need to interfere in the affairs of the Greek world. No foreign power had ever intervened, but that was about to change when the Persian Empire was created in the Middle East and expanded to where it came into contact with the Greeks of Asia Minor.

The Persian Empire or Achaemenid Empire – named after its founding King, Achaemenes – ruled over the city Persis, in the modern day region of Iran. Persis and the Iranian plateau were used as a springboard for further conquest across what we now refer as the Middle East. During the 6th Century BC the Persians, under Cyrus the Great marched west to subdue the declining empires of the Babylonians and the Assyrians, after which Cyrus conquered much of Asia Minor (modern day Turkey) and the Southern Caucasus. Cyrus attempted to add the kingdoms of Central Asia to his empire, but he died while campaigning against the Massagetae in modern day Uzbekistan-Turkmenistan. The kings who succeeded Cyrus later added Egypt and the Greek states in Asia Minor and the Ionian islands into the Persian Empire. At its peak the Persian Empire was the largest empire created up to that point and was considered by its denizens to be the centre of the universe.[3]

Certain Greek states, most prominent amongst them Athens, financed a revolt among the Ionian Greeks which infuriated the Persian king, at that time Darius, who had come to consider himself the king of the entire world. Darius soon furnished an expeditionary force to subdue the 'rebellious' Ionians and to punish those agitators in Greece for their instigation of rebellion within his Empire. This 'instigation' against the Persian Empire (or support for Greek liberty) began the first in a series of Greco-Persian wars in recorded history. After crushing the revolts in Ionia and the Aegean, Darius crossed the Dardanelles straits into Europe. But before Darius moved south into Greece, he turned his army north against the Scythian tribes. Located in modern day Bulgaria, Romania, Ukraine and Russia, the Scythians were a nomadic herding people who did not build permanent structures. In the face of the Persian advance instituted a policy of scorched earth, refusing to do battle with Darius. Unable to force the Scythians into a pitched battle, the Persians fruitlessly pursued the Scythians over the Danube River to somewhere on the Volga River. Darius gave up the chase and returned back to Asia Minor by the way he came, to plan his actions against the Greek poleis.[4]

♦ ♦ ♦

The Persian War began in earnest when Darius sent one of his generals back over the Dardanelles to invade the sparsely locat-

EPIRUS
THESSALY
EUBOE
IONIAN SEA
Ithica
Delphi
BOEOTIA
Thebes
GULF OF CORINTH
ATTIC
Athens
Corinth
PELOPONNESUS
Argos
Sparta

The Classical Greek Poleis

R. DNIEPER
R. DON
SCYTHIA
R. DANUBE
BLACK SEA
MACEDON
THRACE
Sinope
BITHYNIA
Delphi
Thermopylae
Thebes
Corinth
Athens
Sparta
AEOLIA
CAPPADOCIA
Trapezus
LYDIA
IONIA
AEGEAN
SEA
CARIA
ARMENIA
MEDITERRANEAN SEA
CYPRUS
ASSYRIA
R. TIGRIS
SYRIA
R. EUPHRATES
Cunaxa
EGYPT
LIBYA
R. NILE
RED SEA
ARABIA
ETHIOPIA

The Persian Empire

ed poleis of the northern region of the Balkan Peninsula. Unlike the Scythians in the far north, the Greek poleis had nowhere to run and precious little territory to trade for time. The poleis in the north succumbed to the weight of the Persian numbers, but the Persian progress towards the south was hindered by the oncoming winter. While his army in the north was held up, Darius sent another army across the Aegean Sea in ships to attack the island of Euboea and then Athens. This force succeeded in razing Euboea before proceeding towards Athens along the coastline. The Persian general decided he would disembark some of his troops at the beaches of Marathon, a mere twenty-three miles from Athens, in the hope that it would draw out the main Athenian hoplite army* so that the rest of the Persians could sail around to an unguarded Athens and capture the city with the aid of Persian sympathizers within Athens.[5]

The ruse at Marathon worked; the hoplites were drawn out to the beaches as was expected. But something incredible and unexpected (for the Persians) happened next. The Athenian hoplites did not wait and rest before attacking the disembarked Persian force. Instead they plunged into the offensive with their incredibly disciplined phalanx formation and after heavy fighting drove the Persians back into the cover of their ships. The hoplites were heavily armoured and highly disciplined for fighting as a single unit. In contrast the Persians were lightly armoured soldiers, and trained to fight as individual skirmishers.

Under confined circumstances such as the beach of Marathon, the hoplites could dominate the battlefield almost regardless of the numbers arrayed against them. After the surviving Persians retired to the safety of their ships, the Athenians preformed another feat of resilience by counter marching the twenty-three miles back to the city and arrived in time before the

* Hoplites were heavily infantry that were armed with a shield and spear. They were generally made up of the landowning classes, and fought in closely pack lines with their shields overlapping each other.

Persian ships came into view of the city.*[6] Seeing that subduing Athens would require a lengthy siege that was by no means guaranteed to succeed, the Persians opted to withdraw back to their bases in Asia Minor to rebuild their forces for another invasion at a later date. Darius intended to command the next invasion of Greece in person, but his life was cut short†, and so, the job was left to his son Xerxes.

After Darius's death the Persian Empire entered into a period of civil war and anarchy where succession to the throne was hotly and violently disputed. During this time, Egypt broke away from the empire. Order was restored only after Xerxes killed all his competitors and assumed the throne for himself. The Greek poleis were given a few years of reprieve as Xerxes moved to recapture Egypt and his North African territories. After successfully doing so, Xerxes turned his greedy eyes back to his father's unfinished business in Greece. He proceeded to assemble troops from every corner of the empire for the ultimate showdown with the Greek poleis.

In the intervening years the Athenians had discovered rich silver veins in Attica to the east of their city. The democracy was persuaded by the politician-soldier, Themistocles, to spend their newfound riches on the construction of a vast new fleet of triremes‡, instead of their individual material welfare and vanities. The silver was able to construct about two hundred triremes, which was an unheard of number for the small Greek poleis.[7]

Contemporary sources record that Xerxes invasion force numbered in the millions. While this is highly unlikely due to limits imposed by the realities of logistics and geography, it is

* This is where we get the tern 'marathon' from. The length of a modern marathon is also 23 miles, the distance from Marathon to Athens.

† Probably do to over exertion campaigning to put down a revolt against his authority in Egypt.

‡ Triremes were state of the art battle ships during this time period. They employed three banks of rowers on both sides with a massive ram on the prow. The object was to pick up speed via rowing, and raw the prow into the side of a ship, or else board the enemy ship and engage them hand to hand.

none-the-less highly probable that Xerxes could have mustered numbers into the hundreds of thousands.[8] Regardless of the actual number, the invasion force was large enough to require complete logistical support from the Persian navy. With this in mind the Greeks could deduce that the logical route of invasion would be along the coast so that the Persian army could keep in contact with the navy and its source of supply; the Persians did exactly what was expected of them.

Bickering amongst the leaders of the various poleis made it impossible for the Greeks to mount a sufficient defence in a logical and strategic location. The Greeks could have probably stopped the Persian advance indefinitely if they had agreed to commit sufficient manpower resources to the mountain pass at Thermopylae, but alas they did not. The pass at Thermopylae was a narrow path with a cliff running down to the seas on one side and a mountain on the other. It was one of the only feasible routes for an army the size of Xerxes's to cross into southern Greece.

A Spartan King,* Leonidas, defied the Spartan assembly and marched with three hundred hand-picked Spartans to the pass of Thermopylae. The three hundred Spartans combined with about one thousand Greek allies to form a human wall of shields in order to block the Persian advance. For three days which the Persians were unable to break through the wall of shields until a Spartan traitor defected to the Persian side and guided a group of Persians down a goat path into the rear of the Spartans. Once surrounded Leonidas sent the allies home while the Spartans fought and died to the last man. The heroic death of the Spartan king and the loss of Thermopylae gave the Greeks a much needed sense of urgency. Unfortunately, the best place for a common defence had been lost.

The polis of Thebes was shortly thereafter conquered and Athens was quickly coming within distance of the Persian war

* Sparta normally had two kings.

machine. Luckily for the Greeks a successful naval engagement off the coast of Artemisium, on the island of Euboea, wrecked a sizable contingent of the Persian navy. Furthermore, as the Persian navy attempted to sail around Euboea a storm further dwindled the numbers of their navy. Regardless of the losses, the Persian navy still out-numbered the Greeks by roughly three or four to one.[9]

The Spartans and many of the remaining Peloponnesian allies were lobbying the allied council-of-war to build a wall across the Isthmus of Corinth* in order to create another easily defendable barrier. This proposal would leave the polis of Athens out of the protective cordon, without necessarily guaranteeing success to the defence of the Peloponnesus. The Athenians would be welcome to have their ships fight along-side the remaining allied navies, but the Persians would have numerous locations to land their troops, while it would be impossible for the allies to cover them all. The Athenians had consulted the oracles at Delphi for advice as to what course they should take. The message returned from the oracle was cryptic (as usual), the Athenians should 'seek refuge within wooden walls'.[10] Debate ensued amongst the Athenians about the meaning of the oracles' divinations. Some believed they should build a wooden palisade around their Acropolis and make a last stand within the polis. While others believed they should evacuate the people to the nearby island of Salamis and to defend themselves within the wooden walls of their recently built triremes.[11]

The few Athenians, who believed the palisades would protect them remained in the city while the majority were evacuated to Salamis. Those who remained in the city were destroyed when the Persians razed the evacuated city. It was now that Athens faced a truly perilous situation, if the navy retreated with the allies to Corinth their citizens on Salamis would be helpless when

* A land bridge some six miles long that connects the Pelopponeseus to the rest of the Balkan peninsula.

THESSALY
1.
Thermopylae
Delphi
GULF OF CORINTH
Corinth
PELOPONNESUS

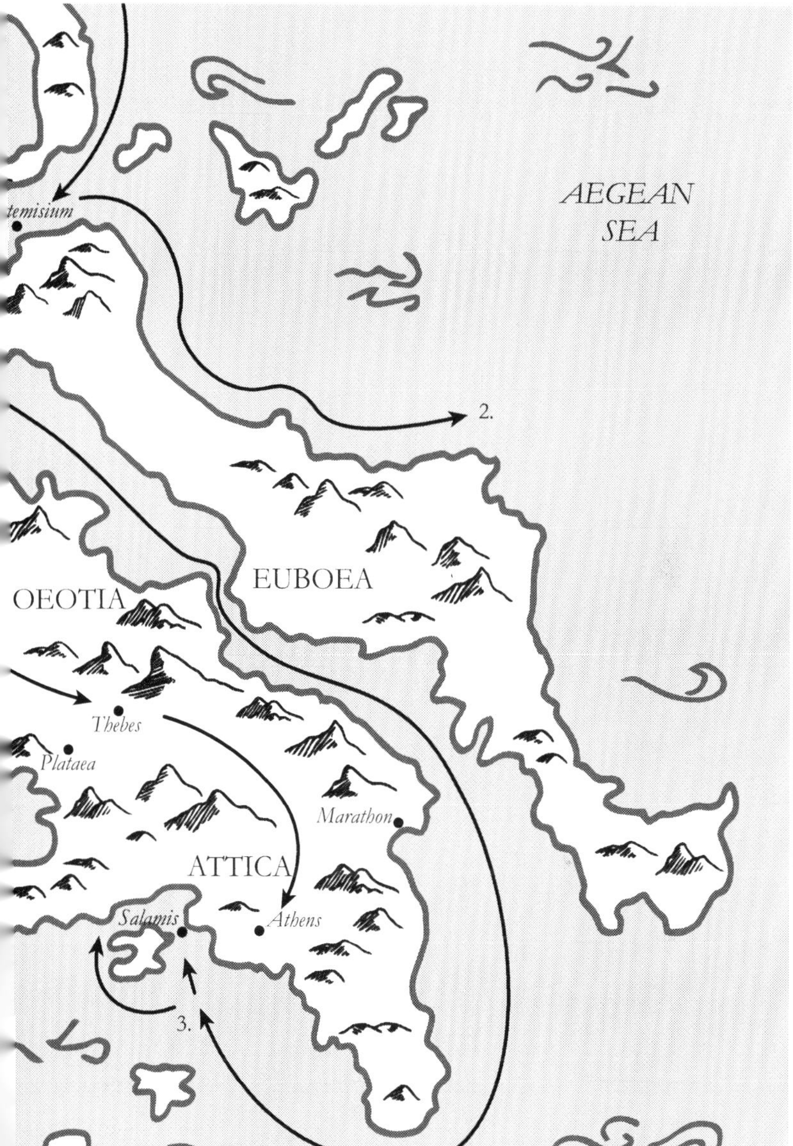

The Second Greco-Persian War

1. Battles of Thermopylae and Cape Artemisium. 2. Storm destroys large detachment of Persian Fleet. 3. Battle of Salamis.

the Persian navy inevitably arrived. On the other hand, it would be difficult to convince the allies to remain in the vicinity of the recently desolated Athens, instead of withdrawing to Corinth. Themistocles, the politician-soldier, sent an envoy to Xerxes saying that the Athenians were ready to defect from the Greek camp if only the Persians would show initiative and cut off the Greek escape.[12] In order to surround the Greek fleet, Xerxes would need to send a sizable detachment around the island Salamis to show up in the Greek rear

Xerxes took the bait; Themistocles was able to lure the main contingent of the Persian navy into the confined space of the Straits of Salamis before the flanking detachment could play upon their rear, thus nullifying the numerical advantage of the Persians. The allied Greeks were forced to commit to the fight instead of retreating to Corinth. The better disciplined and tactically superior Greeks were able to annihilate their Persian counterparts making the Battle of Salamis one of the most decisive naval encounters ever and effectively stole the momentum away from the Persians. The remaining contingent of the Persian navy was ordered to withdraw to safer harbours in the north to defend the boat bridge, while the remaining Persian land forces would be forced to fend for their own supplies. Shortly after Salamis, Xerxes left the campaign in Greece and crossed back over his floating bridge into Asia Minor. The general that Xerxes left in charge withdrew the army to the north where it would be easier to forage for supplies while winter set in.

Once spring returned in 479 BC the Persians marched back south to finish their job, this time the Greeks were unified under the leadership of the Spartans. At the Battle of Plataea in southern Boeotia, the Persians were defeated in pitched battle and forced to retire back across the Dardanelles. The combination of their defeat at Salamis and Plataea had brought Xerxes grand plan for the subjugation of the independent Greek poleis to naught. The liberty and independence of the Greeks had been saved by their two most successful polis; Athens at sea and Sparta on land.

♦ ♦ ♦

With the threatening shadow of Persia now gone from the Greek horizon, the various poleis were once again free to pursue their own destinies. Sparta was quick to give up what ships it had built and the position of leadership it had attained to return to their land locked, insular ways. In contrast, Athens expanded its navy and increased its influence throughout the Aegean and Mediterranean seas by establishing colonies and developing commercial relationships with pre-existing poleis. Athens was, through its constitution a freer, more dynamic society and was becoming an irresistible force culturally, economically, politically and militarily. In addition to the Athenians growing maritime empire, they also constructed a wall around their entire city which ran down to the sea to include their famous port, the Piraeus, within the defensive parameter.[13] During this time period siege craft and the technologies required for effective siege warfare were not highly developed, so these newly built walls made Athens nearly impervious to the threat of invasion and siege as long as its fleet and trade routes remained intact.

Tensions had been simmering for a long time but war amongst the Greek poleis officially broke out when the Thebans (allies of Sparta) invaded Plataea (allies of Athens) and took their city through the use of a ruse.* The small Theban garrison was ejected from Plataea after brutal street fighting. War would now escalate to include all the major Greek poleis. Sparta and her allies, now known as the Peloponnesian League, were the first to make a move after hostilities were officially declared.[14] The league invaded the countryside of Athens (Attica) with a

* Two private citizens opened the gates of Plataea to three hundred Theban soldiers in the hope that the Thebans would over throw the democratic government and bring the city into alliance with Sparta and Thebes. The Theban commander, however, did not resort to violence and instead attempted to persuade the Plataean population.

massive force of hoplite infantry. The Athenian strategy, developed by its ablest leader, Pericles, was to withdraw from Attica into the Long Walls whenever the Peloponnesians invaded and to use their navy to maintain their maritime empire and to sail around the Peloponnesus to harass the Spartans and her allies in the rear.

Even with the Athenian evacuation of Attica, the Peloponnesians found it difficult to permanently desolate the land of Attica. But, the evacuation of Attica created overpopulation within the city walls. Unfortunately for the Athenians, a plague broke out inside the city due to the confined quarters created by the influx of refugees from Attica, and a lack of sanitation infrastructure within the Long Walls. The plague absolutely devastated the Athenian population, possibly killing around one third of its metropolitan citizenry.[15] Among the deaths was the Athenian leader, Pericles. Pericles death began a competition amongst the next best men, or the best connected men to fill the vacant role of wartime leader.

Both Athens and Sparta would persistently change their strategies as the war dragged on, until they found a strategy that would work. After the initial Spartan invasions of Attica, the Athenians began to raid the Spartan coastline, attempting to deprive Sparta of their slave labour force by promising the Messenians freedom if they defected. Meeting with limited success along the Peloponnesian coast, the Athenians next attempted to cut off the Spartan's food supply in Sicily by launching a massive amphibious invasion force against the polis of Syracuse. The siege of Syracuse was a colossal disaster for Athens as it destroyed most of its army and a large portion of its navy as well as making a full time enemy out of Syracuse.* The disaster at Syracuse crippled Athens militarily and the polis was never able to regain the initiative again.[16]

After multiple failed attempts to bring the Athenians out of

* Syracuse owned the second largest Greek navy.

their walls, the Spartans began marching against the Athenian colonies and allies' mainland territories, those primarily being in the northern regions of Greece. Meeting with success there, many of the northern Greek states now aligned themselves with Sparta; the next phase of the war saw the Spartans drawing the Persians into the conflict as the financial backers of the Peloponnesian League's massive naval construction program.[17] With Persian gold and engineering assistance from their maritime allies, Corinth and Syracuse, the Spartans took to the seas and now attempted to strangle the Athenians of their food supply from the agricultural land around the Black Sea and to deprive the Athenians of their colonies and allies in the Aegean Sea.

Even after their disaster at Syracuse, the Athenians still had plenty of fight left in them and most importantly their naval crews and commanders were experts at their maritime trade. The Spartans on the other hand were green when it came to naval combat and this inexperience cost Sparta many losses. However, Persian gold was almost inexhaustible and the Spartans were able to recover the losses they incurred. Eventually the Spartans gained more naval experience and found themselves a capable naval commander, Lysander. Through confusing and deceptive movements Lysander was able to disperse the Athenian forces throughout the Aegean Sea, while he concentrated all his ships at the Dardanelles Straits.[*18] When the Athenians realized where Lysander was, they rushed to the scene to protect their grain supply. At the Battle of Aegospotami, Lysander annihilated the Athenian fleet while it was beached and resupplying. Caught by surprise the Athenian commander, Conon, barely escaped with a fraction of his original fleet. Only twenty out of roughly one hundred eighty ships made it back to Athens.[19] After Aegospotami, Athens' ability to resist was broken. Lysander sailed directly to Athens and forced them to surrender in the spring of 404

* The Dardanelles Straits were the natural chokepoint for grain ships from the Black Sea's shores.

B.C.

The treaty forced the Athenians to tear down the Long Walls and installed thirty pro Sparta, pro Lysander aristocrats, known as the thirty oligarchs, to govern in place of the former democracy. The end of the war was supposed to represent the liberation of the Greek polis from the yoke of the Athenian Empire, but the Spartans were not particularly idealistic nor did they act out of anything short of self-interest. Once the Spartan kings realized that the thirty oligarchs were merely puppets of Lysander and that Lysander was becoming more powerful than themselves, they took action and restored Athens to a democracy.[23] The restored democracy in Athens promised amnesty for those who collaborated with the thirty oligarchs.*

The twenty-seven year conflict ended with the Athenian Empire in ruins and the Spartan led coalition in no place to take over the reins of power. In fact the entirety of Greece was in shambles and the possibility for a war of all against all had more or less returned to the peninsula. The Peloponnesian War exposed the thin veneer that separated the 'civilized' world from that of 'barbarian' and the near total destruction of law, order and the sinews of civilization were unprecedented in the annals of history. Even in times of peace the men of Greece were well trained in the art and arts of war, but now after a long brutal war there was an abundance of well trained, well-armed and socially destabilizing young men looking for work.[20]

♦ ♦ ♦

In a sense, the Spartans owed the Persians a great debt for the gold given to them to finance the construction of their navy. With the death of the Persian King, Darius II, and the subsequent rebellion of Cyrus the Younger against his brother, now king, Artaxerxes II, the Spartans believed they could avoid paying their debt in full by helping to install the friendly

* None-the-less the democracy ended up condemning the philosopher Socrates to death, for his alleged collaboration with the oligarchs and his 'corruption' of the youth with his unorthodox philosophical notions.

Cyrus to the Persian throne. To that end a Spartan commander, Clearchus, raised a mercenary army of Greeks to assist Cyrus in his upcoming battle with Artaxerxes. Amongst the Greeks was the Athenian, Xenophon, who joined the expedition as an observer and friend of one of the commanders. Socrates advised Xenophon to consult the oracle at Delphi as to the advisability of joining the expedition. Seemingly set in his way to go, Xenophon disingenuously asked the oracle what sacrifices he should make before leaving. This would earn Xenophon a stern rebuke from his mentor Socrates. None-the-less Xenophon would embark with the rest of the Greeks on their campaign into Asia.[21] Cyrus hired the Greeks under the pretension of putting down a rebellion in Asia Minor. Once the rebellion was subdued, Cyrus kept marching east through Syria towards the Euphrates River. The Greeks became suspicious of Cyrus' true intention, but were persuaded to continue through a sense of loyalty to Cyrus and by the allure of loot and a privileged position at the court of Cyrus after he became king.

The two Persian brothers met with their armies on the lower Euphrates near the town of Cuxana, a few miles away from the city of Babylon. Cyrus positioned his Greek mercenaries on his right flank along the eastern bank of the Euphrates. Cyrus, himself was in the centre of his line with a body guard of six hundred Persian cavalry, and to his left he positioned his Persian and Asian infantry. Artaxerxes line was much longer than Cyrus' as he commanded almost twice as many men; correspondingly his line was twice as long. When Cyrus' line advanced the Greeks smashed through the Persian left flank, but Cyrus' left wing was scattered as it was outflanked and turned. Cyrus' royal cavalry bodyguard charged headlong into Artaxerxes' bodyguard in an attempt to kill his brother, Cyrus was killed in this action.[22] Upon the news of Cyrus' death, a panic arose amongst his Persian followers and they promptly surrendered to Artaxerxes as a result.

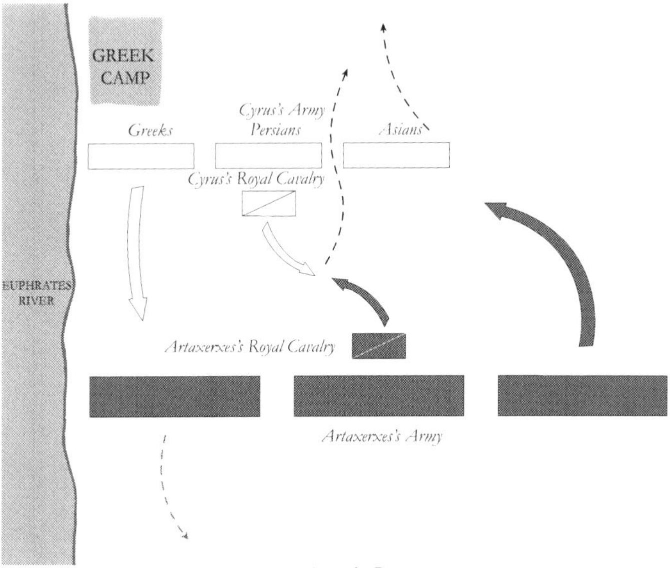

Battle of Cunaxa

The Greeks on the other hand, did not receive the news about Cyrus' death and continued to fight. By the end of the day Artaxerxes had won the battle and was in possession of the Greek camp, but the Greeks had barely lost a man and regardless of their camp property they were still in possession of all their military accoutrements. On the day after the battle, the Persian king called a parlay with the Greeks so there could be peace between the two camps and the Greeks could go home in safety. At the parlay the Greeks and the Persians came to an agreement regarding the Greeks return home; the Persians would provide guides and supply markets while the Greeks promised to leave the country in an orderly and peaceable fashion.[23]

♦ ♦ ♦

On the march to Cuxana the Greeks and Cyrus had ravaged the country side in their requirements of supply, so much so, that it would have been impossible for the Greeks to return home by the same route and expect to be fed. Instead of heading directly back to the Mediterranean, the Persians began by marching the Greeks east over the Tigris River, after which, they went north with the object of following the Tigris to its headwaters through the Armenian mountains to the Euxine (Black) Sea and from there on ships back to their homes in Greece.

All the while, the Persians were guiding the Greeks; both sides would post guards at night and kept themselves in a state of military preparedness ensuring that tensions remained high in both camps. One day the Greek general, Clearchus, and the Persian commander, Tissapherenes, agreed to parlay in an effort to relax the tension. The meeting went well and Clearchus left feeling as if he had gained a friend. Tissapherenes invited Clearchus and the Greek officers to dine with him that evening as friends. At the dinner, the Persians had the Greek officers murdered under the assumption that the leaderless Greeks would fall apart and be easy prey for the Persians.[24] When the Greeks first got wind of what happened to their officers they became extremely demoralized until Xenophon roused them with a fiery speech extolling their hitherto virtuous behavior (as opposed to the example of Persian treachery) and outlined their numerous advantages. Furthermore, the Greeks went on to hold elections to fill the vacant positions left by the murdered officers. One of the four elected to hold the high office of general was Xenophon of Athens.[25] The Greek mercenaries would transform themselves from a leaderless mob into a fighting, marching polis.

The army was first divided into four sections, a vanguard, rearguard, left-wing, and right-wing; each was commanded by one of the four elected generals. Xenophon opted to command the rearguard. As the army began their march home they continued north and crossed the Zabatos River on their first day without Persian guides. While the Greeks were unrivaled as heavy infantry, it quickly became obvious to them that the Persians had superior light infantry and cavalry for harassing the Greeks as they went. At their first encounter the Greek rearguard was effectively engaged by a small band of Persian archers and cavalry. When the Greek hoplites tried to sally forth and attack the archers, the archers would retreat and open fire once again from a safe distance; they were only saved by the coming of night.

Without archers or cavalry of their own, the heavily armoured hoplites didn't stand a chance in catching up with the Persian archers, let alone dealing any damage to them. However, this changed when the Greek commanders were discussing the day's shortcomings and realized that they possessed men from the island of Rhodes who were experts in the use of the sling.* The Greek slingers, though few in numbers, could easily outrange the distance of the Persian bowshot. When the Persians returned with greater numbers of cavalry and archers soon after the first engagement they were met with an unwelcome surprise.

* The sling was a simple weapon consisting of two cords and a pouch in the middle. The user would load a projectile into the pouch and rapidly swing the cord in a circular motion, releasing one of the cords when it was up to speed. Properly used, the sling could outdistance the projectile of a bow.

The Greek slingers had a hard time missing their targets as the Persians came on in such a large body.[26] After the Greeks got the better of them, they were able to continue their march unhindered from the now ineffective Persian skirmishers.

It was at this time that the Greek commanders reorganized their commands and created more divisions at a lower level with junior officers to make the giant square formation more efficient to maneuver when it encountered narrow roads, river fords, bridges or mountain passes.[27] It should be noted here that the Greek commanders and their democratic form of governance allowed for input to come from the lower ranks and be heard and implemented by the upper echelon of command. A combination of discipline and decentralized command provided the Greeks with the mechanisms through which they could quickly adapt their tactics to the changing realities on the ground.

♦ ♦ ♦

Shortly after the initial skirmishes with the Persians, the Greeks were approaching broken terrain. The hills and small mountains were a welcome sight for the Greeks as it would begin to nullify the advantage of the Persian cavalry. Regardless of their nullified cavalry, the Persians had no desire to let off the pressure, and as soon as the Greeks were descending the first hill the Persians appeared on the crest and began to rain arrows down on the unsuspecting Greeks. The surprise and the advantage of elevation kept the Greek slingers and archers within the protective shield wall of the hoplites. The hoplites charged back up the hill, but to no avail, the Persian skirmishers retreated back to safety before the hoplites could come to grips with them. Xenophon kept the hoplites on the crown of the first hill while he sent some slingers from the right wing up the mountain ridge that ran parallel to the road on which the Greeks were now marching. With the slingers now on a higher elevation than the Persians, the hoplites could safely descend the hill and made it safely to the next village to camp.

After recouping their energy for a few days the Greeks set out again and came upon a plain where the Persians could again use their cavalry advantageously. The Greeks were quick to occupy and encamp at another village, believing it would be advantageous for them to withstand an attack from a stationary position, as opposed to taking their chances in the open field. Seeing the Greek defensive preparations from a distance, the Persians decided to withdraw to their own encampments at a distance from the Greeks (as it was their usual practice), so that it would be difficult for the Greeks to affect a night attack. Seeing the Persian withdrawal, the Greeks packed up and stole a night march on the Persians. It was a few days before the Persians would appear within sight of the Greeks again.

Through the use of their own night march, a contingent of Persians was able to occupy a high position dominating the road, while their main army was coming into view of the Greek rear. As the Greek vanguard halted before the Persian blockade on the heights, Xenophon was summoned to the vanguard by its commander, Cheirisophus. The two generals held council and it was decided that Xenophon would take three hundred hoplites and the slingers from the vanguard and ascend a second hilltop that could be used to dislodge the Persians on the high ground. The Persian detachment spied Xenophon's movement and a race to the top ensued.

While Xenophon was urging his hoplites to go faster, one of his subordinates complained that it was easy for Xenophon to do so while mounted on his horse. And so, Xenophon dismounted from his horse and took up the race with his men on foot. However, the rest of the men shamed the lone dissenter and requested that Xenophon remount his horse and lead them on.[28] The Greeks won the race to the top and the Persians fled as quickly as they realized that their advantage of elevation had been nullified. Seeing that the Greeks had sprung the trap Tissapherenes and the main body of Persians turned off the main road and disappeared from sight, while the ten thousand Greeks resumed their march.

The Persians reappeared as the Greeks were settling back into camp and killed some of the Greek foraging parties. The Persians then began to burn villages in the vicinity of the Greeks in order to deny them supplies. Once again the Greeks were stricken with anxiety as they witnessed the burning villages, until Xenophon roused their spirits with a speech. Afterwards the generals called a council-of-war and interrogated some recently captured locals so as to get a better idea of where they should head next.

To the south was the province through which they had just travelled and the main Persian army. To the west was the Tigris River, which was too deep and too wide for the men to cross safely with the Persians in such close vicinity. To the east lay the ancient Persian capital, Persis and Susa. And to the north lay mountains occupied by the Carduchians, a tribal society who were enemies of the Persian king. The prisoners/guides told them that beyond the Carduchians' territory lay the province of Armenia and beyond that lay the Euxine Sea from which they would be able to procure ships for the last leg of the journey home to Greece. Seeing the stupidity or impossibility of going east, south, or west, the generals decided to continue going north.

Another night march by the Greeks brought them to the foothills on the border of the Carduchians territory. As the Greeks ascended the first mountain the Carduchians fell back out of fear and regrouped. The Persians declined to follow the Greeks into the Carduchians' territory as they had previously ventured into these mountains with a large force, barely a man made it back alive.[29]

♦ ♦ ♦

The Greeks had hoped that the Carduchians would let them pass through their country unmolested as they both had a common enemy in the Persians. This was not to be, as the Carduchians fell upon the Greek rear guard as they descended into a valley on their first evening in the new land. During the ambush a relatively small number of Carduchians inflected considerable damage on the unsuspecting Greek rearguard.[30] Knowing this would be an uphill battle (both literally and figuratively), the Greeks prepared themselves for this difficult march by jettisoning any unnecessary possessions and camp followers. After a few days of skirmishing with the Carduchians, the Greeks arrived at an especially difficult mountain pass that the Carduchians had occupied in advance and prepared a defence before the Greeks had a chance.

Luckily for the Greeks, Xenophon's rearguard had captured a few Carduchians and had interrogated them for information pertaining to another route through the mountains. The prisoners advised the generals that there was another, less obvious, route that could be taken, but only if the Greeks seized it before the Carduchians could. And so, the Greeks devised a plan to seize the second path without alerting the Carduchians to their intentions. They called for volunteers to come forth who would take the prisoners as guides and capture the pass in the early evening, while Xenophon would take the rearguard up to the main pass in order to fix the Carduchians attention upon that area.[31] The volunteers were to spend the night on the pass and attack the main body of Carduchian defenders from the flank when the morning came. Before launching their flank attack, they would sound a trumpet as a signal for the main body of Greeks to come up the second pass in support of the volunteers.[32]

The plan worked, except that in the darkness of the previous evening the volunteers did not completely ascend the heights of the pass, but when the morning came they were still able to attack the main body of Carduchians and put them to flight. The Carduchians withdrew to a second hill, which they proceeded to occupy and prepared for a second stand. The Greeks began their advance against the second hill, while Xenophon left a few men to guard the first hill lest the Carduchians return to reoccupy it. As soon as the Greeks approached the second hill the Carduchians evacuated it and withdrew themselves to a third and steepest hill. Once again the Carduchians withdrew upon the Greek advance from the third hill, but unbeknownst to Xenophon, the Carduchians were maneuvering into the rear of the Greek column. When Xenophon had ascended the third hill, he saw what was happening, but there wasn't much that could be done at that point as the Carduchians succeeded in surrounding the Greek guards occupying the first hill and killed those who were unable to escape.[33] Over the next few days, the Carduchians kept up the pressure with light infantry but they were unable to put an end to the Greek advance through their territory. Whenever they would block a pass, Xenophon would come up from the rear and outflank the Carduchians by occupying higher ground. Likewise, when the Carduchians would attack the Greek rear, Cheirisophus would return from the vanguard and outflank them from a higher elevation. Soon enough the Greeks came upon the Centrites River, which formed the border between Carduchian territory and the Persian province of Armenia.

♦ ♦ ♦

Crossing the Centrites River would be another difficult battle for the Greeks. As the Greeks arrived on the river bank, the Persian Satrap* of Armenia arrived with his infantry and cavalry on the river bank opposite the Greeks to dispute their crossing. The Persian Satrap positioned his cavalry down by the river and left his infantry further back from the river on a ridge that ran parallel to it. As the Greeks attempted to cross the river at the first ford, they discovered that it was too deep to ford while under arms. Seeing that they were now stuck in between the Carduchians to their rear and the Persians across the river, the

* A Satrap was a military governor of a province or territory.

Greeks fell into despair as they were ordered to set up camp for the night.

When the morning came, two soldiers reported to Xenophon and the other generals that they had found a shallower ford just a little upriver.[34] With the discovery of this new ford the spirits of the Greeks were revived and the generals devised a plan to cross the river safely. The entire body of Greeks moved towards the second ford, with the Persian cavalry mirroring their movement on the opposite bank. When the Greeks arrived at the ford Cheirisophus began to cross with the vanguard, while Xenophon back tracked to the first ford and pretended to cross the river there. Seeing Xenophon's movement, the Persian cavalry grew anxious that they would be cut off from the support of their infantry, and so, they withdrew from the river bank and were further pursued by Cheirisophus once they were across.

When Xenophon saw the Persian cavalry withdrawing and the Greek vanguard safely across, he proceeded back to the second ford and took up a defensive position in opposition to the advancing Carduchians who were now advancing against him onto the river plain. When the Carduchians came into range the Greek slingers opened fire and the signal for a hoplite advance was given. The hoplites surged forward, knowing that the Carduchians would retreat in the face of such boldness; which was exactly what the Carduchians did. Upon seeing the Carduchians in headlong retreat, Xenophon's rearguard quickly turned around and raced, in an orderly fashion, back across the Centrites River before the Carduchians realized that the Greeks had escaped.[35] After the Greeks had affected their crossing, the Carduchians gave up the hunt and went about with their usual business.

Now in the province of Armenia the Greeks, unhindered by enemies, travelled a few days through relatively flat land until they encountered the Persian satrap again. The satrap, Tiribazus, a favourite of King Artaxerxes, proposed a truce with the Greeks. The Persians agreed not to hinder the Greek advance

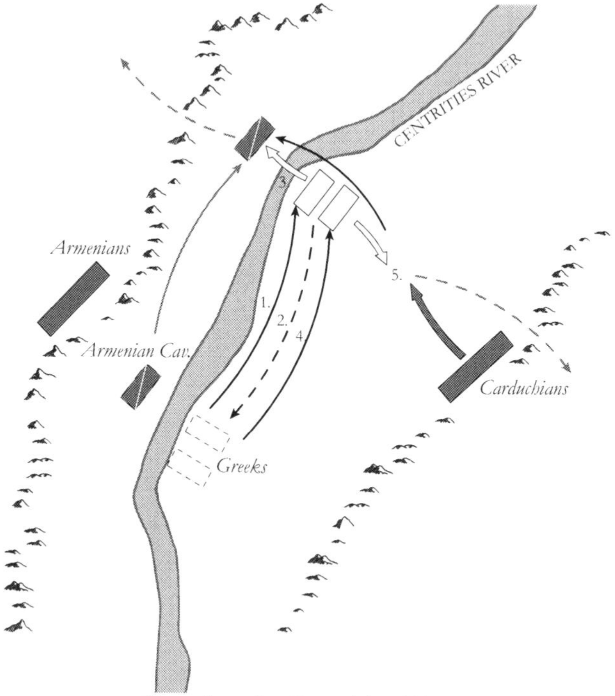

Crossing the Centrities River

1. Greeks maneuver to second ford, Armenian Cavalry shadows movement. 2. Xenophon feignts back to first ford. 3. Cheirisophus fords the Centrites, Amernians flee the battlefield. 4. Xenophon returns to second ford, prepares for Carduchians. 5. Xenophon feignts towards Carduchians. Once Carduchians flee, Xenophon doubles back accross the Centrities.

in exchange for the Greeks not burning down the villages they came across. The truce was mutually beneficial, as Tiribazus was playing for time in order to allow for reinforcements from Tissapherenes to arrive; but any time that passed without hostilities brought the Greeks closer to their objective. After only a few days in Armenia a massive snowfall (probably not by Canadian standards) covered the Greek camp in snow.[36] While some of the men went about scrounging for supplies, they thought they saw campfires in the distance. After the generals sent out a scouting party, they discovered that Tiribazus was concentrating his forces nearby with the objective of occupying a mountain pass through which the only road forward ran.

Upon the return of the reconnaissance party the Greeks hastily set out towards the Persian camp and pre-emptively attacked and scattered the Persians. The Greeks returned to their own camp to collect their belongings before setting out towards the mountain pass. They arrived before the Persians could regroup and occupy the heights. After spending a night camped out on the mountain pass the Greeks proceeded through desert terrain, reaching the headwaters of the Euphrates in the next few days. After travelling through Armenia largely avoiding any serious engagements with the Persians, they now crossed the Phasis River into the lands of the Chalybians.

Shortly upon entering the territory known as Chalybes*, the Chalybians gathered together with the intention of blocking the Greek passage. With a repetition of the tactics used by the Greeks before, they sent a detachment up the mountain to outflank the Chalybians while keeping the main body of troops on the main road to fix the enemies attention on that front. Time and again the combination of flanking maneuver and frontal assault worked and the Greeks were able to pass through the lands of the Chalybians without further hindrance.

* The Chalybes & Taochi territories would now both be roughly located in Eastern Turkey, Western Armenia or Southern Georgia.

As they now entered into the territory of the Taochians, they were beginning to run out of supplies. They were forced by their situation to assault a fortified compound that had only one entrance or exit, as it was surrounded by precipitous cliffs.[37] Whenever the Greeks made their way up the road, the villagers would roll down boulders and hurl stones at the Greeks. It was noticed at this time that the town was guarded by only a handful of men. Four volunteers came forward to accept the challenge offered by the town. The four began up the road and every time the Taochians would begin to hurl their stones and roll their boulders, the four Greeks would take cover in the trees and watch the boulders and stones go by. Every time they re-emerged from cover the Greeks would steal a little more ground until finally they were inside the village. The four men put an end to the boulders and stones, while the main army was able to enter the village without danger. The denizens of the village proceeded to throw themselves off the cliffs to their deaths.[38] With large amounts of provisions secured from the village, the Greeks set out once again through the land of the Chalybians.

♦ ♦ ♦

After crossing over the Harpasus River and passing beyond the land of the Chalybians and Taochians, the Greeks made it to a fairly large city called Gymnias. The city did not resist, but instead aided the Greeks by providing provisions and a guide who promised to direct them safely through hostile territory to a place from which they would be able to see the sea.[39] The Greeks became suspicious when the guide was perpetually prodding the Greeks to desolate the countryside, which was largely hostile to Gymnias. However, on the fifth day of marching with the guide, Xenophon, heard a clamour coming from the vanguard. As he ventured forward to see what the commotion was about, the noise continued to creep backwards until Xenophon could understand it, 'Thalassa! Thalassa!'* At the site from which they

* 'The Sea! The Sea!'

could view the sea, the Greeks immediately set up alters and proceeded to make the sacrifices that they deemed necessary to thank the gods for their deliverance from Persian hands.[40]

Even with the sea within their eyesight, the Greeks still had to travel through tribal lands to get to the coast. Once the Greeks were finished making sacrifices they began their march through the land of the Macronians. The Macronians mustered themselves for a battle but they were talked out of it by an Athenian slave who was of Macronian ancestry. The two sides exchanged vows of good will together, and the Greeks were allowed to pass through in peace.[41]

The next land they came upon was that of the Colchians, who were not about to be talked down from an aggressive stance and promptly fortified a position along the mountain pass. The Greek generals formed their troops into battle formation before holding a council-of-war to discuss their present situation. The problem as Xenophon saw it, was that if the Greeks advanced up the mountain in their line it would break up their formation as some sections would advance faster than others as they encountered rough terrain. As this was naturally bound to happen, it would allow the Colchians to swoop down from the heights and defeat the Greeks in a piecemeal fashion. Xenophon proposed to have the hoplites formed up into columns of company strength (roughly one hundred men) with three larger detachments of slingers; one on the far left, one on the far right and one in the centre. Instead of advancing as a long unbroken line, the hoplites would advance in smaller columns and thus would be able to traverse the uneven terrain with more uniformity and would be able to better protect against Colchian flank attacks.

The new formation worked well, as the Colchians were unable to get in between any of the columns or outflank their formation. Once the Greeks had ascended the mountain ridge, the Colchians turned around and ran.[42]

A short march after scattering the Colchians brought the

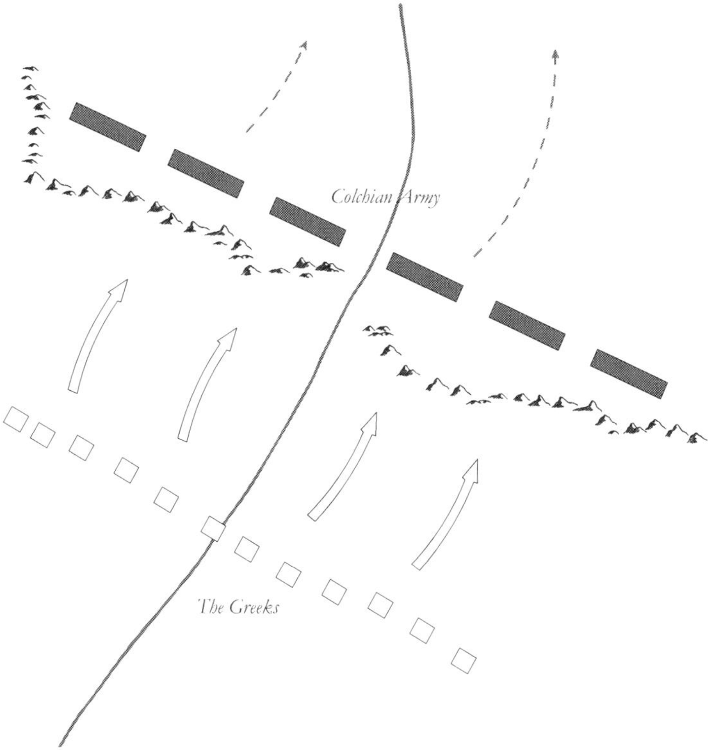

Mountain Fighting

Greeks to the coast of the Euxine Sea in the immediate vicinity of the polis Trapezus, which was a colony of the Greek polis Sinope.[43] The men were ecstatic to be back on the coast,* and as soon as they were welcomed into Trapezus, they began to hold athletic games to celebrate their achievements, and in honour of the men who had fallen along the way.[44] From Trapezus, Cheirisophus set sail to the west in order to gather enough ships from friendly Greek states so that the men could return to their homes on ships as a whole body, instead of in pieces. While Cheirisophus was busy gathering ships in the west, the remainder of the Greeks with Xenophon were forced by necessity to plunder the surrounding Colchian territory before they made their way west by foot and ship. They had captured some ships in the vicinity of Trapezus and loaded their camp followers on board) and eventually made their way to the polis of Cotyora (another colony of Sinope. After staying in Cotyora for over a month, the Greeks had collected enough ships to be able to set sail as a whole body back to Greece.

♦ ♦ ♦

From Cotyora the Greeks sailed west, making it back to their homes in Greece proper after some adventures involving the Greek poleis of the Euxine Sea and Dardanelles region. When Xenophon returned to Athens he discovered that his close friend and mentor, Socrates, had been executed by the restored radical democratic regime on the trumped up charges of heresy, creating new gods and 'corrupting the youth'.[45] Xenophon was disgusted by this act and by the mob like impression that the radical regime left upon him. After leaving Athens in exile, Xenophon went on to live in Sparta, where he became good friends with the nobility and King. He was able to finish writing many of the philosophical and historical works for which he became widely known, thereafter.

Xenophon began the march up country essentially as an ob-

* Most Greeks normally lived only miles from a coastline.

server and a journalist. It was only after the Battle of Cuxana and the subsequent elections that Xenophon assumed a military role with the ten thousand. Although most of the historical record on the Greek retreat after Cuxana comes from Xenophon himself (with all the attendant potential for embellishment and self-aggrandizement), it is none-the-less impressive that Xenophon went from being a journalist with only basic military experience to one of four top ranking general officers taking on the responsibility of effecting the retreat from the gates of Babylon.

The Greek deliverance from the heart of the Persian Empire bought the Greek world some breathing room after the debilitating civil war between the Athenian and Spartan camps. A renewed threat in the immediate aftermath of the Peloponnesian War from Persia could have potentially posed an existential threat to the liberty of the Greek poleis. On top of this, the successful retreat out of Persia showed the world two things. One, that while the Persian Empire was massive in its geographic scope, its core was weak once its defensive outer shell was penetrated. And two, it once again showed the fighting potential of free (Greek) men, who were harnessed into discipline and order with the purpose of protecting their lives and liberty. Greek soldiers were vastly superior in their martial capabilities compared to those of the Persian and various other tribal entities.

The fact that the Greeks made it home largely testifies to the brilliance of their war making capabilities and their political inheritance which was essential for their ability to adapt to their constantly changing situation. The ten thousand Greeks and Xenophon's able leadership gave posterity an example of what could be achieved through valour and determination in the name of liberty and the polis.

BLACK SEA
THRACE
Sinope
BITHYNIA
PAPHLAGON
AEOLIA
R. HALYS
ASIA MINOR
R. HERMUS
Sardis
IONIA
CARIA
RHODES
CYRPUS
MEDITERRANEAN SEA

The March of the Ten Thousand

Epaminondas of Thebes

Epaminondas was born sometime during the Peloponnesian War to an impoverished aristocratic family, his father was Polymnis but his mother's name has been lost to posterity.[1] Much of Epaminondas' early life is unknown to us as the ancient biographer, Plutarch, wrote a biography on him but it has not survived the ravages of time. Some basic information can be gleaned from secondary Roman sources and from Plutarch's biographies of Epaminondas' contemporaries, Pelopidas and Agesipolis. Xenophon, who became increasingly pro-Spartan after his return to mainland Greece, almost went out of his way to not mention Epaminondas in his work, the Hellenica, detailing the end of the Peloponnesian War and the subsequent happenings in Greek international affairs.

What we do know about Epaminondas (as this is corroborated by numerous sources) is that Epaminondas was the faithful student of the Pythagorean philosopher – Lysis of Tarentum.[2] He excelled in his academic studies and scholasticism was something that stuck with him throughout his life. Even while he was an exemplary academic student he was also excellent in his physical education. Epaminondas put his focus on improving his agility as opposed to his brute strength, as it was his belief "that strength suited the purposes of wrestlers, but that agility conduced to excellence in war."[3] It was with this preliminary academic and physical education that Epaminondas began his 'military career' in the service of Thebes. The first battle we have a record of him serving in is the Battle of Mantinea in 385

B.C., Epaminondas was serving in a combined Theban-Spartan force on a mission to enforce the law of Spartan hegemony onto the dissenting polis, Mantinea.

It is said that Epaminondas fought heroically while the wing he was in collapsed, he and his good friend, Pelopidas, refused to retreat and both were wounded as they became surrounded. Pelopidas fell to his wounds, but Epaminondas fought all the more valiantly in defence of his friends' body until the Spartan king, Aegilius, was able to bring up reserves to stabilize the line and save the two Thebans.[4] Thus began one of the greatest friendships of the ancient world, as Epaminondas and Pelopidas would be partners in both political and military affairs for the remainder of their lives. Now we will begin to examine the context of the turbulent era in which Epaminondas lived.

♦ ♦ ♦

With the Spartan coalitions victory over Athens and her allies in the Peloponnesian War came a period of uneasy peace amongst the Greek poleis. The Spartan victory was bought with Persian gold, but afterwards Sparta had attempted to clear its debt with Persia by aiding in the overthrow of its new king, Artaxerxes, and by installing a friendly king, Cyrus, on the Persian throne. After Cyrus' defeat and death at Cuxana and Artaxerxes' failure to annihilate Xenophon and the ten thousand, Artaxerxes decided to reassert his authority over the Greek poleis on the Asian continent. The Spartans did nothing in response to the renewed Persian aggression, effectively selling out the sovereignty of the Ionian Greeks.

Spartan hegemony in Greece was characterized by unilateralism, arrogance and aggression towards both former allies and enemies alike. Their behaviour went far to alienate the various Greek poleis and before long cracks began to appear in their hegemonic system. Alliances against Spartan hegemony would be crafted amongst old enemies and lead to the Corinthian War in 395 BC which pitted Athens, Argos, Corinth and Thebes against

Sparta. For the time being the superiority of the Spartan hoplites kept the Greeks rebellious inclinations in check, but their elite hoplites couldn't do that indefinitely. Sometime around 385 BC the Arcadians dissented with Spartan hegemony, only to be put down by a combined force from Sparta and Thebes at the Second Battle of Mantinea.

Thebes emerged from the Peloponnesian War with more power relative to when the war had started, by consolidating its influence over the neighbouring countryside known as Boeotia. The Spartans increasingly came to view Thebes as a potential rival even though the two poleis had traditionally been allies. In 382 BC, Thebes was divided internally between two political factions, one was democratic, and the other was oligarchic and pro-Spartan. While undergoing a period of civil strife a Spartan band was invited into Thebes by the oligarchic, pro-Spartan party in order for them to carry the day against the democratic faction.[5] The Spartans subverted the ancient Theban constitution and exiled certain members of the democratic faction, believing they would be a constant thorn in the side if left to be in the polis. However, Epaminondas was allowed to stay in Thebes, as the Spartan commander, Phoebidas, believed his poverty and philosophic tendencies did not make him a threat to the new regime. Those who were exiled from Thebes, chief amongst them was Pelopidas, largely went over to Athens to weather the political storm. They would not rest easy whilst in the relative safety of Athens, but rather, they began to conspire amongst themselves for the liberation of their polis from Spartan domination.

While Epaminondas had been left in the city, he still played a part in the political restoration of Thebes. Throughout the Spartan occupation Epaminondas had been rousing the youth of Thebes, exhorting them to intense physical training and discipline.[6] On a stormy winter evening in 379 BC the exiles, led by Pelopidas, returned to Thebes with a force of Athenian hoplites.[7] They snuck back into their polis under the cover of darkness and snowfall. Upon arrival, they assassinated the Spartan generals, who were billeting themselves in the city and blocked the main Spartan force in the Cadmeia, the Theban Acropolis. The next day Epaminondas and Pelopidas addressed the Theban assembly in order to sway the people over to their side, which they succeeded in doing.[8]

With the Theban populace converted to the restoration of their old constitution it was only a matter of time before the besieged Spartan garrison would be forced to evacuate. Once the Spartans, in Sparta, heard what was afoot in Thebes, they sent a relief force to assist their garrison, but it didn't arrive in time. The garrison was allowed to withdraw from Thebes, meeting the relieving force on its way back to Sparta. The Spartan relief force returned home with the garrison and waited for the spring to come for a renewed offensive. When the Spartans returned in the spring, the Thebans evaded a pitched battle and dug themselves into fortifications around Thebes. Invading the Boeotian countryside over a number of years, the Spartans were unsuccessful each and every time in up-rooting them from their fortifications around the city. The Thebans, slowly but surely, consolidated their control over the neighbouring countryside of Boeotia.[9] Eventually, Athens was drawn into the war on the side of Thebes.

The fighting left all sides in a state of exhaustion and so, a convention was arranged to meet in Sparta to discuss the terms of a general peace. Epaminondas was sent from Thebes to act as the signatory for the newly created Boeotian Confederacy (by now Thebes and Boeotia had become politically synonymous although they weren't necessarily recognized by others as such). In an attempt to strip the Confederacy of its legitimacy the Sparta king, Agelisus II, refused to allow Epaminondas to sign as the ambassador of the Boeotian Confederacy saying Epaminondas could only sign for Thebes because the various poleis of Boeotia were nominally independent.

Due to this diplomatic slight, Epaminondas walked out of the peace convention, refusing to sign the treaty at all.[10] War was soon resumed between Sparta and the Boeotian Confederacy. Resorting to their age old strategy, Sparta proceeded to dispatch an elite army to Boeotia to draw the Thebans out into a pitched battle. The rigidity of Spartan society did not allow for strategic innovations; the Spartans were still using the same strategic plans that had consistently failed to achieve their objectives since the Spartan's first invaded Attica in the Peloponnesian War.

In the eight odd years of skirmishing with the Spartans since the Theban restoration, the Boeotians had introduced dramatic changes into the Boeotian military and political structure. Most important of which was the creation of the 'Sacred Band' which was an elite unit of professional soldiers, who were also lovers.* The fact that they were lovers was used to motivate the soldiers into ever greater martial deeds, with the understanding that the men would fight more courageously if their personal lover was fighting beside them.[11] Of almost equal importance to Boeotian morale was the experience and confidence gained from the desultory fighting with Sparta. On the political side of things, the Boeotian Confederacy was governed by eight Boeotriachs from the various Boeotian poleis and were elected by the people for one year terms. Their duties of office were of both a civil and military nature. When the Spartans returned to Boeotia in the year of 369 BC, the Thebans were prepared for it. This time they would be convinced by Epaminondas that it would be prudent to stake their fortune on a pitched battle with the Spartans.

♦ ♦ ♦

The Spartan army commanded by King Cleombrotus numbered around ten thousand men; amongst them were seven hundred elite 'Spartarite' hoplite infantry and roughly a thousand cavalry. They marched into Boeotia from the west, as they had recently

* Homosexuality was common in classical Greece, and much of the ancient world. Infact it was largely seen as normal for men to be bi-sexual.

been campaigning in Phocis, a territory to the west of Thebes. After maneuvering around a Theban ambush party, the Spartan army surprised the Thebans when they appeared within Boeotia and captured a fortification, along with some triremes on the Gulf of Corinth. The Boeotians now came forth to meet the Spartans and before long the two sides were camped outside the town of Leuctra. In a council-of-war Epaminondas, with the persuasive help of his friend Pelopidas, who was in command of the Sacred Band, convinced the other Boeotriachs to adopt his audacious plan.[12]

The Boeotians were outnumbered with only six thousand odd infantry against the Spartan ten thousand, but they had a decided advantage when it came to the quantity and quality of their cavalry. The battle began with a cavalry engagement in which the Boeotians prevailed, sending the Spartan horsemen crashing back into the main Spartan line and disrupting the Spartan formation. The Spartan battle line was conventional for the time period; the line was eight ranks deep with their elite troops on the right wing in order to check the natural tendency of a hoplite formation to drift to the right as the men sought protection from the shield of the man to his right.[13]

In contrast, Epaminondas' battle line was anything but conventional. He put his elite corps, the Sacred Band, on his left wing which he formed into a column some thirty ranks deep, while he purposely left his right wing in a weakened state. When Epaminondas began his advance, he staggered his line, holding his weakened right wing back while he brought forth the column on his left. This would be the first time in recorded history when a general would use the tactic of attacking-in-echelon.[14]

This novel tactical innovation confounded the Spartan left wing who found they could not come to grips with the Boeotian right wing, while the weight and shock of Epaminondas' column broke through the Sparta line on the right. The Spartans on the right, commanded personally by King Cleombrotus, fought valiantly but Cleombrotus was eventually killed in the fighting.[15] The elite Spartarites were able to recover their kings' body, but in doing so they suffered considerable casualties. When the Spartan left wing saw that their right wing had collapsed, they fell into despair and began a disorderly retreat.

The consequences of the battle were enormous for both sides and for the entirety of the Greek world. For Thebes, it meant that their polis was free from Spartan domination and that its leadership of the Boeotian Confederacy was recognized throughout the international system. For Sparta, it was a grievous loss not only to their prestige and their reputation of invincibility, but more importantly, it was a tremendous setback to their ability to put elite infantry into the field. Considering the insular nature of Spartan society, a Spartarite warrior took a lifetime to train, and so they only came in a very finite quantity and took a long time to replenish. For the rest of Greece, Leuctra meant an end to the increasingly despotic rule of Spartan hegemony.[16] It also brought back the potential for a general degeneration into another long multipolar war, unless some power stepped up to fill the power vacuum. If it wasn't for the leadership of Epaminondas, it is entirely likely that Thebes wouldn't have been up to the task of filling that void.

♦ ♦ ♦

Epaminondas wanted to immediately take the war to Sparta by invading the traditional Spartan area of influence within the Peloponnesian peninsula. However, the Boeotians were persuaded by their allies to hold off on their offensive until the next campaigning season. In the meantime, Epaminondas focused his energy and that of the Boeotians on consolidating the authority of the Confederacy amongst the poleis of Greece, causing many poleis that were previously allied with Sparta to switch sides for the coming conflict. At this point the Athenians, who had recently stood by as Sparta went on to attack Thebes, decided to act as the arbiter between the two states and proposed a

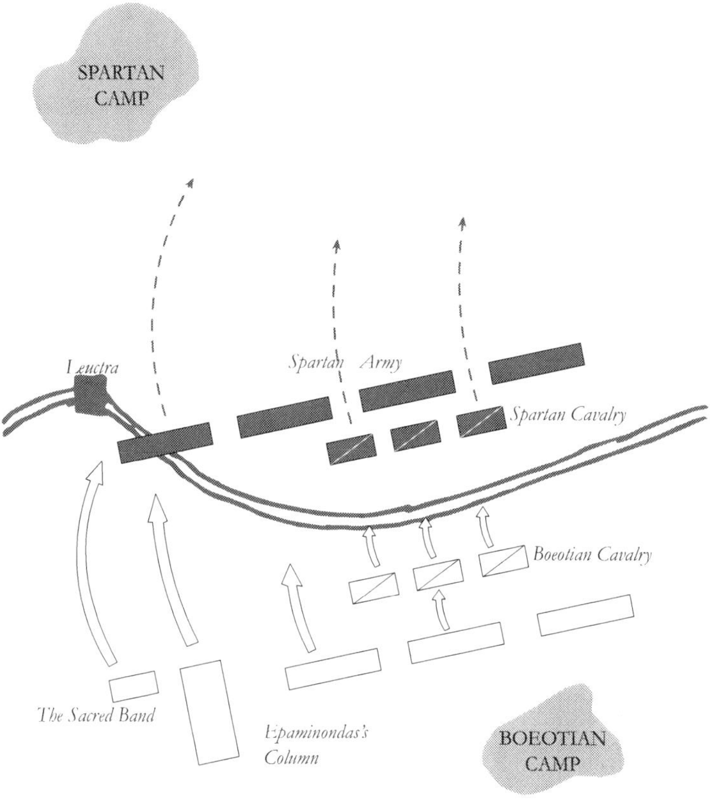

Battle of Leuctra

peace treaty that would make a number of Peloponnesian poleis independent of Spartan domination. Sparta was in no position to resist this diplomatic onslaught, and so, was forced to accept it.[17]

Shortly after the ratification of peace, some of the newly independent poleis led by, Mantinea and , went on to create the 'Arcadian Alliance'. The alliance was designed to limit the potential of a Spartan rebound and was inherently opposed to Spartan interests. The Spartan king correctly feared that this new alliance would put intolerable limits on Spartan foreign policy and further erode the sinews of Spartan hegemony. And so, in an attempt to salvage Sparta's authority on the peninsula and to thwart the new alliance, King Agesilaus, declared war against the member states. The new alliance was quick to send envoys to Thebes asking for their assistance in their war against Sparta. In the New Year's elections, Epaminondas and Pelopidas had been returned and elected (respectively) to the office of Boeotriach and were quickly on their way south to meet the Spartan threat.[18] Gathering allied troops as they went, the Boeotians arrived late in 370 B.C.

When the Spartans saw what the Thebans had arrayed against them some forty thousand soldiers, they decided it was unwise to make a stand against them in the field, and so, they retreated back to their city and dug in. Even with one of the largest armies ever assembled by a Greek coalition, Epaminondas knew an assault on Sparta would be incredibly costly and a siege would take too long to make it a viable option.[19] In the absence of taking Sparta by force, Epaminondas sought to drive a wedge between Sparta and its source of manual labour in Laconia and Messenia.

First, Epaminondas drove his men down to Gythium, the main port of Sparta, liberating minor Lacedaemonian villages along the way. After returning to Arcadia from Gythium, Epaminondas marched south and west into Messenia, which had been conquered and enslaved by Sparta centuries before, and was used as a pool of manual labour allowing the citizens of Sparta to dedicate themselves full time to the training for war. Epaminondas liberated the Messenians, known as helots, and permanently destroyed Sparta's tyrannical hold on Messenia by establishing a fortified city called "" on top of the dominating geographical feature of the area, Mount Ithome. After humiliating Sparta in the campaign of 370-69 B.C. Epaminondas was ready to return with the army back to Thebes.

♦ ♦ ♦

When Epaminondas and the army returned to Thebes, he was put on trial because he had persuaded his fellow Boeotriachs to remain in the field after their year-long tenure of office was up for renewal. His reason for doing so was both logical and legitimate even if it wasn't strictly constitutional. When the tenure was up, the campaign in the Peloponnesus was only half finished at that point and going home would have only shown a weakness that didn't exist and possibly led to the undoing of what had been previously accomplished. In his own defence, Epaminondas half-jokingly told the assembly to inscribe this message upon his resting place.

> "Epaminondas was punished by the Thebans with death, because he obliged them to overthrow the Lacedaemonians at Leuctra, whom, before he became general, none of the Boeotians durst look upon in the field, and because he not only, by one battle, rescued Thebes from destruction, but also secured liberty for all Greece, and brought the power of both people to such a condition that the Thebans attacked Sparta, and the Lacedaemonians were content if they could save their lives; nor did he cease to prosecute the war, till, after settling Messene, he shut up Sparta with a close siege."[20]

After hearing his defence, the courtroom came to its senses and threw out the ludicrous charges against Epaminondas. In a further sign of the goodwill for which the people of Boeotia felt towards Epaminondas, they once again trusted him with the reins of the state; he was returned to the office of Boeotriach through another round of elections.

When the campaigning season began again in 369 B.C. the Arcadian Alliance invited Epaminondas and the Boeotians back into the Peloponnesus to renew the war with Sparta. In light of the recent successful Boeotian actions in the Peloponnesus, the Spartans had gone on a diplomatic offensive and assembled an impressive array of allied poleis to fight on their side. When Epaminondas arrived at the Isthmus of Corinth he found that it was occupied by a combined force of Spartans, Athenians, Corinthians, Megarians and Pellenians.[21] Epaminondas made a breech through the defensive line at its weakest point, guarded by Spartans, which caused the entire line at the Isthmus to collapse. Little strategic value was added to the campaign after breaking the line. Pellene and Sicyon joined with the Boeotian war effort, but it proved impossible to capture Troezen and Epidaurus, in the northeast of the peninsula. Furthermore, an expeditionary force was sent from Syracuse, a polis on Sicily, to help aid the Spartan cause. After the arrival of the Syracusians, Epaminondas decided to withdraw the army back to Thebes as not much else could be done in the face of such resistance.[22]

After returning home, and without achieving any spectacular result in the previous campaigning season, Epaminondas was once again persecuted by his political rivals. This time, they were able to ruin Epaminondas' chances of re-election to the office of Boeotriach. There is not much recorded legal explanation as to why Epaminondas was excluded from the office in 368 BC, but two reasons can be deduced even without any historical sources to confirm their validity. First, was his failure to achieve a humiliating defeat over the enemies of Thebes in the previous campaign. While breaking through the Isthmus was an impressive feat, the subsequent failed sieges dampened morale and eventually brought Syracuse into the fight against Thebes. Secondly, Epaminondas' greatest political asset and friend, Pelopidas, was away from Thebes on a diplomatic mission in Thessaly* and was unable to throw his weight into the political fray to assist him.

Pelopidas' diplomatic foray in the north was a failure, with the king of Pherae, Alexander, taking the ambassadors as prisoners and declaring war on Thebes. The Boeotriach sent to avenge this outlandish slight and to rescue Pelopidas failed to accomplish the release of the diplomats and was further embarrassed with casualties as the army returned to Thebes.[23] After this set back, the Boeotian Assembly elected to have Epaminondas sent out with a second force to affect the rescue of Pelopidas and to punish King Alexander. Epaminondas' reputation for superb generalship frightened Alexander, and after Epaminondas maneuvered his army into surrounding Pherae, Alexander surrendered and returned the envoys to Epaminondas without a fight. After being rescued, Pelopidas was sent to the Persian court where he was able to foil the creation of an alliance between Athens, Sparta and Persia. Once again Pelopidas brought war back into Thessaly against the tyrant Alexander and was mortally wounded in battle.[24]

In 367 B.C. Epaminondas was returned to the office of Boeotriach where he would stay for the rest of his life. Prior to a renewed military effort in the Peloponnesus, Epaminondas requested the Agrives (from Argos) to occupy the Isthmus ahead of time so as to allow the Theban army to march through to the peninsula unhindered.[25] Once Epaminondas arrived in the Peloponnesus he directed his army west to Achaea in an attempt to convince the ns to switch sides. Epaminondas was

* Thessaly was a region to the north of Thebes, in what is now central Greece.

GULF OF CORINT
ACHAIA
Pellene
ELIS
Elis
ARCADIA
Mantinea
Megalopolis
LACONIA
Sparta
Messene
MESSENIA
Boeotians & Allies
Spartans & Allies
Corinth & Allies
Athens & Allies
MEDITERRANEAN SEA

Theban Hegemony

not opposed in the field and was quickly able to convince the governing aristocracy of to switch over to his side. After they had done so, the radical democratic ideologues within the anti-Sparta alliance began to push for ideological conformity within the alliance (against Epaminondas' better judgement) arguing that the Achaean oligarchs should be thrown out of power and a democracy set up in its place.[26]

Ideological conformity proved to be a bane for overall grand strategy, as the oligarchs in the nearby poleis banded together to reinstate the exiled and ousted Achaean aristocrats. Once the aristocrats were reinstated in Achaea, they became steadfast enemies of Thebes, and served as a warning to other oligarchies sitting on the fence of what might happen to their hold on power if they aligned themselves with Thebes. With that, the action of 367 BC campaigning season was largely over and the diplomatic offensives were once again about to resume.

The Greeks called upon the Persian king, Artaxerxes II, to guarantee a peace amongst the poleis. The king's peace was but a brief and meaningless respite to the conflict as both sides used the time to muster their forces. Furthermore, the Persians had no intention of getting mixed up in another messy Greek war just to keep the peace. The political situation in Greece was becoming increasingly confused, while Sparta and Thebes fought it out on land, Athens decided to remain aloof. Instead Athens was busy rebuilding its fleet and reconstructing the old Delian League* at sea. In 364 BC the Boeotian Assembly voted to send Epaminondas out to sea with a force of one hundred triremes in an effort to disrupt (or control) the Delian League. The naval expedition met with limited success, and within the year Epaminondas was back on the mainland getting prepared for another invasion of the Peloponnesus.[27]

♦ ♦ ♦

* The Delian League was Athens's informal empire of islands and coastal enclaves which had evolved in the aftermath of the Greek victory over the Persians.

As Theban influence began to turn into Boeotian hegemony, the ancient jealousies of the various Greek poleis reasserted itself and began to work against the designs of Epaminondas and Thebes. In the campaign season of 362 BC Epaminondas brought down his Boeotian force into the Peloponnesus and was joined by his allies from Thessaly, Euboea, Messenia, Argos, Tegea and a few poleis from the Arcadian confederation. The immediate casus belli for this years' invasion was to bring Mantinea into line with Boeotian Hegemony. In response, Mantinea requested and received assistance from the remaining Greek powers, namely, Sparta, Athens, Achaea and the parts of Arcadia not beholden to Thebes. The two opposing sides were roughly equal in numbers and quality and so stalemate ensued.

With time running out in the campaigning season Epaminondas had to move quickly to break the stalemate. Upon receiving intelligence that a Spartan force was en route to Mantinea, leaving Sparta largely without a garrison, Epaminondas through a night march, attempted to seize Sparta by surprise but he was frustrated when the Spartans were tipped off to his maneuver and backtracked to re-occupy Sparta.[28] After a light skirmish outside of Sparta, in which the Spartans got the better of the Boeotians, Epaminondas double backed towards Mantinea and attempted to capture Mantinea while its garrison was trying to trap Epaminondas in between Sparta and their army. Frustrated again, after the Mantineans reoccupied their city before Epaminondas could arrive, stalemate once again ensued. Time was running out for Epaminondas, as it was almost the time of season when the Boeotians would have to leave the Peloponnesus; thus ruining the credibility of Thebes within the anti-Spartan alliance.[*29] With this in mind, Epaminondas decided to stake his reputation and that of his polis on a pitched battle.

Epaminondas was not a rash or irresponsible gambler when

* Sieges were impossible, considering that Boetotian commanders had one year term limits.

he decided to stake his fate on a battle. His decision was based on his well-grounded confidence of his tactical aptitude for creating an element of surprise, and his ability to handle his troops in battle. The battle that ensued would be the largest set piece hoplite battle up to that point in classical Greece. Epaminondas had a numerical advantage with something like thirty thousand infantry and three thousand cavalry, against the oppositions twenty thousand infantry and two thousand cavalry.

Once the two forces faced each other in their lines of battle, Epaminondas had his men switch from battle line to marching column with an about face to the left, making it look as if they were about to march somewhere else. When the column started marching the Spartans and their allies began to relax their readiness as it seemed as if the battle would not be fought that day or in that place.[30]

After marching a short distance Epaminondas switched the column back into battle line with an about face to the right before having the men relax their arms furthering the impression that there was not to be a battle that day. While the men were relaxing their arms, Epaminondas marched some of his infantry from his extreme right wing to reinforce his left wing; imitating his tactical formation at Leuctra.[31] The reinforcing of his left wing went unnoticed by the Spartans as they were almost entirely convinced that the battle would be delayed, and they were far from a state of physical preparedness as much of the infantry began to take off their armour and relax their arms.

When his left wing was in position, Epaminondas ordered his troops to take their arms back up and begin their advance in the same fashion as at Leuctra; with the weakened right wing not committing itself to the general action and using his strengthened left wing as a battering ram. Before the infantry engaged, Epaminondas' cavalry, that was stationed on both wings, advanced to the attack against their counterparts opposite them. The Boeotian cavalry bested the opposing cavalry as Epaminondas attached light skirmishers to his cavalry wings which greatly assisted with the cavalry's assault. The clash of infantry that followed the cavalry skirmish unfolded in much the same fashion as the Battle of Leuctra. Epaminondas used his reinforced left wing to batter into the Spartan right wing. The opposition's infantry were rushed back into formation and took up their arms once they saw the Thebans advancing.[32] Regardless of their haste and valiant actions, the battle had already been won through Epaminondas' efforts at deception and his tactical preparations.

While the action was going favourable for the Thebans, the Spartans focused their efforts onto Epaminondas personally, and were successful in striking him with a spear jab. The wound he received was not immediately fatal and his close companions were able to evacuate his body to a safe area, but it was only a matter of time before Epaminondas would breathe his last breath. As the Spartan line was breaking and withdrawing from the field, Epaminondas' life expired on the field of battle outside Mantinea.

♦ ♦ ♦

With Epaminondas dead the Boeotians and allies did not have the leadership or the resolve to aggressively pursue the Spartans. And so, after the main action of the battle, as Xenophon recounts, both sides were allowed to collect their dead and set up trophies as if both sides were simultaneously defeated and victorious.[33] In an odd way both sides were victorious as Thebes saved its honour, while Sparta avoided complete destruction. But both victories were pyrrhic in the sense that it left both sides in such a weakened state that it would be almost impossible for any of them to recover.

Xenophon ended his history of the Peloponnesian war after the Battle of Mantinea, and in a way it was the final act in the war that began in 431 B.C. During that sixty-year period the realities of Greek geopolitics had gone in full circle with each major

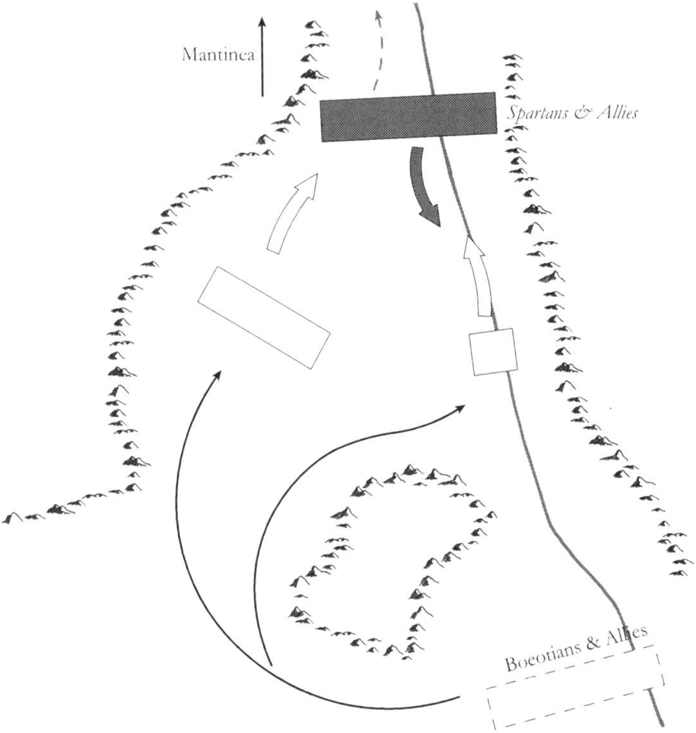

Third Battle of Mantinea

power briefly taking its place in the sun before being replaced by another. After the death of Epaminondas Theban power began to wane until it finally collapsed. The Athenians recreated their Delian League and briefly enjoyed predominance in Greek affairs until an outside interloper, King Phillip of Macedon, unified the Greek peninsula by conquering the various poleis, destroying their independence and subverting their ancient liberties. While the Greeks went on to achieve great things in the lands of the Persian Empire under the leadership of Alexander the Great of Macedonia, King Philips son. They achieved those great feats of arms for the purposes of greed and revenge under the banner of a tyrant.

Epaminondas passed away at the height of his career, while surrounded by his fellow countrymen at the apex of a magnificent tactical victory. The tactical innovations brought about by Epaminondas' ingenuity saved Thebes from destruction before turning Thebes and Boeotia into the pre-eminent power of the Greek world. While the nature of the Boeotian political construct and constitution didn't allow for power to be consolidated under one man or office, it is telling of Epaminondas' character that he never attempted to subvert the constitution and rule as a tyrant despite his incredible popularity amongst the people and the loyalty felt for him by the troops.

Another testament to Epaminondas' leadership was the fact that the Boeotians geopolitical hegemony fell apart almost as quickly as he had died. As further proof to the thesis of this work, that without effective military and political leadership it is almost impossible for liberty to exist on the world stage. The ancient Theban constitution was subverted by the Macedonians not even a generation after his expiration. Epaminondas and the Boeotian Confederacy were classical Greece's last hope for the survival of ancient liberties of the poleis. Quickly after the death of one of liberty's greatest lieutenants, the Macedonian tyrants, Philip and Alexander, built upon Epaminondas' tactical innovations and perfected them in their quest to subvert and conquer the ancient Greek poleis.

And so it is here at the end of what historians generally refer to as the 'Classical Age' and the beginning of the 'Hellenistic Age' that we shall move our discussion away from the heroes of Greece and onto the great commanders of the Roman Republic.

Publius Cornelius Scipio Africanus

Publius Cornelius Scipio* was born in the year 236 BC to one of the Roman Republics most celebrated and successful families. His father, also named Publius Cornelius Scipio was a politician and military commander as was his paternal grandfather and numerous other relations.[1] The Scipio's were a successful subset of the even more successful family line of Cornelius. They were aristocrats in the fullest meaning of the word and their status was based entirely in their long tradition of public service (in the military and senate) to the Roman Republic. Even on his mother's side of the family, the Pamponia, there was nobility as her family enjoyed equestrian status,† a sort of knightly officer class.[2]

As a member of the elite upper class, Publius was expected to join, train and one day hold a leadership position within the citizen militias, known as legions, of Rome. Publius grew up in the time period after the First Punic War and was coming of age when the Second Punic War erupted onto Rome's doorstep. His first commission was in his father's consular army when it was stationed in a defensive posture against Hannibal's Carthaginians in northern Italy. He first saw combat at the Battle of Ticinus where he saved his father's life as the Carthaginian cavalry were about to affect their envelopment of the Roman flanks.[3]

Publius's level headedness in combat and his ability to learn from mistakes (both his own and those of others) allowed him

* Africanus was added later.

† Meaning they could afford horses.

to quickly rise through the ranks before he was able to convince the Senate to appoint him to an independent command in 211-210 BC. According to legend, before Publius's father set off to the Iberian (Spanish) theatre he made his son pledge that he would not cease in his efforts until the Carthaginians military capabilities ceased to exist.[*4] We shall now turn our attention to the unfolding realities of world politics as they existed in the western Mediterranean and how they shaped Publius into the man that he would become.

♦ ♦ ♦

The island of Sicily lay in between the toe of the Italian peninsula and the North African stronghold of Carthage. It was in the middle of the lucrative east-west and north-south Mediterranean maritime trade routes and had the potential to control that trade. For almost as long as history was recorded, the island was divided between Greek poleis and Punic (Carthaginian) settlements, both ethnicities were maritime traders who used the natural harbours of the island for their commercial enterprises. Throughout the Classical Age and into the Hellenistic Age, both sides vied for supremacy on the island, but neither side was ever successful in dominating the entirety of the island.

The Greek polis of Syracuse was the pre-eminent entity on the island, it was successively ruled by demagogic tyrants who were never able to unite the other Greek poleis or conquer the Punic settlements on the island. Throughout its early history the tyrants of Syracuse attempted to garner support amongst the mainland Greek poleis by exaggerating the Carthaginian threat; claiming that Carthage was the equivalent of the Persian Empire in the west.[5] The centuries long power struggle on Sicily was usually interrupted by deep lulls in military activity where both sides sought to heal their wounds and continued to expand their commercial enterprises.

* This being almost identical to the pledge Hannibal made, makes it seem unlikely.

The Carthaginians were Phoenician colonists from the Levantine city of Tyre. The Phoenicians and Tyrians in particular were world class merchants who expanded their commercial networks throughout the entirety of the Mediterranean Sea. Archaeology suggests that the Tyrians established a colony at Carthage sometime around 800 BC. As the location had an excellent harbour, and was well positioned to control the Maritime trade along the east-west axis as well as the north-south route that ran along the coasts of Italy.

Carthage itself was located on the northeast coast of modern day Tunisia, and had one of the ancient world's best natural harbours improved upon through architecture and engineering. While the Carthaginians had excellent access to the sea, they had very little influence over the hinterland of North Africa, which was controlled by the nomadic desert kingdoms. The Carthaginians had always enjoyed a certain amount of autonomy from Tyre, due to the distance from the mother city, but it became a de-facto independent state when Tyre became subsumed within the Babylonian Empire in the sixth century BC.[6] With independence came increased trade and increased trade meant more settlements.[7] But while Carthage increased its area of influence it did not seek to consolidate its trade networks into a centralized empire, instead it preferred to stay along the coastal areas in fortified harbour settlements leaving the hinterlands relatively politically undisturbed.[8] The major Punic settlements included Gades in the southwest of Spain, the Balearic Islands, Corsica, Sardinia and Lilybaeum on the western extremity of Sicily. The Punic settlements in the western Mediterranean were governed by a sort of laissez-faire understanding that it was in everyone's best interest to keep the shipping lanes open and commerce flowing. The responsibility of securing the sea-lanes fell to the Carthaginian navy.

Even if Carthage wanted to establish a formal empire over their Punic kinsmen and neighbours they would have found it extremely difficult to do so as they lacked a significant reserve pool of manpower. Instead of relying on citizen soldiers to fight its wars, Carthage used its material wealth, generated through trade, to pay for mercenary armies that would be commanded by the Carthaginian upper class.[9] The mercenary armies were reasonably successful at defending the existing Punic settlements and had the added bonus of exempting the male Carthaginian population from the dangers of military service. However, the disadvantages of relying solely on mercenaries were numerous. Mercenaries could be incredibly fickle and unreliable, constantly requiring to be paid in cash. Beyond a paycheck and the chance for booty, the mercenaries almost always held no loyalty for the state or generals that employed them, and so, it was difficult to inspire the mercenaries with patriotic zeal. Generally speaking, the Carthaginians were not involved in any major expansionary wars, but rather were satisfied with their coastal enclaves and by expanding their influence over the hinterlands through the indirect benefits of trade and commerce, the notable exception was Carthage's involvement in Sicily.

By this point in history Rome was an emerging power house on the Italian peninsula, but it had never ventured past its Mediterranean coastline for a fight. What started out as a small settlement on the Tiber River, sometime in the Eighth Century, ruled by its legendary founder Romulus, continued to expand for quite some time until it held domination over the entirety of the Italian peninsula. Traditional ancient sources tell us that Rome was ruled by seven monarchs from the beginning of its foundation to the year 509 BC.[10] Legend has it that after a war with the neighbouring Latin tribes around the foundation, Romulus created a council of one hundred noblemen known as the Senate (which included men from the neighbouring tribes), to act as an advisory body for the king. After the revolution of 509 BC, the Roman state would be governed by the Senate.

The Estrucans, a highly advanced Italian tribe to the north, became the dominant power on the Italian peninsula around the Sixth Century BC. The Etruscans succeeded in subverting the Roman state, incorporating Rome into their dominion as they conquered their way into the south.[11] The hegemony that the Etruscans ushered in began to falter after they ran into resistance and even defeat at the hands of Greek poleis in the south of Italy. Rome was able to rebel from their Etruscan overlords after their weaknesses had been exposed in the south. After restoring independence to their city, the Romans established a republican government after a group of noblemen, led by Lucius Junius Brutus, overthrew the reigning king, Tarquinius, who was an Etruscan collaborator.[12] The new government drew from the pre-existing political infrastructure of the Senate and further devolved responsibility onto the popular assemblies called the tribunes allowing all freemen to have a say in the direction of the government.

In contrast to Carthaginian military policy, the Roman armies were made up of citizen militias and allied Latin/Italian tribesmen. The militias had the benefit of paying for their own accoutrements and fighting zealously in defence of their homeland.[13] The downside was that any severe battlefield losses would negatively affect the population of Rome and its allied territory. This was partially offset by the enormous reserve pool of manpower to be found in Italy.

Shortly after the introduction of republicanism into the city a new foreign threat arose out of the north to replace the Etruscans. The Gauls were a tribal entity that occupied most of western and northern Europe; they invaded Italy and went on to sack Rome, but quickly evacuated the city as they had no intention of occupying the area. Instead of wallowing in their destruction, the Romans rebuilt their city and went back on the offensive conquering territory from the Etruscans in the north and the neighbouring Latins in the south.

After a series of wars with their Latin neighbours throughout the early third century BC, Rome had expanded to occupy the central area of the peninsula which now brought them into direct contact with the Greek poleis in the south.[14] The Greeks invited a warrior king from the western coast of northern Greece, Pyrrhus of Epirus, to land in Italy and defend them from the advancing Romans. Pyrrhus was an excellent tactician and commander but he lacked a sufficient reserve of manpower in comparison to that of Rome. Furthermore, the Greeks came to suspect that Pyrrhus was planning to expand his dominion over southern Italy. Several victories were won by Pyrrhus, but they came at such a high cost in causalities that it led Pyrrhus to exclaim "If we win one more such victory over the Romans, we shall be utterly ruined".[*15]

In the war with Pyrrhus, the Romans were displaying the strengths that would become characteristic of their state and people; defiance and resolve in the face of adversity and their ability to tap into an almost limitless supply of manpower in Italy. The Greeks eventually disowned Pyrrhus after he was unable to secure their safety and independence, and Pyrrhus was forced to abandon Italy and return to Epirus.[16] With Pyrrhus out of the picture for now, the Romans were free to complete their domination over southern Italy in the late third century, which now brought them up to the doorstep of Sicily and into the neighbourhood of Carthage.

♦ ♦ ♦

The Greek poleis and the Punic settlements on Sicily were intermittently at war for control over the island until during one war in the mid-third century, the independent polis of Messena had defected to the Carthaginian side. The citizens of Messena came to regret their decision and decided to call in help from the Republic of Rome to the north.[17]

After almost two centuries of successful expansion Rome

* This is where we get the term 'Pyrrhic victory', which is essentially a tactical victory, but a strategic loss.

was full of itself and feeling generous; Rome landed at Messena in 262 BC and took it through subterfuge two years after Carthage had acquired Messena. It was now that the Carthaginians and Syracusians put aside their differences to deal with the new Roman threat. The Carthaginians and Syracusians quickly laid siege to the Romans in Messena, but the Romans were able to breakout.

At this point the Carthaginians barely had a field army in Sicily and were assembling a fresh army back in Africa to meet this new Roman threat.[18] After Messena the Romans moved south quickly to lay siege to Syracuse causing the government there to sue for peace and switch sides to Rome. The land war on Sicily would drag on and teeter-totter between the two sides; consisting mostly of sieges, the local geography being mainly hilly or mountainous made pitched battles a rarity.

When the war began, Rome had a decided advantage in land forces, while Carthage was the dominant naval power. Both sides tried to augment their weakness to match their enemy's strengths; in this, Rome was the more successful of the two. While the war bogged down on the island it became obvious that the only way around the island was by way of the sea.[19] Seeing their weakness at sea, the Romans began a massive naval construction program in an attempt to match the Carthaginians. The Romans suffered numerous naval setbacks throughout the war, but they were able to quickly make good on their losses and build more ships when necessary.[20] The historian, Polybius, puts the final casualties at seven hundred ships for Rome and seven hundred for Carthage.[21]

The Carthaginians fought at sea in the traditional way, they used speed to maneuver around and ram their opponents to death. For this purpose, they had pioneered the development of new naval vessels that built upon the existing technology of the trireme but instead of three banks of oars, there would be five.[22] These 'quinqueremes' were faster and more maneuver-

ATLANTIC
OCEAN
GAUL
GARONNE R.
DOURO R.
IBERIA
EBRO R.
TAGUS R.
GUADIANA R.
Saguntum
BALEARIC ISLES
JUCAR R.
GUADALQUIVIR R.
Ilipa
Baecula
New Carthage
MAURITANIA
NUMIDIA

The Western Mediterranean World

able than any other ship on the sea, but in the event that they were boarded they were susceptible to attack by marines. The Romans eventually came to the understanding that it was impossible to best the Carthaginians at their own game, and so, they devised a new game to play.

The Romans had been lucky enough to capture a shipwrecked Carthaginian quinquereme, which they reverse engineered, taking the technical knowledge for themselves. After taking the shipwreck the Romans made two important innovations to naval construction that would play to the Roman strengths. The first innovation, was copied from the Carthaginians, was to construct the ships with pre-fabricated parts; which made construction and repair cheaper and quicker to replace their losses. This would prove vital as the Romans would lose entire fleets through the course of the war.[23] The second innovation was to install a hinged boarding plank with a spike on the extremity onto the bow, called a corvus, which would attach itself to an enemy ship upon its descent. The corvus, once deployed, would make escape impossible and would allow the Romans to dispatch their marines onto the enemies' ships; effectively turning naval combat into an extension of land warfare.[24]

These new developments allowed the Romans to turn their initial naval weakness into a strength by adapting and applying their infantry advantage to the high seas. In contrast the Carthaginians were too stubborn and stuck in their traditional ways (at times they were also successful) to introduce reforms into their navy and so they began to suffer catastrophic defeats at sea, most notably the Battles of Mylae and Cape Ecnomus in 260 and 256 BC.[25] Even with these defeats Carthage was far from exhausted, and with the war on Sicily turning against them they were able to concentrate a sizable army at their fortress Lilybaeum on the western extremity of Sicily. The Romans went on to expand the war to the islands of Corsica and Sardinia and won naval victories near the two islands, but they were unable to take either island by force from the Carthaginian populations and garrisons.

With Rome now in possession of much of Sicily and stalemate sinking in, the Romans planned and executed an amphibious invasion of the Carthaginian mainland in North Africa. Initially the Romans were successful and won a victory at the Battle of Adys, the victory caused the fickle Carthaginian Council to sue for peace.[26] The Romans set out heavy terms for a peace treaty which were rejected out of hand and the war resumed in earnest. The Carthaginians now turned to the Spartan mercenary general, Xanthippus, who was able to defeat the Romans at the Battle of Tunis in 255 BC. The Romans who survived were forced to withdraw back to Sicily but were destroyed en-route by a storm.[27]

Sicily returned as the main focus of the war, but fighting was largely confined to sieges along the coast. The Carthaginians began a policy of strengthening their garrisons on Sicily in an attempt to hold on to what remained in their possession. The Romans continued to show incredible resilience when it came to making good on their losses; whether due to bad weather or defeat on the sea, the Romans would rebuild their fleets whenever they were destroyed.

Beginning in 250 BC, the pace of the war slowed down as both sides began to be strained by the cost of rebuilding so many ships. Carthage sent a new general to Sicily, Hamilcar Barca,* to conduct a guerilla campaign aimed at disrupting the Roman advance. In the year 244 BC it seemed as if the war would peter out. A leading Carthaginian politician, Hanno, convinced the council to decommission a large portion of their navy, so as to save money; believing that the Romans couldn't possibly continue building more ships.[28] However, the Romans did construct another fleet of warships in 242 BC, forcing the Carthaginians to scramble in their attempt to rebuild their navy. The Romans

* Father of Hannibal Barca.

went on to win a crushing victory the next year at the Battle of the Aegates Islands off the western coast of Sicily. The Carthaginians were unable to make good on their losses and feared that their garrisons on Sicily and throughout the Mediterranean would starve. The Council sued for peace and accepted Rome's terms,* thus ending the first Carthaginian war in 241 BC, twenty-three odd years since it began.[29]

♦ ♦ ♦

The peace that followed wasn't particularly magnanimous for the losers. In fact, it created a number of problems for the Carthaginians and these problems would later be exploited by the Romans for their own advantage; which would lead to feelings of resentment and mutual distrust between the two powers. The treaty required Carthage to pay an indemnity to Rome to make up for the costs of war. While these war reparations were heavy, they would be entirely within the ability of Carthage to make the payments. The final payment occurring in 228 BC, thirteen years after the wars end.[30]

The problems really began for Carthage when it was required to evacuate its mercenary army from Sicily. For the mercenaries, the end of the war meant the end of the prospect for loot and the beginning of their demands for getting paid. The mercenaries rebelled from their commanders as they had no quick way of paying their wages. Hamilcar Barca was able to assuage their fears for a short period as the Council invited them back to North Africa to await their payments. But once they arrived back in North Africa, payment was not forthcoming and the mercenaries mutinied and stumbled into a full on war.[31] While the Carthaginians were distracted putting down the revolt in North Africa, their mercenary garrisons in Sardinia and Corsica also revolted from Carthaginian rule. Seeing the rebellions in Corsica and Sardinia and with Carthage's attention fixated solely

* The Roman terms were for Carthage to pay of an indemnity for the cost of the war and to completely evacuate Sicily and renounce their claim to it.

on North Africa, Rome decided to get involved and pacify the islands, taking them for themselves. Carthage was powerless to do anything as Rome conquered the Phoenician settlements on the two islands.[32]

In 237 BC Hamilcar Barca ended the mercenary war by defeating them in pitched battle. However, after the loss of Sardinia Corsica and Sicily, Carthage started to feel the pinch in their wallet and their bellies; they needed to expand their economy somehow to make up for its lost territory.* Carthage did this in two ways; first it expanded agricultural production within its North African hinterland. Secondly, the Carthaginian general Hamilcar Barca took an army over to the Iberian Peninsula (Spain) and began to conquer the tribal 'kingdoms' along the east coast and its immediate hinterland, gaining the rich silver mines and man power reserves located there.[33]

Before leaving for Iberia, Hamilcar's son – Hannibal (aged 8), asked his father if he could join him in Spain to which Hamilcar replied that he could come on the condition that Hannibal would pledge to be a lifelong enemy of Rome. Hannibal pledged his life to the destruction of Rome and was off to Iberia with his father.[34] The Carthaginians enjoyed success in Iberia, using the newly founded 'New Carthage'† as a staging point for further access into the hinterland and the rich silver and gold mines were used to pay off the indemnity to Rome.

In the year 228 BC Hamilcar Barca died in battle while on campaign in Iberia. The army elected to have the young Hannibal take over his father's command in Iberia and after a fierce opposition to his appointment from the Barca clan's supreme political opponent, Hanno; the Carthaginian Council confirmed Hannibal's appointment and allowed him to rendezvous with the army in Iberia.[35] The Carthaginians in Spain were overjoyed

* The three lost islands, Corsica, Sardinia and Sicily, had traditionally been the bread basket of Carthage but it was no longer possible to profitably import food from them.

† Todays Cartagena, on the southeast coast of Spain.

with Hannibal as they knew him and saw the image of his father in his personage.[36] Hannibal intensified the pace and expanded the scope of Carthaginian dominion over Iberia until it encompassed almost all the land in-between the Atlantic and Mediterranean coast south of the Ebro River. All the land that is, except the city of Saguntum.

Rome and Carthage had signed a treaty that recognized everything south of the Ebro as belonging to Carthage effectively blocking Carthaginian expansion into Gaul. After the treaty had been signed Rome became an ally of Saguntum vowing to come to its defence if ever it was needed. Saguntum stuck out in Iberia like a sore thumb for Carthage, its treaty with Rome was viewed as another example of Roman duplicity. While Carthage itself was governed by an aristocratic council, (and to a lesser extent a public assembly) Iberia was becoming a loyal but de-facto independent fiefdom of Hannibal and the Barca clan.[37]

As most of Carthage's good fortune was due to Hannibal's and the Barca clan's leadership, Hannibal came to view the Iberian Peninsula as his own personal possession. He increasingly began to disregard orders from the Council in favour for his own personal prerogatives. And so, when the city of Saguntum began attacking its Carthaginian allied neighbours, Hannibal took the initiative and laid siege to Saguntum, breaking the treaty between Rome and Carthage.

♦ ♦ ♦

Caught unprepared, the Romans dithered as Hannibal laid siege to Saguntum. They knew what needed to be done, they were just slow in doing it. First they sent an envoy to Hannibal's camp demanding that he desist in his action against Saguntum. Hannibal told them that he was too busy to have his attention diverted and sent the envoy away.[38] So instead they set sail for Carthage intending to plead their case in front of the Council. The Roman envoy demanded that the Carthaginian Council immediately recall Hannibal and send him to Rome for trial; giving them the option to accept peace or prepare for war. The Council, with the exception of Hanno and his faction, refused the Roman envoy and enthusiastically clamoured for the resumption of war.[39]

The war that began in 218 BC after Saguntum would be fought very differently from the previous Punic War. The Romans had all but complete control over the Western Mediterranean, so much so, that the Carthaginians would not contemplate renewing the struggle on the waves. On the Carthaginian side(s) there was effectively two independent commands, one in North Africa with the Carthaginian Council the other in Iberia with Hannibal himself. Hannibal had extensive resources in Iberia that allowed him to recruit and maintain a mercenary army out of his own treasury, the Barca clan had actually started minting coins with his likeness on them.[40] The strategy of the Carthaginian Council was inherently defensive; they intended to maintain their holdings in North Africa while putting a meager effort into capturing parts of Western Sicily. Hannibal on the other hand was planning an offensive strategy that would see the war brought to the doorstep of Rome in Italy itself.

After Saguntum had fallen, Hannibal brought his army back to New Carthage to stay the winter with the intention of having them outfitted and ready to move when the spring campaigning season began. When ready, Hannibal proceeded to march his army north through Iberia over the Pyrenees Mountains into Gaul, then over the Rhone River through treacherous Celtic tribal areas. By the time Hannibal had taken Saguntum, the Romans had sent a consular army, under the command of Publius Cornelius Scipio,* by way of the sea to intercept Hannibal in Iberia.

Scipio landed in Massalia† and discovered that Hannibal had already crossed the Rhone River and was on his way towards the Alps.[41] Unable to catch up with Hannibal, Scipio sent the major-

* Father to Scipio Africanus.

† Modern day Marseille.

ity of his command onto Iberia, but himself returned to Italy to raise another army for when Hannibal had completed crossing the Alps into Italy. With the advent of spring in 217 BC came Hannibal's descent from the Alps into Italy and the beginning of the war in earnest.

Hannibal's sudden appearance in Italy caught the Romans relatively unprepared. Scipio had raced back to northern Italy from Massalia and raised a new army; these men were raw recruits without much training or discipline. On the other hand, Hannibal's men were depleted from their trek over the Alps, but they were battle hardened veterans who had fought with him for the better part of a decade. Included in Hannibal's army was a contingent of elephants that were used as a sort of super heavy cavalry, much like a modern tank.[42] The people of Italy had never seen elephants and were shocked when they first saw them thundering onto the battlefield. Overtures had been made by Hannibal to the Celtic tribes of northern Italy to rise up and assist the Carthaginians in their attempt to overthrow Rome. The Celts were receptive to the idea, but did not want to get caught in between the two sides, and so, they decided it would be prudent for them to hedge their bets until one side had proved themselves over the other.

♦ ♦ ♦

Hannibal and Scipio first came into contact with one another along the Ticinus River (a tributary of the Po). The day before the battle both sides had scouted out the other side and both advanced with the entirety of their cavalry. Along with his cavalry, Scipio also brought with him his javelin throwing light infantry. When the two sides met in the field, they formed up into lines and prepared for a battle.

Scipio formed up his line with his skirmishers out in a line in front of his horsemen.[43] Hannibal's line was formed with his heavy cavalry in the middle and his light cavalry on either wing. When Hannibal saw Scipio's javelin men setting up he had his cavalry charge them before they could get a volley off. The Roman skirmishers scattered before the onslaught of the Carthaginian horse and disrupted the Roman cavalry line as they retreated. The Roman line held fast and put up a good fight, but the Carthaginian light cavalry maneuvered around their flanks and surrounded the Roman force. Scipio himself was cut off from retreat and wounded. He would have fallen dead had it not been for his son Publius Cornelius Scipio and his body guard coming to the rescue just in the nick of time.[44]

The Romans who survived withdrew from the Ticinus River back to the Trebia, another tributary of the Po River. Feeling the urgency of the situation, the Senate in Rome recalled the consular army bound for Sicily and joined it with Scipio's legions. With the two consular armies now joined together there was bound to be another battle before long. Scipio was not anxious for another battle and advised a cautious approach, he preferred to wait and train the men throughout the coming winter. Tiberius Sempronius Longus, the second consul, was itching for a fight and believed that Scipio's caution was borne out of fear from his earlier defeat.[45]

The Celts were still sitting on the fence as they believed that the Battle of Ticinus had not proved who was the strongest. Their obfuscation angered Hannibal, and so, he dispatched some of his cavalry to lay waste to their land within the immediate vicinity. In response, the Celts sent envoys to the Roman camp to ask for their assistance, which prompted Tiberius to dispatch some of his troops to rescue the Celts. After a cavalry skirmish, the Romans emerged victorious and full of confidence.

The two consuls now held a meeting with themselves to discuss what their next action should be. Scipio restated his belief that the troops wold be better served by settling in for the winter (it was now December) and by continuing in their training. Sempronius was confident that now was the best time to strike; they had just won a skirmish and it was almost time for consular elections to take place. Hannibal was informed of Sempronius's temperament and planned an ambush for the Romans on the opposite bank of the Trebia.[46] He concealed a combined force of some one thousand handpicked infantry and cavalry in brambles perpendicular to the river to the south of the ford while he deployed his main battle line parallel and in front of the river crossing. Once the trap was set, Hannibal lured the Romans across the Trebia by sending his Numidian cavalry to harass the Roman camp in the early morning.

The Romans took the bait and advanced over the cold swollen river. They had their cavalry routed when the Carthaginian horsemen wheeled back around and renewed their attack. This left the Roman heavy infantry unsupported, hungry and cold on the west bank of the river. Once the Roman infantry had advanced far enough, the concealed men to the south sprung their trap and moved against the Roman's left flank. The Romans formed into a hollow square and were able to avoid complete destruction but they were morally beaten and had to retire back to Placentia under constant pressure from Hannibal. With the winter now in full force, Hannibal settled his men down into camp; the Celts and many of the cities of Northern Italy now came over to the Carthaginian side.[47] The next campaign would find Hannibal's army in full fighting strength and Rome inching its way into the abyss.

♦ ♦ ♦

In the elections that were scheduled to take place, the Romans elected two new consuls to replace Scipio and Sempronius. The new consuls were Gnaeus Servilius Geminus and Gaius Flaminius. They took command of the two armies in the north while four new legions were raised and split between the two commanders in an attempt to bolster their chances in subduing the threat. The two old armies were recalled from the north to prepare a defence closer to Rome; once Hannibal saw their movements he set his army in motion.

Hannibal's plan was to somehow place himself in between Rome and Flaminius and thus provoke Flaminius into a battle on ground of Hannibal's choosing. Flaminius, like Sempronius before him was rash and over confident in his ability. Through the use of a forced march over marshy terrain, Hannibal entered into and began to desolate the territory Flaminius was sent to protect.[48] At the sight of the smoke and with the added motivation of reproach in Rome, Flaminius set out in force to put an end to Hannibal's deprivations.

On the northern shore of Lake Trasimene, Hannibal was prepared to meet Flaminius in ambush, and he was further aided by a thick fog that had descended over the area. He had spent the previous night deploying his light skirmishers and Celtic allies along the forested slope to the north. While on his right he deployed his cavalry out of sight and on his left he posted his heavy African infantry perpendicular to the road in order to block the Roman column when they advanced. As the Romans came forward along the road, Hannibal had a detachment of skirmishers harass their van guard without fully engaging them so as to separate their vanguard from the rest of their column.

When the Romans were sufficiently advanced along the road, Hannibal gave the signal to launch the ambush; his Iberian and Celtic light troops came out from concealment and engaged the Roman centre while the cavalry swung around and engaged the Roman rear.[49] The Romans were now trapped on three sides by Hannibal's forces and on their forth side was the lake. After hard fighting the Roman vanguard was able to force their way out through the front but the rest of the Romans were not so lucky. Many of them preferred to drown themselves than to fight the Carthaginians; the Roman commander, Flaminius was amongst the dead.[50]

With nothing standing in the way of Rome, the people and Senate were put into a panic and forced to elect another consul, who they made into a dictator for the duration of one year. The man they made dictator was Fabius Maximus and the strategy he initiated was a radical break from the headstrong offensives that were the norm for Roman generals. Fabius first sought to avoid pitched battle with Hannibal on level ground by occupying the high grounds of the central Apennine Mountains. His strategy wasn't entirely defensive as he also strove to dislocate Hannibal from his Celtic and Latin allies through pin prick attacks on his supply lines.[51] To the Roman psyche, Fabius's strategy was outrageous and unmanly; as long as an invader was on Italian soil the invader was to be directly confronted no matter what the cost. Fabius's strategy was working, slowly but surely, but the Romans demanded a direct confrontation with Hannibal's army. When Fabius's one-year term as dictator expired there was no shortage of Senators who would promise Rome the decisive action they so eagerly desired.

In the year 215 new consuls had been elected, Gaius Terentius Varro and Lucius Aemilius Paullus. As well, the Senate authorized an unprecedented army of eight legions to be recruited and put under the command of the two consuls, each consul taking his turn at command on alternate days.[52] The Romans marched south against Hannibal when they heard that he had captured the stockpile of supplies at the town of Cannae. A few days later the two forces were within marching distance on or around the Aufidus River close to the town of Cannae. The engagements began with a cavalry skirmish in which the Romans got the better of the Carthaginians. Buoyed with confidence after the skirmish the Consul, Varro, was eager for a set piece battle which he set about to arrange on his day of command by placing the army in close contact. For his part, Hannibal was prepared and desired to oblige Varro with a battle.[53]

When battle came Hannibal had positioned his best African infantry on either wing of his centre. While his centre comprised of his Iberian, Gallic and Latin allies, he deployed his infantry in a bow shape with the centre closest to the Roman lines. On Hannibal's extreme right wing he placed his swift Numidian cavalry, while on his far left he positioned his heavy Gallic horsemen.[54] The Romans formed up their battle lines in their conventional order with three lines one behind the other and with two detachments of cavalry on either side. The battle began with the Romans advancing their first line forward against Hannibal's centre. Hannibal's auxiliaries in the centre fought hard, but gradually gave up ground as was the plan. The Carthaginian cavalry achieved success on both wings. After scattering the Roman horse posted against them, the Gallic cavalry circled around the Roman rear and attacked the Roman cavalry engaged with the Numidians; effectively scattering both wings of Roman cavalry.[55]

The Roman infantry believed they were enjoying success in the centre and pushed forward unbeknownst that they were falling into Hannibal's trap. As the Roman infantry advanced into Hannibal's centre the heavy African troops turned into the center and attacked the Roman infantry in their flanks. Once Hannibal's cavalry had finished their business against the Roman horse, they turned against the Roman rear and completed the encirclement. Now surrounded on all sides and with no room to maneuver the Romans became so crowded that they were barely able to use their own weapons and were eventually cut down almost to the last man. Of the eighty odd thousand Romans that began the battle, a mere five thousand found their way back to Rome.[56]

After the utter destruction of the Roman army, the Romans were once again seized with a panic and soon brought back Fabius as their dictator. Fabius reinstituted his old strategy and brought the army back to within the walls of the city. Unable to assault the walls of Rome directly (due to his lacking an adequate siege train and a lack of forthcoming reinforcement's from Carthage or Iberia), Hannibal was forced to continue his policy of attempting to detach the Latin cities from their obli-

Ticinus
Trebia
Massilia
CORSICA
MEDITERRANEAN SEA

Hannibal in Italy

gations to Rome. While Fabius's strategy had retrieved the situation of Rome from its desperate state after Cannae, it was only capable of creating equilibrium amongst the two powers and not a decisive victory for Rome.

A new strategy would be required if the Romans were to evict Hannibal from the Italian peninsula and achieve a meaningful victory. Scipio the Elder was sent to Iberia in an attempt to deprive the Carthaginians of their base there, but he was killed during a battle against Hannibal's brother, Hasdrubal.[57] Once news of the Elder Scipio's defeat and death reached Rome it appeared as if the Iberian theatre had been lost to Rome as no one appeared ready, willing or qualified to take up a command in the theatre. However, there appeared to be a glimmer of hope in the person of the young Scipio, who at this dark moment of the Republics history stepped into his role that destiny had ordained.[58]

♦ ♦ ♦

When Scipio offered his service to the Roman Senate he was, according to custom, too young to hold the office of proconsul. But due to the severity of the situation and the zeal with which he conducted himself, Publius Cornelius Scipio the younger was elected to the office of proconsul for the Roman army sent to Carthaginian Iberia. Upon his arrival at the mouth of the Ebro River in 210 BC, Scipio learned that the three Carthaginian generals in the theater were situated in the south, and west interior of Iberia, leaving the capital of New Carthage largely undefended. Scipio moved quickly along the coast from the Ebro and captured New Carthage where he was able to requisition the military provisions that were stored there.[59]

While occupying New Carthage, Scipio was forced to make some difficult decisions that would show posterity his practical magnanimity and good statesmanship that would become characteristic of his career. The Roman Senates first priority was the Italian theatre, and so, precious few reinforcements would be available for Scipio in Iberia. He would have to make do with what he had and with what he could recruit amongst the locals. It was with these considerations in mind that Scipio released hostages of the Iberian chieftains that the Carthaginians had been holding, including a princess, back to their tribes.[60] This act of magnanimity attracted certain Iberian tribal elements over to Scipio's side as he was preparing to move west to engage the Carthaginian generals.

Scipio and Hasdrubal found each other's armies around the village of Baecula on the upper portion of the Guadalquivir River. This would be Scipio's first set piece battle with himself at the highest level of independent command. Scipio's dilemma was that he couldn't spend time maneuvering as the other two Carthaginian armies would converge with Hasdrubal and overwhelm Scipio. In the absence of time, Scipio was forced to make a frontal assault up a hill with his heavy infantry, Scipio instilled his soldiers with hope by reminding them of how they had scaled the walls at New Carthage. The assault in the centre took casualties as they proceeded up the hill, but they did not falter forcing Hasdrubal to call in his reserves to retrieve the situation. While the attack in the centre was unfolding and distracting Hasdrubal's attention, Scipio had sent two divisions around both flanks to effect a double envelopment.[61]

The flanking maneuvers caught Hasdrubal by surprise and forced him to withdraw from the battlefield. Hasdrubal and his army was not completely destroyed and were able to make their way north with the intent of reinforcing Hannibal in Italy.[62] Scipio was unable to pursue Hasdrubal as there were still two Carthaginian armies operating out of Gades in southern Iberia. Before Hasdrubal could link up with Hannibal he was intercepted and destroyed by another Roman army in northern Italy. In the meantime, Scipio was busy getting Iberian tribes to switch over to the Roman cause; in this endeavour he met with moderate success getting two of the more powerful tribal entities joining his side. After two years of both sides recouping their energies they both went out looking for a battle again.

Scipio used the time to drill his forces into a high level of tactical efficiency with an emphasis on the maneuverability of his formations. The two remaining Carthaginian generals, Hasdrubal Gisco and Mago Barca, used this time to marshal their forces together, but they were hindered from garnishing significant reinforcements from North Africa as Carthage was busy putting down revolts in Numidia. The upcoming battle would prove decisive for the winning side as both armies represented the sole available-remaining forces their governments could muster for the Iberian theatre.

The two forces met around the village of Ilipa in southwest Spain not far from where Scipio's father and uncle had died; victims to the treachery of their Iberian allies. Both sides attempted to gain an advantage over the other through skirmishing, which was to cost the Carthaginians dearly in cavalry when Scipio laid a trap for them outside his camp. For a few days both sides would arrange their forces into battle formation but neither side wanted to take the initiative. However, Scipio noticed that the Carthaginian formation was the exact same every single time they were led out.[63]

Everyday Gisco and Mago would deploy their elite infantry in the centre, their light troops on either flank, their cavalry on the far wings and their elephants screening in front of their light troops. Every time the armies were called out Scipio would mirror this formation and lulled the Carthaginians into believing that this was how Scipio intended to fight the battle.[64] After having drilled his forces in battlefield maneuverability for two years Scipio was supremely confident in the abilities of his troops; Scipio had no intention of attacking the Carthaginian position in the conventional way.

On the day Scipio had chosen for battle, he had his men wake up before dawn and eat their breakfast before they took to the field. This time Scipio assembled his army in a different fashion, with his Roman infantry on the flanks and the Iberian auxiliaries in the center and then advanced his cavalry and skirmishers towards the Carthaginian line to act as a screen for the advancing infantry.

Caught by surprise, and unable to see what Scipio was up to, the Carthaginians were mustered in their usual deployments. When the dust settled it was too late to make any changes. Scipio's cavalry was the first to make a move, they attacked the Carthaginian flanks and drove their elephants back into the Carthaginian lines. As the Carthaginians became confused, Scipio completed his maneuvers of encirclement which mimicked Hannibal's deployments at Cannae, but with an offensive twist. As Scipio's heavy infantry attacked the Carthaginians flanks (made up of Iberian auxiliaries), their elite African troops in the centre were not engaged by Scipio's Iberian allies, but they were unable to come to the aide of their flanks as Scipio's Iberians constantly threated to pounce on them if they did.[65]

Scipio's deception and skillful tactical maneuverings confined the Carthaginians within their original deployments and were unable to maneuver or fight within their own lines and before long they were forced to withdraw. Initially the withdrawal was orderly, but it quickly degenerated into a rout. Gisco and Mago were able to escape from their disaster but the next day Scipio aggressively pursued the remnants of their force and caught up with them the day after. Once again Gisco and Mago affected their own escapes, but the Carthaginian imperial project in Iberia was effectively destroyed for good when Mago and Hasdrubal set sail for Africa and abandoned their last port of entry at Gades to the Romans.[66]

♦ ♦ ♦

With the war wrapped up in Iberia, Scipio was slated to return to Rome, but before he set sail he made a quick trip to the North African kingdom of Numidia. Situated to the west of Carthage

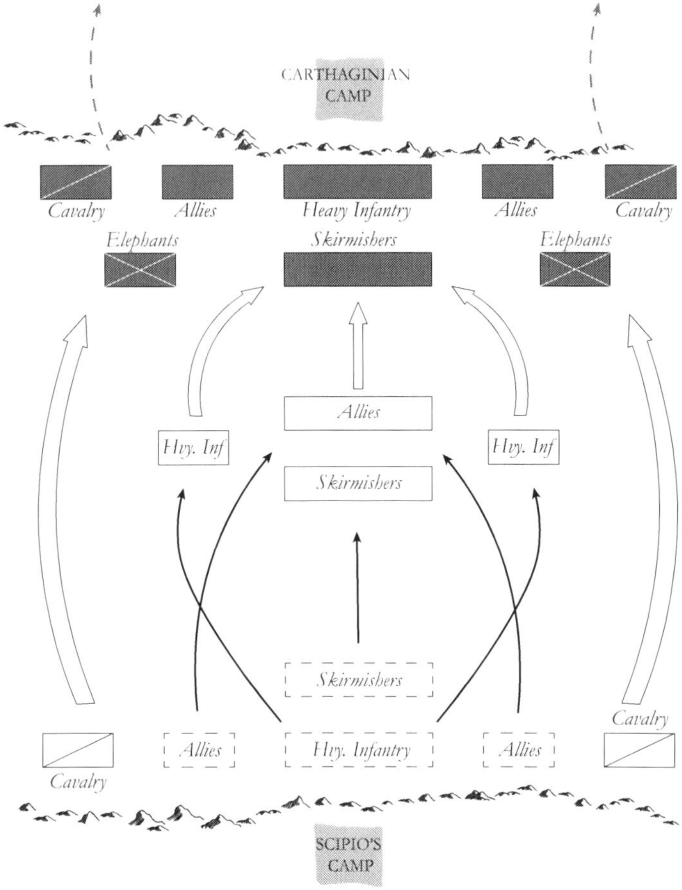

Battle of Ilipa

in modern day Algeria and Morocco, Numidia was an important ally of Carthage and was a vital source of mercenaries and elite cavalry units. While Scipio was visiting the Numidian capital, his rival Hasdrubal was also in town on an identical mission to secure assistance from the Numidians. Scipio was successful in getting the rival kings Syphax and Massinissa to sign a treaty pledging to aid the Romans in the event of Scipio landing an army into North Africa.[67] For the time being, Scipio had to return to Rome to secure his position there and to convince the Senate to raise another army for him to invade Africa; all the while Hannibal was busy consolidating his position in southern Italy.

After Scipio's successful campaign in Iberia and his opening of diplomatic channels with Numidia he was finally able to return to Rome as a conquering hero. While in Rome, Scipio relinquished his command over the Roman troops and began to lobby for command of an army he planned to bring to the doorstep of Carthage. A number of influential senators, chief amongst them was Fabius Maximus, were opposed to Scipio's plan for invading North Africa while Hannibal was still at large in Italy. This opposition was partly out of jealousy but also out of a legitimate fear of Hannibal's marauding army still at large in Italy. While Scipio was elected to the office of Consul in 205 BC, he was only allotted the command over the Roman garrison of Sicily.[68] His political opponents believed that such limits would restrict his ambition and doom him to failure.

Before setting off for Sicily, Scipio used his own funds and called in favours from his aristocratic friends to raise a force of volunteers numbering some seven thousand men and thirty warships, which he took with him to the island of Sicily. As soon as he was in Sicily he began training his new army. The garrison in Sicily were veterans from the great Roman disasters in Italy.*

* Rome used garrison duty in Sicily as a punishment of sorts for perceived failure.

Scipio had common ground with his new charges as they had all seen action against Hannibal at Cannae or elsewhere. Knowing that the disasters were not the fault of the men, Scipio took pity on them and brought them the hope of redemption through future service. The rank and file were receptive to his message and took a liking to their new general.

Scipio also took measures towards creating a Roman cavalry corps that would be a rival for that of Carthage. He began by conscripting local Sicilian noblemen into service. The Sicilians were anxious to avoid military service to their Roman overlords, so when Scipio suggested they could pay to equip and send a replacement in their stead, the noblemen eagerly accepted Scipio's offer.[69] Around this time rumours had made it back to Rome that Scipio's forces on Sicily were nothing more than an undisciplined rabble, idling their time away in relative safety and comfort. The Senate decided to send a group of commissioners to investigate the army's condition. When the commission arrived in Sicily, they found the rumours to be utterly false. Scipio was at the head of a well quipped, highly trained and motivated force that was eager to see action in Africa.[70]

Still the Roman Senate was skeptical of Scipio's plan and only granted him permission to cross into Africa if it appeared to be in the interest of Rome. The orders from Rome were ambiguous enough for Scipio to interpret them to suit his own designs. And so, in 204 BC, Scipio believed that he was sufficiently prepared for the expedition and he set off towards the Carthaginian heartland.

Scipio landed his army to the west of Carthage near the city Utica. Utica was ideal for its port facilities and also it was conveniently within a reasonable distance of his Numidian allies. While Prince Massinissa stayed true to his earlier pledge of assistance to Scipio, Prince Syphax was convinced by the Carthaginians (Hasdrubal's daughter was married to Syphax) to remain on their side.[71] After disembarking his forces, Scipio promptly laid siege to Utica, but was forced to abandon the siege when Syphax and a Carthaginian army arrived in the vicinity. Scipio was then forced to retire to a thin peninsula nearby in order to nullify the Carthaginians numerical superiority. And so, the attackers became the defenders and both sides settled in for a protracted siege.

Scipio concocted a novel plan to raise the siege and break out of the beachhead by attacking the Carthaginian camp at night when they least expected it. The Carthaginian camp consisted of mud and reed huts that were extremely flammable if someone were to put them to the torch. Through the use of a night attack Scipio set fire to a portion of the camp which spread out of control and caused a panic amongst the soldiers. Amidst the chaos Scipio was able to annihilate the majority of the Carthaginian army and caused Syphax to withdraw his forces from the vicinity.[72] The following day Scipio dispatched his cavalry and those of Massinissa to pursue Syphax and to eliminate him as a future threat. At the Battle of the Great Plains in 203 BC, Scipio destroyed another hastily assembled army of Carthaginian citizens reinforced by mercenaries from Iberia. The Iberians were the only ones who gave much account of themselves, but as the native Carthaginians abandoned their positions the Iberians were in turn outflanked and annihilated.[73]

With their army in shambles and Syphax no longer of any assistance the Carthaginians had no immediate hope other than to improve their cities fortifications and to sue for peace. While the denizens frantically prepared for a siege and attempted to negotiate with Scipio, they also sent an envoy to Hannibal requesting that he and his army return to Africa to save them from Scipio. Although reluctant to abandon Italy, Hannibal felt an obligation to return to his mother city to organize its defence.[74] After sixteen years of tramping through Italy, Hannibal was finally made to evacuate the peninsula due to Scipio's strategy of taking the war first to Iberia, then directly to Carthage's doorsteps. Scipio

Carthaginian North Africa

had learnt well from Hannibal's invasion of Italy and now the student was turning the lesson back on the master.

♦ ♦ ♦

With Hannibal and his veterans back in Africa, the peace negotiations between Scipio and Carthage were broken off as it was obvious that fighting would soon resume in earnest. Southwest of Carthage on the plain outside the city of Zama the two armies met each other. In an attempt to resume the peace talks, Hannibal requested and received a parlay with Scipio to see if they could negotiate a peaceful solution. The negotiations broke down once again as both sides believed they would be successful in a pitched battle.

For this battle Hannibal had a slight numerical advantage in infantry with nearly thirty-six thousand infantry to Scipio's thirty thousand. However, Scipio had a decided advantage in the quality and quantity of his combined Roman and Numidian cavalry with roughly six thousand horsemen to Hannibal's four thousand cavalry and eighty elephants.[75] Both Scipio and Hannibal resorted to relatively simple tactical formations, as compared to the complex tactical maneuvers they had employed on other commanders. This was probably out of respect for each other's ability to handle their troops on the battlefield.

When Hannibal arrived on the field he proceeded to deploy his infantry in three successive lines. Mercenaries in the first line, Carthaginian conscripts in the second and his elite veterans from Italy in the third line, with cavalry contingents on either wing and his elephants out in front.[76] Seeing Hannibal's deployment with his elephants out front, Scipio arranged his forces to deal with the inevitable charge. Instead of deploying his infantry in the long unbroken lines as Hannibal had, Scipio created pathways that ran perpendicular to his lines so that the elephants could be brought through the lines without doing excessive damage. In addition to these dispositions, Scipio placed his cavalry on either wing reinforcing his right wing to make it stronger than the left.[77]

The battle began with Hannibal's elephants charging at Scipio's lines, the Romans scared some of the beasts away by blasting trumpets which sent a number of them charging back into Hannibal's infantry mass. Still some elephants were undaunted by the noise and continued towards the Romans. The remaining elephants were either herded through the Roman lines along the pathways, or were dealt with by the Roman skirmishers. The Elephants managed to inflict minimal damage on the Roman infantry, but this was offset by the damage and chaos that the panicked elephants had also inflicted upon Hannibal's lines.

The next phase of the battle saw the engagement of both the cavalry and infantry of both sides. After heavy melee combat amongst the opposing infantry both sides were becoming exhausted and their most experienced of troops were called on to engage with their opposite members. Stalemate was seemingly about to be reached, but at this moment Scipio's superiority in cavalry began to pay dividends. After scattering the Carthaginian horse, the Roman cavalry returned to the main fray and began their work upon Hannibal's rear. With Scipio's veteran infantry engaging Hannibal's front and his cavalry now engaged in his rear, Hannibal's men fell into a panic and were routed as they attempted to retreat back to Carthage, as they had nowhere safe to rally and reform.[78] Scipio now moved his men towards Carthage itself, from where he would be able to give the city his terms for peace; this time they would not be able to refuse.

♦ ♦ ♦

In another act of magnanimity Scipio, after his defeat of Hannibal at Zama, offered the Carthaginians relatively lenient terms for peace.[79] The treaty required the Carthaginians to give up their claims on any overseas possessions (which was already a reality), also to surrender their warships and to pay and indemnity to Rome over a period of time. Scipio allowed Hannibal to remain in Carthage as their civic leader, but his political enemies in the

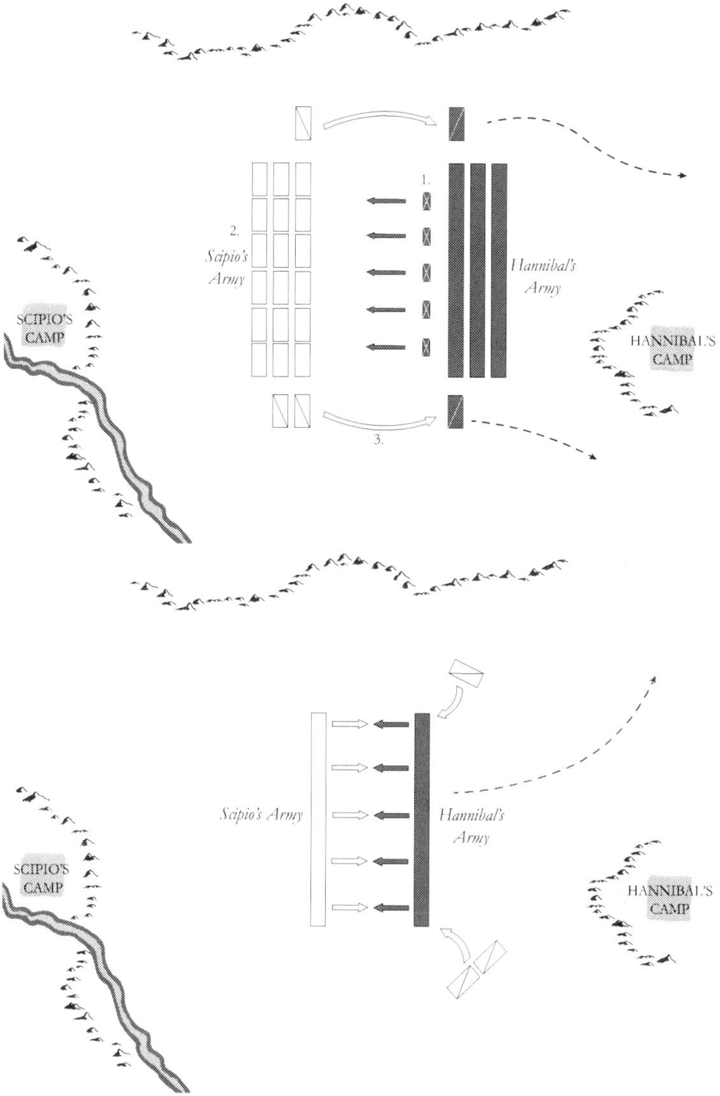

Battle of Zama

1. Elephants charge, infantry follows. 2. Roman infantry create gaps in their lines for elephants to pass through. 3. Roman cavalry best their Carthaginian opponents.

city would soon force him into exile. When Scipio returned to Italy he was greeted as a conquering hero and was celebrated with a triumphal procession through the streets of Rome.[80]

The citizens of Rome, in their delirium wanted to crown Scipio as consul or dictator for life, but Scipio turned down the offer. Instead, Scipio chose a quiet life in the country. However, he did accept the title of Africanus being added to his name. Scipio's rural life was interrupted when it was found out that, Antiochus III - King of the Seleucid Empire, had hired Hannibal as a mercenary general, who was believed to be planning on retaking Carthage.[81] Scipio was dispatched to assist his brother, Lucius Cornelius Scipio (later Asiaticus), in the Syrian theatre. In 190 BC, the same year as war was declared the two Scipio brothers brought the war to a successful conclusion after the Battle of Magnesia.[82]

After the Syrian campaign, Scipio once again attempted to return to the simple country life, but he was brought before the courts by his political enemies in 185 BC. They claimed that he had been bribed by Antiochus to accept a peace, in his defence Scipio appealed to the public reminding the Romans that it was an anniversary of his victory at Zama. The court of public opinion instantly forgot the charges of wrong doing brought against him.[83] Scipio returned to his estate in the country, but he lived under the constant threat of legal annoyances. He even attempted to save his old enemy Hannibal from the wrath of the Roman Senate; Hannibal was eventually tracked down to the kingdom of Bithynia (on the Black Sea) where he killed himself rather than be paraded through the streets of Rome. When Scipio died (probably in 183 BC) he refused to have his remains transported back to Rome for burial, because he felt that Rome had been ungrateful to him.[84]

Scipio's military accomplishments were considerable in their scope and in their consequences. At the time when he was first given independent command, the Roman strategic situation was incredibly bleak; Hannibal had free reign in southern Italy and the War seemed all but lost in Iberia. If Rome strictly adhered to Fabius's strategy (which could avoid disaster) there would be no decisive victory for Rome. Scipio tempered the tradition of head on Roman aggression with the subtle tactic of exposing the enemy's weakness into a policy of indirect offensives that first knocked the Carthaginians out of Iberia, and then forced Hannibal to evacuate Italy in order to defend his homeland. Instead of waiting on his enemies, Scipio took the initiative and forced the Carthaginians to react to the tempo of his offensives. Scipio's strategy was essential for Rome's decisive victory.

The defeat of Carthage secured Rome's dominance in the Western Mediterranean and allowed for the continuation of Rome's mixed constitution. Along with making Rome phenomenally rich, it also allowed Rome to look beyond its traditional neighbourhood in search of land and fortune. In a way Scipio's success in the Second Punic War and the massive introduction of wealth helped bring about the social changes that would one day rock the Republic to its very foundations. But for now, peace and liberty reigned within Rome and throughout much of the Mediterranean world. The new Roman world order had been brought about and secured by Scipio's actions and brilliance.

Marcus Junius Brutus

Marcus Junius Brutus was born in 85 BC to his father Marcus Junius Brutus the Elder and his mother Servilia Caepionis.[1] His paternal family was directly descended from Lucius Junius Brutus who was the leading Roman in the coup d'état that disposed of the last king of Rome in 509 BC and established Rome as a republic.[2] Marcus's father, Brutus the Elder, was a skilled politician and commander of men, but he was assassinated by an agent of Gnaeus Pompeius Magnus (Pompey) after having sided with the populares faction in a rebellion/civil war.[3] When his father was killed, Marcus was extremely young and he was adopted by a maternal uncle, Quintus Servilius Caepio. Under his uncles wing Marcus learned the ropes of the political scene in Rome.

Luckily for posterity, Plutarch's biography of Marcus's life has survived as have numerous accounts from his contemporaries. The accounts agree that Marcus was a very well rounded and agreeable young man. Plutarch tells us that Marcus excelled in his 'liberal education' especially the in the field of philosophy.

> "Brutus… having to the goodness of his disposition added the improvements of learning and the study of philosophy and having stirred up his natural parts, of themselves grave and gentle, by applying himself to business and public affairs, seems to have been of a temper exactly framed for virtue."[4]

Generally speaking, none of Marcus's peers ever had a bad thing to say about him including the people who had openly fought against him. "...they who were most his enemies upon account of his conspiracy against Caesar, if in that whole affair there was any honourable or generous part, referred it wholly to Brutus..."[5] Julius Caesar who was a good friend of Brutus once said of him. "I know not what this young man intents, but whatever he intends, he intends vehemently."[6]

Marcus first cut his political teeth while serving under another maternal uncle, Cato, during Cato's term in the office as governor of Cyprus. While in Cyprus, Marcus was able to amass himself a small fortune by lending money at a high rate of interest.[7] During his time there, Marcus was ordered to take charge of King Ptolemy's treasure after the Romans had subdued his agitation. The man Cato had originally tasked with the duty of guarding the treasure turned out to be a scoundrel and was suspected of skimming off the top. Brutus was not overjoyed with the duty given to him (he felt it beneath him) but he executed the mission none-the-less and brought the treasure into Rome personally.[8]

Once back in Rome, Marcus was a rich man with a noble family background stretching back to the foundation of the Republic. He became a Senator and true to his class aligned himself with the conservative 'optimate' faction against the emerging 'first triumvirate' which was a three-way political pact between Pompey, Crassus and Caesar. Before venturing any further into Marcus Junius Brutus's political and military career we shall first review the world in which the Roman Republic had existed since the time of Hannibal and Scipio.

♦ ♦ ♦

The results of the Second Punic War left Rome in the position of undisputed master of the Western Mediterranean world. But before long, Carthage had been able to pay off the war indemnities that were part of their terms for surrender after the

Second Punic War. Even with Carthage confined to its North African hinterland, it had once again grown quite prosperous. The Senate in Rome grew suspicious of Carthage's economic revival and would jump at any pretext to renew the war against its old nemesis.

That pretext came when a border dispute erupted between Carthage and the Numidian kingdom; the peace treaty stipulated that Carthage must seek the permission of Rome before going to war with anyone. The Senate immediately sent an army to demand that Carthage surrender its arms. Carthage submitted to Rome, but then Rome made new demands which would prove impossible for the once proud Carthaginians to accept.[*9] When the Third Punic War began, it was little more than a protracted siege in which the Carthaginians mobilized their entire metropolitan population in a frenzied attempt to rearm themselves. All their efforts were for naught as the Romans utterly destroyed every block of the city after a brutal three-year siege ending in 146 BC.[10]

In the same year as the annihilation of Carthage, Rome also sent a message to the Eastern Mediterranean world through the annihilation of the ancient Greek naval power, Corinth.[11] The message was clear: quarrel with Rome at your own peril. Rome had become the dominant power throughout the entire Mediterranean basin, but this new found hegemony and infusion of wealth did not come about without radical rifts to the social fabric of Rome and Italy.

The series of long wars going back to the initial conquest of Italy and the subsequent introduction of immense wealth after their favourable outcomes tended to benefit the well-to-do disproportionately. A lengthy campaign took the smaller landholding men away from their farms, which would then fall into disrepair, debt and idleness and would sooner or later be

* Chief amongst those provisions was the relocation of its population away from the sight of Carthage.

bought up by the larger agricultural estates, to be run by slaves introduced into Italy from the wars. The loss of their land and livelihood forced families into the city(ies) to look for work and more often than naught to become dependent on the handouts from the aristocratic elite.[12] These displacements created political discontent and allowed for unscrupulous political leaders to prey on the votes of desperate individuals who would vote for whoever promised them the most (much like democracy in the contemporary world). And thus, we began to see the rise of domestic political factions who would pander to the whims of class interests, and politicians who would use the desperations for their personal rise to power. Demagoguery was quickly becoming the name of the game in Rome.

The populares and optimates factions emerged to represent the interests of the landless plebeians and the aristocratic patricians respectively. As they migrated into the city, the plebeians had been steadily expanding their influence while the Patricians were constantly working to maintain their position of power. What began as a lively political debate quickly solidified into class warfare and threatened, at best to paralyse the legislative process and at worse to drag the Republic into open rebellion and civil war.

The Senate was politically and legally attacked by the Gracchi brothers, Tiberius and Gaius, when the two acting as Tribunes of the people (one after the other) attempted to subvert Rome through legal machinations from a form of mixed government into a direct democracy.[13] The Senate resisted these reforms with each and every means at their disposal; eventually including the assassination of the two Gracchi.[14] The death of the brothers actually succeeded in stalling the momentum towards popular rule for a time. However, the populares faction was still a powerful meddling force within the political scene at Rome. The populares became emboldened again when they found a new leader in Gaius Marius, a minor nobleman and successful general (from Southern Italy), returned from the recent 'Jugurtha War' against a usurper in Numidia. Marius became entrenched in power with the loyalty of his legions paid for (by himself), while the Senate had no experienced military man who could effectively challenge Marius's position.

When war broke out in 88 BC to the east with the expansionist kingdom of King Mithridates of Pontus*, the aristocracy and Senate saw their chance to revive their position of authority. The Senate elected one of their own (an optimate), Lucius Cornelius Sulla to command the expeditionary force sent to deal with Mithridates.[15] Almost as soon as Sulla had left the city, a tribune (acting at the behest of Marius) declared Sulla's commission void. Sulla was forced to return to the city with his army to confront the agitators, and while he was in Rome he passed some legislation aimed at curbing the growing influence of the populares.[16] With the crisis dealt with (or so Sulla believed), Sulla was able to resume the war in the east. Once again, without Sulla in Rome the populares returned to their status of influence in Rome under the leadership of Marius and Cinna, this time going so far as to perpetuate violence against members of the Senate.[17]

When Sulla had successfully concluded a peace treaty with Mithridates in 85 BC,† the pendulum was ready to swing back against the populares with a vengeance. Sulla returned to Rome and ejected the Tribunes from their seat of power before going on to kill Cinna and his supporters, leaving no populare resistance openly declaring itself.[18] After the destruction of the opposition Sulla made himself dictator in an attempt to restore order to the city. As dictator, Sulla brought the Senate back to

* Pontus was a Greek kingdom along the southern coast of the Black Sea, located now in modern day Turkey.

† Mithridates had united much of Asia Minor under his banner and brought the war into Greece. It began when Mithridates order the murder of all Roman citizens living in Asia Minor. Mithridates was eventually pushed back into his original borders, but was left in control of the Kingdom of Pontos. There would be two more wars fought against Mithridates.

its position of prestige and introduced reforms to permanently weaken the Tribunes. Once he had accomplished these goals he resigned the dictatorship and practically quit public life before he died in 78 BC.[19] It would seem as if balance had been brought back to the government of Rome, and that the trouble with the populares were put on the back burner.

Even with the political situation in Rome decided for the moment there were still rebellions and uprisings within the empire that threatened to destabilize the government. The most important of which took place in Iberia.* One of Sulla's former lieutenants, Pompey, was sent in 77 BC to retrieve the situation for Rome.[20] In Italy itself, a former slave/gladiator, Spartacus, had been ravaging the countryside in Hannibalistic fashion and had soundly defeated a few Roman armies that had been sent against him and his followers. Another of Sulla's former lieutenants, Crassus, was dispatched from Rome to end Spartacus's depravations.[21] By 71 BC, both Crassus and Pompey returned to Rome after having successfully concluded their respective campaigns.† They found that the populares were once again agitating for their political reforms. In an attempt to placate the masses, Crassus and Pompey (once elected to consul), began to reform some of the more obnoxious parts of Sulla's constitution, like restoring the office of the tribune to its previous status.[22]

Not to be bought off by such trinkets, the populares began to demand even more. Once the well of goodwill in the Senate had run dry, the populares began to conspire for an open rebellion to use violence to achieve their desired ends. The populares rallied around a new aristocratic leader, Catiline, and began to muster their forces for an assault on the city.[23] The Senate, under the direction of acting Consul, Cicero, mobilized an army and put the rebels to the sword. With the rebellion subdued, it seemed that once again the Senate could return to business

* The revolt in Iberia was led by the Populares faction in response to Sulla's actions in Rome.

† Pompey took part in the Spartacus campaign at the end.

as usual. But now with the populares largely discredited (once again), the Senate would have to deal with the fractures that were opening up within their own social strata.

♦ ♦ ♦

With the aristocracy drunk on its own success, the Senate proceeded to reverse the reforms to Sulla's constitution that Pompey and Crassus had ushered in. Pompey was now stripped of his power, but not his wealth or the potential for influencing events. Pompey, Crassus and the upstart, Julius Caesar entered into a private agreement with the understanding that they would assist each other in their pursuance of political power.[24]

This alliance would come to be known as the First Triumvirate. While it's immediate aim was the attainment of power and wealth for the three members, its endgame was unknown. Once Caesar was elected Consul he proceeded to reintroduce Pompey's legislation (regarding the settlement of territories in the east), overcoming resistance with every single tool in the Roman toolbox (including assassination).[25] After his tenure as Consul was over, Caesar was awarded by being given the governorship of three contiguous provinces; Illyricum, Cisalpine Gallia, and Trans-Alpine Gallia.* His term in office was to last for five years, during which time Caesar intended to vastly increase his own wealth and prestige through the conquering of the various Celtic tribes to the north.[26]

With Caesar now established along Rome's northern frontier, all he needed was a pretext to make his plans for military conquest seem legal in the eyes of the Senate and the people of Rome. The pretext arrived when a Germanic tribe, the Helvetti, began to migrate en-masse from the high Alps and German Alps into the area of Gaul in the immediate vicinity of the Roman province.[27] After the Helvetti tribe had been defeated and evicted from Gaul, Caesar (according to his own account) was greeted as a hero and a saviour by the Celtic tribes.

* North western Balkans, northern Italy, and southern France.

Caesar's success against the Helvetti sparked anxiety amongst the Germanic tribes to the east of the Rhine who now began to escalate their military preparedness. Itching for a real conquest, Caesar was ready to bring the war to the Germans.[28] With both the Germans and Romans moving into northern Gaul, the Celtic tribes began to hedge their bets and take sides. After initial success against the Germans in the north some of the tribes began to suspect Caesar's motives and realized the potential staying power of the legions.[29]

Before long the remaining independent tribes of Gaul rallied around the charismatic chief Vercingetorix and were in open resistance against Caesar and his legions. After achieving a victory over Caesar at the Battle of Gergovia and with much of Gaul in arms against the Romans, Vercingetorix believed that he could outlast Caesar without having to fight him in a pitched battle, and so, he collected his tribesmen together and prepared to hold out at the stronghold of Alesia.[30] Caesar returned to face Vercingetorix and laid siege to the Gauls in Alesia. Unbeknownst to Caesar, Alesia was a trap as there was another Gallic army on the prowl outside the siege walls.[31]

Caught in-between a rock and a hard place, Caesar did something unheard of, he built a second wall around Alesia; the first to keep Vercingetorix in and the second to keep his own rear secure. Although outnumbered and seemingly defeated, Caesar emerged victorious out of the melee at Alesia, owning much to the superior discipline and field engineering of his troops.[32] After Alesia, the entire area of Gaul fell into the hands of Rome and made Caesar rich beyond the imaginations of anyone in Rome.

During the past eight years a lot had happened in Gaul, Rome and elsewhere. Caesar's campaign had brought him to invade the British Isle's on two occasions and to cross the Rhine once. When Caesars first five-year term as governor was over the triumvirate was able to extend it for another five years.[33] In

NORTH SEA
BRITANNIA
THAMES R.
ATLANTIC OCEAN
GERMANIA
RHINE R.
SIENE R.
GAUL
Alesia
RHONE R.
GAUL
PO R.
DOURO R.
HISPANIA
TAGUS R.
EBRO R.
GUADALQUIVIR R.
Gades
Cartagena
Massilia
Mutina
ITALY
TIBER R.
Rome
MAURETANIA
AFRICA
MEDJERDA R.
Carthage
SICILY
Syracuse
NUMIDIA

The Empire of the Republic

addition Pompey and Crassus were elected to Consul and were able to place their friends in the office of Tribune.[34] It would seem as if the Triumvirate was secure in its position of power, but at its pinnacle the seeds of its unravelling were being sown.

The first undoing was the death of Caesar's daughter, Julia, who was also the wife of Pompey and the cement of their alliance.[35] The second fracture was the death of Crassus who fell whilst on campaign against the Parthians (Persians).[36] The two men were now in an uneasy détente, neither wanted to make the first move, but both knew there wasn't enough room in Rome for the both of them.

♦ ♦ ♦

By the time Caesar had completed his conquest of Gaul, the optimate faction in the Senate were growing anxious of his incredible wealth and influence that he was buying amongst the lower classes of Rome. They feared that Caesar would be swept onto a throne by a wave of popular goodwill, and that once he was installed on the throne he would proceed to subvert the republican constitution and bring back monarchy. Towards their purpose of resisting Caesar's power, the noblemen enlisted Pompey into their cause (through a marriage alliance) and had the Senate declare Caesar as an enemy of the state once his second term as governor was over.[37] The resolution of the Senate demanded that Caesar disband his legions and to return to Rome unaccompanied by his military camp to answer the charges being brought against him. Caesar had no intention of complying.

In 50 BC Caesar had brought a single legion (roughly five thousand men) to Ravenna on the border of Italy to camp for the winter, while he left the remainder of his army in Gaul. He intended to open negotiations with the Senate, but after the Senate had declared him an outlaw he had no choice but to take up the war against Pompey and the optimates. During the course of the winter, Pompey was busy mustering his legions together but they were still mere recruits. Before spring fully arrived, Caesar marched his Thirteenth Legion across the Rubicon River and on towards war,* scattering Pompey's green troops as he went. Before long Caesar was in Rome and Pompey and his aristocratic party were in flight. From Rome, Pompey went south then crossed over to Greece where his support was strongest, with the hope that they could raise another army and be able to put up a real fight against Caesar.

Even with Caesar in control of Rome, Italy and Gaul, Pompey still controlled much of the periphery of the empire including Spain, North Africa, Greece, Asia Minor and the Near East.[38] Caesar knew he held the interior lines on a strategic level and would use them to his advantage. He wasn't about to wait around in Rome for Pompey to overwhelm him. Taking the initiative, Caesar never gave it up; first he went for Spain and either killed Pompey's legions there or converted the men to his cause.

After Spain, Caesar returned to Italy before crossing the Adriatic Sea into Greece. Once in Greece, Caesar found himself outnumbered and surrounded by Pompey's legions and forced to call on his friend, and lieutenant, Mark Antony,† to bring reinforcements over from Italy.[39] Antony came to Caesar's aid and although still outnumbered, the two men together were able to defeat Pompey at the Battle of Pharsalus in 48 BC Pompey and the majority of the Senators either escaped or surrendered to Caesar after their defeat. Resistance to Caesar continued amongst those who had escaped, but Pompey was assassinated by some Egyptians when he landed along the coast. The remainder of Senatorial resistance became scatted and was snuffed out after Pompey's death; Caesar was able to deal with them in a timely, piecemeal fashion. With the Civil War over, Caesar returned to Rome in 45 BC as a hero and was allowed to resume his consolidation of power.

* Even in that day the Rubicon was hardly a river, but rather more of a stream. This is, however, where we received the term 'cross the Rubicon', as in crossing a point of no return.

† Antony had been left in charge at Rome.

After the Battle of Pharsalus, Brutus was amongst those who surrendered and sought the mercy of Caesar. The two men had been good friends before and Caesar was eager to forgive Brutus after his surrender to appear magnanimous in an attempt to regain aristocratic good will. While Caesar was still busy hopping about the Mediterranean sweeping up the final pockets of resistance, Caesar had Brutus appointed as the governor for Gaul. Brutus excelled as the acting governor of Gaul.[40] In contrast to other Roman provincial governors, who used their office as a means to enrich their own coffers, Brutus took a genuine interest in the well-being of the population now under his authority.

Through the promotion of stability, economic growth and good government Brutus increased the prosperity of the province and thus its overall worth to Rome. By rebuilding the war torn province, Brutus also gained the affection of the Celtic inhabitants whose admiration he directed onto the glory of Caesar. In the three short years that it took for Caesar to wrap up the civil war, Brutus had returned a semblance of normal life back to Gaul and that fact was not lost upon the people of all classes in Rome.

When Caesar returned to Rome after the Civil War, it became increasingly obvious that he had kingly ambitions. His popularity amongst the lower classes was at a fever pitch; it was as if Pompey never existed at all. It appeared as if no one cared that Caesar was still dictator for life even though the crisis (of Caesar's own making) was at an end. On the face of things, Caesar was making every effort to not be seen in a regal light, but with nearly every passing day his autocratic tendencies were being revealed. A good many Senators (some who had been pardoned by Caesar, some not) began to become anxious of Caesar's power and ambitions and thus they set in motion a plot to take Caesar's life.

It is unclear who the primary mover of the plot was. William Shakespeare's great drama on the subject gives credit to Cassius, a good friend of Brutus for setting the plan in motion. Whoever began the plot is not as important as that the plot was underway. Brutus's reputation and honourable name leant the conspiracy his gravitas and infused it with a noble purpose that without him, it would be lacking.

The various Senators had been urged on out of their own fearful, greedy self-interest or because of some injury Caesar had inflicted upon them or their property. In contrast, Brutus considered Caesar a good friend and had gained much through this friendship. For Brutus this cause transcended personality; he would act solely for the liberty of his country and its ancient republican constitution.[41] The assassination took place on the 'Ides of March' (March 15th) in the 44th year BC, it was carried out by a small band of high profile senators at a meeting of the Senate. "Sic Semper Tyrannis" (thus always to tyrants) were the words that reportedly came out of Brutus's mouth after he had plunged his blade into Caesar's body. After the deed was done the Senate declared the action to be lawful (as opposed to declaring it a murder) and granted those who took part an amnesty.[42] At first sight the population went along with the new regime. However, there were those who longed for the return of a monarchical regime and to avenge the death of Caesar.

♦ ♦ ♦

The conspirators had made a few key decisions that would later come back to haunt them, although at the time they were undoubtedly the honourable choices to make. Perhaps the most fatal of which had been the decision to not kill Mark Antony along with Caesar and furthermore to allow Antony to speak at Caesar's public funeral. After Brutus gave the crowd the conspirator's reasons for the assassination and left the scene giving his permission to allow Antony to say some words over the body of their mutual dead friend. "Friends, Romans, Countrymen, lend me your ears"[43] with those words Antony began his famous speech that reminded the ordinary Roman of the love they once had for their general Julius Caesar.

Antony's speech succeeded in turning the Romans against the conspirators which forced Brutus, and company to vacate the city for safer quarters; leaving Antony in charge of the city for the moment. Although Antony was a skilled tactician and an excellent lieutenant of Caesar's, he was a wastrel and a rake better suited towards leading an army but was in no way capable of governing the city of Rome for long. Caesar's nephew, Octavius (or Octavian), was an extremely intelligent and calculating, strategic thinker and had been named as Caesar's benefactor in his will. He proceeded to use his new found wealth to muster an army and take Rome away from Antony, in this endeavour he was encouraged by Cicero.[44] With Octavius marching on Rome, Antony decided he would take up the governorship of Gaul, even though it was currently governed by Decimus Brutus.* Antony laid siege to Brutus at the city of Mutina in northern Italy. The Senate declared Antony an enemy of the state and commissioned an army to relieve Brutus.

Octavius succeeded in winning over the Roman Senate and public and was allowed to join his private army with the force raised to relieve Mutina. Although they were victorious at the battle that ensued Octavius was the only commander of the Republics forces left alive. Antony was forced to flee and take refuge in Gaul. Octavius, now sole commander followed Antony and laid siege to his camp.

All the while this was going on in the west, Brutus and Cassius had been busy in the east raising an army for their attempt to restore the Republic to his ancient constitution. had established his base at Athens and from there he was in a good position to administer the mustering of legions in the eastern Mediterranean. From Greece, Brutus travelled north and secured the allegiance of the Macedonian commanders before swoop-

* Not to be confused with his distant cousin Marcus Junius Brutus, Decimus Brutus was a fellow conspirator in the assassination of Caesar. He was also a distant nephew of Caesar.

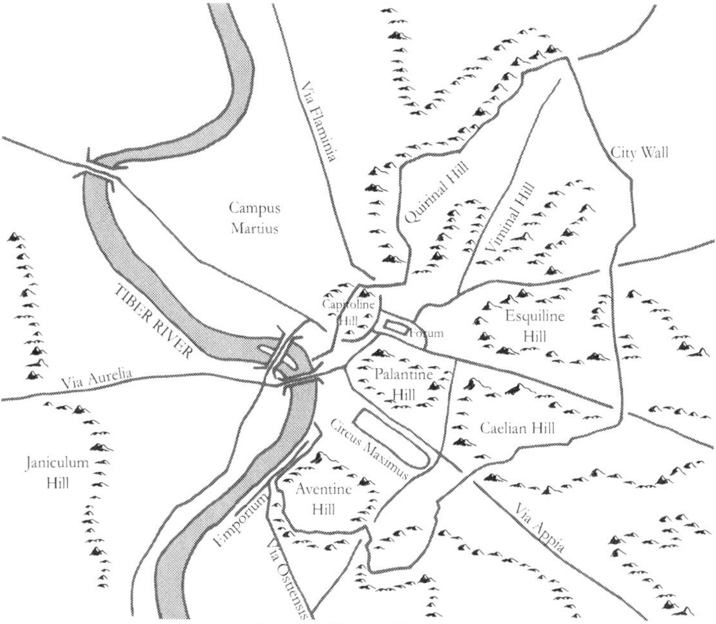

Republican Rome

ing east along the coast of Asia Minor gathering money and treasure along the way. Cassius had split off from Brutus after Athens and was tasked with raising men from the province of Syria and Egypt. But before Cassius could reach Egypt, Brutus had received word from Cicero (and the Senate) of the warfare currently raging between Octavius and Antony in Gaul. Upon hearing this Brutus believed it was time to rendezvous with Cassius's forces so as to affect a united march on Rome; they met at the city of Smyrna in Asia Minor.[45]

Once Octavius found out what was transpiring in the east, he proposed a peace treaty with Antony so that they could resist the advance of Brutus and Cassius. Octavius, Antony, and Marcus Lepidus came together to form the Second Triumvirate. In an effort to consolidate their positions in Rome the three men created an enemies list of some two hundred Senators and aristocrats who were suspected of having goodwill towards Brutus and Cassius, now being called the Liberators. They proceeded to have all men on the list executed, and their property confiscated to pay for the legions.[46] The trio agreed in principle to divide the provinces amongst themselves in the event that they were victorious over the Liberators. With any semblance of Senatorial resistance destroyed or placated in Rome, the Triumvir left the junior partner, Lepidus, to govern the city whilst Antony and Octavius crossed their legions over into Greece in search of a decisive victory.

♦ ♦ ♦

The two forces met each other to the west of the ancient city of Philippi in lower Macedonia. The Triumvirate's advance guard had been able to occupy the pass along the Via Egnatia well before the remainder of their forces could arrive. With a flanking maneuver, the Liberators had been able to push them back and take up their position on the dominating high ground. In possession of the high ground, the Liberators dug into a strong fortified position and planned to use their naval superiority to cut off Antony and Octavius's communications and supply lines with Italy; so as to avoid a direct confrontation. Their position along the Via Egnatia was strong, with a seemingly impassable swamp to the south and rough mountain terrain to the north. The road divided Brutus's and Cassius's camps with Brutus on the north and Cassius on the south, as it also divided the Triumvirate with Octavius on the north and Antony to the south.

The numbers of the opposing forces were roughly equal, around the one hundred thousand mark; sources say there was a slight advantage going towards the Triumvirate in this respect.*[47] Another slight advantage for the Triumvirate was that their forces were almost entirely made up of 'proper' Roman and Italian legions. In contrast, the Liberators were forced to rely on native levies from the eastern provinces and in some cases legions of questionable loyalty who had served under Caesar's banner during the First Civil War. However, time and local geography was on the side of the Liberators and the Triumvirate was beginning to feel the pinch of long supply lines.

The battle began when Antony started to build a causeway through the swamp so as to outflank Cassius's position and threaten his communications with the sea. Seeing this movement, Cassius began to construct a counter mole to extend his line and obstruct Antony's movements. But now, with Cassius's forces out of their camp, Antony began his assault on Cassius's main line. At around the same time, Brutus's men had been provoked by Octavius into attacking. Without waiting for Brutus to give the order, his men advanced in an undisciplined fashion. None-the-less, the rashness of Brutus's men took Octavius's soldiers by surprise and they were beaten back beyond their camp. Brutus's men fell into further disorder at Octavius's camp as they and began to plunder the camp thus allowing Octavius's forces to reform their lines in relative safety. On the southern

* It is fairly difficult to verify the numbers. One hundred thousand is certainly within the logistical capabilities of the Romans, but it still seems on the high side.

front the opposite result befell the Liberators fortunes, as Antony's advance against Cassius was a success. Antony proceeded to dismantle Cassius's field works and plunder the tents once he had gained possession of his camp.[48]

The movements of the two armies had kicked up such a dust that none of the four commanders could tell what was happening outside of their immediate sector. The dust prohibited Brutus from understanding the danger that Cassius was in, and it prevented Cassius from knowing that there was still hope and that reinforcements could be expected to relieve his situation. Unfortunately, Cassius believed that Brutus's position had also been overrun and became so overwhelmed with grief that he mistook Brutus's incoming reinforcements to be those of Antony's. Cassius took his own life by plunging his sword through his chest,* rather than be captured by the enemy. Brutus's troops managed to drive Antony back into his own camp and the fighting ended in stalemate for the day.

On the same day as the first battle, the Liberators fleet (under the command of Pompey's son, Sextus) had successfully engaged the Triumvir's fleet in the Ionian Sea as they attempted to bring reinforcements and supplies over to Greece from Italy.[49] This defeat caused great concern amongst Antony and Octavius as the region had largely been denuded of its forage already, and caused them to desire a speedy resolution.[50] Unfortunately for Brutus, the good news from the Ionian Sea did not reach him and the loss of Cassius (who was considered the better commander amongst the two) caused a great deal of anxiety to play on his mind and increased the rate of desertions amongst the soldiers, even though in hindsight he was in a stronger position than his opponents.[51]

Knowing that they would need to attack Brutus sooner rather than later, Antony continued construction on his causeway

* Suicide by ones own sword was considered a proper, manly, Roman suicide.

to the south, in order to threaten the flank of Brutus's position. Brutus extended his lines to the south so that they were parallel to the Via Egnatia. His position was still strong, but without the knowledge of the naval victory there was a threat that his men would defect to the Triumvir enticed by better pay and because in the moment it was believed that Cassius's death doomed their cause.

Under threat of mass desertion, Brutus ordered his lines to attack almost three weeks after the first engagement at Philippi. Before marching into battle, Brutus was reported to have said "I seem to carry on war like Pompey the Great, not so much commanding now as commanded."[52] The battle that ensued consisted mainly of a brutal, close quarter melee between highly trained and experienced veteran soldiers. Initially Brutus was successful on his left, but the officers on the right wing had extended themselves too far and were thus weakened in the centre. Brutus's center was the first to collapse, and to make matters worse Octavius was able to capture Brutus's camp before he could reform his lines. By the end of the day, Brutus was forced to seek refuge in the hills to the north where he intended to make his last stand. Seeing that the situation was hopeless, Brutus made the decision to take his own life (in the same fashion as Cassius) instead of being taken alive and paraded through the streets of Rome.[53]

♦ ♦ ♦

Antony was the first to the scene of Brutus's death. At the sight of his body Antony covered him with a purple blanket out of respect for the man and the fact that Brutus had spared Antony in the aftermath of Caesar's assassination. The majority of aristocrats surrendered their arms to Antony as he was the more respected and senior of the two enemy commanders. Octavius was also considered a bloodthirsty, ruthless upstart after the enemies list and executions he sanctioned. The Triumvirate continued to operate as per the agreement, with Antony travelling

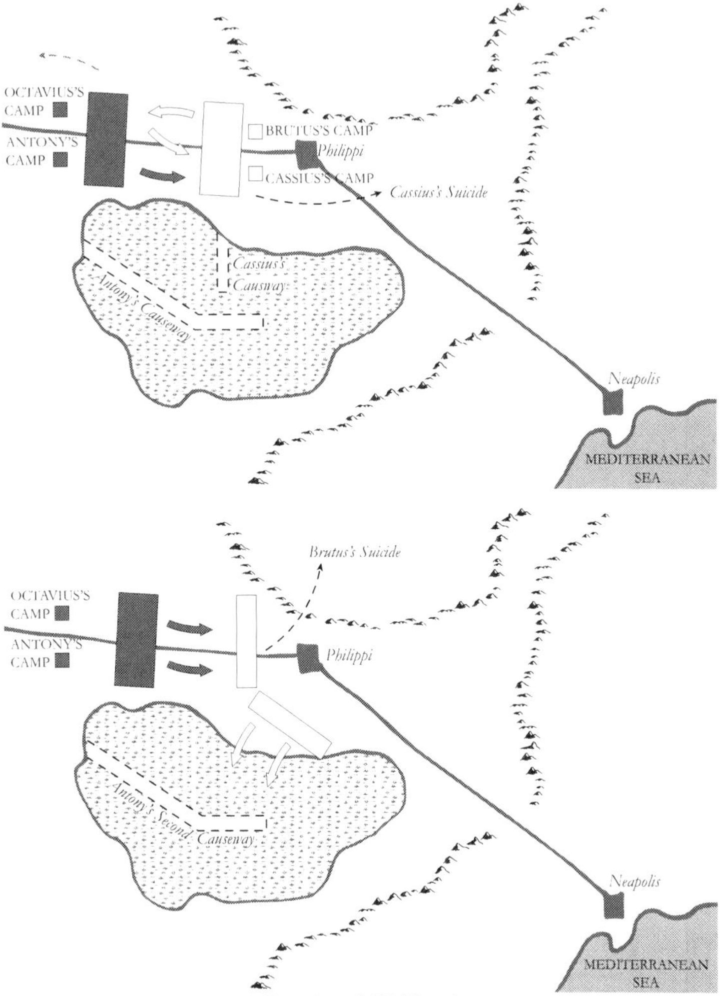

Battle of Philippi

on to the eastern provinces where he took up his residency in Egypt with Queen Cleopatra. Lepidus was given control over Hispania and the North African provinces while Octavius took command over Greece, Italy and Gaul.[54]

Much like the First Triumvirate, the second one was unstable and unable to endure the power hungry personalities that it involved. Before long, Antony and Octavius came to despise each other to the point of open warfare. Lepidus took Antony's side but was easily brushed aside by Octavius and forced to switch sides. Antony came to be vilified in the eyes of the Romans because of Octavius's gratuitous use of propaganda; broadcasting to the Romans that Antony had become orientalised and no longer considered himself a Roman. For his part, Antony played into Octavius's depiction of him; choosing to stay put in Egypt, taking on Egyptian dress and fathering a litter of children with Cleopatra.[55] When war eventually came, Octavius was anxious to avoid labelling it as a 'civil war' and instead declared the official war to be against Cleopatra.

After a naval engagement off Actium, Greece in 32 BC, Octavius emerged as the victor and pursued Antony and Cleopatra back to Alexandria, where the two committed suicide. Cleopatra took her life by poison, Antony in the good old fashioned Roman way.[56] Octavius returned to Rome in triumph and completed his domination of the political scene by having himself declared as emperor. The continuity of the republican form of government had been in mortal danger for nearly a century, but now it was finally dead; monarchy had officially become the law of the land. Rome, the city would continue to dominate much of the known world for nearly another five hundred years. It would give its dominions relative stability, commerce, law and order but this was gained at the cost of an autocratic, arbitrary and odious dictatorship; what would come to be known as the 'Augustan Age'.

Brutus began his service to Rome as an aristocratic politician, but circumstances and his own personal convictions forced him to make the difficult decision between a comfortable life as the friend of a despot and the uncertainty of what would happen if the conspiracy ran its course. The assassination of Caesar was not an event that Brutus took lightly, he was a long-time friend of Caesar, who, when defeated at Pharsalus was forgiven, his property and person left fully intact. The only thing Brutus stood to lose by abiding Caesar's regime was his liberty and the liberty of his country. While the decision was difficult for Brutus to make, the decision was never in doubt in his mind. Liberty was the most valuable principle for Brutus, more important than safety, glory, power or wealth.

Brutus was not a first rate military genius like the other subjects of this book, but his skills as a politician and an administrator were second to none. When the situation required it, Brutus excelled at organizing the creation of the Liberators forces.

When Brutus came across Cassius's dead body at Philippi, he commented that Cassius was "the last of the Romans".[57] But when Brutus lay dead on that same battlefield there were no true 'Romans' left to say the same thing about him. The truth is, Brutus was the last hope for liberty and for the survival of the republican constitution. No one else had the gravitas or the scruples to make it work. With the death of Brutus and the defeat of the Liberator's cause at Philippi the Dark Age for liberty began and it would take over a thousand years for even a semblance of it to be revived.

Renaissance and Revolution

"Necessity is the pleas for every infringement of human freedom. It is the argument of tyrants; it is the creed of slaves"

-William Pitt the Younger, British Statesman

The Magna Carta

The Thirteenth Century was a period of time much different from our own, but none-the-less it is of paramount significance to our discussion of liberty. It was well over a thousand years since the heyday and fall of Athens, Thebes and the Roman Republic. Since then the people of Europe had reverted to a simpler more secure form of despotic governance; but a new era was about to begin. The Thirteenth Century was a time of feudalism; a system of organizing society and government around kings, queens, barons, dukes, priests, knights, freeman and peasants. Most importantly and disturbing it was a time of almost limitless discretion and sovereignty for the monarch. There was almost nothing a ruling monarch could not do, not only were they the physical embodiment of the law they were also not subject to the law; in short the king was completely above the law. The institution of law, beyond the power of the sword, was only beginning to re-emerge throughout Europe.

Part of the British Isles was conquered by the Roman Empire.* After the Romans brutally suppressed the druidic religion at the climactic invasion of the island of Anglesey in 77 AD, the process of conquest and Romanization continued apace. With the exceptions of much of Scotland, the Welsh mountains, and Ireland, the British Isles had become a province within the Roman Empire by 96 AD. Under Roman occupation, the native

* As previously mentioned, Julius Caesar had briefly invaded the island during his campaign in Gaul. It wasn't until around 43 AD, that the Romans returned. The mission of the initial invasion purpose was to restore a friendly British king to his throne, but the Roman's didn't leave.

Britons lived in relative peace and prosperity for the next few centuries to come.*

When the Empire began to feel the pressure from the barbarian invaders from the east, the Roman legions were withdrawn from the Isles† leaving the Romanized Britons to fend for themselves. The occupation had left the Britons soft and weak. In the wake of the power vacuum left by Rome, the Britons hired mercenaries from the Saxon and Angle tribes in Germany to counter the threats from Scotland and Ireland. What began as a single boat load of Saxons quickly turned into a full scale migration into the Isles.The Britons and Saxons fought intermittently over the next few hundred years, with the Saxons eventually gaining the upper hand. The Saxons went on to occupy much of the same territory as the Romans had carved out for themselves. The Isles remained in a state of disunity for a few centuries with multiple independent British Kingdoms in Wales, and the Anglo-Saxon kingdoms in England.

This was the situation when the Norsemen arrived.‡ One by one the Saxon kingdoms fell, until there was only one left, the kingdom of Wessex, along the southern coast of England. The Norsemen came from the lands adjacent the Baltic Sea, including todays Denmark, Norway, and Sweden. The Norse constructed ships of shallow draft that allowed them to cross the high seas as well as travel up rivers.§ The King of Wessex, Alfred was beaten in battle by the Norse, but rallied his kingdom from a swamp on the Severn Sea. Afterwards Alfred took the fight to the Norse and eventually succeeded in bringing them to heel, as well as uniting the former Saxon lands into one kingdom, that

* Christianity was introduced during the Roman period, but it wasn't until the advent of the Norseman invasions that it became the dominant religion over paganism.

† Around 410 AD.

‡ The term 'Viking' is a verb describing an action, which is raiding.

§ The ships would take them from the Baltic to Newfoundland, through Russia to the Caspian Sea, and everywhere around the Mediterranean Sea. Their richest targets were the British Isles and France.

of England.* For his life's work, Alfred was given the title, 'the Great', and remains the only British monarch to have that title added to their name.

The British Isles weren't the Norsemen's only conquest, in fact one of the territories in which they succeeded in setting down roots was in the north of France, what would become known as Normandy. The Normans were nominally subjects to the French king, but in reality they remained completely independent. They were also successful in mixing with the bloodlines of the Western European nobility. So when the English king, Edward, died in 1066, William the duke of Normandy had as legitimate a claim to that throne as any.

William launched an invasion of England and was successful against his rival claimant at the Battle of Hastings, he was shortly after crowned king of England.† The new Norman administration wasn't particularly benevolent for the inhabitants. The main concern of King William was the taxation of his new realm, and to that end he commissioned the doomsday book, a register of who owned what in England. On top of taxation the Normans brought French influence, and took over the important positions within the government. The Anglo-Saxons, who were the vast majority of the population, chafed under the weight of government as they saw their ancient liberties trampled upon.

Marriage alliances were a chief instrument in international diplomacy, and dynastic politics of the day. It was through such marriages that the Angevin Empire sprang into existence. When William died he had four sons. Eventually the fourth, Henry, came to reign over England. Henry had a daughter, Matilda, who was married to Geoffrey Plantagenet, Count of Anjou.‡

* England comes from Angle land, the Angles being one of the main Germanic peoples to have migrated to Britain after the Romans had vacated the islands.

† This was the last successful invasion of the British Isles.

‡ All this was occurring amidst a recurring backdrop of war among the major noble families in France.

They produced a son, Henry, who was later to consolidate much of northern and western France and England into the Angevin Empire. Henry married Eleanor of Aquitaine* securing much of Western France to his banner, soon after he set sail for England to take up his claim for the throne.

Henry was able to expand his possessions in France, at the expense of the other noble families, but his greatest challenge came from his own flesh and blood. His son rebelled and was able to capture his father in 1189 with the help of King Philip of France. Henry died a few days after learning that his son John had betrayed him and sided with Richard and Philip.

Richard was another warrior king, and soon he and King Philip were fighting each other in France. Hostilities ceased when the two kings left for the Holy land to Crusade.† When the Kings returned, hostilities in France and England resumed. Richard didn't have long left on earth. Five years after his return to his kingdom, Richard fell while leading an attack on a castle in central France. When he died he was without an heir, and so his brother John ascended the Throne of the Angevin Empire.

♦ ♦ ♦

King John was by all accounts a bad king and a wicked tyrant. Unlike his father and brother, Henry II and Richard, John was ineffective at being a tyrant. Henry II and Richard the Lionheart were respectively gifted administrators and commanders who were able to hold together and expand their family possessions through their abilities. John on the other hand was lacking in aptitude for either governance or war.[1] Instead of effectively ruling or conquering lands John chose to commit nearly every indecent

* Who had recently been divorced from Louis VII, King of France.

† The Crusades were a war against the heathen Muslims who were occupying the Levant. Islam had sprung out of the Arabian deserts just as the Roman Empire was disintegrating. The Arabs swiftly conquered the Middle East, and cut a bloody swath across North Africa, into Spain. Their invasion of Europe was halted by the Franks at Tours, in France. It would take hundreds of years before the Christians would be able to expel them from Spain.

Angevine Empire

act and crime imaginable in those days including but not limited to murder, adultery, sacrilege, treachery, cruelty, corruption and perhaps most importantly incompetence.[2] And so, the nobility who had long strafed under the oppressive rule and high taxation of John's father and brother began to consider rebellion in order to put an end to the lawlessness of their king.

John's ascension to the throne was contested by his nephew, Arthur, who was backed by King Philip of France. At first the war went well for John, he knocked Arthur out of the fight at the Battle of Mirebeau, and was able to capture him and the rest of the nobles with him. The victory at Mirebeau was ultimately his undoing. He quickly alienated the local nobles when he mistreated the prisoners. It was so bad that thirty of them died in captivity. Fresh revolts ensued in Brittany and Anjou, which effectively cut his French holdings in two.

The situation further deteriorated when John had Arthur killed* while Philip was pushing on Normandy from the east, the Rebels were causing trouble to John's west. John attempted to raise Philip's siege of Chateau Gaillard with an amphibious assault, but failed. He next turned west to stamp out the rebels, and failed again. John withdrew to England to recuperate his forces. By August 1204 Philip had conquered Normandy, and in the wake of Eleanor's death (a few months earlier), Philip invaded John's possession to the south. By the end of 1204 only the Duchy of Aquitaine remained of John's French territory, a mere rump of what he had inherited.

For the next ten years John attempted to retake his holdings in France. He was successful in reconstructing his brother's alliance with the powers in Belgium, and the Holy Roman Empire in Germany. After almost yearly uprisings in the British Isle, that required John's attention, he was able to land in France in 1214. The campaign called for John to Advance from his holdings in

* It is unknown how Arthur actually died (some said it was John in a drunken rage), but it is certain that he died while John's custody.

Aquitaine in the south, while his allies would advance out of Belgium in the north.

The campaign began well enough, John was able to retake the county of Anjou, but his advance was stalled when the Aquitaine nobility refused to continue any further. Meanwhile, Philip was busy on the north western front. He managed to make contact with the enemy forces and beat the decisively at the Battle of Bouvines. The Alliance collapsed afterwards and John was forced to withdraw back to England.

The exact beginning and causes of the rebellion are clouded to posterity. However, general assumptions can be made about its causes. While the barons had previously chaffed under the rule of Henry II and Richard they still enjoyed some of their ancient liberties that were a mish-mash of traditions and codified laws.[3] Through acts of stupidity and poor management he frittered away much of his inherited lands on the European mainland. In attempts to regain his lost lands he turned to oppressive taxation and levying feudal armies,[*] only further fueling baronial opposition.

Consistent acts of treachery, greed, knavery, guile and immorality frittered away the remaining goodwill and loyalty normally reserved for the monarchy. In one of his more infamous dealings he forcibly auctioned off his first (infertile) wife to an earl for twenty thousand marks, an immense sum at the time. The earl had no realistic way of paying such a fine and thus it drove him into the camp of the rebels.[4] Another example of his immorality occurred when one of the generals was captured in France; King John attempted to seduce his general's wife instead of paying for his release.[5] In an act of extreme sacrilege King John willfully confiscated church property. Much to John's indifference, the pope ex-communicated John from the Roman Church.[†6] But perhaps his gravest misfortune was the destruc-

* Armies raised at the expense of the barons.

† Excommunication was a very serious matter in a very religious society, as it meant that the churches would be closed to all worshippers.

tion of his army at the Battle of Bouvines in 1214 which sapped the English treasury and ended his attempts at conquest on the mainland.[7]

♦ ♦ ♦

Lack of baronial support for his recent continental adventures created the perception that a growing opposition existed against the King and his government in England. After the defeat at Bouvines and the collapseof the alliance, John had few supporters left in England and little means by which to purchase new ones. The Northerners, barons with land in the north of England, were the most aggrieved and the first to act out in rebellion. Support for the Barons became widespread and King John was quickly brought to the negotiating table.[8] On June the 15th, 1215 in the meadow of Runnymede outside London, King John fixed his seal to the 'Articles of the Barons'. On the 19th of June the barons once again swore fealty to King John, thus ending the rebellion. The 'Articles' became the 'Great Charter' or in Latin the 'Magna Carta'. Among the many provisions of the Charter, the most important principle – even in a rather primitive form – was the idea that the king would now also be subject to the laws of the land.[9]

Even with the sealing of the Charter the battle for liberty was far from over. In another act of extreme duplicity, John appealed to the Pope, his onetime enemy, asking to declare the Magna Carta null and void, as he claimed it had been violently forced upon him. The Pope did what John requested and the Baronial War resumed in earnest.[10]

The Baron's controlled much of northern England and had captured London the month before the Magna Carta was signed. The castle of Rochester, just east of the city, was quickly occupied by the Barons after John had broken his side of the treaty. The King of Scotland also aligned himself with the Barons as well as the remaining independent Welsh kingdoms in the north of Wales. John, on the other hand, had support in Dover, Windsor, Winchester, Nottingham, and Lincoln. As well John had the loyalty of the Marcher lords in the south of Wales.*

When the war resumed John was based out of Dover, where he was easily able to purchase mercenaries from Europe. He took the imitative and besieged Rochester, taking it by November 1215. From Rochester he moved quickly to disrupt the Barons in the north. At London he split his force in two. The first part would stay and keep the Rebels in place at London. King John and the second part would head north to attack the Barons holding and deal with the king in Scotland. By January of the new year John was on his way back to help subdue East Anglia, after beating the Scots at Berwick. It was now that John's luck began to run out.

In February a small French force hand resupplied London and brought news that Prince Louis, of France, was on his gathering a larger army to assist the Barons against John. John attempted to block the French crossing with his navy, but a storm in May wrecked a number of the ships and they had to return to port. Prince Louis effected his crossing days later. Louis captured Rochester after a brief siege, and moved to attack John at Winchester. John evacuated Winchester for the castle at Corfe before Louis arrived, and Winchester fell to Louis without a fight.

It was now Louis turn to split his forces in two as he moved to besiege Windsor and Dover castles. With the Baron's army stalled, it was now John's turn to wield the initiative. He struck north out of Corfe, and feigned an attack towards Windsor, but instead maneuvered to relieve the Rebel siege at Lincoln. From Lincoln he made his way into East Anglia to resupply.† It was at Kings Lynn, in East Anglia, that John contracted dysentery. He

* The 'Marches' were on the borderlands of England and Wales. The 'Marcher Lords' had quasi-regal powers within their own lands, more powers than a regular baron in England possessed.

† Along the way he lost his baggage train to the tide. The treasure has never been found.

died on October 19th at Newark Castle.

John's death didn't end the war, but it made some of the Anglo barons reconsider their allegiance to Louis. John's son was crowned king as Henry III, and William Marshall appoint as his regent. In a masterstroke Marshall reissued the Magna Carta, albeit without some of the more contentious points, further causing more of the barons to switch sides. The more barons defected to Marshall, the more Louis was forced to rely on soldiers from France, which only infuriated the Anglo barons more.

The spring of 1207 witnessed a French army depart from London to attack Lincoln. They succeeded in taking the city, but were prevented from taking the castle. Marshall got word of the French whereabouts and moved to intercept them. Marshall emerged victorious at Lincoln, Louis' cause in England was all but destroyed. The French still held out in London.

Louis was forced to call on France for reinforcements. They didn't make it to him, but were destroyed by Marshall's navy at the engagement off Sandwich. Stranded in England, without reinforcements, Louis was forced to negotiate with Marshall. At the treaty of Kingston, Henry III was recognized as king, and Louis was forced to evacuate to France. The war was over.

♦ ♦ ♦

When Henry III came of age he 'voluntarily' reissued a version of Magna Carta, only to continuously debate its validity with the barons through force until the end of his long reign.[11]

Even though the principles of the Magna Carta have been repeatedly contested, a precedent was set in 1215 that would eventually begin to become a permanent fixture of English and global politics. While the original Charter initially only protected the liberties of the church, nobility and freemen from the arbitrary whims of the monarch, it slowly and surely, distilled those liberties down to the common man until the entirety of society was covered by its benefits. Although the Magna Carta was not perfect in 1215, the few days at Runnymede and the subsequent

First Barons' War

war brought the concept of liberty through law and order back onto the fore step and began a new era of governance for mankind that had been lacking from civilized history for the previous thousand years.

William Wallace

Very few facts are known about William Wallace's early life. This is partly due to the legends that arose from his later career, and the lack of any objective history written by his contemporaries. What we do know is that William was born as the son of a minor, land owning, nobleman somewhere in the southwest of Scotland.[1] His exact place, and date of birth as well as the names of his parents are still in dispute today. However, this information is largely irrelevant to our discussion of his career and his contribution to the cause of liberty.

It is entirely likely that William had some formal (or informal) military training in his youth. There is some evidence to suggest that William served as a mercenary archer in one of the many Welsh uprising against the English.* Which side William fought for (and if he fought at all) will probably never be certain. None-the-less it would be hard to believe, considering his later career, that William had no military experience prior to the Scottish uprising. So while nothing can be proved definitively, it is reasonable to believe that William was a seasoned veteran and commander by the time he heeded his country's calling.

There is also vague speculation that suggests Williams's father was killed fighting against the English when William was still young.[3] Once again, although it is impossible to ascertain, this assumption is not hard to believe as the late Thirteenth Century was rife with low intensity skirmishing and all out warfare throughout the British Isles (and much of Europe). But, we

* William had archer insignia on the seal he used as the 'Guardian of Scotland'.[2]

shall now turn our attention to the wider context of that era, so as, to give a fuller explanation of the events that brought William to the brink of his destiny.

♦ ♦ ♦

Scotland was a wild and untamed land, with a fertile soil but mountainous geography. Similar in some respects to Classical Greece, the mountainous topography fostered the creation of isolated political communities. Instead of poleis, the inhabitants of Scotland were organized along more tribal lines, referred to as clans. The people of ancient Scotland were of Celtic stock. Along with the Celts of Ireland, they were the last holdouts in Western Europe against the encroachments of the Roman Empire. Since time immemorial, the Scots had lived according to their ancient liberties, untainted by the yoke of a foreign overlord. But with the fall of Rome in the 5th Century and the advances of Christianity that followed, the Scots eventually abandoned their pagan ways to join the family of civilized nations. During the medieval ages the neighbouring land to the south, England, was quickly becoming a centre of power in its own right. While it was one thing to successfully resist the expansion of Rome from far off Italy, it would be another thing entirely to resist the burgeoning powerhouse next door.

Scotland was essentially in the same condition as England when the Romans left the isles; it was divided along tribal lines. The Pictish tribe eventually achieved dominance, and expanded their authority over much of today's Scotland.* The Saxons largely left Scotland alone. The Norse made small inroads in the north, around Inverness, and the Shetland, and Orkney islands.

The Normans were much more successful. Instead of a military invasion, they were successful at peacefully intermingling with the nobility. This was especially true in the more populated, hospitable south. With the influx of Anglo-Norman people Scotland underwent a transformation and set off what came

* It was during this time that the kingdom was named Alba, or Scotland.

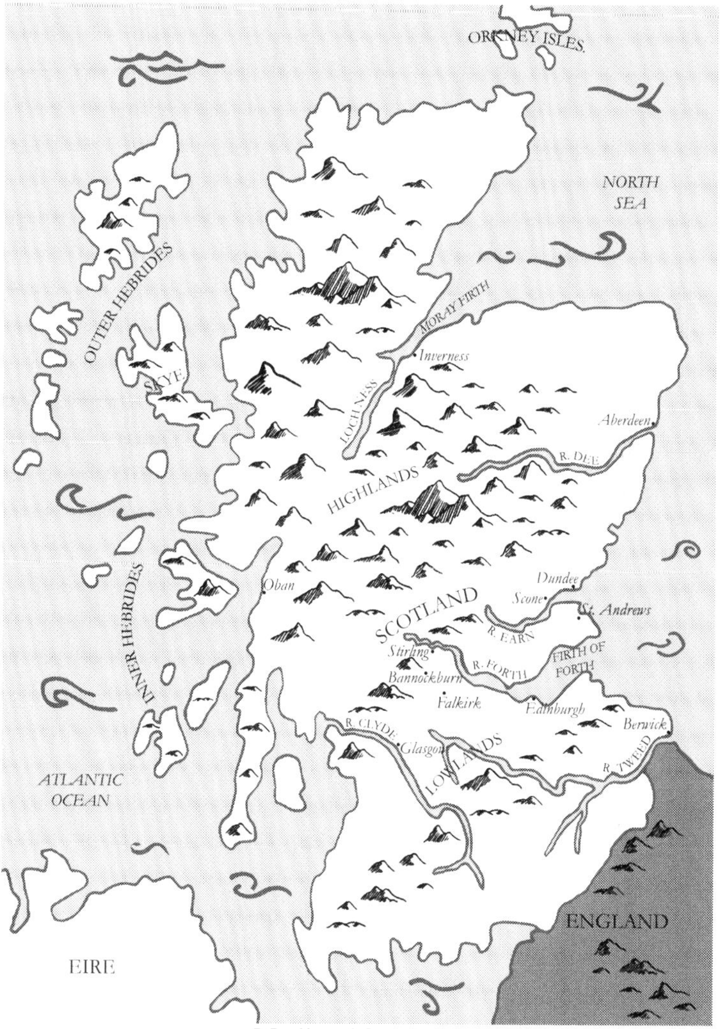

Medieval Scotland

to be known as a golden age. For almost two hundred years Scotland experienced peace, stability and economic growth, as well they were able to take back the mainland territory that the Norsemen had occupied. Every golden age comes to an end.

In the year 1286 the King of Scotland, Alexander III, died without an heir, leaving the throne empty and the question of succession open to dispute.[4] Alexander's reign had been long and was successful on many accounts. He governed over a period of economic growth and was able to consolidate the territory under his control by prying much of the northern region and islands away from the Norse kingdoms.[5] Only the major island chains, the Orkneys and the Shetlands remained in servitude to the Norse from across the North Sea. Upon Alexander's death the King of England, Edward I, or Longshanks as he was to become known, was asked by the Scottish nobles to intervene and set himself up as the arbitrator who would judge the claims of the leading men. Edward ended up supporting John Balliol, and so, John was crowned in 1292 ending a period of six years without a king.[6] Edward's support came with a heavy price and he proceeded to undermine the authority of the Scottish king, by calling upon him, as a feudal lord would, to levy troops for a campaign in France.

King John and the leading Scottish noblemen grew weary of this relationship with the English king, and so, they devised a council of twelve guardians who assumed control of the affairs of state. King Edward, as you might assume, was not pleased with this political development and so he invaded Scotland in 1296, and beat a feudal Scottish army that was raised by King John and the nobles at the battle of Dunbar. Victorious, Edward took King John prisoner and removed the 'Stone of Destiny' located at the Abbey of Scone, back to London and declared the war over.[7] The stone was symbolically used by the Scottish nation in their coronation ceremony and thus Edward's appropriation of it represented English usurpation of Scottish sovereignty. With victory declared and Edward returned to England, events in Scotland were beginning to take on a life of their own. The war with Scotland had only really just begun. The year 1297 witnessed the rise of Wallace's patriot volunteer militia in the southwest and another militia under the banner of Andrew Moray (or Murray) in the northeast.[8]

It is hard to ascertain what exactly pushed Wallace and the Scots into 'rebellion', as Wallace never left a written recording or verbal account for posterity. Some sources say that Wallace was outlawed and had turned to banditry before igniting the rebellion, while others point to the execution of his wife at the hands of the local English sheriff.[9] It is reasonable to assume that there were multiple causes; at least three reasons can be logically deduced from the nature of the uprising Wallace led. For one, there was anger over the King Edward's recent demands on Scottish sovereignty under the reign of Balliol. Secondly, there was outrage over removal of the Stone of Destiny, with all the symbolism attached to it. And third, there was a genuine desire for liberty, peace and the love felt for the homeland from which Wallace and his 'rebels' had sprung. Wallace's insurgents began their campaign with pinprick attacks on Scotsmen who were collaborating with the English monarch.

Now in control of much of Scotland north of the River Forth and rapidly gaining momentum and soldiers as they continued, Wallace's raids quickly gained the attention of King Edward who became sufficiently alarmed at the deteriorating situation and resolved to send another invasion force.

♦ ♦ ♦

The Battle of Stirling Bridge on the eleventh of September, 1297, was the first known major battle that Wallace took part in. Leading up to the battle Wallace and Moray combined their militia forces to resist the incoming English invasion.[10] The English force commanded by John de Warenne, sixth Earl of Surrey and Hugh Cressingham, King Edwards's treasurer for Scotland wanted a quick and economical victory over the Scottish insurgency. The combined Scottish forces were deployed on the northern bank of the River Forth and waited for the English host to begin crossing. A native Scottish nobleman, who had sided with the English, suggested to de Warenne that the River Forth could be crossed further downstream at a ford that was wide enough for sixty horses.[11] However, Cressingham insisted on speed, and instead of the wide flanking maneuver he ordered the army to cross at Stirling Bridge; which was only wide enough for two horses abreast.[12]

Wallace and Moray waited for roughly half of the English army to cross the bridge before launching their attack. Hand-to-hand combat ensued. The Scottish assault pinned the English vanguard to the northern bridgehead, creating a bottleneck and making it impossible for the rest of the English army on the southern bank to cross the River Forth. The English vanguard became completely isolated when the bridge collapsed under the weight of the reinforcements attempting to cross, and was annihilated by the energetic volunteers of Wallace and Moray.[13] The remaining English withdrew from Scotland, leaving Wallace's militia in control and Scotland once again unified. Moray was wounded in the battle and shortly afterwards succumbed to his wounds, making Wallace the sole commander of the militia army.[14]

Within a month of the Battle of Stirling Bridge Wallace cleared out all but a few of the remaining pockets of English resistance from their fortified castles before commencing his invasion of Northern England.[15] Wallace decided to turn his army south to exact reparations from the English living in the northern counties, he did not intend on occupying and subjugating the land and people, his only purpose was to pillage and devastate the area while avoiding any serious engagement. The raid being a success, Wallace returned to Scotland during December of 1297 where he was formally knighted and appointed 'Guard-

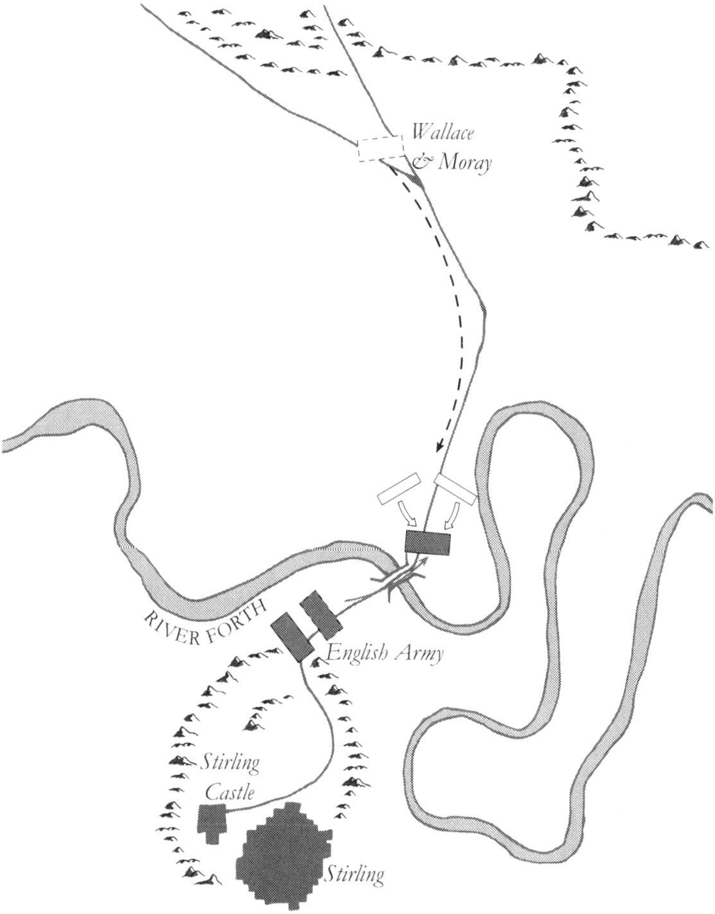

Battle of Stirling Bridge

ian of Scotland', leader of its armies.*[16]

The nature of the Wallace government is a curiosity compared to its contemporaries. In many ways it was a throwback to earlier times, but it was also extremely cutting edge and a harbinger of trends that would slowly develop throughout Europe centuries later. The new regime borrowed much from the feudal system of government (such as land distribution and the privileged position of the nobility) with the fundamental exception that it was not a kingdom in the traditional sense. Much like Wallace's army, Wallace's government did not owe allegiance to a king, but rather to the idea of the nation. The army was a microcosm of the nation; the government was a prototype for the nation-state that was very gradually coming into competition with the feudal system. It might not have been perfectly democratic, but it was significantly more representative than feudal governments of the past.

In the limited time that was available, Wallace scrambled to find supporters amongst the neighbouring kingdoms connected by the North Sea.† As well, Wallace attempted to reopen the trade networks that Scotland had historically been a part of.[17] Time, however, was not on Wallace's side; his hitherto successful insurgency was gaining the complete attention of King Edward. The spring of 1298 would witness a reinvigorated assault on the liberty of Scotland by a newly raised army of King Edward.

♦ ♦ ♦

After the embarrassments at Stirling Bridge and in the northern counties, King Edward decided to overwhelm the 'Scottish rebellion' with the superior resources of his kingdom. He assembled a conscript army from the various regions of his kingdom including contingents of Irish, Welsh, French and English soldiers and decided to lead the force himself. Contemporaries put

* Since King John was still in English custody, Wallace would have likely been knighted by one of Scotland's earls or other nobility.

† To name a few, envoys were sent to France, the Catholic Church, and the German free cities along the North Sea coast.

the total figure at around 90,000 men, but other writers' dispute that figure saying it was actually much lower.[18]

Regardless of the actual numbers King Edward had a definite numerical advantage, as well as a technological edge over Wallace's force. The English possessed contingents of longbow men to outdistance the shot of Scottish archers, as well as heavy cavalry to which the Scots had nothing comparable to match. On the other hand, food was difficult for the English to supply and this almost caused the contingent of Welsh archers to mutiny.[19] In general the morale of the English army was poor. On the verge of ordering a retreat, Edward was advised by a reconnaissance that the Scots were encamped a few short miles from the English army. After a quick march by Edward the two forces found themselves opposite each other near the town of Falkirk, with swampy ground and a minor stream in between them.

The precise location of the battle continues to elude historians, and there is still much debate. Wallace decided to give battle and had drawn up his troops into a defensive formation, consisting of four schiltrons (circles of pike men) with archers drawn up in lines in-between the schiltron circles. A line of men-at-arms (swords-men) was drawn up behind the schiltrons and archers; to the rear of the men-at-arms a line of light cavalry was posted.[20] The Scottish army was facing downhill and to their rear there was a slight incline and a forest. Standing on the defensive the Scots waited for the English to launch their attack.

Initially the Welsh longbow men refused to open the battle, King Edward then sent two groups of heavy cavalry to attack both flanks of the Scottish position.[21] The cavalry charges were dashed upon the schiltron formations as they held fast and their long pikes could stop any charge a few yards short from of the actual men. Whether due to treachery or cowardice (is still debated today) the Scottish light cavalry fled at the sight of the initial charge of the English heavy cavalry.[22] Both groups of English cavalry realized that attacking the schiltron formations was both futile and reckless and so changed their tactics. The group on the English left targeted the Scottish archers, while the group on the English right pursued the fleeing Scottish cavalry and manoeuvered its way to the top of the hill, blocking the natural route of escape for the Scots.

At this point, Edward committed his English and Irish foot soldiers to the attack. They crossed the swampy stream and engaged the Scottish front, while the Lancastrian (English and Welsh) longbow men begin to break up the cohesion of the Scottish schiltron formations.[23] The battle was turned into a massacre once the English bowmen broke up the schiltrons and the heavy cavalry charged into the gaps of the Scottish formations creating a panic in the Scottish army.[24] The Scots become scattered and were unable to reform to offer any meaningful resistance. Wallace managed to escape from capture but this defeat marked the end of armed rebellion and the Wallace led Scottish government.[25]

After the defeat at Falkirk, Wallace abdicated his role as guardian of Scotland and fled to France where he continued to fight minor skirmishes with King Edwards's possessions on the continent.[26] Two Scottish nobles were invited to share the responsibilities of the state when Wallace vacated the position; John Comyn, brother-in-law to John Balliol, and Robert the Bruce, also of noble lineage, succeeded Wallace as the Guardians of Scotland.[27] Joint guardianship was rather unstable as the two men were rival claimants to the Scottish throne. Some measure of stability was introduced when a third guardian, William de Lamberton, the Bishop of St. Andrews, was invited to share in the responsibilities of governing; Lamberton was seen as a neutral player who could increase diplomatic pressure from the Catholic Church.[28]

Instead of focusing on military policy, the new regime intensified its diplomatic aid, seeking to draw King Philip IV of France and the Pope onto the side of Scottish independence.

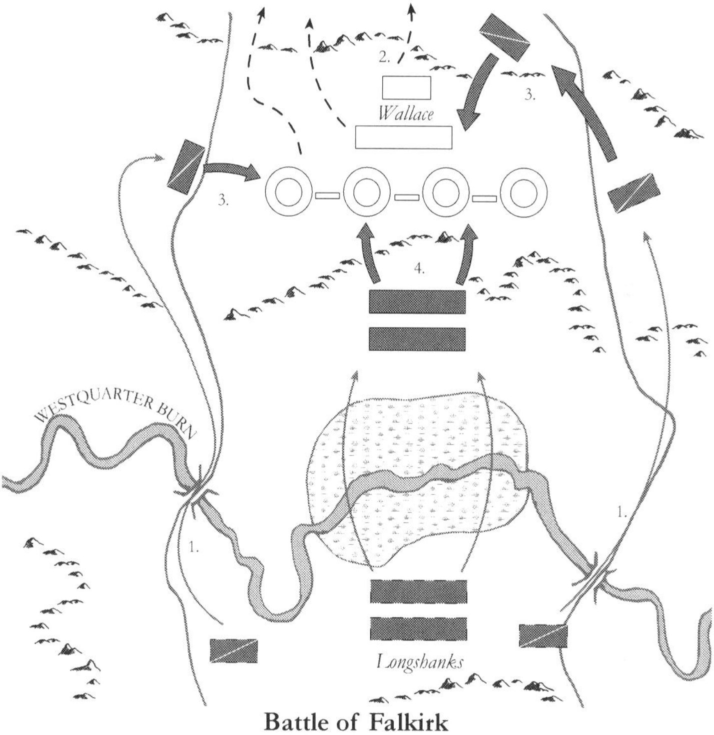

Battle of Falkirk

1. English Cavalry manuever onto the Scottish Flanks. 2. Scottish Cavalry flee the field. 3. English Calvary launch their attacks. 4. English Infantry attack along the Scottish front.

Even in exile, Wallace played a role in Scotland's cause, which included service to the French king and probably even a diplomatic tour to the Pope in the Vatican.[29] Wallace probably returned to Scotland in 1304 and was betrayed by his fellow countrymen to the English. King Edward brought Wallace to London where they tortured and quartered (i.e. butchered) him, then sent out his body parts to the four corners of the kingdom as an example of the wages of 'rebellion'.[30]

♦ ♦ ♦

William Wallace came from a humble, yet noble land owning family and achieved great notoriety by rallying the common Scotsman into an armed resistance against a foreign usurper. Wallace loved his country and he wanted Scotland and its people to enjoy liberty and peace, thus he attempted to rid Scotland from the tyrannical grip of a foreign overlord. However, in the end his efforts were unsuccessful and he died a tortured, un-thanked and lonely man in London. None-the-less his example of personal heroics and selfless devotion; his governments example of political independence and unity gave his contemporaries and future generations an ideal to live up to.

The death of Wallace seemed to bring the hope of victory and stability to King Edward. However, passion still burned hot in the hearts of the Scots. Accounts vary, but for one reason or another Robert the Bruce killed John Comyn during a secret meeting at the Greyfriars church in Dumfries.[31] Bruce was shortly thereafter crowned as the King of Scotland, which ignited another war with the aging English monarch. After initially being defeated by Edward in a pitched battle, Bruce sought to place a barrier of water in-between himself and King Edward. Bruce spent his winter on one of the many Scottish Isles (accounts vary as to which one) where he decided to adopt a military policy of guerilla tactics to oppose the encroachments of the English.[32]

In 1307, King Edward died while on the march and was

succeeded by his son Edward II who proceeded to scale down the English war efforts against the Scots (he had problems with his Barons to reckon with). Even with some of the pressure relieved, Bruce still had to contend with domestic enemies who persisted in their loyalty to the English or the late John Comyn. After making steady inroads in the northern portion of Scotland, by 1314 Bruce was even able to launch raids into the northern counties of England.[33] Bruce's lieutenants had captured the remaining English held castles in the years 1313 and 1314, now only Stirling Castle held steady in its defiance to the Scottish King. Edward II mobilized an army to come to the relief of his Stirling garrison. The two kings met each other on the field of Bannockburn, not far from the battlefield of Wallace's great victory at Stirling Bridge.

In 1314, nine years after Wallace's execution in London, Robert the Bruce rallied his Scottish army and decisively beat the army of Edward II at the Battle of Bannockburn.[34] The spirit and memory of William Wallace were still alive and well in Scotland. Robert the Bruce now recognized as the rightful King of Scotland by his enemies both external and internal. Although England would be constantly preying on her weaknesses and looking for an opportunity to intervene, freedom from foreign oppression and political unity was restored to Scotland for generations to come.

John Churchill: Duke of Marlborough

John Churchill was born to an impoverished noble household in the year 1650 to his parents Winston and Elizabeth Churchill.[1] John's father, Winston, had fought in the English Civil War (1642-51) on the side of the monarchy, and was heavily fined by parliament after the royalists had lost. After the parliamentary regime, run by Cromwell, had run its course and Charles II was restored to the English throne, Johns father Winston was rewarded with a position in the government of Ireland.[2] The young John followed his father to Dublin where he attended the Dublin Free School. In 1664 Winston returned to London and was able to secure John a page's position in Prince James'* household.[3] Once, while John and James were reviewing some troops, James asked John what he would like more than anything in the world. Johns reply was that he would like a battalion, James then procured John a commission in the Kings Guards.[4] At that point in time the English army was extremely small and "…numbered under 6,000 men…The English army was employed mainly as guards, or in garrison … It knew little of Continental warfare, for war with the principal enemy, Holland was usually fought at sea - with soldiers as marines."[5] Thus began John's career in the military.

John's first overseas duty was on a cruise through the Mediterranean as a marine in 1670. When he returned to England he served on James flagship in the 1672 war against the Dutch "…

* James was brother of King Charles II and future king.

where his bravery earned him a captaincy."[6] In 1674 John was sent to fight as an auxiliary for the French against the Dutch* and Germans (both Protestant kingdoms), where he served under the storied French Commander Turenne – with whom, John would later square off against. John's ability as an officer during his time with the French earned him the praise and recognition of the French King, Louis XIV, something Louis would no doubt come to regret.[7] When John returned to England he was a Lieutenant Colonel, and upon his return, John met his future wife Sarah at the Royal court; he would marry her a few years later. Sarah was a close friend and maiden at the court of Princess Anne, James younger sister.

♦ ♦ ♦

The competition between France and England had a long history stretching back to the fall of the Roman Empire in the fifth century AD. It continued largely unabated and intensified up to its climax in the 18th and 19th centuries. The culminating conflicts between France and England were reminiscent of the classical Greek rivalry between Sparta and Athens, in which a predominately land based power, Sparta later France, squared off against a predominately sea based power, Athens, later England. Throughout these conflicts France's strategy, guided by the fact that it was a continental power, was to dominate continental Europe while also attempting to strangle England's overseas possessions and trade. On the other hand, England's position as an island kingdom guided its overall strategy. England aimed to cut off and or capture France and its overseas colonies, while subsidizing France's continental enemies with the money it generated through trade. All the while England would also contribute small expeditionary forces to the alliances against France on

* The English and Dutch fought a series of wars in the mid to late 17th Century. The wars were mostly fought at sea over trade, and colonies. The wars were largely inconclusive, and would end with the Glorious Revolution, only to be revived shortly a century later. Churchill served alongside the French in the Third Anglo-Dutch War.

the continent.[8]

In addition to the classic rivalry between land and sea was added the antagonisms of religion, and systems of government. The French state was becoming increasingly centralized under the monarchy, which came to sees its rule as being ordained by God, a very Catholic God. In contrast to France, England had been proceeding along a more decentralized trajectory, beginning with the introduction of the Magna Carta and the establishing of Parliament; then later by throwing off the shackles of popery and the embracing of the Protestant reformation.

England was one of the countries who had split with the Roman Catholic Church during the great schism of Western Christianity known as the Reformation; France remained loyal to the Vatican in Rome. On top of the religious division within England came the Civil War between the monarchy with its 'Royalist' supporters and parliament and its 'Roundheads'* supporters. Reminiscent of the struggle for the Magna Carta, the Civil War produced a victory for parliament led by the Puritan Protestant soldier Oliver Cromwell. This victory did not conclusively settle the rivalry between parliament and monarchy or the rivalry between Protestant and Catholic forces.

After Cromwell's death in 1658, disorder reigned in England until the English army commander of Scotland, General Monck, marched on London and reinstated order. General Monck prepared England for the resumption of monarchy under Charles II, who returned in 1660.[9] Problems re-emerged between parliament and the crown after Charles was succeeded by his Catholic brother James II in 1685. James increasingly alienated the Protestant population with his pro-French and pro-Catholic views, and frustrated the upper classes by exclusively appointing Catholics to high places of influence and authority.[10]

The tipping point came when James produced a Catholic

* The supporters of Parliament were referred to as the 'Roundheads' because of the helmets they wore, which were round.

heir. Faced with the prospect of an indefinite pro-French and Catholic dynasty, the leading Englishmen in Parliament opted for a rebellion to dispose of James. Parliament invited William of Orange, the Protestant Dutch Stadholder (king) and leader of the anti-French confederation on the continent, to invade England and claim the English throne. James II fled to France after his regime collapsed almost upon William III's arrival in England.[11]

In 1688 William III became the King of England and his wife Mary became Queen. This succession became known as the Glorious Revolution for the relatively small amount of bloodshed. The Dutch provinces were already at war with France when William assumed the throne of England, now with William on the throne of England the British Isles became pro-actively involved in the continental war on the side of the coalition against France and its King XIV.

While in exile in France, James attempted to raise trouble for the new English king. With the assistance of his French ally Louis XIV, James invaded (Catholic) Ireland as a preliminary to taking back his kingdom. In response, the English forces under William III invaded Ireland and effectively ended the uprising at the Battle of the Boyne in 1690.[12] The uprising was broken, but continued on in the remote places of Ireland for a while longer. In Scotland, Catholic forces (calling themselves Jacobins) also attempted to raise trouble for the new English King, but they were also put down in due time. With the upstarts subdued, turned his attention back to the conflict with France on the continent.

Louis XIV had been expanding the French Kingdom, at the expense of his neighbours, for the better part of his reign as King. An alliance formed to resist Louis's ambitions known as the 'League of Augsburg', later to become known as the 'Grand Alliance' once The British Isle's became involved. The alliance included the Dutch Republic, England, Scotland, the Holy Roman Empire, Prussia, Spain, Austria and Piedmont– Savoy. The 'Nine Years War' (1688-97) largely ended in a stalemate with negligible territorial differences compared to when it began. With nothing decided the peace resembled more of a ceasefire where both sides used the time to marshal their strength for when the fighting would inevitably resume.

The cause of war for this round of fighting was the dispute over who would inherit the Spanish Crown after Charles II of Spain died without an heir. On the one side Louis XIV favoured his grandson Philip as the candidate, while the members of the Grand Alliance favoured Archduke Charles VI of the Holy Roman Empire. On his death bed King Charles II of Spain willed his crown to Philip, which did nothing to settle the dispute between the two sides.[13] King Charles' will would have certainly been ignored regardless of who he chose as long as it favoured one side over the other. The war would become known as the 'War of Spanish Succession' and was largely a continuation of the 'Nine Years War' except that France would have a powerful ally, as the French and Spanish Crowns were effectively fused together when Louis XIV installed his nephew as Philip V of Spain.

At this point in history the kingdom of Spain was declining in power, but still held vast domains in Europe, Asia and the Americas. The members of the Grand Alliance rightly feared the unification of France to the vast Spanish domains and the material resources that would become available to France with it. And so they decided to reignite the conflict with France. Early on in the war King William died in 1702, his wife Queen Mary had died in 1694. They were without an heir and so the throne passed to Mary's sister, Anne. Anne was a Protestant and continued to prosecute the war against Catholic France.[14]

♦ ♦ ♦

When James II ascended to the English throne in 1685, Churchill was appointed to the head of the Hudson Bay Company;

he was granted a barony and promoted to Brigadier General.[15] Churchill assisted with putting down the Monmouth Rebellion (1685) which was started by Duke Monmouth, the bastard son of Charles II as he attempted to claim the throne for himself. After initially being promised independent command by King James, Churchill was superseded by Lieutenant General Feversham.

Feversham emerged victorious from the Battle of Sedgemoor, thus ending the rebellion; the Duke of Monmouth was captured shortly thereafter and put on trial. Churchill continued to serve King James loyally and was promoted to Major General after the rebellion was subdued. When William III was invited to invade England and take the crown, Churchill was promoted to "…Lieutenant General but was without specific command duties…"[16] However, King James vacillated and refused to heed Churchill's advice even while Williams invasion was fully underway. King James' incompetence and indecision led Churchill to switch his allegiance over to William. Churchill's defection effectively destroyed the morale of King James' army and his regime dissolved shortly thereafter. Churchill's timely defection was important in averting a battle between the two forces and thus he contributed to the relatively restrained level of violence involved in what would become known as the Glorious (bloodless) Revolution.

Churchill kept his rank and occupation under the new regime of William and Mary, but he was not trusted by the king because of his overly ambitious nature. King William increasingly came to rely on his Dutch retainers all the while sidelining Churchill.[17] After William's victory over James' Irish levies at the Battle of the Boyne, Churchill commanded the English forces tasked with retaking the ports of Cork and Kinsdale, in 1690. With the two ports now in English hands, James' Irish insurgents were cut off from logistical support from France. The rebellion in Ireland was all but crushed, William now turned his attention back to

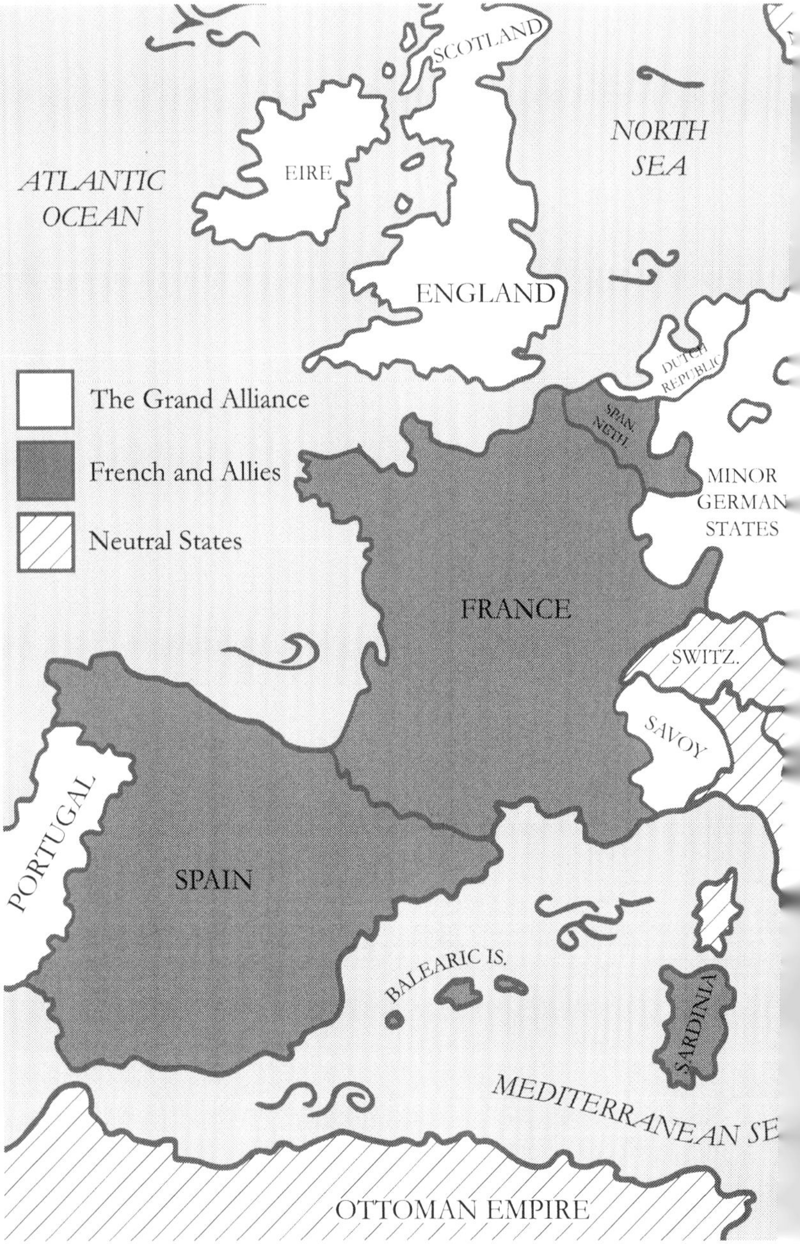
SCOTLAND
NORTH SEA
ATLANTIC OCEAN
EIRE
ENGLAND
DUTCH REPUBLIC
SPAN. NETH.
The Grand Alliance
French and Allies
Neutral States
MINOR GERMAN STATES
FRANCE
SWITZ.
SAVOY
PORTUGAL
SPAIN
BALEARIC IS.
SARDINIA
MEDITERRANEAN SE
OTTOMAN EMPIRE

War of Spanish Succession

the continent and the war against the French there.

Churchill was sent to Flanders, but was not given any meaningful independent command. In 1691 King William's plan to attack Dunkirk was leaked to the French. Churchill was implicated in the treasonous plot and was stripped of his positions and thrown into the Tower of London.[18] After posting bail, Churchill was further implicated with sending James II (and thus Louis XIV) open information (as in not secret) about an impending allied attack on Brest. Although he was cleared, Churchill was never again trusted to lead troops for King William. With King William's death (1702) and the ascension of Queen Anne, Churchill's time had finally come.

With Churchill's military ability and his wife's influential position at the royal court of Queen Anne, Churchill was promoted to the rank of Captain General of all English forces (army and navy) a rank that had never been issued before, or has ever been succeeded in the scope of its responsibility since Churchill held the position.[*19] Churchill moved an army commanded by himself into the Dutch Provinces. While Churchill was supreme Commander-in-Chief of the English forces, there were still the armies of the various alliance member states who were not under Churchill's direct command and who all had their own states interests to protect.

Naturally, it was difficult for the allies to agree upon a common strategy.[20] The Dutch, being in such close proximity to France were naturally and understandable reserved about going too far afield from their country. Churchill on the other hand knew that if the separate alliance members pursued their own (often diverging) interests, they could be isolated and destroyed in detail by the French King. Churchill was determined to not let this happen and towards this end he was forced to employ all his skills as a general and a diplomat.

* Churchill also came to command the Dutch military as their Deputy Captain General, presaging Dwight D. Eisenhower's roles as Supreme Allied Commander.

♦ ♦ ♦

Deception was a key part of every strategy that Churchill employed in his campaigns and battles. In his march to the Danube River, Churchill deceived both friend and foe alike. Churchill's objective was to save the Austrian capital, Vienna and the states of southern Germany from the clutches of the French and their allies in Bavaria. The campaign to save Vienna and the southern Germany states would turn out to be the longest march from a secure base for an English army in close to five hundred years.[21]

Churchill began his campaign at Maastricht on the Maas River from which he went east to Cologne in the spring of 1704. From Cologne he moved his army upstream (south) on the Rhine to Coblenz at the confluence of the Moselle and Rhine river. It was here that the campaign took its first surprising twist for Churchill's contemporaries. It was supposed that Churchill would march up the Moselle and into the rear of the French forces who were threatening the Dutch Republic. Instead of this, Churchill decided to cut his lines of communications with the sea and continue south along the Rhine.

At Mainz he sent his siege train of artillery up the River Main and onto Nuremberg. Churchill continued up the Rhine with the main body of his army, until Manheim where he switched to the River Necker, from which he marched through Swabia over the hills and into the Danube River Valley.[22] Once he had descended into the Danube River Valley he was shortly thereafter joined by an Austrian army under the command of Lewis of Baden, who it should be noted did not share the same offensive spirit as Churchill. Continuing eastwards along the Danube to Bavaria and Austria; Churchill marched his men with speed, in order to prevent a junction of the Bavarian and French forces in the hopes of negotiating with the Bavarians to switch sides. In order to prevent his enemy's junction, Churchill needed to cross the bridge over the Danube at Donauworth which was guarded by a fortress on the hill called the Schellenberg. The hill and fort overlooked the town and was garrisoned with a detachment of the Bavarian army numbering some fourteen thousand men.[23]

Churchill stormed the Schellenberg fortress on the second day of July 1704, before the Bavarians were able to complete their improvisations to the fort and receive more reinforcements from their allies. Churchill's assault succeeded in taking the Schellenberg, but not without heavy losses. The Bavarians were forced to retreat back into their capital, Augsburg. With the Bavarians holed up in Augsburg, Churchill was presented with somewhat of a dilemma.

Augsburg was too well fortified for an assault without a formal siege and Churchill was without adequate siege artillery as his train was slow in coming up. Any delay on the part of Churchill would mean the French would enter the Danube theatre and tip the balance of power to the side of the Franco-Bavarian alliance. Negotiations to get the Bavarians to switch sides were going nowhere, and every moment brought the French closer. Churchill decided, against his own moral objections, to spoil and pillage the Bavarian country side in an attempt to speed up the negotiations.[24] However, this tactic largely failed to bring the Bavarians into the allied camp. The Bavarians and French armies joined forces in early August 1704 without any further molestation.[25]

The French had exhausted themselves with their march to the Danube, as their commander had not done the same meticulous logistical planning as Churchill. Prince Eugene of Savoy, an allied state located on the southeast frontier of France, had been following the French with an army of his own, and managed to join Churchill's army shortly after the convergence of the Franco-Bavarian forces.[26] Lewis of Baden and Churchill diverged in their plans on how to deal with the new threat. But now with Eugene on the scene,* Churchill devised a new plan.

Lewis wanted to attack the Bavarian city Ingolstadt, which

*Eugene shared Churchill's enthusiasm for aggressive actions.

was sufficiently fortified as to require a formal siege. Lewis preferred to have Churchill direct the siege with himself commanding the covering force. Churchill was convinced that Ingolstadt was not an important objective and was worried about relying on Lewis to provide cover, Churchill convinced Lewis to siege Ingolstadt himself. In this way, Churchill rid himself of Lewis's non aggressive ways, and prepared the rest of the army with Eugene for battle against the newly arrived French.

The one beneficial aspect of Churchill's campaign to spoil Bavaria was that it got the Elector of Bavaria* to disperse "… at least 16,000 of his troops…"[27] to locations he felt were vulnerable to Churchill's raiders. As well the deprivations began to sow the seeds of dissension between the commanders of the Franco-Bavarian army, as the French commanders, Tallard and Marsin, thought it was foolish to split off small detachments for this purpose.[28]

♦ ♦ ♦

The Elector of Bavaria was becoming anxious and wanted to get the Anglo-Austrian forces out of his country. However, the French commanders Tallard and Marsin were content to wait knowing that Churchill, being so far from his secure base in the Netherlands was going to be quickly diminishing his supplies. The French commanders deferred to the Elector, and so, they moved their forces down the Danube valley. The two opposing forces were to engage each other on the northern bank of the Danube to the west of Donauworth around the village Blenheim.†

The Danube runs slightly from the south west to the north east. There are wooded hills to the north with numerous creeks running their way south into the Danube. In between the hills to the north and the Danube to the south, the country is practically flat from Donauworth to Ulm.[29]

* The elector of Bavaria was the sovereign of Bavaria, although the office nominally owed its allegiance and sovereignty to the Holy Roman Emperor.
† Or Blindheim, we shall refer to it as Blenheim.

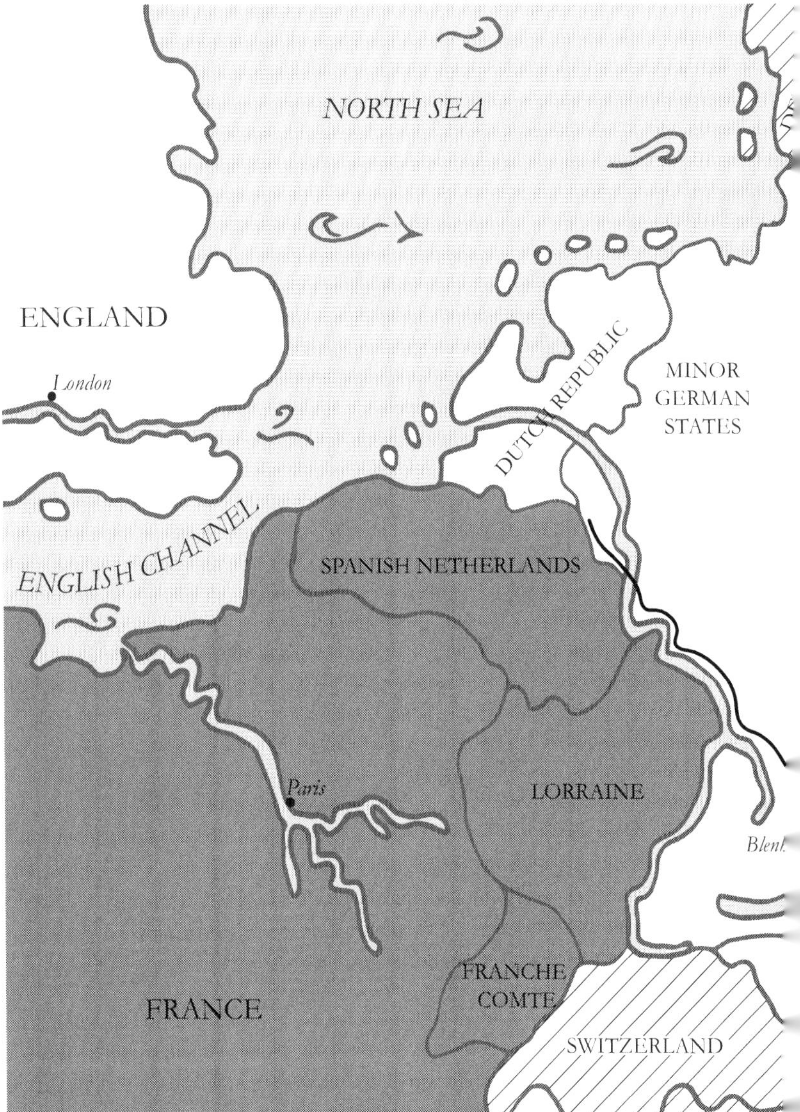
NORTH SEA
ENGLAND
London
DUTCH REPUBLIC
MINOR
GERMAN
STATES
ENGLISH CHANNEL
SPANISH NETHERLANDS
Paris
LORRAINE
FRANCHE
COMTE
FRANCE
SWITZERLAND
MILAN
SAVOY
PIEDMONT

March to the Danube

Consistently throughout the campaign, Churchill had paid handsomely for good intelligence. He also was well known for doing his due diligence when it came to reconnoitering the enemy forces before him.[30] At Blenheim, Churchill noticed that the French and Bavarians had positioned themselves in two separate bodies without much of their force held in reserve. Both sections were respectively garrisoning a town, Blenheim in the south and Oberlaugheim and Lutzingen in the north. There was a significant gap in the middle of the French lines that was covered by some cavalry squadrons. To the front of the French was the small river Nebel running north to south into the Danube.

Seeing the disposition of the opposing forces, Churchill devised a plan and divided his troops into two separate commands. The right wing in the north was under the command of Eugene, while the left wing in the south was commanded by Churchill himself. The French commander decided not to contest Churchill's crossing over the Nebel in close quarters, so Churchill had a relatively easy time of crossing it. Eugene's crossing was more difficult as the French and Bavarians were positioned closer to the western bank of the Nebel.[31]

The assaults on both wings had the effect that the French commanders called in their reserves to reinforce the northern and southern sectors (to the neglect of the centre section). This movement was not lost on Churchill, and once he saw it happen Churchill scrapped together his reserves and threw them into the centre. The French and Bavarians had no fresh units to rescue the center and so Churchill's maneuver succeeded in capturing the center gap in between the two French commands, effectively splitting the French line in two.[32] The town of Blenheim became exceedingly crowded as the French reserves came in, so much so that it was nearly impossible to maneuver or disentangle the units. Eventually the remaining troops in Blenheim were forced to surrender, as they were cut off and pressed from all sides. After the troops in Blenheim surrendered the French and Bavarian troops in the northern sector either retreated or were captured. The remnants of the army (probably about one third) had a hard journey back to France.[33]

After the victory at Blenheim, Churchill pursued the remaining French forces that were in full retreat back to the Rhine. Late in the fall there were two separate sieges to finish off the fighting season, one at Landau, and the second at Trarbach.[34] The Battle of Blenheim had destroyed Louis XIV's best army. It decisively decided the campaign in southern Germany and saved Austria from a Franco-Bavarian attack on their capital, Vienna. The destruction of the French army effectively sealed the French into their own territory, and forced Louis XIV to rethink his grand territorial ambitions and look for a dignified way to end the war.[35] Victory at Blenheim did not entirely defeat the will of the French king, but at least it put a temporary halt to his more expansionist impulses. However, the success, although much needed had a negative effect on the Grand Alliance, in that, they became satisfied and lost their sense of urgency deluding themselves into thinking they could relax their efforts and take it easy with regards to the Sun King.

♦ ♦ ♦

As mentioned before, the members of the Grand Alliance on the continent all had their own individual problems to deal with, and after the removal of the overwhelming French threat in 1704 they felt safe enough to do so. It was one of Churchill's responsibilities to persuade the member states to maintain a unity of effort. Before returning home to England, Churchill toured around the allied "…courts of northern Germany… from Wissembourg, Frankfurt, Kassel, Berlin… [travelling] over 400 miles in sixteen days…"[36] drumming up support and discussing allied plans and policy for the next fighting season.

The Emperor of Austria had earlier promised to make Churchill the Prince of Mindelheim, after the victory at Blenheim the Emperor bestowed this gift upon him.[37] Churchill had problems

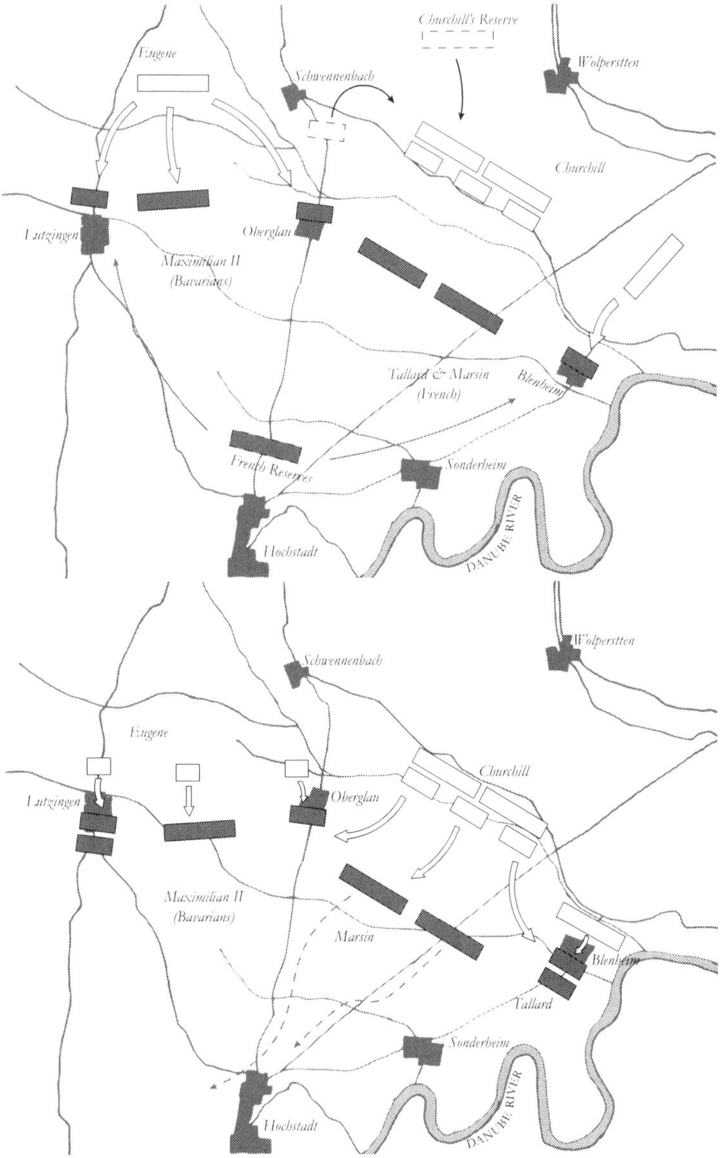

Battle of Blenheim

of his own with the parliament in England; these would become known to him as time proceeded.

Upon his return to London during the Christmas of 1704 Churchill was greeted as a hero and was congratulated first by Parliament, and then by Queen Anne. The Queen vested in him the "…royal park at Woodstock together with an act for the [funding] construction of a new palace."[38] After the initial jubilation which accompanied Churchill's return, the underlying political differences once again assumed the forefront. The members of the Tory party were opposed to the policy of fighting a continental war, its large armies meant high taxes, and they preferred a policy of fighting it out in the colonies of the Americas and through a blockade of the major French ports.[39]

The members of the Whig party supported the policy of fighting the French on the continent, but the Whig party was losing power in parliament. Churchill a Tory by birth, but a Whig by inclination (and the fact that the Whigs supported the policy of continental war) was strictly non-partisan. The Queen was non-partisan and desperately wanted a united wartime coalition government with broad popular support, to be formed in parliament.[40] However, when it came to elections her hands (as well as Churchill's) were tied.

The year 1704 bore witness to successes for the preferred policies of both parties. The Grand Alliance had concluded a treaty with Portugal, which gave England an important naval base at Lisbon from which to launch naval operations into the Mediterranean.[41] In early August 1704, a week before the victory at Blenheim, a combined force of British infantry and warships assaulted and captured the strategic rock of Gibraltar. The rock was situated at the western extremity of the Mediterranean Sea, which narrows to some fifteen miles before opening up into the Atlantic Ocean. The mountain is easily cut off from the mainland of Spain, and once properly fortified it guards (or hinders) any transit into or out of the Mediterranean. Even today it is still a part of British territory. Victory at Blenheim was seen as a vindication of the Whig policy, while the capture of Gibraltar was the equivalent for the Tories.

♦ ♦ ♦

Once Churchill arrived back on the European continent in 1706 he received intelligence of the allied setbacks in northern Italy and along the Rhine front. The French king sensing that a purely static defense would be insufficient against the aggressive Churchill deployed an army with the finest equipment under the command of Marshall Villeroy and instructed him to immediately seek out an engagement with Churchill. At the same time Louis XIV warned Villeroy of the shock value and firepower of the English troops in battle and advised him to be wary of the section of his line that would receive the English attack.[42]

The Battle of Ramillies was to take place considerably closer to the English and Dutch bases of operations. And thus it did not require the same logistical preparation or planning as did the campaign on the Danube. However, the same was also true in respect to the position of the French. Churchill began the campaigning season by concentrating his forces around the city Maastricht. The French under Villeroy were based out of Louvain, and proceeded to cross the Dyle River then headed east to Tirlemont on the Geete River from whence they headed south. When the two opposing forces met around the village of Ramillies both sides were surprised to meet each other in the field so soon.

The terrain around Ramillies was hilly but did not slope in any particular direction. There was the Mehaigne River to the south of Ramillies that ran from west to east and the village of Taviers, which was located on the northern bank of the Mehaigne River. There was a road connecting Taviers and Ramillies and in-between the two towns there was a road running west to Charleroi. To the north of Ramillies was the Little Geete River, with its steep banks, running south to north with the village of

Autre-Eglise on a tributary of the Little Geete River. There were two roads that connected Autre-Eglise and Ramillies that ran roughly parallel to each other although they were on either side of the Little Geete.

The French line was facing east in a large arched line. Their right wing was anchored at Taviers, perpendicular to the River Mehaigne. Their line continued north, their center occupied Ramillies, and further north the left wing was anchored on the town Autre-Eglise and was positioned behind and parallel to the Little Geete River. Facing the French, Churchill's army was drawn up looking west. Churchill utilized the blind spots created by the hilly landscape to hide the movement and dispositions of his troops from the French.[43] Once in position, Churchill immediately took the offensive against the French.

His first move was to concentrate his forces on his left wing and attack in depth along the axis of the River Mehaigne. Soon afterwards, Churchill's right flank (which consisted of his English troops) moved in to engage the French in the northern sector. Once the English troops had crossed the Little Geete River, the French appeared upon the crest of the steep western bank and poured musket fire down into the English ranks. The highly disciplined English troops did not panic, but returned fire and drove the French back to their lines.[44]

Remembering what Louis XIV had told him about the shock power of a regular British infantry line, Villeroy began to call in his reserves and redeploy troops from the center of his line for the expected attack on his left. With the French center denuded of its strength, Churchill sensed his opportunity and quickly seized it. He threw in his cavalry and reserves and assaulted the center of the French line. The attack in the center overwhelmed the French line and isolated their right wing that was now pinned down in Taviers. Once the cavalry had broken the French center, they wheeled to their right and threatened to outflank the main French line, while some infantry and dismounted dragoons (mounted infantry) wheeled to their left and began to envelop the French in Taviers. At this point the battle was essentially won for Churchill, and the spoils were as great as those of Blenheim.

Blenheim and Ramillies share commonalities not only in that they were great tactical successes, but also in that they were of the greatest importance on the level of grand strategy. Blenheim saved Austria and the southern German states from the menace of the French, while Ramillies saved the Dutch Republic and liberated much of the Spanish Netherlands. Numerous important Belgian cities and fortifications capitulated to the Grand Alliance upon the news of the French defeat.[45]

The victory in 1706 was desperately needed good news, considering the setbacks suffered by the Grand Alliance along the Rhine and in northern Italy earlier in the year. However, as happened before, the members of the alliance believed they could rest on their laurels and once again return to pursuing their own interests. Louis XIV had other plans for the Grand Alliance. Although Louis was looking for a way to end the war, he desired an end that would leave France in a position of strength, and with its honour intact. From the perspective of the Grand Alliance this would mean that France would still be in a position to (once again) threaten the peace of Europe at a later date. If the Grand Alliance wanted a lasting peace, they would need a decisive victory on French soil; to do this they required a united effort and Churchill in command of an army.

♦ ♦ ♦

By the time of the campaign of 1711 Churchill's position had been ruined among the ruling political elite. His close friend and ally in parliament, Godolphin, had been dismissed from office and replaced by the Tory Robert Harley. His wife Sarah, a hyper partisan Whig, had once been Queen Anne's closest friend and a maid at court, but was replaced because of her extreme partisan views.[46] The Tory party had been swept into power in the gener-

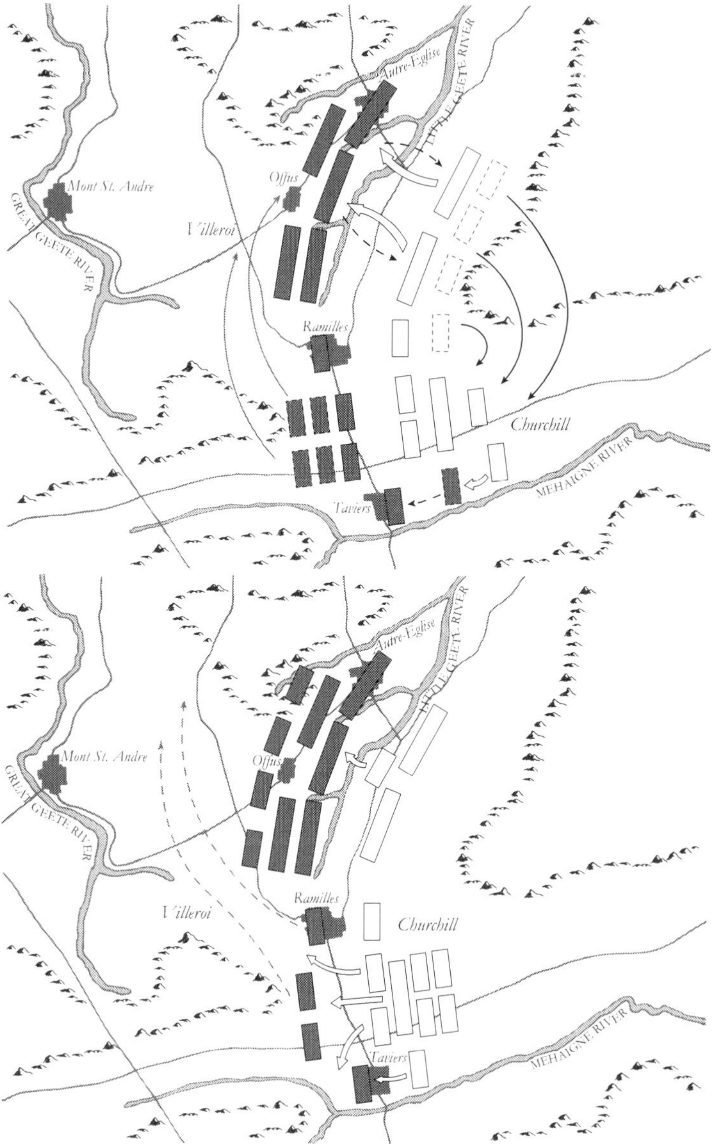

Battle of Ramilles

al election of 1710 on a wave of war weariness and opposition to the high taxes required to pay for the continental war and also as a result of the campaign of 1709 which culminated in the Battle of Malplaquet. Malplaquet had been extremely costly in terms of causalities for the Grand Alliance (especially the British), and the campaign of 1710 had produced no positive decisive results for the alliance either.[47]

The sinews that held the Grand Alliance together were beginning to break down. The Austrian Emperor Joseph died, leaving the question of future Austrian policy up in the air. Amongst other tensions and unbeknownst to Churchill, as well as the other members of the alliance, the new Tory government was entering into secret negotiations with Louis XIV. Churchill intended for 1711 to be the final campaign where he would break through the French lines, march on Paris and onto a final peace.[48]

As soon as Churchill landed on the continent he was overwhelmed with problems. The Prussian king was arguing with the Dutch and English governments over the payments of subsidies, and was withholding his contingent of troops. As well, the Secretary of State, St. John, gave Churchill instructions to send "...five infantry regiments to leave Flanders for an expedition against Quebec."[*49] Poorly planned and executed, the Quebec expedition failed in its objectives and sapped the strength of the forces on the continent that would be needed for offensive operations against France.

The campaign of 1711 was to be fought on French territory. After a long series of defeats, Louis XIV tasked his chief military architects and engineers, led by the famous Vauban,[†] to construct a series of impenetrable fortifications along the French

* Quebec was a French Province in North America.

† Vauban brought the science of fortifications to its apogee. Much of his work, or that of his followers, is still standing today, and can be found in Europe, and around the world.

and Belgian frontier. Dubbed the 'Lines of Ne Plus Ultra',* the fortifications stretched from the English Channel in the west to the Ardennes Massiff (hill country) at Namur in the east. The lines utilized the natural barriers of four rivers; from left to right, starting with the River Canche, Gy, Sensee and the River Sambre.[50]

Churchill arrived relatively late in the season, close to the end of April, even then bad weather and rain set in to further delay his plans. The French who were behind secure lines had no intention of engaging Churchill in a battle, but rather intended to either allow him to waste his army in an attack on the lines or burn through his supplies. On top of the troops sent to Quebec, Prince Eugene and his contingent were detached from Churchill's army because a French force had been sent to the Rhine.

At Arleux, there was a fort and a causeway of strategic importance, which connected to Douai by a canal. Douai had switched sides numerous times during 1711 with the French eventually being left in control of it. In an infamous move the French commander stripped naked the four hundred prisoners they had captured and marched them behind their lines. This gesture filled Churchill with disgust and a burning desire for vengeance.[51]

On July the 27th Churchill made a theatrical demonstration with his leading generals by personally inspecting the French defensive lines on the high ground west of Arras in between the headwaters of the River Gy and the River Canche. Villars took the bait, and knowing that Churchill had attacked fortified positions before, and was willing to accept causalities, he began to concentrate his forces opposite Churchill. Concentrating his army in the Arras sector for what appeared to be an assault on the French line, Churchill was also discreetly gathering a force outside of Douai to assault the causeway at Arleux and create a bridgehead on the other side. When midnight came on August

* In English it means 'go no further'.

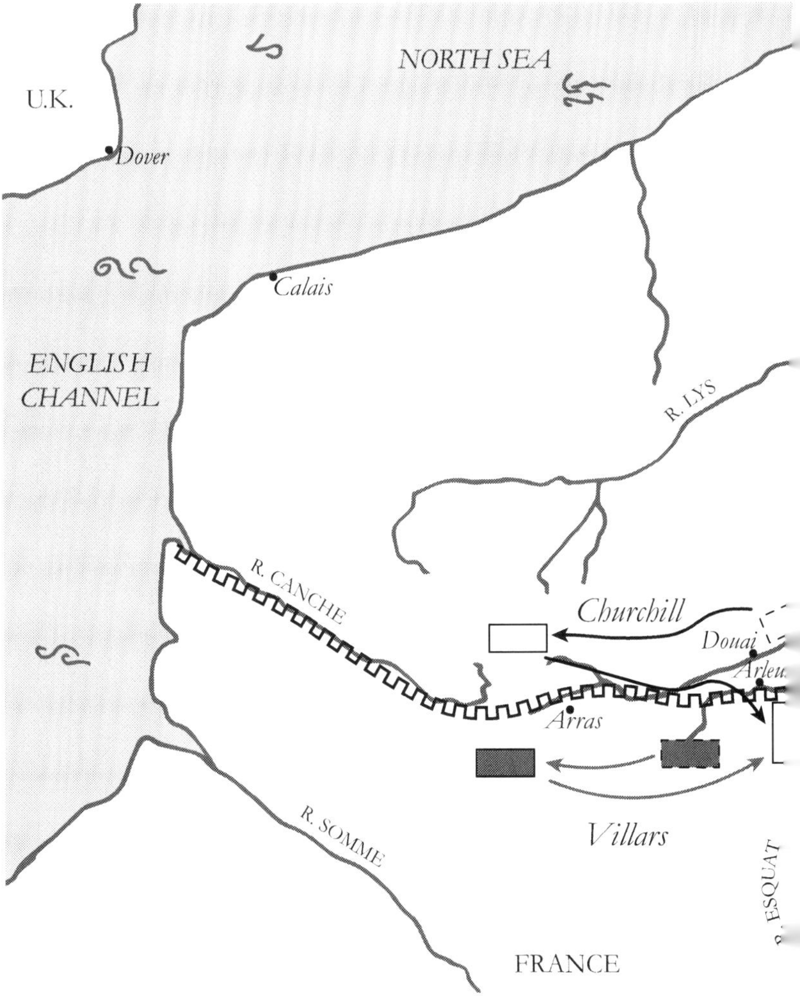
NORTH SEA
U.K.
Dover
Calais
ENGLISH
CHANNEL
R. LYS
R. CANCHE
Churchill
Douai
Arras
Villars
R. SOMME
FRANCE

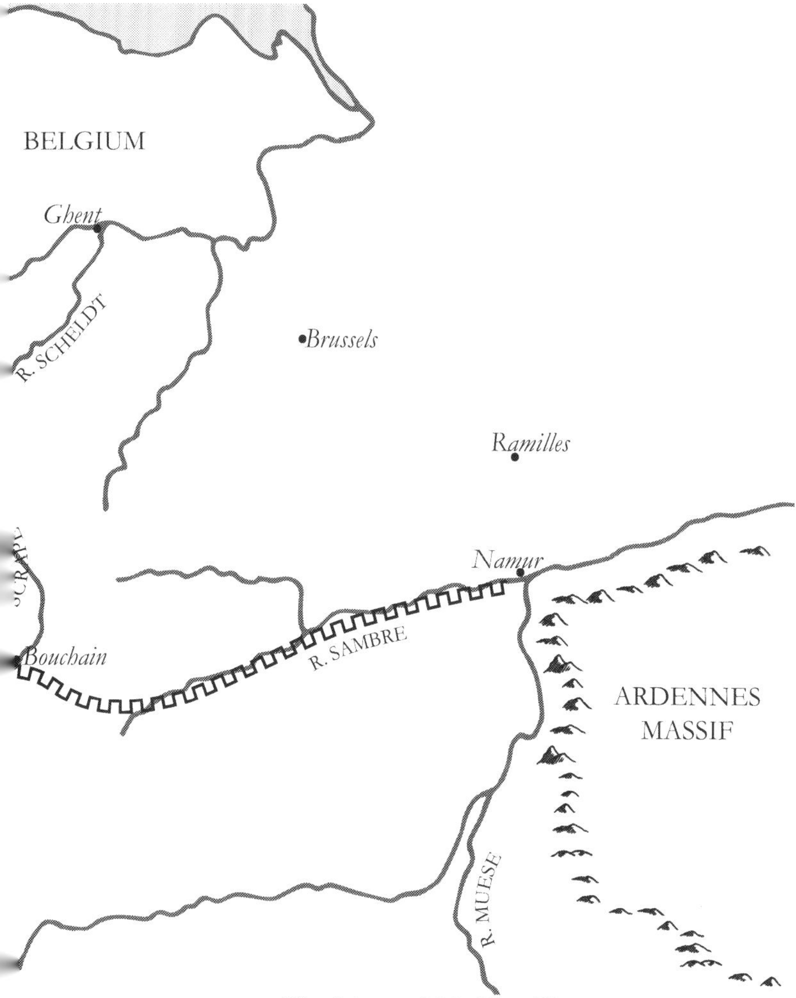

The Lines of Ne Plus Ultra

the 4th Churchill sent word for the men outside Douai to attack the causeway, while the main army camped near Arras began their march east towards the causeway.[52]

Villars was half expecting a night attack in the Arras sector and was on high alert. He eventually realized he had been tricked and was forced to race Churchill's army to Arleux. But Churchill had a head start and his army was prepared for the march with his fastest units marching in the front of the column (i.e. cavalry, infantry, and then the artillery). That morning Churchill passed through the Ne Plus Ultra without losing a single man to French action.♦♦♦[53] Even his Tory detractors in government had to concede this glory to him. Secretary of State St. John wrote to him, "I most heartily congratulate with your Grace on this great event, of which no more needs I think be said than that you have obtained without losing a man, such an advantage as we should have bought with the expense of several thousand lives, and reckoned ourselves gainers."[54]

After crossing the causeway, the army formed up in line for battle in anticipation of a French counter attack. Villars, who was thoroughly embarrassed, decided against battle as his troops were exhausted from the counter march and instead formed up his lines in a strong position to the south of the causeway. It was now that Churchill turned east towards Bouchain on the River Escaut.[55] The River Escaut provided an excellent route to Paris, in an age when roads were generally poor and military supplies were much more efficiently carried over water. Bouchain was thus of great strategic importance to Churchill.

The siege of Bouchain was thought to be impossible by most of Churchill's subordinates, but Churchill understood that the strategic location of the fort made it worth the effort of a siege. The land surrounding Bouchain was swampy and Churchill's artillery still needed to arrive; none-the-less Churchill proceeded to surround the fort. He then split his forces between those besieging the fort and those that would cover the siege. Villars had the advantage of not needing to divide his larger army, but he was still afraid of Churchill and he did not act with a sufficiently aggressive spirit. Villars eventually moved his forces to the River Sensee to threaten Churchill's supply lines, but the move was too little too late.[56]

Churchill's covering force managed to keep Villars at bay, while workers from Belgium arrived and completed the lines of circumvallation. On the 21st of August Churchill's siege train arrived and the artillery bombardment on Bouchain began on the 30th.[57] Villars responded by bombarding the allied army, but it was too late, Bouchain's garrison surrendered on the first of September. With Bouchain secure, the army was exhausted and retired into winter quarters, Churchill returned home to England.

This would be Churchill's last campaign as his political opponents had finally discredited him at court. "For ten years he led the armies of the Grand Alliance, and during all that period he never fought a battle he did not win, or besieged a town he did not take. Nothing exists like this in the annals of war."[58] Churchill's career in the military was effectively over and he was replaced by the Duke of Ormonde, but the peace treaty with France was yet to be signed.

♦ ♦ ♦

After the replacement of Churchill in 1712, the Grand Alliance suffered military setbacks which offset the gains made by Churchill in 1711. The Tory government was already eager for peace and began secret negotiations that would allow Louis XIV to save face and end the war in an honourable fashion.[59] A treaty was negotiated in the city of Utrecht in the year 1713, between France and Spain on the one side and Great Britain, the United (Dutch) Provinces, Savoy and Portugal on the other side.

The peace of Utrecht was shortly followed by individual treaties with the rest of the members of the Grand Alliance. While the war of Spanish Succession did not permanently end the possibility of French domination of Europe, it at least set the project back for a generation. Ending a war that had been waged, almost without interruption, for twenty years the Treaty of Utrecht guaranteed the liberty of the European countries for the next generation to come.

John Churchill grew up in an impoverished aristocratic household during a turbulent period of human history. Through his luck and skill as a military commander, Churchill was able to reverse his father's bad fortune and insured the good standing of his family's name for generations to come. On the field of battle, Churchill's well planned march to the Danube River and his brilliant victory at Blenheim stopped the tide of French expansion to the east of their natural frontiers. As the ensuing battles of later years were progressively fought closer and closer to French territory, Churchill can justifiably be considered the arch-nemesis of Louis XIV's political and territorial ambitions.

The Battle of Ramillies was as brilliant in its result as was Blenheim. Crossing the 'Ne Plus Ultra' lines was a masterpiece of organization and deception. Churchill's battlefield successes translated into political victories for the concept of constitutional monarchy and the parliamentary system over that of arbitrary, absolutist monarchy. Louis XIV was famously quoted as saying "l'etat, c'est moi", which translates into English as, 'the state, it is I'. The French King believed himself to be the entirety of the state and that his rule over men was naturally ordained by the Supreme Being, God. The same old conflict that began with the Barons and King John was playing itself out on the international stage.

The questions raised by the Manga Carta were not definitively decided in either direction by the end of the War of Spanish Succession. However, Churchill's contributions to the ultimate victory of the Grand Alliance at least insured that the liberty of man would not be destroyed by the 'Sun King's' ambitions. By the time Churchill returned to the British Isles in 1711, the people of the Isles were tired of the war and the ensuing costs of fighting it out on the continent. Churchill retired from public life to the country as somewhat of an unwanted hero in Great Britain. In 1713 he travelled to Europe to inspect his principality in the Holy Roman Empire, and was greeted as a hero there. After his European tour, he returned to the Isles and was able to occupy one wing of his yet to be completed palace named 'Blenheim', before passing away in 1722.*[60] Churchill's body was entombed on the premises.

* Blenheim Palace was the birthplace of the more familiar Sir Winston S. Churchill. While today's Duke of Marlborough still occupies the house as the family's principal residence, the gardens are open to the public and the palace grounds have been recognized as a UNESCO World Heritage Site. More recently part of the Palace was used as a set in the 2015 James Bond movie, Spectre.

George Washington

George Washington was born on February 11, 1731* in Virginia to his parents, Augustine and Mary Ball Washington. He was the first child born to Mary, who was Augustine's second wife.[1] Augustine had two sons older than George with his first wife, Lawrence and Augustine Jr. who went to England for college before going on to serve in the Virginia Colonial militia.

Augustine Washington passed away in 1743, when George was 12, leaving George as the de facto man of his half of the family. George inherited various properties in Virginia from his father, including Ferry Farm across the Rappahannock from Fredericksburg. His eldest brother, Lawrence inherited the property called Mount Vernon that would later become George's upon the death of Lawrence.[2]

His father's death ended George's childhood early and dashed his hopes for a higher education abroad like his older brothers whom he admired. However, the next stage of George's early manhood proved equally effective as a college education would have been in preparing him for the later challenges in his life. Although he cherished books and longed for a college education, he was a very athletic and outdoorsy boy.

> "He loved to swim in the deep waters of the Rappahannock. He excelled in riding, liked to hunt, later learned fencing, attended a dancing school, played billiards, fre-

* This is according to the old Julian calendar. The British Empire, including the American colonies adopted its use in 1752. The changed moved George's birthday to February 22, 1732.

quented cock fights and horse races, and experimented with his first flirtations."[3]

Through the connections of his eldest brother, George landed a spot as a surveyor at the age of 15, which enabled him begin to rise through the social strata in earnest. Surveying provided an excellent means for George to provide a living for his family and to gradually amass a fortune for himself. Various surveying jobs around Virginia allowed George to buy himself several thousand acres in the Shenandoah Valley, marking his first major investment.[4]

In the summer of 1752, George's eldest brother Lawrence died from tuberculosis while in Bermuda trying to regain his health. George had gone to Barbados with Lawrence (before Lawrence continued onto Bermuda), but George came down with the small pox and so returned to Virginia. Lawrence's property, Mount Vernon, and its twenty-five hundred acres were left to George's stewardship on the condition that if Lawrence's wife and daughter were to die without an heir it would be left to George.[5]

Lawrence's death also left his military position in the Virginia militia vacant, which George promptly pressed his case to succeed his brother to the post. In "…February 1753, just before his twenty-first birthday, George Washington took the oath of office and became district adjutant, which paid one hundred pounds annually and crowned him with the title of Major Washington."[6] Just as George had assumed his military position, trouble began to brew in the Old World and the New.

♦ ♦ ♦

The Seven Years War was another chapter in the century's long Anglo-French rivalry and French attempts at European hegemony. This new episode built upon the previous conflicts, but expanded the intensity and geographic scope. The Seven Years War also included numerous smaller territorial wars overlapping with the larger European one. The military and economic strategies of Great Britain and France remained the same as before. By and large little changed in the system of alliances except that Austria was now allied with France against Great Britain, Prussia, Sweden, Portugal and Spain (to name the most important). The conflict was not contained to the European continent; indeed, it even began in the back country of North America. It was perhaps the first truly global war, as it quickly spread to every region on Earth where Europeans had colonies.

The previous wars in North America were miniscule in scope compared to what would become known as the French and Indian War to the American colonists. Both sides would deploy significant manpower and economic resources to the region and were expecting to achieve decisive results. In comparison to the war on the European continent where the 'rules' regulating warfare had been long established and were rigidly adhered to by all sides; the French and Indian War resembled a form of total war that would become increasingly common later on in history, in that the European rules of war did not apply or were largely ignored.[7] The French and British empires in North America would escalate their means and goals from minor territorial advantages, to the complete destruction of their rivals' imperial systems in North America.

The thirteen British colonies in America were all situated along the eastern seaboard facing the Atlantic Ocean and hemmed in by the Appalachian Mountain range in the west. The territory to the west of the mountains was claimed by both the French and British. New France was hinged in the centre on the Great Lakes. Going in the southern direction from the Great Lakes took you along the Mississippi River to New Orleans on the Gulf of Mexico. To the north and east of the Great Lakes the French empire stretched along the St. Lawrence River down to Montreal and Quebec City and into the North Atlantic. New France was an imperial system dominated by rivers and lakes with few access points to the Atlantic Ocean, other than the mouths of the two great rivers. The French empire in North American was not as densely populated as the Thirteen Colonies, but the French still effectively held up the British advance to the west.[8]

♦ ♦ ♦

The French decided they would begin building forts in the Ohio River region, which was claimed by the French, the British and their respective native allies. The French wanted to better control the region connecting their main colonial interests in North America, Quebec (the St. Lawrence River Valley), and New Orleans (the Mississippi River Valley). The British responded by sending Washington as an emissary directly to the French commander of the Ohio. He headed west over the Allegheny Mountains with instructions to tell the French to immediately leave the region or prepare to face the consequences.[9]

Washington was also tasked to reconnoiter the headwaters of the Allegheny, Monongahela and Ohio Rivers for an ideal location to build a fort to block French expansion into the Ohio region. The French told Washington they had no intention of leaving. And so, Washington returned to Williamsburg, Virginia,* and reported to the House of Burgesses (a sort of parliament/congress) on the French intransigence. He also reported on the locations of the French fort system and their state of martial preparedness.[10]

The mission to the Ohio had tested Washington's physical and mental stamina, but it had proved that he was not wanting. The undertaking and completion of the diplomatic mission enhanced his reputation as a hardworking, diligent and reliable young officer. As the adjutant of the northern sector of Virginia, it was now Washington's duty to raise and train one hundred men for the colonial militia and the upcoming fortbuilding expedition into the Ohio lands.[11]

* Williamsburg was the colonial capital of Virginia.

Washington received his first experience in battle, when a small group of Frenchmen had been stalking his militiamen through the wilderness. Tracking them down with his scouts, Washington found the French camp hidden in a gully. He ordered the French to surrender, but they opened fire instead. The Virginians, and Indian allies with them, returned fire and killed about half of the French party before the survivors surrendered. Among the dead was a supposed envoy sent to deliver a message to Washington saying 'leave Ohio or face the consequences'. The supposed French envoy was the brother of the French commander in the Ohio region; the brother claimed righteous indignation and wanted revenge.[12]

Washington had good reason to believe that the French envoy was a fraud, seeing as how the French band had been stalking his group of men (presumably an envoy would approach directly). Regardless of the Frenchman's commission the French now had a reasonable pretext for declaring war against Great Britain. The Virginians dug into a position and constructed a fort, later named Fort Necessity.* Washington was forced to retreat back to the British colonies after being assaulted by a large French force sent to avenge the dead emissary and evict the British from the region. Washington's battle in the Ohio wilderness witnessed the first shots fired in what would become known as the Seven Years War.[13]

The colonial militias of the thirteen colonies assisted the British in defeating the French Empire in North America. Fighting was generally brutal as both sides employed their Indian allies as auxiliaries, who did not engage in war with any regard to European values or rules of engagement. Often towns and villages were raided and razed with women, children and the elderly murdered and scalps taken as trophies. Initially the British and the Thirteen Colonies suffered the worst of the fighting,

* Fort Necessity is now located south east of Pittsburg. Fort Duquesne is now located within Pittsburg.

British North American Imperial System

but the tide turned rapidly as the British Royal Navy made it difficult for New France to keep a steady stream of reinforcements and supplies coming from France.

The war in the New World ended after an amphibious operation up the St. Lawrence laid siege to Quebec City. In an example of superb British generalship, General James Wolfe succeeded in taking the city by maneuvering his army up a cliff near the city under cover of darkness and winning a battle on the Plains of Abraham. Wolfe died of wounds received during the battle.[14] The French were chased up the St. Lawrence to Montreal but were able to recapture Quebec City from the British. Starving and ill-supplied, the governor of New France was made to surrender once he realized France could not reinforce them. The French and Indian War decisively knocked the French out of the North American continent and cemented the position of the British. However, the fruits of the British victory were to be relatively short lived, as the seeds of the American Revolution were sown in the French and Indian Wars and the peace that followed it.

♦ ♦ ♦

Having acquired the Ohio River valley and the rest of New France, Great Britain proceeded to block the westward expansion of the Thirteen Colonies with the Royal Proclamation of 1763. The proclamation gave the land to the Indian allies of the British while depriving the colonial land speculators and veterans of the land they were expecting.[15] Notwithstanding the Royal Proclamation illegal settlers from various European lands continued to pour into the western lands without the official consent of the Royal or colonial governments.[16]

The Seven Years War forced the British government to spend a considerable amount of money and to accumulate a considerable amount of debt. King George III and his government in Parliament (led by the Tories) believed that since the American colonists had benefited from the French defeat that they should then help bear the burden of the debt. The British government proceeded to impose taxes on certain imported manufactured goods while also increasing inspection of shipping to thwart smuggling.[17] The Sugar Act (1764), Stamp Act (1765), and the Quartering Act (1765) incensed the American colonists and in response they created boycott associations to stop buying non-essential goods from Great Britain.[18]

Parliament rescinded the unpopular acts when the old Whig politician, William Pitt, was elected to be the Prime Minister. Pitt's tenure was short lived as he was ill and died in 1768 shortly after assuming office. While Pitt was sick a subordinate minister, Charles Townshed independently attempted to safe guard the prerogative of parliament and the crown to levy taxes. In 1767 Townshed introduced new legislation that was much the same as the 'sugar' and 'stamp' acts called the Townshed Duties.[19]

While the Townshed acts were also repealed, parliament and the crown reaffirmed their right to levy taxes in the colonies with the Declaratory Acts. The Declaratory Acts created a colonial revenue collection bureaucracy called the American Board of Customs Commissioners.[20] The Declaratory Acts were also repealed, but the duty on tea was kept. In response to what the British government was increasingly seeing as rebellion they sent four thousand troops to Boston to help pacify the situation. The leading men in the colonies disputed the British parliaments supposed right of taxation over the colonies without the colonies having any representatives in parliament.[21]

As mentioned above, a duty on tea had been left in effect, although the duty was lowered in 1773. Despite the lowered tax the Americans were still incensed by the concept. In December of 1773 a Boston mob dressed up as Indians and threw a cargo of tea into Boston harbour as an act of political protest against the Tea Act. The British government and King now considered the colonies and especially Boston to be in rebellion. In response to the Tea Party the port of Boston was shut down to commerce and the colony of Massachusetts was placed under direct Royal rule.[22]

In a show of solidarity with Massachusetts the rest of the colonies, save Georgia, sent representatives to the first Continental Congress in Philadelphia in 1774. While this Congress "…denounced the Coercive acts, approved a boycott of British imports and authorized military preparations… they continued to profess their loyalties to George III and their disapproval of Parliament's actions."[23] In truth, their blame was misplaced as Parliament, now under a Tory government, was heavily influenced by King George and they were little more than puppets of the King.

The newly formed Colonial Congress was impressed with George Washington's military resume and his devotion to the cause of independence, and so, they appointed Washington as commander-in-chief of the continental forces. He was somewhat reluctant in accepting the commission because he understood the responsibility and gravity of the position,* but never-the-less he accepted and was quickly off to the siege at Boston.[24]

♦ ♦ ♦

The British in Boston had attempted to seize a known arsenal that the colonists had stockpiled at Concord, but the militia† came out in force to harass the British regulars and made them retreat back into Boston. The minutemen went on to try to occupy Bunker Hill, which dominated Boston harbour, but the British were able to beat them off it, although with very high casualties. After the battle of Bunker Hill, the colonists laid siege to Boston and stalemate ensued. For months each side was within eyesight of each other. When Washington arrived he was confronted with disorder and haphazard discipline. To add

* As Washington put it himself, "But as it had been a kind of destiny that has thrown me upon this service, I shall hope that my undertaking it is designed to answer some good purpose."

† The militia came to be known, or nicknamed as the minutemen for their ability to deploy at a minute's notice.

another danger to the situation the colonials were desperately short of gunpowder.[25]

Washington began by reorganizing the siege entrenchments, which he had found to be wanting and attempted to instill some discipline into the men. In January artillery that had been captured from the British at Fort Ticonderoga and been dragged mostly overland on sledges to Boston.[26] The city was completely surrounded from the land side, except for in the south, where there was a hill called Dorchester Heights that had not been occupied by either side. Once Washington considered his entrenchments sufficient he launched his plan to assault Boston.

February 1776, the fresh water surrounding Boston had frozen, making it possible to launch an attack on the city. In a council of war, Washington was dissuaded by his subordinate commanders from making a frontal assault.[27] Instead a plan was made to quickly fortify Dorchester Heights in one night and thus present the British with the problem of assaulting the heights at great disadvantage or having their positions in the city bombarded by the colonists. The Americans constructed prefabricated obstructions to place on the heights and also wrapped their wagon wheels in leather to soften the noise of carrying their cannon and other implements up the heights. On March 2nd Washington ordered a light bombardment of Boston to serve as a distraction.[28]

On the night of the 4th of March, a twelve-hundred-man work force set about building the entrenchments on Dorchester Heights.* The morning of the fifth, the British woke up to the sight of what had been constructed overnight. The British commander, General Howe, decided it was not prudent to attempt an assault on the hill and instead decided to withdraw to a more secure harbour. With the relatively bloodless capture of Boston, Washington won the first great victory in the war and bolstered faith in the cause of the colonists.

* They were aided by a thick fog which further softened the noise.

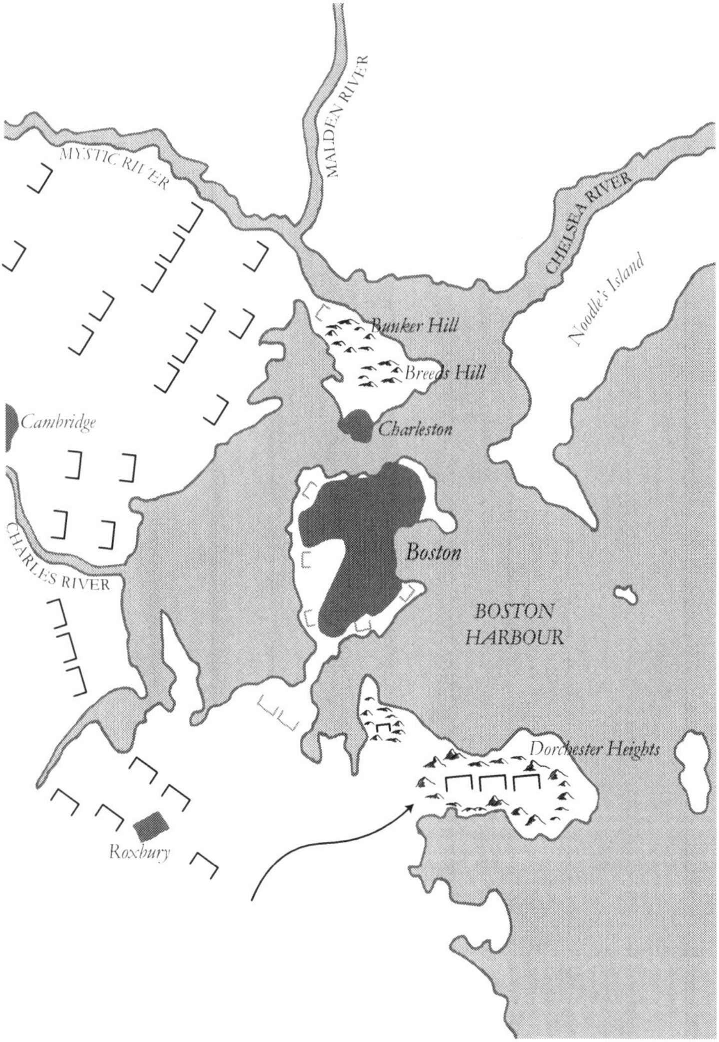

Siege of Boston

♦ ♦ ♦

From Boston, the British retreated to the port of Halifax to regain their strength. Washington believed correctly that New York City would be their next target.[29] General Howe was reinforced by a force under the command of his brother, Admiral Howe; he brought with him a larger army and fleet than had ever been deployed to the North American theatre by any European power before. The British arrived offshore from New York in July 1776 with 20,000 troops.[30] New York City would prove exceedingly difficult to defend against a British attack as it was completely surrounded by water. However, giving it up without a fight would signal weakness and strike a severe blow to the morale of the army and the nation, especially since the Declaration of Independence had only recently been signed by the Continental Congress. The defense of New York was all but doomed from the beginning, but putting up a fight for it would show the British that subduing the colonies would be a costly affair.

The capture of New York City in 1776 forced Washington to concentrate upon blocking the Hudson River, as it, if under British control, would cut the communications between the northern and southern colonies or at least make it extremely difficult. The colonists had two forts built opposite each other on the Hudson, Fort Washington on the east and Fort Lee on the west bank. Fort Washington fell to the British before its garrison could be evacuated to the west bank. After the fall of Fort Washington, Washington was forced to abandon Fort Lee and evacuate New York State before marching his army across New Jersey into Pennsylvania. The British were satisfied with the year's campaign and decided to retire to the comforts of their new headquarters in New York, while leaving a detachment of German mercenaries, known as Hessians, in the New Jersey border town Trenton.

Smarting from the losses of New York City and the Hudson

River Valley, Washington needed a victory, however small, to bolster the morale and spirit of the Independence movement. The British garrison of Hessians at Trenton provided him with that opportunity. Crossing the Delaware (which separates Pennsylvania from New Jersey) would not be easy, but Washington had gained experience in such amphibious operations from the campaigning on Long Island, New York and the recent crossing into Pennsylvania. He would now put that experience into action.

Washington split his army into three separate parts and crossed the Delaware at different points so as to converge upon Trenton from different directions. The crossing took place on Christmas night 1776 and after some delays the troops reached Trenton in the morning. The attack took the Hessians by surprise and Washington took Trenton within the day. The surprise worked almost perfectly, over a thousand Hessians were taken prisoner for only four American casualties; two American officers and two privates wounded.[31]

While two parts of the army had managed to rendezvous for the attack on Trenton, the third part was unable to link up with the others due to delays, bad weather and the fog of war. The third division was still on the New Jersey shore after Trenton was taken. Once Washington realized where his third division was, he reembarked his army and crossed back to Pennsylvania. The third division crossed over to Trenton and found the town evacuated. Washington was soon back at Trenton with his entire force and began to prepare for the British counterattack.[32]

General Cornwallis was sent from New York to deal a counterblow to Washington; Cornwallis entered Trenton to find Washington formed up for battle behind the Assunpink Creek east of town. Cornwallis wanted to rest his men after the march and declined to attack until the next day. Washington had no intention of waiting around for Cornwallis to attack him. With a night march on a little known road, southeast of the main pike that connected Princeton and Trenton, Washington turned up in Princeton the next morning. While Cornwallis woke up in Trenton wondering where Washington had gotten to, Washington was raiding the supplies of the British after pushing back a small British detachment at Princeton. Once Cornwallis got word of what happened in Princeton, he sensed he was cut off and proceeded to retreat back to New York City.[33]

Washington wanted to push on and take the British magazine at New Brunswick, New Jersey, but his men were exhausted by the successive night marches and realistically could not be pushed to go any further. The battles of Trenton and Princeton buoyed the patriots cause and Washington finally settled into winter quarters at Morristown, New Jersey in January 1777. The Americans were now firmly in control of New Jersey when only a few days earlier the exact opposite could be said for the British.[34]

♦ ♦ ♦

Part of the reason why Washington struck at Trenton was to stem the tide of the British advance towards the Continental Congress's seat of government in Philadelphia, Pennsylvania. While Washington's foray into New Jersey denied the use of the overland route to the British, their navy gave them the flexibility to disembark their army at any point along the coast of their choosing. With that being said, there were only so many places within a reasonable vicinity of Philadelphia in which they could disembark an army with all its accoutrements. While the British held the element of surprise, Washington had the advantage of interior lines, and he had the intuition to deduce the object of the upcoming British campaign.

The spring of 1777 witnessed the British embarking their army onto their ships at New York harbour. Instead of sailing up the Delaware and directly to Philadelphia, they took a more indirect route up the Chesapeake Bay and disembarked at the head of Elk River.[35] Washington had marched his army through

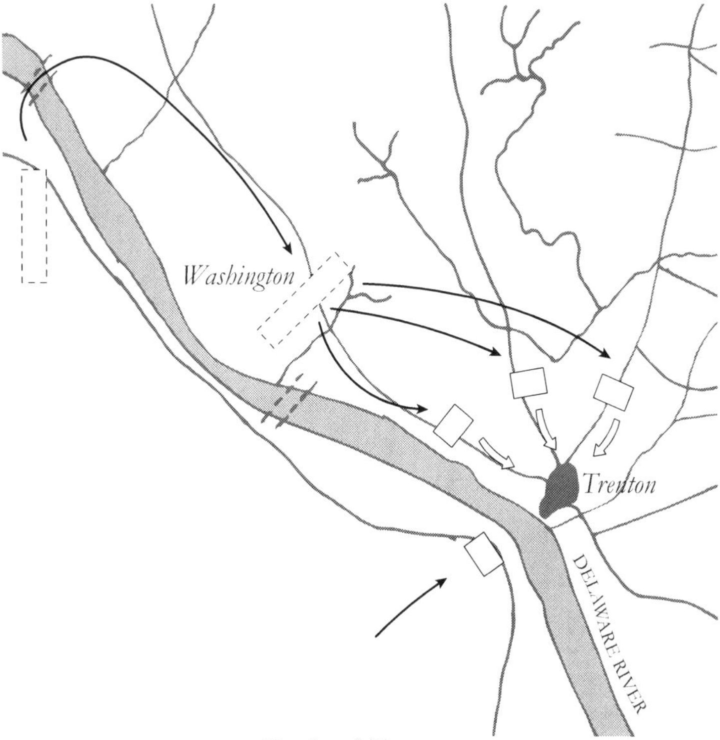

Battle of Trenton

Philadelphia, when he heard the news of their landing at Elk River he marched his army south to the Brandywine Creek, over which the British would need to travel on their way to Philadelphia.

The Brandywine was naturally good for a defensive posture, with its steep banks, no bridges and few places to ford. Regardless of there being few usable fords, Washington failed to adequately reconnoiter the area and a ford to the north of his position went unreported.[36] Once the British arrived at the Brandywine they split into two groups, one group engaged the Americans along the most obvious route, while the second group swung north and discovered the undefended ford for themselves. This maneuver became Washington's downfall, when the British suddenly appeared upon his right flank Washington redeployed his troops, but it was too late. The flanking maneuver caught the Americans off guard and they were eventually made to abandon their position along the Brandywine.[37]

In September 1777 the British entered Philadelphia after outmaneuvering Washington at the Battle of Brandywine. The Continental Congress had been warned of their imminent arrival and had managed to slip out of town avoiding capture. Washington positioned himself at Pott's Grove on the Schuylkill River between Howe in Philadelphia and the new seat of government at Lancaster Pennsylvania. The British sent a detachment north and west of Philadelphia to Germantown, where they would have an advanced force in between Philadelphia and Washington's army.

Seeing this detachment Washington believed he could score another victory like Trenton before the winter arrived. He divided his army into four separate units for the assault on Germantown and marched his men on through the night. Unfortunately for Washington, a thick fog descended in the morning making it extremely difficult for the separate units to coordinate their attacks, the British were also on guard lest Washington attempt

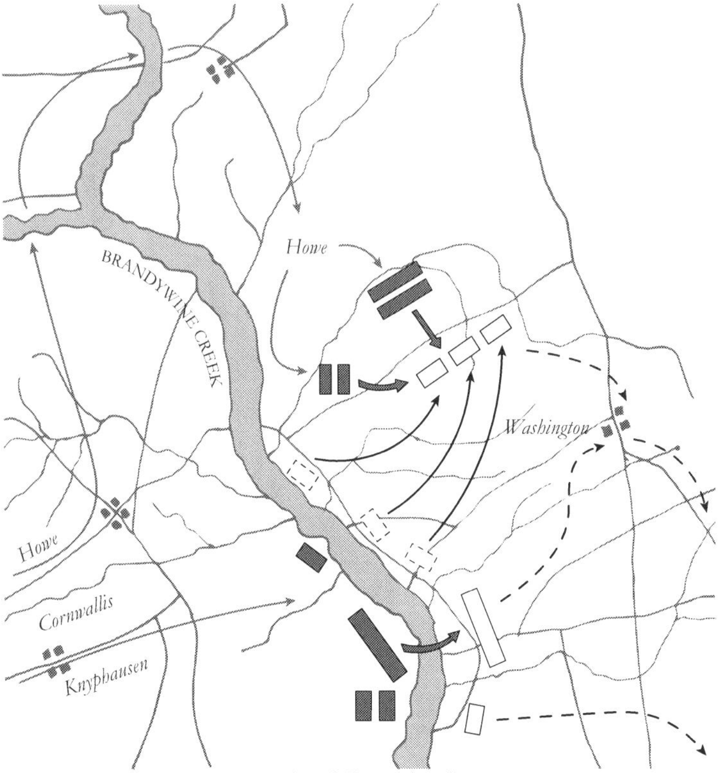

Battle of Brandywine

to hatch another surprise. The Hessians put up a stubborn defence of Germantown and the Americans could not capture the city due to their inability to coordinate their attacks. They were forced to retreat back up the Schuylkill River to a place that Washington had picked for their winter quarters called Valley Forge, they arrived in December 1777.[38]

♦ ♦ ♦

The winter at Valley Forge became extremely desperate for the continentals. Located on a plateau surrounded by ravines the camp was naturally suited for the defence and could be further fortified through the construction of trenches and earthworks. When the army arrived it became necessary to construct shelters for themselves. While Valley Forge was ideally located in an agricultural region, Washington, ever respectful of private property, was loath to simply requisition the supplies needed.[39] The state of Pennsylvania had numerous loyalists and opportunists in the state that were eager to sell their produce to the British whose currency was in good standing. The devaluation of Congress's money further confounded the army's ability to purchase the stores that it needed, commissary agents were effectively issuing 'I owe yous'.

To add to Washington's difficulties a faction in Congress, known as the 'Lee-Adams junta aided by a few generals,[*] began to call Washington's leadership into question, by criticising the results of Brandywine and Germantown.[40] On the heels of Washington's defeat at Germantown, came the news of an American victory in the northern theater at the Battle of Saratoga, the continentals, under the command of General Gates defeated an invasion force sent from Canada. After bitter political wrangling, Washington emerged victorious over the conspiring party and remained in his position as commander-in-chief.

The supply situation began to improve when the previous Quartermaster General was replaced with Nathaniel Greene,[41]

* Namely General Charles Lee & General Horatio Gates.

a trusted General and aide-de-camp of Washington's.* Furthermore, the arrival of Baron von Steuben of Prussia also marked a turning point for the army. Steuben began to drill and discipline the troops, teaching them complex field evolutions and steadiness under fire.[42] This was to Washington's liking as he himself had been trained in the British and European methods of war. By the time the campaigning season had arrived the physical requirements of the army were being met with some regularity, and their discipline had never been better. Washington became eager for a battle.

♦ ♦ ♦

The survival of Washington's army at Valley Forge and General Gate's victory at Saratoga marked a watershed for the independence cause, in that it prompted France, and later Spain to recognize the United States as an independent state. While France had pledged to support the independence of the American colonies, their assistance, in the form of declaring war on Britain and sending military aid, was still a long way off. However, overt French support greatly buoyed the morale of the army, its commander and the nation, as well as forcing Great Britain to completely rethink its strategy as her Atlantic supply lines were now far from secure.

General Howe was recalled to England for a possible cross channel invasion of France, leaving General Clinton in charge of the British army in North America. Clinton now believed that Philadelphia had become indefensible and therefore he planned to retreat through New Jersey back to New York City. Once Washington caught wind of the planned British retreat, he understood this to be a great chance to score a victory.

At a council of war with his generals, Washington decided to strike at the British in New Jersey even though some of his most senior generals were pessimistic. General Charles Lee, an-

* Even though Greene was largely responsible for the debacle at Fort Washington.

other member of the failed conspiracy to dispose Washington, even commented that instead of offering battle, the Americans should build 'a bridge of gold' for the British to cross back to Manhattan Island, Washington was amazed and repulsed by the suggestion.[43] The British were slow moving, bringing their wagons and sick and were easily caught up to by the unencumbered continentals. However, Clinton was expecting an American attack and prepared his army for it.

Washington had tasked Lee with commanding the advanced guard to attack the British rear. Lee's force ran into the British rear guard, commanded by General Cornwallis, around Monmouth Courthouse. Cornwallis put up a stiff resistance and counter attacked causing Lee to loose heart and retreat in disorder. Washington was bringing up the main body of troops when the retreating Americans began streaming back his way. Perplexed to see his troops in such disorder, Washington was furious at Lee's lack of aggression and lack of control over the troops. Washington sent Lee back to the rear to regroup any of the men who made it that far.[44]

After putting a halt to the retreating vanguard, Washington formed them up for battle in a line perpendicular to the road that ran west from Monmouth. The British advanced to the attack along the pike but were stopped by Washington's reformed line. After repulsing the attack of the British along the pike, Washington sent his right wing under Greene to advance west and parallel to the pike and hit the British on their left flank from the heights of Combs Hill.[45] The flanking maneuver had the desired effect and the British were forced to abandon the field and continue their retreat back to New York. While the battle of Monmouth Courthouse failed to destroy the British or capture their supplies, it succeeded in roughing them up and showing that the Continental forces were still formidable and could stand up to the best of the British army.

♦ ♦ ♦

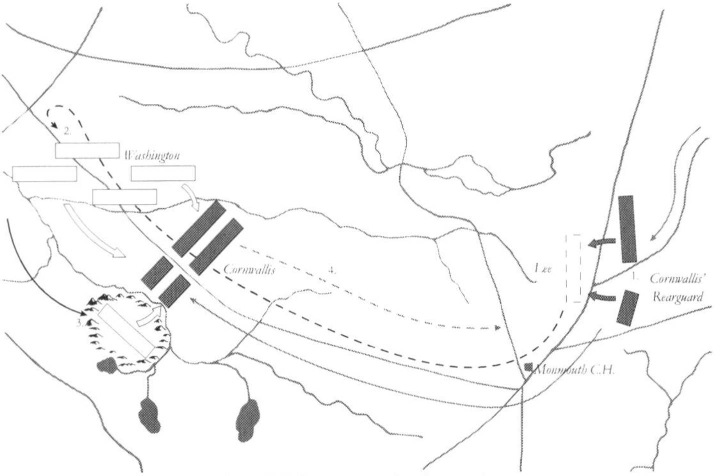

Battle of Monmouth Courthouse

1. Cornwallis' rearguard attacks Washington's vanguard (commanded by Lee) 2. Lee's retreating troops are rallied by Washington in the rear. 3. Washington launches his attack on Cornwallis' left flank. 4. Cornwallis is forced to withdraw from the field.

After the Battle of Monmouth Courthouse, the war in the north was essentially over as the British, largely confined to New York City, now focused their attention on the southern colonies, and their possessions in the West Indies. The northern and central commands for which Washington was responsible became largely inactive. Congress had actually restricted his authority in the southern theatre; he could only observe, comment and later recommend a commander for the theater. Washington's role for this portion of the war would largely be hands off.[46]

The first British target in 1780 was Savannah, Georgia, then the great seaport of the South; Charleston, South Carolina. Charleston was at that point the largest and most important city in the southern colonies The British had very little trouble capturing Charleston and after the battle and surrender of Charleston, Clinton moved back to New York City and left Cornwallis in command of the southern theatre. Not only did the British capture most of the five-thousand-man strong garrison in Charleston, but they went on to soundly beat a numerically superior American army, commanded by Gates,* at the battle of Camden, South Carolina.[47]

There was no longer any regular continental army left in South Carolina after the Battle of Camden. Responsibility for the defence of the southern colonies descended onto the irregular and unorthodox militias. After Camden, Cornwallis began his invasion of North Carolina, and General Gates was relieved of his command by Congress. With the position now vacant, Congress asked Washington if he would suggest a replacement; Washington's nominee was General Greene. Once confirmed, Greene was able to turn things around for the American cause in the Southern theatre. Under Greene's command, the continentals won victories at the battles of Kings Mountain and Cowpens, but most importantly Greene kept his command intact and was able to replenish his numbers quicker than the

* Hero of Saratoga, and a participant in the conspiracy against Washington.

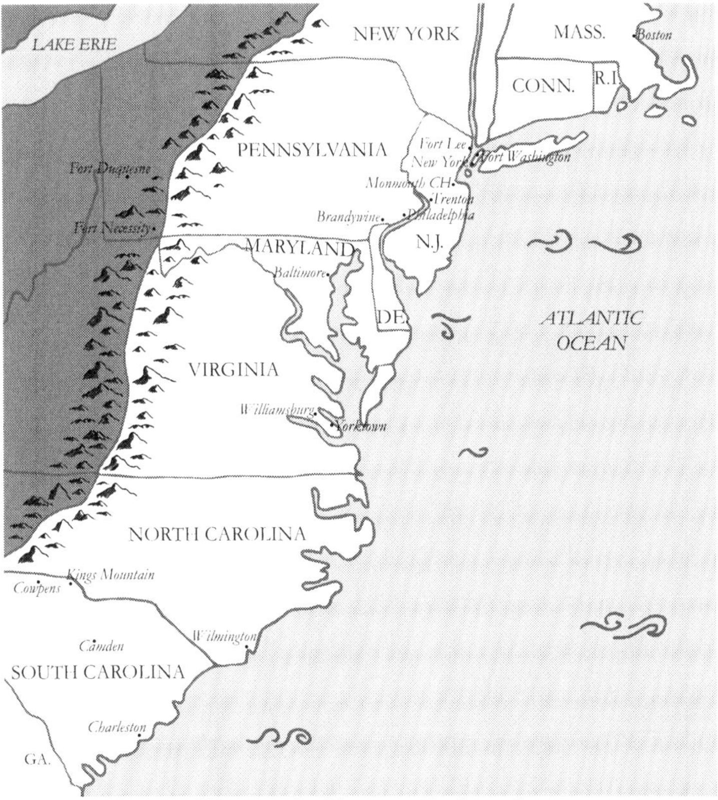

War on the Eastern Seaboard

loyalists.[48]

Along the way, Greene was greatly assisted by the use of famous irregular militia men, such as "…Thomas Sumter ("the Gamecock"), Francis Marion ("the Swamp Fox"), and Andrew Pickens (who, sadly for his historical reputation, never acquired a memorable nickname)".[49] At the battle of Guildford Courthouse, North Carolina, Cornwallis defeated Greene, but at a tremendous cost, he was forced to abandon the interior of the state and retreated to the coast at Wilmington, North Carolina and then eventually north to Virginia. Washington sent General Lafayette and General 'Mad' Anthony Wayne to help Greene stalk Cornwallis' movements in Virginia. Cornwallis was unable to destroy the elusive American army in Virginia, and so, General Clinton ordered Cornwallis to construct a fortified naval outpost to await reinforcement or evacuation.[50]

Since the battle of Monmouth Courthouse, Washington had desired to retake New York City from the British. However, in 1781 it became known to Washington that a French Naval squadron would be sailing for the Chesapeake Bay area. Washington decided to exploit the new (and possibly temporary) balance of power in the Southern theatre. He gave up his plan to retake New York City, in favour of marching south and taking his French allies, who were with him in the vicinity of New York. Washington deceived Clinton into thinking an American attack on New York City (via New Jersey) was imminent, by repairing bridges and making other preparations for such an attack.[51] By mid-September Washington and his French allies were in Virginia besieging Cornwallis in Yorktown.

Yorktown lies on a peninsula, named after the river, with the York and James Rivers running from the northwest of the city to the south east and emptying into the Chesapeake Bay. Northwest of the city was a swamp and another swamp lay to the west. There were two roads that connected to the city, one running to the northwest and the other running west; each road went through a swamp. Once Washington arrived with his French allies, regular siege operations began in earnest. Washington's deception operations in New Jersey succeeded in deceiving Clinton into believing an attack on New York was imminent from the direction of New Jersey. By the time Washington was at Yorktown it was too late for Clinton to come to Cornwallis' relief.

The French fleet arrived from the West Indies and defeated the British fleet that was stationed on the York River in the Battle of the Chesapeake in September of 1781. The remainder of the British fleet retreated to New York City, which effectively isolated Cornwallis in Yorktown. All the while Washington's siege operations were squeezing in closer and closer to the British lines around the city. Cornwallis attempted to break out through Gloucester across the James River.[52] However, the attempted break out through Gloucester failed as it proved impossible to ferry the troops across the water (due to bad weather) and as the Americans had surrounded it as well. Bottled up in Yorktown and knowing that Clinton could not come to relieve him Cornwallis surrendered on the 19th October 1781.[53] Negotiations for peace between Great Britain and the United States began in good faith shortly afterwards. Washington returned to the fortifications at West Point, New York after Yorktown as the British remained in control of New York City until negotiations were finalized in Paris.

♦ ♦ ♦

Upon entering the war on the side of the colonists, France and Spain had recognized the thirteen colonies as independent and legitimate states. With the possibility of cross channel military actions and the surrender of Cornwallis at Yorktown, the British were forced to concede the impossibility of subduing the lost colonies. The Americans had told their French and Spanish allies that they would not sign a separate peace treaty, but when the time came Great Britain and the United States signed their

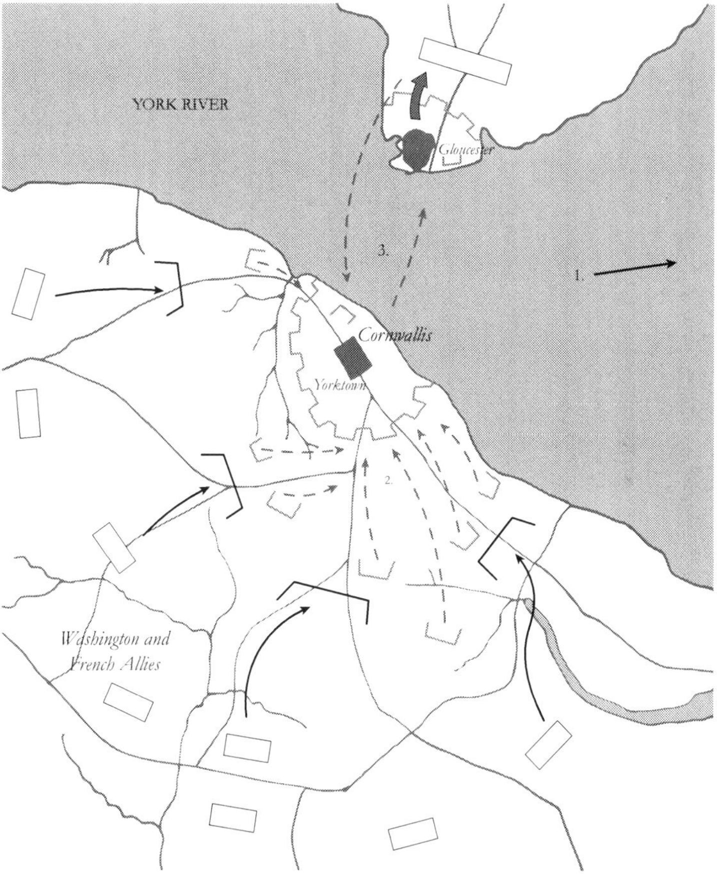

Siege of Yorktown

1. British and French fleets engage to the east in the Battle of Chesapeake Bay (Virginia Capes). 2. British forces withdraw into Yorktown, after the arrivial of Washington's forces. 3. Cornwallis crosses to Glouchester, and attempts to breakout but is replused and returns to Yorktown.

own bilateral treaty.[54]

The treaty recognized the new fact of colonial independence and set the new boundaries between British North America (Canada) and the United States. The United States was allowed to annex the Ohio Valley region, south of the Great Lakes and east of the Mississippi River, as well, New York City was evacuated by the British. This clever diplomatic maneuver allowed the British to protect themselves against the possibility of the French and Spanish capturing certain valuable British possessions and using them as bargaining chips in the treaty process.[55] It was well known that the Spanish were incredibly interested in recovering the British held fortress at Gibraltar. Shortly after the Americans and British had come to terms, treaties with France and Spain were also signed at Versailles.

George Washington came from a respectable, well-to-do family and rose through the ranks of society to become the first man and father of his country. In the War of Independence, Washington began with a rag-tag assortment of colonial militiamen, farmers, bankers, shopkeepers, and citizens. He transformed them into a regular army capable of resisting the premier world power, Great Britain. While Washington's military record does not run unblemished by defeat, he was never beaten so badly that he could not continue. Furthermore, when Washington was victorious, his victory was never bought with a high price in blood, at Boston, Trenton, Princeton, Monmouth and Yorktown the casualties on both sides were relatively low. Washington was a builder of nations, not a butcher of men.

From beginning to end, Washington's high quality of leadership and his devotion to his cause, piloted the colonies through the stormy waters of rebellion and independence to safety.

By the end of the war, Washington's reputation was so legendary that when there was talk of using force against the congress to exact money owed to the officers, a speech from Washington was enough to quell the thought of rebellion.[56] Instead,

Washington wanted the newly independent United States to be free from the whims and absolute discretion of one man. Washington believed that Americans should enjoy their hard earned liberty and be governed as a republic.

When the time came for elections to be held for the position of president, Washington was swept into office on a wave of gratitude for his earlier service. During his tenure, he sought to limit American involvement in overseas alliances and to limit European influence in North American affairs. Ideally the new republican government would also be limited at home, so as to foster the enjoyment of liberty for its citizens.

It is important to remember that the United States is not a democracy, even though it allows the democratic process to shape many of its institutions. It is a republic, with checks and balances built into place so that one institution can never completely trump the others. The founding fathers understood that a complete democracy could be just as arbitrary and tyrannical as an absolutist monarchy or dictatorship could be. While Washington was not the sole, or even the primary author of the new republican form of government, he agreed with it in principal and endeavoured to make it succeed in practice.

After his term as president was over Washington and his wife Martha retired to their home at Mount Vernon, Virginia. They produced no children which only helped to reinforce his reputation as the father of his country. George and Martha lived in peace at Mount Vernon, being visited by numerous members of their extended family and friends until George passed away in December of 1799. George Washington has been immortalized in many ways since his passing, his image appears on the American dollar bill, in stone at Mount Rushmore and in countless work of art. When the American capital was moved to its current location in the District of Columbia, within the state Maryland, the new city built for the purpose was named after its greatest benefactor, George Washington.

Arthur Wellesley: Duke of Wellington

Arthur Wellesley was born as Arthur Welsey on May 1st 1769 in Dublin, Ireland. He was the third of five sons (who survived birth) to his parents Garret and Anne Wesley. Garret Welsey was the 1st Earl of Mornington, a minor nobleman at the Anglo court in Dublin.* When Arthur was merely a boy his father died, leaving his eldest brother, Richard (now Lord Mornington), in charge of the family's affairs.[1] Once old enough, Arthur was sent to school at Eton, but he was rather introverted and did not fit in with the other boys and did poorly with the curriculum. After spending a year at Eton, the Welsey's were facing financial troubles. Because Arthur wasn't considered a budding intellect and an expensive education would've been wasted on him, Richard was forced to remove Arthur from Eton and moved him and his mother to Brussels.[2] A year or so later Arthur was enrolled at the French Royal Academy of Equitation (horsemanship) at Angers. When he returned to the United Kingdom in 1786, he was a completely different person with a renewed purpose in life.

Shortly upon returning to the British Isles, his brother Richard helped him to purchase a commission in the army.† He also got his first taste of politics when he was elected to the Irish Parliament for the constituency of Trim.[3] During this early pe-

* Garret had a talent for music, specifically the violin, which he imparted to Arthur.

† Richard was by now a Member of Parliament at Westminster, and a rising star in the Pitt (Tory) government.

riod of his life he met his future wife, Catherine (Kitty) Pakenham, the daughter of an 'Irish' (Anglo) lord. Catherine's family turned down his request to have her hand in marriage as Arthur, at that point had few obvious prospects. After that rejection, Arthur burned his violin (he had hitherto been an aspiring musician of sorts) and fully dedicated his life to his military career.

Shortly afterwards Arthur bought himself a commission as a major in the 33rd Foot.* As was the practice in those days, he was quickly promoted to Lieutenant Colonel after his brother lent him the money to purchase his way up the military ladder.[4] Before we delve any further into Arthur's active military career, we shall first examine the context of the French Revolution and the Napoleonic Wars.

♦ ♦ ♦

After the recent successive military defeats of France in the War of Spanish Succession and the Seven Years War, France had been going through a turbulent period. A combination of bad harvests, high and arbitrary taxes, oppressive, corrupt and inefficient government and a stimulating intellectual discourse, stirred up by the enlightenment, created a perfect storm for revolution. Intervention in the American colonies had been an expensive undertaking, the French government was on the brink of collapse; its finances were in extreme disorder. King Louis XVII was forced to convene a 'parliament' called the 'Estates General' at Versailles in order to raise the necessary funds required to operate the government. In those days' French society was rigidly divided into three classes which comprised the Estates General; the monarchy was the first, the nobles and clergy comprised the second, while the third class was made up by the bourgeois (middle class) and the peasants.

Parliament was inteded to placate the population, but rather, events quickly took on a life of their own. There is still some controversy, and by no means a consensus over what transpired

* The 33rd Foot was, and is a regiment of infantry in the British Army.

at Versailles as Parliament was convened and subsequently prorogued. Royalist sympathizers claim that Parliament was shut down because the Royal Family was in mourning over the death of one of its members, or because the room was being prepared by carpenters for an upcoming Royal speech.[5] On the other hand, the revolutionary sympathizers claim that the third estate was locked out of the meeting by the Kings men for their radical proposals.[6] Either way the Third Estate was locked out of their meeting hall and decided to pursue a radical course independent of the first two estates. The representatives assembled their own parliament in an indoor tennis gymnasium where they swore an oath, promising to not stop convening themselves until France had adopted a new constitution (presumably one drafted by themselves).

Things quickly began to spiral out of control for Louis XVII. The Bastille, an imposing prison in the middle of Paris and a symbol of the 'Ancient Regime', was stormed and over run by a mob of Parisians. From Paris, the disorder spread throughout the country. The monarchy would hold onto power for two more years as a sort of constitutional monarchy, but the 'Ancient Regime' was unable to bring order back to the country – not least the capital – and a radical government called 'the Directorate' violently usurped control of the state.[7] The Directorate, led by a succession of directors[*] had no grand solution to the multifaceted problems of running France and it was forced to resort to the brutal tactics of repressive policing and terrorism. Sham trials for members of the Ancient Regime which more often than not resulted in the execution by guillotine (including the king and queen) were the main accomplishments of the Directory period.

The excesses of the French Revolution shocked and appalled the monarchies throughout Europe. 'Grand Coalitions' were formed amongst the major European powers to quash

* The most radical & infamous member was Robespierre.

the revolutionary regime and ironically, in light of the past two major European wars started by the Bourbon monarchs, to re-instate the exiled Bourbon family to the French throne. In reaction to the Grand Coalition's impending invasion of France, the Directorate resorted to universal conscription of French manpower (a first in history) and created a massive citizen militia to defend Frances frontiers and the revolution from the re-imposition of monarchy.[8] Conscription and the newly formed citizen armies were an incredible improvement on the traditional way of supplying manpower for the military; in essence it affected a revolution in military terms equivalent to what the French Revolution had brought to the realm of politics.[9] France's militias repulsed the initial coalition armies and were soon on the offensive on the usual European battlefields of war; the Rhineland and Northern Italy.

♦ ♦ ♦

The Directorate used terrorism, the threat of foreign invasion and mass conscription to keep the population loyal to its rule. But even the hard hand of government had its limits and soon the citizens in Paris and France grew weary of the extreme measures imposed on them by the Directorate.* When another Parisian mob, riled up by Royalist sympathizers, threatened to overturn the government, no one in the government or army seemed to know how to handle the situation. No one that is, until a little known general from the backwater island of Corsica, arrived on the scene.

Fresh from successfully reclaiming the French port of Toulon from the British on the Mediterranean, Napoleon Bonaparte took command of the Directorates defences just in time to save it from the mob. Through the gratuitous use of musket fire, grape shot and a cavalry charge the mob was repulsed and brought back to order.[10] Saving the revolution and the Director-

* There were revolts in the Vendee (Brittany), and in the south of France that were brutally supressed.

ate's regime on the streets of Paris launched Bonaparte's career in earnest.

Success in Paris allowed Napoleon to pick his next field assignment. He decided on tackling the threat emanating from the Austrians in northern Italy. The Directorate considered northern Italy to be a strategic side show and thus did not allocate sufficient resources to the theatre. In spite of the logistical deficiencies, Napoleon's audacity and superior generalship humiliated the Austrian army in that theatre and within a short period of time forced them to surrender their claims on Italy. With France's southeast frontier now secure, Napoleon was allowed to plan even farther reaching campaigns and was now given the resources to implement them.

With dreams of Alexander the Great in his head, Napoleon turned his attention to Egypt, his ultimate purpose being to threaten the position of the British in . Although this was an extremely farfetched and impractical idea strategically, Napoleon included a scientific team on his expedition to study the country for good measure and the potential for good public relations. After initial success at the Battle of the Pyramids against the Ottoman Mamelukes, the tide quickly turned against the French in Egypt. On the same day as the Battle of the Pyramids, a British naval squadron, under the command of the illustrious Admiral Nelson, engaged the French transport armada and decisively beat it at the Battle of the Nile.*

Without his ships Napoleon was stuck in Egypt and the Levant, confined to the major cities and surrounded by enemies. Disease quickly began to spread throughout the French ranks; morale was sinking lower every day. Luckily for Napoleon, he was able to sneak past the British blockade in a small frigate and make his way back to France.[11] Notwithstanding the disaster that befell his army, the scientific expedition was a success, and helped to turn the strategic failure into a propaganda coup that

* Situated near Alexandria.

increased Napoleon's reputation amongst the French citizenry.

The France Napoleon returned to was still in terrible shape, the Directorate was once again in need of a saviour. Instead of perpetuating the ineffective revolutionary regime, Napoleon decided to dispose of it and usurp the powers and responsibilities of the state for himself. In order to appear as if he was in fact the saviour of the revolution, he took the title of 'first consul' and appointed two other figure heads (who in fact had no real power) as co-consuls.[12] Regardless of the supposedly 'democratic' title, Napoleon had installed himself as the supreme dictator of France; in all save the name. With time, the name also came with the position.

By 1805 Napoleon crowned himself as the hereditary Emperor of the new French Empire. In a symbolic coronation ceremony Napoleon took the crown from the Roman Catholic Pope and literally crowned himself before crowning his wife Josephine. His ascendance to the throne was overwhelmingly supported by the franchised citizens of France in a popular referendum.[13] However, the return to a 'monarchy' under Napoleon did not restore stability to France. While Napoleon's regime did not rely on torture or terror to the extent that the Directorate did, it did depend on ever expanding conquests to fill its coffers, and Napoleon was never short of territorial ambitions.

Napoleon's ambitions only fueled suspicion and animosity amongst the powers that be, creating enemies amongst the royal families who viewed the revolution and his regime as a threat to the stability of their own. Numerous strategic and tactical victories seemed to be proof of Napoleon's genius and invincibility. Late in 1805 another British fleet under the command of Nelson* destroyed a combined French and Spanish fleet off the coast of Spain, in what would become known as the Battle of Trafalgar. Any hope of a cross channel invasion of the British

* Nelson was the hero of the Battle of the Nile.

Isles for Napoleon was destroyed at the Battle of Trafalgar.* But it would take more than a decisive naval engagement to bring Napoleon's empire to its knees. Around the same time that Napoleon was gaining notoriety in Europe, a new star was rising in the East – one that would come to rival that of Napoleons. The 'Scourge of Europe' would one day be confronted by Wellesley the 'Sepoy General',† but Arthur's career was yet to take flight.

Arthur was sent to Flanders in 1794 with the 33rd Foot to support the Duke of York's campaign in northern France, as part of the first Grand Coalition. The campaign was a failure as the new French militias easily pushed the coalition forces out of France. Arthur barely got a chance to command in a battle as the British expeditionary force withdrew to northwestern Germany – but as he later remarked "Why, I learnt what one ought not to do, and that is always something".[14] In 1795 the Duke of York's expeditionary army was evacuated to the British Isles and the coalition was in shambles. However, peace with France was not forthcoming. The British government decided to send Arthur's regiment to the West Indies to conquer the rich French possessions in the Caribbean. But after several weeks of rough trans-Atlantic weather the government decided to send him East to India. Arriving in 1797, India would become the theatre where Arthur's military reputation would be built.

♦ ♦ ♦

Landing in Calcutta, Arthur was made to endure a period of inactivity before being sent on a fruitless expedition to the Spanish held Philippines with the intention of depriving the Spanish crown of that valuable colony.[15] The expedition to the Philippines was recalled before it even arrived at its intended target. When Arthur returned to India he found that his eldest brother Richard had been appointed the Governor General for the British possessions on the sub-continent.[16] With Richard, who

* The gallant Nelson died at the apex of his victory.

† A Sepoy was a native Indian who was trained and fought for the British in India as an infantryman.

was now Lord Mornington, also came the news that the family name had been changed from Wesley to Wellesley.[17] In the days of extreme nepotism and patronage, Lord Mornington's arrival in India came with obvious advantages for Wellesley's career. However, as we shall see, Wellesley advanced his career far more on his own merit than due to anything family connections could ever do.

Conflict on the sub-continent would first flare up in the southwest of that country when the Sultan Tippoo of Mysore (provoked by French advisors) declared war against the British held territory. Wellesley was serving under General Harris as the Colonel of the 33rd Foot, in addition Lord Mornington (Richard Wellesley) appointed him to the position of chief advisor to Nizam of Hyderabad, an allied prince of the British.[18] General Harris's forces defeated the Sultan in his capital of Seringapatam, after a siege in which Wellesley was instrumental. After the capitulation of Seringapatam Wellesley was then temporarily appointed Governor of Mysore. Amongst his duties he was charged with subduing the Mysore guerillas that had sprung up in the jungles of south central India after their defeat at Seringapatam. Although outnumbered and operating in unfamiliar terrain, Wellesley overwhelmed the guerillas in a matter of months.[19]

Late in the year of 1802, Wellesley learnt that he had been promoted to the rank of Major General in the British East India Company at the age of thirty-three; not quite the same as the regular army, but none the less an impressive feat for someone so young.* He continued in his capacity as Governor of Mysore until he was summoned in November for his first independent command in preparation for the Second Anglo – Maratha War.

The Maratha Confederacy was a native Indian power primarily located in the north and center of the sub-continent of India. As the name would suggest, the Confederacy was comprised

* Wellesley was 33 at tht time.

NORWEGIAN SEA
SWEDEN
RUSSIA
St. Petersburg
BALTIC SEA
NORWAY
Moscow
EXTENT OF FRENCH ADVANCE INTO RUSSIA
Copenhagen
DENMARK
NORTH SEA
PRUSSIA
POLAND
Leipzig
Jena
AUSTRIA
Austerlitz
RHINELANDS
BLACK SE
GREAT BRITAIN
Waterloo
OTTOMAN EMPIR
ITALY
FRANCE
NAPLES
Toulouse
CORISCA
ATLANTIC OCEAN
Vittoria
MEDITERRANEAN SEA
Alexandri
Corunna
Salamanca
SPAIN
Madrid
Oporto
OTTOMAN AFRICA
PORTUGAL
Cape St. Vincent
Gibraltar
Trafalgar
SPANISH MOROCCO

Eurasia in 1810

of numerous nominally independent kingdoms. The Maratha leaders were persuaded, like the Sultan of Mysore, by French advisors* that the British should be attacked in their strongholds and expelled from India. War was delcared in the late months of 1802, but the fighting did not begin in earnest until the spring of 1803. The British strategy was executed in two parts. One force was operating out of Calcutta in the north commanded by Lord Lake, was to attack and seize Delhi. The second force operating our of Bombay on the west coast, commanded by Wellesley, was to secure the Deccan Plateau,† and protect the newly acquired lands in Mysore.[20]

Wellesley was confronted by the superior manpower resources and the home court advantage of the Marathas. He quickly realized that a purely defensive strategy would ultimately be destructive to British interests in the theatre. Regardless of his disadvantage in manpower, Wellesley possessed the advantage of a unified command and well-disciplined troops. And so, he was able to rapidly mobilize and take to the field on the offensive.

He first assaulted the Maratha fortress at Ahmednuggur with scaling ladders, and took it. The Maratha commander of the fortress had expected Wellesley to lay siege to the fort, and was thus completely surprised by audacity of so rapid an assault. Ahmednuggur opened up the Maratha heartland to Wellesley's army. However, the Maratha's maneuvered to invade the recently conquered lands of Mysore, and so Wellesley was forced to pursue the main force of Maratha's. Wellesley marched his army east in pursuit of the Confederate host, along the way detaching garrisons to protect the bridges and secure the fords to keep his communications open with his base of supply on the west coast of India. He further divided his forces in order to pin

* French advisorys were largely responsible for training the natives in modern tactics, as well as fanning their hatred of everything British.

† The Deccan Plateau dominates central and India, and extends into the southern portion of the subcontinent. It is triangular in shape, similar with the subcontinent itself.

the Maratha's down when he recieved intelligence they were nearby. The intellegence wasn't entirely accurate, the Marathas were closer then was thought. The Confederates had converged around the village of Assaye, and had dug into defensive lines behind the River Kaitna.[21] At this point Wellesley's troops were outnumbered by almost six or seven to one.[22]

♦ ♦ ♦

Scindia, the Marathas commander, had formed up their lines on the northern bank parallel to the River Kaitna, and then returned to his camp as he didn't believe the fight would take place when that day. Antony Pohlmann, a European advisor, assumed commanded of the Maratha army at Assaye. The Marathas had a ford, what was thought to be the only one, in the middle of their line near the town of Taunklee. As far as anyone knew, the ford in front of Taunklee was the only ford over the Kaitna in the immediate vicinity and it was pretty well covered by the Maratha's defensive position. Wellesley's own native scouts even failed to detect another ford. However, Wellesley deduced that there must be a ford further downstream, seeing as there were two villages directly opposite each other on either bank of the Kaitna. It would follow a certain human logic that no two settlements would be founded so close together without a convenient line of communication between them, be it a bridge or a ford.

Wellesley's deduction proved correct, there was another ford, and he was able to cross his army while under fire from the Maratha artillery.[23] Once across, Wellesley wasted no time in forming his troops into line. His infantry was mainly posted on his left flank along the Kaitna axis, while Wellesley's cavalry was divided into two groups. One group of cavalry he posted on his right flank along the southern bank of the Juha, while the other Wellesley posted on his left flank along the southern bank of the Kaitna. Just as Wellesley wasted no time in forming his lines, he wasted no time in assaulting the Maratha positions.

Wellesley's manoeuver across the Kaitna forced the Maratha's to reposition their forces, with both flanks now being anchored on a river. Pohlmann's left flank now occupied the village Assaye on the Juha River and his right flank was cemented on the River Kaitna. Regardless of the Maratha's change of position, Wellesley's maneuver into the confined space between the rivers Juha and Kaitna afforded Wellesley an important advantage; the confined space restricted the use of the enemy's numerical superiority, especially when it came to their cavalry arm.

At first the British believed the Maratha's were still in their original positions, they soon found out about Pohlmann's redeployment.[24] Wellesley's infantry advanced in a steady disciplined fashion along the axis of the Kaitna. The courage and discipline of the British infantry's advance along the Kaitna forced the Maratha's to abandon most of their artillery. The Maratha's right flank crumpled and retreated under the assault of the British left flank. The Maratha left flank occupying Assaye held fast.

The infantry that had been tasked with extending the British right flank had pushed too far and had come under heavy cross fire from the garrison at Assaye and the Maratha guns in the centre of their line. Wellesley's right flank was forced to retreat in the face of a Maratha counter attack, but he was able to restore order when he ordered up his cavalry from the reserve. Not only was Wellesley's cavalry able to save his right flank from the counter attacking Maratha's they went on to force them out of Assaye and across the Juha, killing a great many of them in the process.[25] Both Wellesley's left and right flanks succeeded in breaking the Maratha's line and scattering the forces opposite them.[*]

Wellesley wasn't alone in victory during the campaign of 1803; the British forces had also been successful in the north, resulting in the capture of the great city Delhi. Defeat of the Maratha's at Assaye in the south and at Delhi in the north effec-

* Wellesley went on to fight and win another battle at Argaum before successfully assaulting the remaining enemy at the mountain fortress of Gawilghur by mid December of 1803.

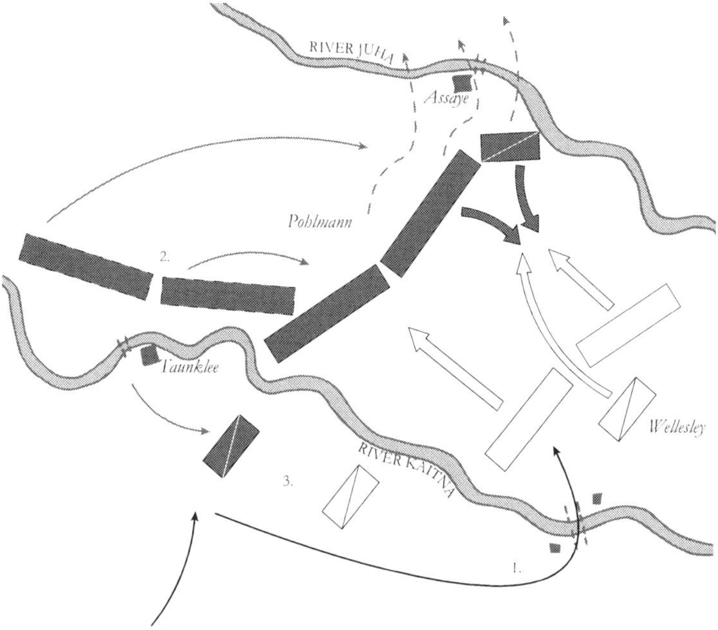

Battle of Assaye

1. Wellesley's manuever after discovering second ford. 2. Pohlman manuever's into second position. 3. Cavalry engages on the south bank of the River Kaitna tively ended the Second Maratha war and destroyed the power of the Confederacy. The Maratha Confederacy was effectively disbanded and the balance of power on the sub-continent was definitively tipped in the favour of the British. Soon afterwards Wellesley was recalled to Great Britain.

When Wellesley returned to Great Britain he had amassed a great fortune from the spoils of conquest in India, as well he was rewarded with a knighthood in the Order of the Bath. On the return voyage by ship to the British Isles, Wellesley made a stay on the island of St. Helena and ironically commented that he found it to be quite enjoyable (the irony will be understood shortly). While Wellesley had achieved the highest rank of independent command in India, back in Great Britain he was outranked by numerous senior officers, and so, he was forced to endure another period of inactivity.

One day in London while waiting for an interview with the Prime Minister, Wellesley's path briefly crossed with that of Admiral Nelson, hero of the Nile* and soon to be of Trafalgar. Almost as if passing a torch, the two stars of the British nation eclipsed each other.[26] Nelson was about to end his career in glory, while Wellesley's European triumphs were still to take place. Wellesley returned to Ireland, at the post of Chief Secretary, where he was married to his adolescent sweetheart, Catherine 'Kitty' Pakenham in 1806. He was also elected to the British House of Commons for the seat of Rye in southeast England.[27]

In 1807 Wellesley was sent to Denmark in command of an infantry brigade as part of a combined arms expedition to capture the Danish fleet, and keep the ships from the hands of the French Emperor. Wellesley's brigade was the only one to see action as it was ordered to intercept and cut off an advancing force of some nine thousand Danes, which he did with a minimum of bloodshed.[28] The expedition succeeded in capturing the remaining ships of the Danish fleet and the troops were

* Also known as the Battle of Aboukir Bay.

evacuated before a French army could be brought to bear on them. After Denmark, Wellesley was put in command of a small but respectable force that would eventually be sent to the Iberian Peninsula at the beginning of what would become known as the 'Peninsular War'.

♦ ♦ ♦

Napoleons French Empire had jumped from one victory to another ever since Bonaparte had crowned himself Emperor. Napoleon had defeated every major power on the continent; Prussia, Austria, and Russia had all in due course succumbed to the pressure of his armies. The battles of Ulm, Austerlitz and Jena had made Napoleon's name feared and admired; only the British Isles remained unbeaten and unconquered. The age old rivalry between sea power and continental power would once again be played out. With the destruction of the French and Spanish fleets at Trafalgar and later the capture of the Danish fleet, an amphibious invasion of Great Britain was all but impossible. Napoleon then turned to the only weapon he could use against the unconquerable British Isles; that being trade or in the case of France a boycott of commerce between the U.K. and the rest of Europe.

In 1806, Napoleon issued the 'Berlin Decree' – which created the 'continental system' in effect an internal trading network aiming to nullify the British blockade of France and banning trade between the Continent and the British Isles.[29] Hurting from the economic consequences of the trade embargo, the government of Portugal decided against applying the continental system in 1808 and instead sent envoys to the U.K. to request military assistance against the French. The Spanish government all but gave up trying to enforce Napoleon's system. Such an obvious disregard for Napoleon's 'authority' could not be abided by the Emperor, and so he invaded the peninsula.

Initially Napoleon allowed King Ferdinand VII to remain on the Spanish throne as a puppet, on the condition that Ferdinand would tolerate the installation of French military units and advisors and allow the free movement of French troops en route to Portugal. However, by 1808 Napoleon disposed of Ferdinand and replaced him with his brother Joseph. The puppet king and his French puppet masters inflamed the Spanish people who would now rise up in resistance to what they saw as intrusions onto their sovereignty.[30] The peninsula was too much of a backwater to require Napoleon in person, and so he left the invasion of Portugal to his subordinate Marshalls. To conquer Portugal the French armies were required to climb over the Pyrenees into Spain, cross over the barren countryside of Spain then traverse over another mountain range that divided Spain from Portugal and onto the coastal plain of Portugal.

By the time Wellesley arrived off the coast of Portugal, he received the bad news that the initial intelligence regarding the number of French committed to the invasion of Portugal was inaccurate, the French had brought more troops than expected. More troops from Great Britain were being sent along with two senior officers that would, upon arrival outrank Wellesley.[31] Knowing that he would soon be outranked, Wellesley decided he would endeavor to defeat the French before his superiors could arrive and assume command. One of his superiors arrived off coast on the very eve of the Battle of Vimeiro, Wellesley, attempted to persuade his superior into a bold flanking action Wellesley's request was denied, but the general remained on his ship while Wellesley returned to camp.[32]

The French Commander, Junot, had no intention of remaining static while the British were disembarking their soldiers, so if the British wouldn't attack, Junot would come to them. The engagement that took place at Vimeiro was a triumph for Wellesley and if he had been given permission to pursue the French, even greater spoils would have been had. However, as both of his cautious superiors were now on the scene he was refused permission to pursue the French any further.[33] They even went on to negotiate an exceedingly generous ceasefire treaty with the French, which made provision to transport the remaining Frenchmen (on British ships) out of Lisbon to French ports with all their accoutrements and loot.[34] Wellesley was made to sign the treaty, which once made known to the British public enraged them. The commanding officers, including Wellesley, were recalled to London to account for their actions. Wellesley's two superiors were black listed and were never again given a field command. Wellesley was also put in the bad books, regardless of the fact that he was blameless. However, in early 1809 Wellesley was exonerated and given a second chance when King George III appointed him to be the supreme allied commander in Portugal.[35]

♦ ♦ ♦

During Wellesley's absence from the peninsula, the Spanish rose in revolt against France. It started in Madrid when members of the Spanish royal family were arrested and sent to France. The rest of the country rose up in revolt. Napoleon personally led an army into Spain to put down a rebellion in Madrid. The British forces on the Peninsula, commanded by General Moore, were en route to assist the uprising in Madrid, but upon hearing of Napoleon's arrival in Spain thought it better to withdraw to the port of Corunna in the northwest of Spain. Moore was doggedly pursued by the French Marshall Soult and although the army was successfully evacuated, he fell during the fighting at Corunna.

After Corunna, Napoleon once again left the theatre to his subordinates and Soult proceeded to invade Portugal from the north. Initially Soult was resisted by the rag-tag Portuguese militias, but he easily seized the important port of Oporto* in the north, even though his own forces had been worn out since his campaign had begun. During the French capture of Oporto, the birdge over the Douro collapsed under the weight of the

* The Portuguese refer to the city as Porto.

BAY OF BISCAY
Corunna
ASTURIAS
GALICIA
Burgos
Valladolid
LEON
OLD CASTILLE
R. DOURO
Oporto
Almeida
Fuentes D'Onoro
Ciudad Rodrigo
Salamanca
Busaco
Coimbra
Madrid
Talavera
R. TAGUS
PORTUGAL
Torre Vedras
Lisbon
ESTREMADURA
NEW CASTILLE
Badajoz
R. GAUDIANA
Baylen
R. GUADALQUIVIR
Seville
ANDALUSIA
Cape St. Vincent
Cadiz
ATLANTIC OCEAN
Cape Trafalgar
Gibraltar

The Peninsular War

civilians as they attempted to flee. There was no other bridge over the Douro, so Soult was effectively stuck at Oporto for the moment.

Soon after the beginning of 1809, Wellesley arrived in Lisbon and took command of the Anglo-Portuguese forces. He immediately set off north to attack Soult. When Wellesley arrived opposite Oporto, the bridge was still destroyed, and the French were guarding all the boats on the northern bank the river.

It appeared as if there was no way across the Douro. But then it was discovered that some Portuguese had hidden a boat and some wine barges a little further upstream. The boatmen were persuaded to cross over and ferry the British across. Wellesley also sent a force to cross the river further east, and to block the French line of retreat should he succeed in pushing them out of the city.

Almost miraculously a British company made it over without being noticed by the French, and they quickly occupied the well-built Seminary. With the seminary in British hands, it was safer to bring more troops across. By the time the French realized what had happened the Seminary was strongly defended, and able to repulse the French counter attacks. Soult was asleep when attack began, when he awoke he ordered the men on his right flank (guarding the ships) to assist with the attack on the Seminary. As the French abandoned the ships, the Portuguese citizens took them over to Wellesley, allowing him to cross the Douro with the majority of his force.

After the French realized they couldn't take the Seminary, they began to withdraw from the city. The retreat turned into a route once Wellesley's main force were deployed and attack the French rear.

Unfortunately the force Wellesley sent to prevent the French escape failed in its mission. However, Wellesley pursued Soult vigorously and was able to capture the main roads leading back to Spain. The French were forced to abandon their cannons and wagons in order to escape over the mountains. Of the 11,000 troops Soult had at Oporto, a little more than 4,000 made it back to Spain. Wellesley lost under 200 men. With Portugal once again secure from the menace of a French invasion, Wellesley turned his attention to his first invasion of French occupied Spain and the army of Marshal Victor.

Marching his army east, along the valley of the Tagus River Wellesley united with the main Spanish rebel army. The Spanish, in characteristically unreliable fashion, were reluctant to join forces with Wellesley to do battle with the French. Because of Spanish indecision Soult was allowed to reinforce Victor around Madrid. When battle was joined around the village of Talavera on the Tagus River the French assumed the offensive and advanced in three massive columns, which was standard French tactics in the Napoleonic era.* The French column was typically thirty men wide and forty to fifty men deep. The column could be used as a hammer to break through a line formation with the shock of its mass as opposed to its fire power as only the first three or four ranks could effectively fire their weapons. The column could also be used as a means to quickly advance the units into the fight, before contact they would be deployed into a line formation.[36]

Wellesley had conceived of a novel tactical concept to counter the shock and mobility of the French column. He utilized the local geography of the land, the skill and discipline of the British infantry and the maximization of his manpower and firepower. Wellesley endeavoured to position his troops behind the crest of a hill in the prone position, so as, to be hidden from the enemy and to form them up in long thin lines two or three rows deep (which were typical of British infantry tactics) with a line of skirmishers in front of the main force. The British would

* The French column has standard tactical procedure for the French by the time Napoleon was Emperor, but it had been revolutionary only years prior at the beginning of the French Revolutionary Wars.

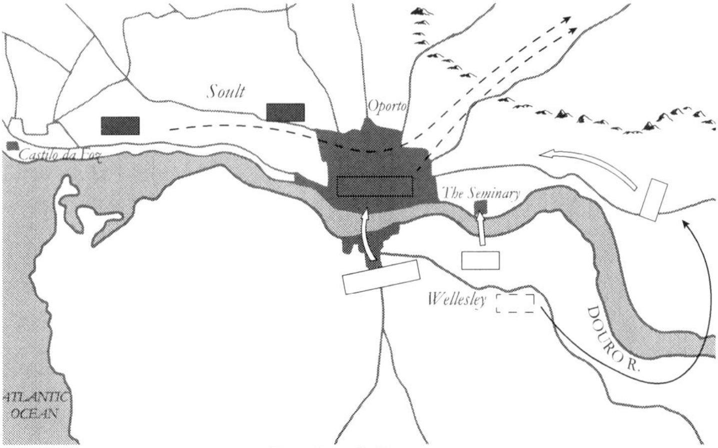

Battle of Oporto

keep out of sight of the advancing French column until the moment of truth, when the French would arrive at the crest of the hill, the British would be ordered to stand up and open fire.[37] The wide British line did not waste any of its potential firepower because every row of men could open fire when given the order. The skill and discipline of the British soldier, which was derived from intensive drill, enabled them to fire three to four rounds a minute and most importantly it instilled in them the courage to stand up to the shock of a French column.

Wellesley's skillful deployment of his infantry lines repulsed the attacks of the French columns and gave him the victory at the Battle of Talavera. The Spanish allies, who had been so timid and indecisive before the battle, now advised Wellesley to advance and retake Madrid. Wellesley was skeptical of an advance as that would put his lines of communications with Portugal in greater danger and so he opted for a strategic retreat in the face of numerous French armies converging on him from almost every direction.[38]

When Napoleon received the news of Talavera he dispatched his most competent commander, Marshal Massena, to the Iberian theatre. In the meantime, Wellesley was completing the construction of the defensive lines around the Portuguese capital Lisbon that were to become known as 'the Lines of Torres Vedras'. Beginning in the autumn of 1809, the construction of the Lines of Torres Vedras, which consisted of three fortified lines arching from the River Tagus to the Atlantic Ocean, had been an extremely well-kept secret.[39] So much so, that when the French under the command of Marshall Massena arrived in Portugal and pushed Wellesley back towards Lisbon, Massena was completely taken by surprise at the sight of them.

In addition to the defensive lines, Wellesley instituted a policy of scorched earth north of Lisbon destroying all crops and forage north of the city in anticipation of a third French invasion of Portugal. The French began their invasion by capturing the border fortress of Badajoz and Ciudad Rodrigo along the Spanish-Portuguese frontier. These weren't suppose to be easy sieges,* but the Spanish troops garrisoning them barely put up a fight.

Tragedy struck at the fortress of Almieda, which had been strengthened by British troops. A lucky French artillery shell started a chain reaction that set off the powder magazine and obliterated the fortress's citadel. The garrison was forced to surrender. Wellesley's army fell back to the ridge at Busaco, the French advanced on his position in columns. They were repulsed with heavy losses, but Wellesley was forced to retreat when he recieved reports that Massena had sent troops around his flank to the North. The withdrawl was orderly, and Wellesley fell back behind the Lines of Torres Vedras.

The French, who were notorious for living off the land, found it difficult to keep their army fed in the newly desolated region north of the lines. After a month of scavenging for supplies, Massena was forced to withdraw his army from Portugal. However, the French occupation force in Spain continued to hinder Wellesley's campaign for the liberation of the Iberian Peninsula.

In the spring of 1811 the French still held the two fortified towns that guarded the main roads connecting Portugal and Spain, Ciudad Rodrigo in the north and Badajoz in the south. Wellesley needed to secure both in order to protect his communications for when it came time to invade Spain. First Wellesley moved towards Ciudad Rodrigo and won a victory on the Portuguese side of the border at Fuentes de Onoro, causing the French to retire from Almeida to their Spanish fortress at Ciudad Rodrigo. At this point Marshall Massena was sacked from his position and replaced by Marshall Auguste Marmont.[40]

Instead of assaulting Ciudad Rodrigo, which was closer,

* Badajoz, and Ciaudad Rodrigo had been building using state-of-the-art architectural designs inspired by Vauban.

Wellesley maneuvered towards Badajoz and combined his force with a mixed British-Portuguese army commanded by Wellesley's subordinate General Beresford. A fresh French army appeared in the vicinity of Badajoz and relieved the fort from Wellesley's siege. From Badajoz Wellesley went back north to Ciudad Rodrigo, but was once again forced to retire in the face of another French relief force.[41] Little other activity occurred in 1811 between Wellesley and the French. The main actions were between various Spanish guerilla (irregular) forces and the French occupiers, most importantly in Catalonia (Barcelona), Valencia, Aragon and Andalusia (Cadiz).[42]

Spanish guerillas would take on an increasingly important role that would spread French manpower thin and drain the morale of their forces in Spain. Whenever the French advanced or occupied a new province, the Spanish guerillas (aided by the British) would appear upon the French supply lines or wherever they were weakest. The guerillas added a new dimension and level of intensity to the conflict on the peninsula; it was one that Napoleon had not accounted for in his plans for conquest. The guerilla war dominated the Spanish theatre, the French usually had two hundred fifty to three hundred thousand soldiers in the country usually with only fifty thousand being directed against Wellesley.[43]

The year 1812 was fated to be a turning point for Wellesley's Peninsular War and the allied war effort in Eastern Europe. Starting with Ciudad Rodrigo, which fell to Wellesley early in 1812, Badajoz was next. Both fortresses fell after brutal sieges and storming operations that were (and are) typical of siege operations, regardless of the period of time. In Badajoz Wellesley captured the French pontoons and promptly destroyed the floating bridges across the Tagus near Almaraz. The French Marshals in the north and south were now separated by the Tagus, the only crossing they controlled was a few hundred miles to the east in Madrid.[44] After Ciudad Rodrigo and Badajoz were secure Wellesley marched northeast to the town Salamanca and defeated Marshall Marmont's army at the Battle of Salamanca. Wellesley was finally building up an unstoppable momentum in the theatre; his victory at Salamanca created a panic in 'King' Joseph Bonaparte's court in Madrid and Joseph soon fled to safety on the eastern Mediterranean coast of Spain.

Joseph's withdrawal from the capital of Spain prompted the French army in the south to lift their siege of Cadiz and retreat out of the fear of being cut off. Wellesley's liberation of Madrid did not induce him, or allow him, to rest on his laurels as the French withdrawals allowed them to regroup in strength. He quickly advanced on the northern sector and laid siege to the town of Burgos. Sieges take time, and so, the French were allowed to regain the offensive and force Wellesley to lift his siege of Burgos; he retired back to Portugal in good order.

♦ ♦ ♦

Events in Russia, combined with those in Spain began to drastically affect the strategic balance of power on the continent.* In July of 1812 Napoleon marched eastward with some five or six hundred thousand French and allied troops in an attempt to bring the Russian Czar back into the fold.[45] The French won easy victory after easy victory as the Russians retreated eastwards towards Moscow, scorching the earth as they went. The Russians took a stand a little west of Moscow at the village of Borodino, while losing the battle they were able to inflict considerable causalities on Napoleon's Grand Army, and thus further delaying the Emperors march as winter settled in.[46]

The Russians withdrew from Moscow heading north to St. Petersburg. Napoleon entered Moscow shortly thereafter to find that the Russians had left arsonists behind who had been given orders to engulf major parts of the city in flame.[47] With the Russian army still intact and safe in St. Petersburg, Napoleon

* The Czar had decided to pull out of Napoleons Continental System and resume trade with Great Britain.

was unable to bring the Czar Alexander I to terms and as the harsh realities of the Russian winter began to set in, the French, far beyond their means of supply and so used to living off the land, were forced to retreat.

Once the French retreat was underway, the Russian counterattack began in force. Utilizing guerilla tactics, Russian cavalry forces, called Cossacks,* descended upon the freezing and slow moving French columns; keeping up a constant pressure. Napoleon's Grand Army barely made it back to their point of departure on the Niemen River with a fraction of its original strength. One of the boldest invasions up to that point in history was almost completely annihilated by a combination of inhospitable weather, poor logistical planning and capabilities, and a tenacious pursuit by irregular forces. The consequences of the 1812 invasion of Russia were soon to be felt dramatically in the Iberian Peninsula.

Fearful from his recent defeat in Russia, and the possibility of his client kingdoms in Germany defecting from their subservience to France, Napoleon withdrew much needed veterans from Spain to bolster his forces in Northern Europe. With the remaining French in Spain stretched thin from Valencia on the Mediterranean to Bilbao on the Atlantic, and the Spanish back in control of much of their country the tide had definitively turned. Spring of 1813 witnessed Wellesley marching over the Spanish – Portuguese frontier for the last time. His army was bigger than he had ever commanded with some fifty thousand British, twenty-five thousand Spaniards and twenty-eight thousand Portuguese, totaling around one hundred twenty-five thousand men.[48]

Wellesley's army swarmed over Northern Spain and seized Burgos in the late spring. Moving on to Vitoria he out maneuvered Joseph Bonaparte's army and forced him to commit to battle on terms unfavourable to the French.

* Cossacks were horsemen from the steppes of central Asia.

King Joseph and Marshall Jourdan believed that Wellesley could only attack up the valley which narrowed to a small defile west of the city. Jourdan positioned the majority of his forces on two ridges that over looked the defile, and a smaller force on a ridge further south. As well the French had positioned some forces to guard the bridges closest to Vitoria itself.

Wellesley did have part of his army advance through the defile, while another force attacked the French on the southern ridge. With the French attention fixated firmly on the defile and the southern ridge, Wellesley let loose his attack on their flank. Descending from the northern ridge of the valley, the force struck where the French least expected. The most important of which was the attack on the bridges closest to the city. The French put up a stout defence but the British carried the bridges none-the-less.

At this point the French guarding the defile flew into a panic as they heard the fighting at the bridges. Their retreat quickly turned into a rout as the French lines lost all cohesion. To make matters worse, the route of retreat was blocked up by King Joseph's baggage train, which was loaded with all the loot he had managed to squeeze out of Spain.

The retreating French soldiers were the first to sack the wagons, but they were quickly seen off by the advancing British. The British fell into disorder as they ransacked the wagons, and were unable to properly pursue the French. Wellesley was furious at the disorder, but regardless the victory was complete.

Once victorious, Wellesley was free to shift his main lines-of-communication to the northern coast of Spain and also to lay siege to the two remaining French fortifications at San Sebastien and Pamplona.[49] After Vitoria, the two forts hindered Wellesley from vigorously pursuing the retreating French. While Wellesley laid siege to the forts the French had been regrouping on the French side of the Pyrenees. The French launched a counter-attack in late July, but was stalled short of Pamplona

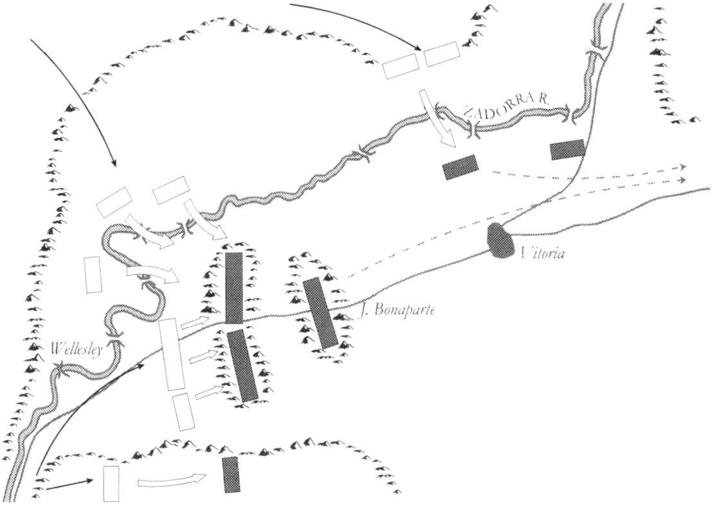

Battle of Vitoria

before being repulsed by a Spanish army at the Battle of San Marcial.[50]

In hindsight the repulse of the French at San Marcial ended any hope of French victory in Spain, although if Napoleon was victorious in the north he could have transferred troops back to stabilize this front somewhere south of the Pyrenees. For Wellesley and his allied army, who in the moment did not have the benefit of our hindsight, a victory for Napoleon in the north was still a very real possibility. Napoleons only hope, other than a decisive victory in the north was the possibility of the Allied nations falling out of concord with each other and into petty squabbling.

With this in mind, Napoleon attempted to sign a separate peace with Spain by releasing King Ferdinand from captivity and reinstalled him on the Spanish throne in the hope that he would sign a peace treaty with France and thus alienate Wellesley's army on the peninsula. Luckily for Wellesley, Napoleon's attempt to divide came to nothing as the Emperor had done too much to aggrieve the Spanish population. It is unclear that even if King Ferdinand allied with France at this point the population would loyally follow their king back into the French camp, in all likelihood the average Spaniard would have rebelled from the king.

Napoleon's armies still held two important advantages. First, they held the interior lines of strategic communication between their northern and southern fronts. And second, they had a unified national command structure controlled by Napoleon. Fortunately, the differences between the allies, both in their ambitions and geographic positions, did not cause a falling out amongst their ranks. Furthermore, the eastern powers, Prussia and Russia, had avoided loosing decisively to Napoleon at the Battle of Dresden (in Germany) and they were rewarded with Austria rejoining the Coalition.[*51] With Austria now counted

* By this point Napoleon had divorced his first wife, Josephine, and married the princess of Austria. However, this marriage alliance did nothing to stop Austria from joining the coalition.

amongst their ranks the eastern allies went on to beat Napoleon at the Battle of Leipzig,* which ended the campaigning of 1813.

With Napoleon's attention fixated upon Frances northeastern frontier, Wellesley was free to pursue the French armies that he had pushed out of Spain into France itself. Napoleon actually used his interior lines to Wellesley's advantage by further stripping experienced units form his southern front to bolster his army in the north after the costly draw at Dresden, and loss at Leipzig. In the spring of 1814 Wellesley moved against Marshall Soult across the northwestern mountain pass into France. The two generals did battle along the River Nive around Bayonne before Soult retired into Toulouse. Wellesley lost no time in laying siege to Toulouse and after a brief but none-the-less tenacious defence Soult surrendered Toulouse to Wellesley.[52]

The first evening Wellesley spent in Toulouse the news came of Napoleon's surrender. The combined armies of Prussia, Russia, and Austria had decisively defeated Napoleon at the Battle of Leipzig and laid siege to Paris. Napoleon was forced to surrender his armies and abdicate from the throne. For the time being the war against Napoleon was over; Napoleon was exiled to Elba, a Mediterranean island to the south of France. Before leaving, Napoleon vowed to return to France just as the flowers would return to the fields in the spring of 1815.[53] In the meantime Wellesley had been commissioned as the British ambassador at the new French court of Louis XVIII in Paris.† True to his word, Napoleon managed to escape from Elba in a small skiff in a scene reminiscent of his escape from Egypt. When Napoleon landed in Marseille, French opinion had swung back in favour of the former Emperor. The British government reassigned Wellesley to the allied Congress of Vienna out of fear for the safety of his person.[54]

* Also known as the 'Battle of Nations'.

† Louis' regime was plagued with incompetence and corruption, and engendered no loyality amongst the French people.

Landing in Marseille, Napoleon marched north to Paris gathering soldiers for his new army along the way. The old allies wasted no time in reassembling their forces for the inevitable battle. The British and Prussians were the first to arrive on the scene, being as that they were the closest to the French frontier. The Russians and Austrians being considerably further from the theatre took longer to assemble and were unable to arrive in time. To further confound Wellesley's problems his peninsular veterans had mostly been sent to fight across the Atlantic Ocean in the 'War of 1812' against the Americans.[55] His new army was made up mostly of new recruits, troops who had been a part of the home defence forces stationed in Great Britain and Dutch troops serving under the Prince of Orange.[*56] Napoleon's forces began moving north in late May, early June with the intention of attacking the allied armies separately before they could combine and outnumber him.

Wellesley and his forces were based out of Brussels, with their supply lines stretching back to Ostend and other Channel ports. The Prussians commanded by their storied commander General Blucher, of Dresden and Leipzig fame, were not far off to the east. Napoleon's army marched quickly, with Brussels as its objective, feinting towards the coast to threaten Wellesley's supply lines, forcing Wellesley to move west to protect his lines. The feint worked and Napoleon was able to maneuver himself into a central position between the British and Prussians.[57]

Napoleon first attacked the Prussians with his centre and right wing, pushing them back at the Battle of Lingy. Napoleon directed his left wing, commanded by Marshall Ney, to take the crossroads at Quatre-Bras. An advanced guard commanded by the allied Prince of Orange initially held Ney off, but he was pushed back until Wellesley arrived with reinforcements and recaptured the crossroads. By having to retake Quatre-Bras,

* The Dutch, and Belgians had, until recently served under French command.

Wellesley's advance was slowed down and he was unable to be of any assistance to Blucher.

Napoleon did not have the time or the resources to pursue the Prussians in force, and so they were allowed to withdraw in order while Napoleon turned his attention to Wellesley. The next day Napoleon joined Ney for an assault on Quatre-Bras but found that Wellesley had withdrawn to safer ground to the north. After a brief cavalry skirmish, a heavy rain set in which halted Napoleon's advance and gave the allies some much needed time to regroup.

That evening Napoleon belatedly ordered his right wing, commanded by Marshall Grouchy, to pursue the Prussians who had withdrawn from Ligny to the north and were amassing at Wavre where they could support Wellesley should they be required. The rain had saturated the ground and so Napoleon was forced to delay his offensive actions until the next morning when the ground would be dry. Wellesley was in a strong position to the south of Brussels outside the village of Waterloo, where he waited for Napoleon to advance.

Wellesley occupied a long ridge that ran east to west with a road running parallel to the ridge behind the crest, and was bisected by the main road to Brussels. Wellesley drew up his line in depth out of view from Napoleon on the opposite crest of the hill. In front of Wellesley's line there were three well-built farmhouses, which Wellesley promptly occupied and fortified. On his right flank stood the farmhouse called Hougoumont, on his left was the hamlet of Papelotte and in the centre was the farmhouse called La Haye Sainte.[58] Wellesley's forces were strongest on his right and centre as Wellesley had good reason to believe that the Prussians would be marching to reinforce his left.[59] Still fearful of a wide ranging flanking maneuver by Napoleon to cut off his communications with the sea, Wellesley sent a sizable detachment to Hal and Braine le Comte on his far right to protect his line against such a flanking move.[60] Oppos-

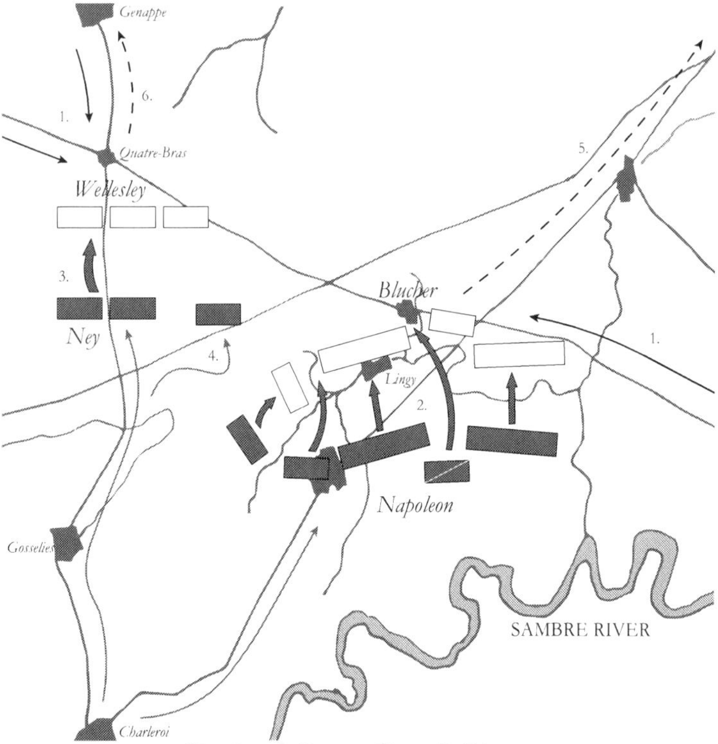

Battle of Quatre Bras & Ligny

1. Wellesley's and Blucher's forces converges on Quatre-Bras and Ligny. 2. Napoleon engages Blucher at Lingy. 3. Ney launches attack against Quatre Bras. 4. D'Erlon is ordered to assist both attacks, but fails to assist either. 5. Blucher is forced to withdraw in the face of Napoleon's assault. Instead of retiring to the east, he takes his army north. 6. Ney's attack is repulsed, but Wellesley withdraws in the evening.

ing Wellesley, Napoleon had his army drawn up into columns on a ridge parallel to Wellesley's position to the south.

Before Napoleon's assault began he sent another order to Grouchy to pursue the Prussians to Wavre. Napoleon's assault began sometime between 10am and 11:30am, with a massive barrage of artillery upon Wellesley's lines.*[61] The majority of Wellesley's forces were out of sight from the French, but they still took casualties from the bombardment. Napoleon's first attack was directed against Hougoumont on Wellesley's right. The French made it through the forest to the south of the farmhouse before being repulsed by fresh British reinforcements. Fierce fighting would continue around Hougoumont for the duration of the battle, but the French would never succeed in taking it. Napoleon's main effort was now to focus his attention on Wellesley's centre and left flank so as to drive a wedge in between the British and Prussians before driving Wellesley back into the sea.

Another massive artillery bombardment began around 1pm on the British centre, followed by French columns of infantry and cavalry. The attack in the centre isolated La Haye Saint farmhouse, but the French were stalled when they ascended the ridge only to find the British line lying in wait. The surprised Frenchmen pressed their attack and nearly succeeded in breaking Wellesley's line, were it not for Wellesley's second in command ordering the heavy cavalry to support the faltering infantry.[62]

The heavy cavalry succeeded in driving the French assault back, but in their frenzy they also pushed too far and were decimated by the French infantry who were at the base of the hill formed up in squares.† However, some of the British cavalry pushed further and were able to disable a number of the artillery pieces in the 'Grand Battery' before they too were driven off

* Curiously enough, for such a well documented battle there is no agreed upon time.

† This action became famous as the 'charge of the Scots Greys'.

by a French counter-attack. Regardless of the losses sustained by the British cavalry, Wellesley succeeded in holding his line against the massive French assault as he played for time until the Prussians could arrive on the scene.

Before the French had assaulted Wellesley's centre, Napoleon had spied through his glass the Prussians a few miles distant, but they were still a few hours away. He was now pressed for time and at a loss for men after being repulsed twice. Napoleon, or one of his subordinates now ordered his cavalry to assault the centre again as he believed he saw the British withdrawing from La Haye Sainte, they were in fact evacuating their wounded.* In response to the incoming French cavalry, the British infantry formed into squares and beat off the successive waves of French charges.[63] The French Cavalry, unsupported by its infantry, did little damage to the British squares, and so Wellesley's center remained unbroken. It was only after the British garrison of La Haye Sainte ran out of ammunition and were forced to retire, that the French ended up in possession of the farm. Once the French were in control of the farm they brought up horse artillery and inflicted considerable damage upon the British squares.[64]

Even with the fall of La Haye Sainte, Napoleon was grasping at a fleeting chance for victory. The Prussians were arriving in force on Wellesley's left flank and were beginning to drive in Napoleon's extended right flank before he was able to stabilize this front at the Village of Plancenoit.[65] Napoleon was now faced with an almost impossible situation, yet he was not ready to give up the fight until all his options had been exhausted. He still held his 'Imperial Guards' in reserve, which he now committed to the battle.

The Guards were initially successful in their assault on Wellesley's centre, but they did not have the necessary manpower or momentum to achieve their objective of crushing Welles-

* It is still debated today as to who was responsible for the order.

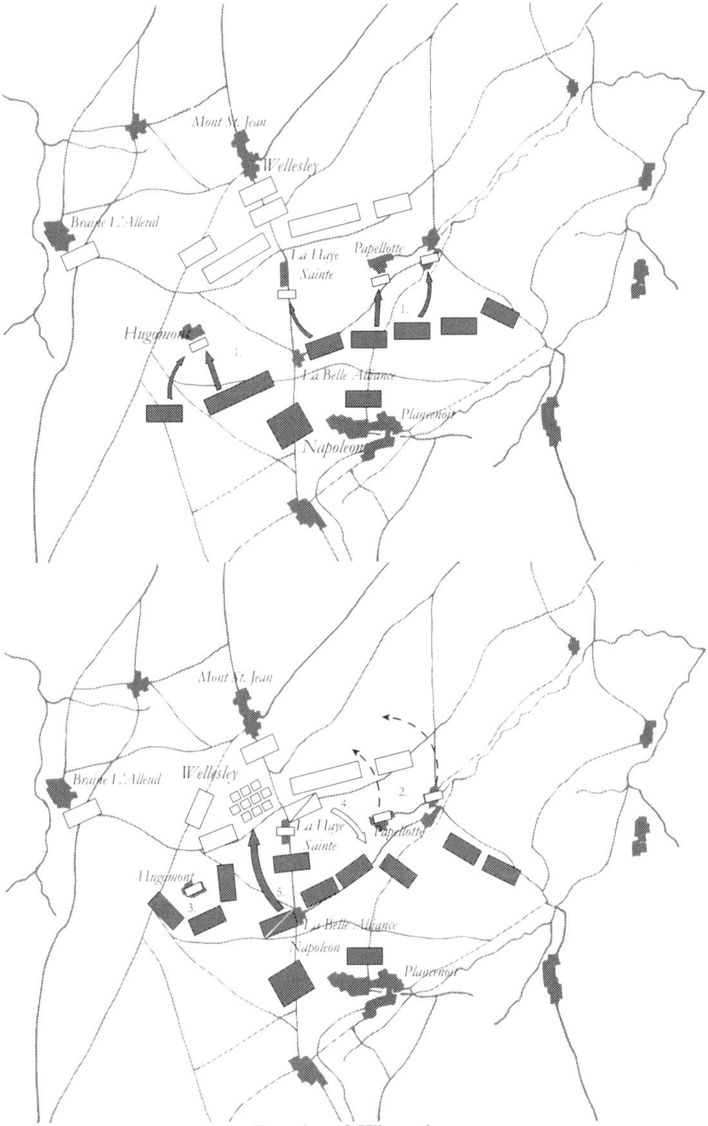

Battle of Waterloo

1. Napoleon launches his attack on the British lines. 2. Allied troops withdraw from Papellotte. 3. Hugomont is surrounded, but holds out. 4. Charge of the British cavalry. 5. Charge of the French cavalry, British infantry form squares.

ley's centre. The Imperial Guards were forced to retreat, and by doing so they caused a panic amongst the remaining French ranks. They attempted to regroup on their reserves south of La Haye Sainte, but Wellesley could sense that victory would be total if he acted decisively, and so, he ordered his entire line to advance.[66] At roughly the same time the Prussians began to make progress through the streets of Plancenoit completing the disintegration of Napoleon's army. The 'Old Guard' (part of the Imperial Guard) created a rear guard around the village of La Belle Alliance, but the majority of the army was in head long retreat and Napoleon was unable to reform any cohesive resistance in the face of Wellesley's and Blucher's incoming armies.

♦ ♦ ♦

Wellesley, who had never before faced Napoleon, the Scourge of Europe, in battle now stood victorious and poised to invade France. Napoleon was once again forced to surrender and to abdicate from the French throne. This time his place of exile would be considerably further from France than Elba was. He was now escorted to St. Helena* where he would spend the rest of his life until he died in 1821.[67] After Waterloo, Wellesley returned to the British Isles as the most celebrated commander since John Churchill, Duke of Marlborough had commanded armies in the field. Unlike Churchill, Wellesley was not to simply retire to home and hearth. By now, Wellesley had become the Duke of Wellington, a Field Marshall (the highest military rank possible) and was also a sitting member of Parliament for the Tory Party.

Wellesley became Prime Minister of the United Kingdom late in his life and was a vocal and active member in support of restoring the franchise (the right to vote) to Great Britain's Irish subjects, who had been disenfranchised as they were Catholics and had continuously attempted to throw off the rule of

* The irony is that Wellesley found the island enjoyable, while Napoleon hated it.

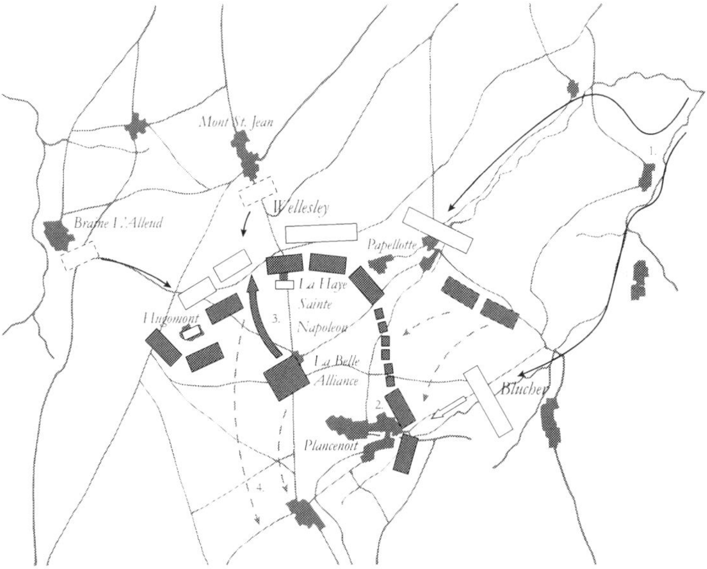

Battle of Waterloo

1. Blucher's Prussians arrive on the field. 2. Part of Napoleon's Imperial Guards occupy Plancenoit. 3. Napoleon orders the Old Guard to assault Wellesley's lines. 4. Napoleon fails to dislodge Wellesley, and is forced to retreat.

the British crown and government. Regardless of his military reputation, there was much opposition to his policy regarding the Irish, and so his tenure as Prime Minister was indeed rather short, he did go on to serve with distinction in the House of Lords.[68] His insight into military affairs never left him and Wellesley was retained in the rank of commander-in-chief until the day he died, the 14th of September 1852. While Napoleons career is generally considered as the more spectacular of the two, Wellesley's by far outpaced Napoleons in both length and durability.

To briefly recap, Wellesley's victories in India first stabilized and then expanded British hegemony on the sub-continent. The Peninsular War drained French resources before reuniting the peninsula against the Bonapartist regime, and then was finally used as a springboard into the French country side. Wellesley's army was the first hostile foreign army to grace the soil of France almost since the war against the revolutionary regime had begun. It was Napoleon's opinion that the Peninsular War did more than any other even to bring down his empire. Victory at Waterloo proved beyond a shadow of a doubt that Wellesley was a first rate rival to Napoleon's military genius, as Waterloo decisively defeated the Emperor's designs for a French Empire in Europe. Furthermore, the wars end, brought about by Wellesley, effectively ended the century's long rivalry between France and the British Isles and turned the two arch enemies into allies. Although there have been trying times and mutual suspicions, the two nations have never again fought against each other since the Battle of Waterloo.

The peace that followed Waterloo lasted for well over a generation in Europe and allowed for great strides to be made in all aspects in the societies of Europe. Not least in Great Britain whose society and economy was to profit handsomely from the dividends of peace. With these consequences considered, Wellesley goes down as one of the greatest military commanders and protectors of liberty against the wicked tyranny that Napoleon sought to impose upon Europe and the world.

Robert E. Lee

Robert E. Lee was born on January 19, 1807, the son of 'Light Horse' Harry Lee and Anne Hill Carter in Virginia. His father Harry was a hero of the American Revolution who had served with George Washington and at one point served as Governor of Virginia and a representative to the U.S. Congress.[1] Robert was the fifth child of Harry and Anne; Harry had been previously married to another and had three children to his first wife. Robert's father left the family in debt after he was attacked and mutilated by a mob over his political views regarding the War of 1812.* Shortly thereafter Harry left Virginia for the West Indies.

His father's leaving at such an early age scarred Robert's early life because he did not really have a father figure to grow up with and live up to. Robert attended West Point Military College after receiving an appointment from U.S. Secretary of War, John C. Calhoun.[2] He graduated second in class in 1829 and accepted a commission as second lieutenant in the corps of engineers. He was married in 1831 to Mary Anna Custis, a great granddaughter of George Washington. In his capacity as an engineer Robert travelled across the United States reinforcing fortifications on the Atlantic coast, the Mississippi River and in New York City.

When in 1845 the United States and Mexico went to war, Robert volunteered for active service. He won praise from the commanding officer, General Winfield Scott, for his construction of artillery emplacements and his successful efforts at reconnoitring the enemy positions.[3] In 1852 Robert was appoint-

* Harry had been a vocal opponent of hostilities, the mob in Baltimore vigorously disagreed with him.

ed superintendent of the U.S. Military Academy at West Point. After three years at West Point, Robert was promoted to second-in-command of a cavalry regiment stationed in Texas. His mission in Texas was to protect settlers from Indian raids and to subdue rebellious tribes. Robert was largely unsuccessful at subduing the tribes, due to the large open expanses in which the tribes could easily seek refuge in.

In 1857 Robert was recalled to Virginia to manage the estate of his recently deceased father in law. His father in laws estate included vast tracks of farmland, numerous slaves, and considerable debt. Robert was forced to take a leave of absence from the army to sort out the estate, much of his time was spent attempting to emancipate his inherited slaves.

In 1859 Robert commanded the troops assigned to the retaking of Harpers Ferry arsenal from the self-styled messianic terrorist, John Brown.[4] Brown intended to use the arms captured at the arsenal to incite rebellion and revolution amongst the black slaves of the South. John Brown's failed crusade into the South stirred up emotions and tensions on both sides of the Mason-Dixon Line. This tension was only further exasperated by the upcoming presidential election of 1860.

♦ ♦ ♦

Ever since the founding of the British colonies along the eastern seaboard of North America there had been division between the slave holding and non-slave entities. Tension had existed between the two entities prior to the American Revolution, but was exasperated after the founding of the United States of America as an independent nation-state. A political balance had been struck in Congress called the Missouri Compromise before the 1845 war with Mexico, in which, for every new 'slave' state admitted into the Union, a new 'free' state would also be admitted.[5] The Compromise insured a state of equilibrium in the number of senators representing the two regions in the Senate, which could then stifle any radical legislation that came through the House of Representatives that could upset either side.

Politics were tenuous at the best of times. But with the territorial gains from the 1845 Mexican War California, Arizona, New Mexico and Texas further strained the equilibrium in the Senate. The states of the South naturally, for the sake of geographic continuity and economics, wanted the newly conquered territories to be admitted as 'slave' states.[6]

The potential for statehood of the Kansas territory in 1855 further ratcheted up the tension, as it was located in between the North and South. The 1854 Kansas-Nebraska Act made it law for residents of territories to decide whether to be admitted as free or slave. Both sides proceeded to send settlers into Kansas in an attempt to influence the vote within the state. The contest between settlers quickly degenerated into savagery and small scale guerilla warfare.* The Northern faction eventually gained the upper hand, but Kansas wasn't admitted into the Union as a free street until January 1861.

The presidential election of 1860 was another extremely polarizing, and unique event. The Democratic Party had a falling out amongst three of their leading men, and all three ended up running for president for three separate 'Democrat' parties thus splitting the votes that would have conceivably gone to one unified party.[7] The Republican Party's† candidate for president, Abraham Lincoln, was a vocal abolitionist of the slave system. Furthermore, Lincoln did not waste his time, money, or energy campaigning in the Southern 'slave' states instead focusing on a strategy of extreme northern sectionalism. When the time came to vote Lincoln didn't win a single Electoral College vote south of the Mason-Dixon Line.[8]

Lincoln legally won the election by carrying nearly every Electoral College seat in the 'free' states of the North and Pacific coast. Foreseeably the vote was split in the South among the

* John Brown got his start in Kansas.

† The Republican Party was a new political party, only a few years old at that point.

three Democrat parties, which deprived the opposition of any chance of beating Lincoln in the Electoral College.

The election of Lincoln understandably enraged the people of the South, and before Lincoln could be inaugurated as President of the United States, certain states in the South began to secede from the Union. South Carolina was the first to make its move followed by Mississippi, Florida, Alabama, Georgia, Louisiana and Texas.[9] These seven states formed themselves into the Confederate States of America with their capital in Montgomery, Alabama and elected Jefferson Davis (of Mississippi) as their President.[10] The Confederate Constitution was almost identical to the original Constitution of the USA,[11] the Confederates sincerely believed that if they had to fight what remained of the Union they would be fighting the 'Second War of American Independence'.

Most of the federal forts located in the South surrendered themselves, including a substantial portion of the old U.S. army garrisoned in Texas.* However, Fort Sumter, located in Charleston Harbour South Carolina refused to surrender itself. Once Lincoln was officially inaugurated, he decided to send a shipment of food to relieve the fortress under siege. The Confederates sent the ship away and once again demanded the fort surrender. Surrender was refused and on April the 12th, 1861 the Confederate General Beauregard ordered a bombardment, Fort Sumter surrendered the next day, war would now commence.[12]

♦ ♦ ♦

With the attack on Fort Sumter, Lincoln had his pretext to wage an aggressive war against the break-away states; he ordered the states still loyal to the Union to raise their own volunteer armies to subdue the South. After Lincoln had called for his volunteers the remaining states of the South who had not yet seceded from the Union, were repulsed with the thought of attacking their

* Lee was stationed in Texas at the time, and was returned in Washington, as part of the surrenders.

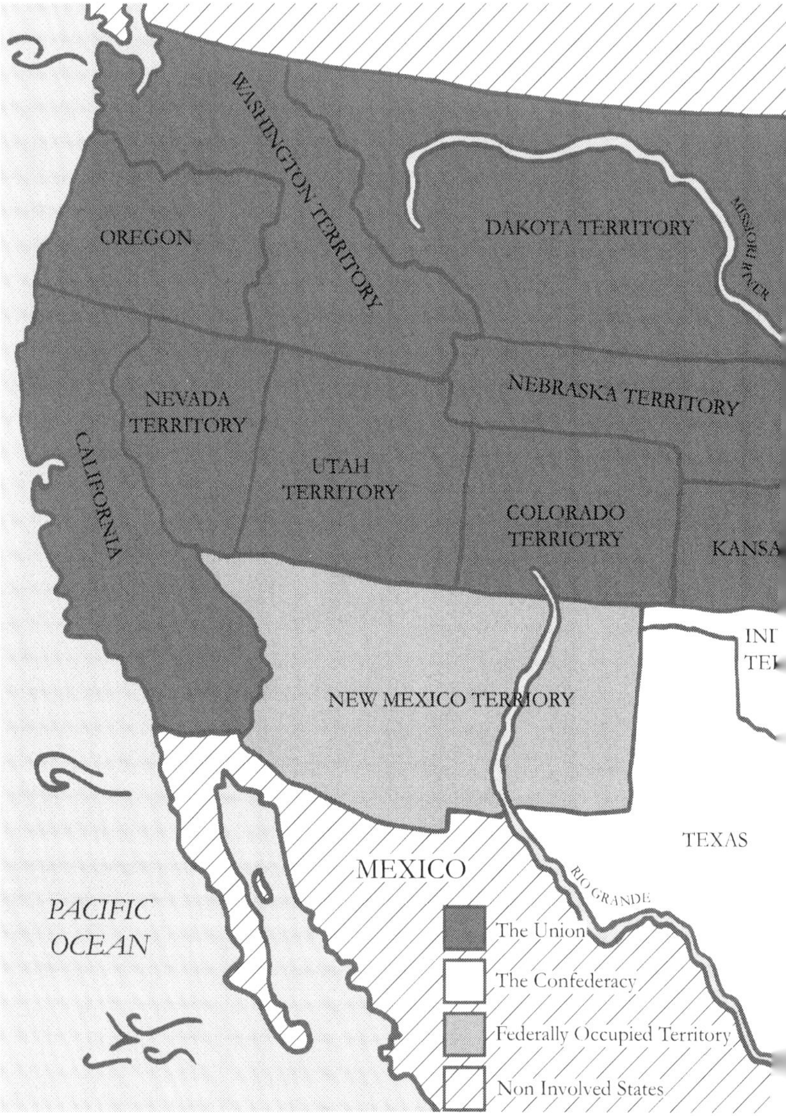
WASHINGTON TERRITORY
OREGON
DAKOTA TERRITORY
MISSOURI RIVER
NEBRASKA TERRITORY
NEVADA TERRITORY
CALIFORNIA
UTAH TERRITORY
COLORADO TERRIOTRY
NEW MEXICO TERRIORY
MEXICO
TEXAS
RIO GRANDE
PACIFIC OCEAN
The Union
The Confederacy
Federally Occupied Territory
Non Involved States

Secession of the Confederate States

sister states. Virginia, Arkansas, North Carolina and Tennessee seceded and joined the Confederate States of America.

Kentucky and Missouri were quickly invaded by Union forces and their legitimate elected state governments were forced into exile in the South.[13] Maryland and Delaware remained loyal to the Union, but declared themselves neutral. Stating they wouldn't allow soldiers from either side to cross their states, Lincoln quickly sent Federal troops to occupy them anyways. The stage was now set for what both sides expected would be a quick, painless and glorious war. It would turn out to be the bloodiest and bitterest conflict in the history of the United States, where fathers would fight against sons and brothers against brothers. It would change the very fabric of the United States forever and left the slave holding Southern States in a state of cultural and economic desolation.

At the commencement of hostilities Winfield Scott was the Commander-in-Chief of the U.S. Army, but with the crisis on the horizon Scott realized the Union would need a younger man and he was conveniently about to retire. Once Lee returned from Texas, where he was stationed after the incident at Harpers Ferry, Gen. Scott called Colonel Lee into his Washington Office and offered Lee the command of the Union field army, with the full consent of President Lincoln.[14] Lee, who was morally and politically opposed to the institution of slavery,* declined the invitation to command the Union armies citing his reservations against raising his sword against his native state of Virginia.[15]

After the decision of Virginia to secede and join the Confederacy, Lee decided he would accept and share the destiny of Virginia regardless of his personal convictions. The Governor of Virginia quickly invited Lee to accept the command of the Virginian forces. Lee did so reluctantly, but immediately.[17] In a rare public speech to the Virginia State Convention, Lee, ever

* Even though he inherited and owned slaves, he was in the process of freeing his inherited slaves as the Civil War was erupting.[16]

the gentleman stated that this would be the last time he would raise his sword. Unlike many, Lee knew this war wouldn't be quick or glorious, he advised his fellow Southerners to prepare themselves for a long and bitter war.

The first major action of the war was at Manassas Junction.* The citizens of Washington expected a good show and came to the battlefield to watch. The Union forces were routed after the Confederates put up a staunch defence. The confusion was exasperated by the intermixing of the soldiers and civilians. Exhausted, the Confederates were unable to pursue and they Union troops were permitted to regroup themselves back in the capital. Lee was right; the war wouldn't be quick or glorious for either side.

At first Lee was engaged as a military advisor to the President of the Confederacy, Jefferson Davis. Lee was also employed in strengthening the Confederate fortresses on the eastern seaboard.[18] In the spring of 1862 the Union crafted a new plan to capture Richmond. General McClellan and 100,000 soldiers were to embark on ships from Washington, and land on the Yorktown peninsula, before making their way to Richmond. The advance was slow, as McClelland made it a habit of overestimating his opponents, but made steady progress until it was within sight of Richmond. And then the Confederates attacked. At the battle of Seven Pines Joseph E. Johnston, the highest ranking Confederate officer,† was wounded and incapacitated. As Douglas S. Freeman so eloquently puts it, Johnston's incapacitation

* The Confederates and Federals usually named the battles differently. As a general rule, The Federals named battles after the nearby natural geographic features such as rivers, hills and &c. while the Confederates named battles after the nearest town, village or city. For the sake of simplicity and consistency this book shall refer to the battles after the Confederate designations.

† Johnston commanded with General Beauregard at the Battle of First Manassas.

> "…was a grim price to add to the toll of the mismanaged battle. A birthday present of ill omen to the army, men might say it was, but there was another gift: To the command that Johnston laid down, to resume no more, the President on June I named General Robert E. Lee."[19]

It was now Lee's time to shine.

♦ ♦ ♦

Upon assuming command, Lee was immediately faced with Union forces threatening from two opposing directions. Union General George McClellan was still on the York Peninsula and General John Pope was amassing strength along the northern border of Virginia. However, Lee held the interior lines and he knew he could concentrate his forces quickly to deal with each threat in detail. Lee's first target of choice was the largest and most imminent threat to Richmond; McClelland's army occupying the York Peninsula. This was the first time Lee would command an army of considerable size in battle. McClelland (a naturally cautious commander) was being pressured by Lincoln and Lincoln's advisors to attack Lee, Lee for his part feigned weakness in front of McClellan in an attempt to get McClelland to attack his lines. Giving into the pressure from the President and deceived by the perceived weakness in his front, McClelland began his offensive on the 25th of June.[20] It was to be a short lived offensive; Lee staunchly defended his lines and then aggressively counterattacked.

The Seven Days Battle was a collection of sequential battles at a collection of locales over seven days. After McClellan's initial offensive at the Battle of Oak Grove, McClelland began to overestimate the number of men under Lee's command and succumbed to what would later become known as 'Lee-phobia'. Lee's counterattack began on the 26th at the Battle of Mechanicsville, it continued on the 27th at Gaines Mill, and Garnett's Farm. June 28th saw action at Golding's Farm, on the 29th it was

Savage Station, the 30th at Glendale and it ended on July 1st at the Battle of Malvern Hill. At the end of the seven days, McClelland had been exhausted and defeated mentally by Lee's vigorous assaults, and so, he began to withdraw from the peninsula* and therefore ended the threat to Richmond emanating from the Yorktown Peninsula. McClelland's subsequent evacuation from the York Peninsula allowed Lee to turn his attention towards Pope's forces in northern Virginia.

In the brief time allotted after the Seven Days Battle, Lee undertook a radical reorganization of the Army of Northern Virginia (ANV) which essentially consolidated the army into two corps; one under the command of General 'Stonewall' Jackson, the other under General James Longstreet.[21] Prior to the reforms introduced by Lee, the Confederates didn't have a level of command in-between General Lee and the division commanders.[22] The de-facto creation of corps in the ANV was felt necessary by Lee to fix the armies greatest deficiencies. Those being the division's inability to coordinate and support one another and the inability of the divisions separate artillery attachments to concentrate.

After the Seven Days Battle, Lee dispatched General Thomas Jonathan Jackson,† north to screen Pope's advance south. Jackson's force met with Pope's advance guard and did battle with them at Cedar Mountain, south of Manassas Junction. Both sides received reinforcements after Cedar Mountain. Once Lee and Longstreet had linked up with Jackson, Lee decided to split his army once again. Jackson was sent on a wide flanking maneuver to the west of the Bull Run Mountains up to Salem on the Manassas Gap Railroad then east along the railroad to descend upon Manassas Junction from the west.[23] Jackson's flank march enabled him to capture the Federal stores located at

* It wasn't until the 14th of August that McClelland's forces were completely evacuated.

† Jackson was nicknamed 'Stonewall' after his gallant performance at First Manassas.

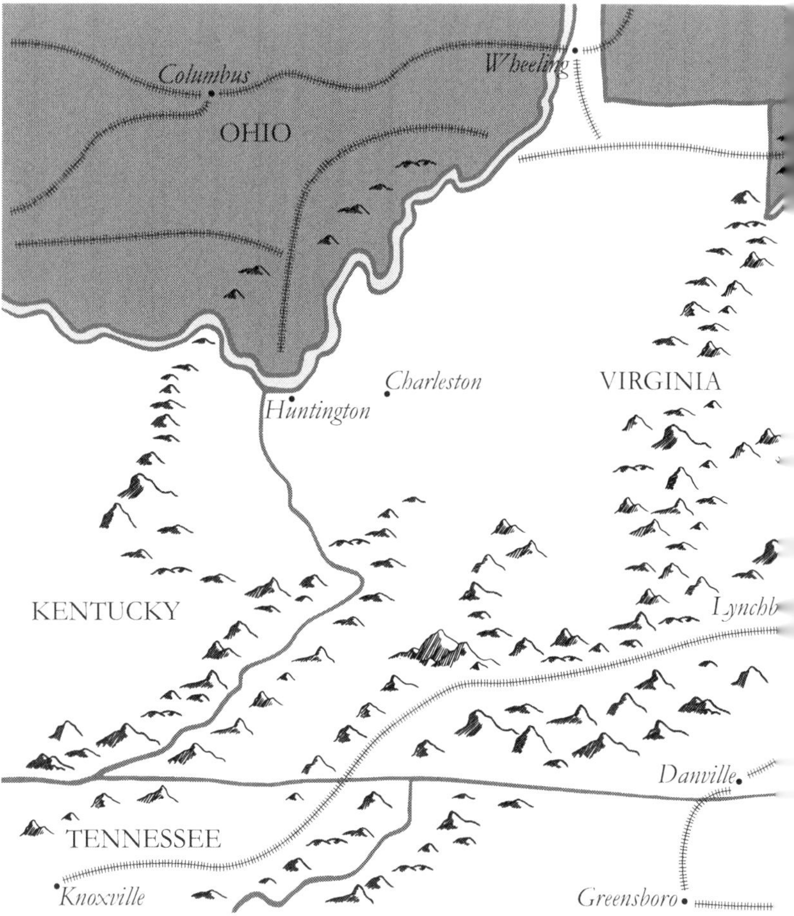
Columbus
Wheeling
OHIO
Charleston
Huntington
VIRGINIA
KENTUCKY
TENNESSEE
Danville
Knoxville
Greensboro

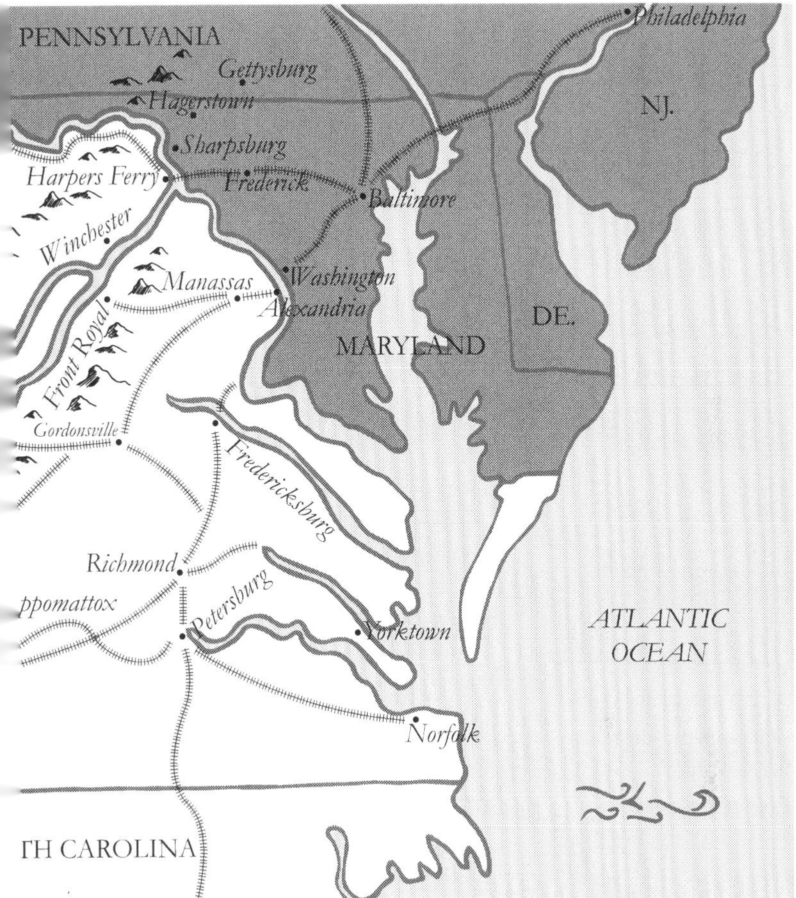

The Old Dominion

Manassas Junction before withdrawing to the northwest where he dug into a defensive position on Stony Ridge.

The remainder of the Army of Northern Virginia was being brought up along the Manassas Gap Railroad by General Longstreet following the same route as Jackson's flanking maneuver. Arriving at White Plains on the Manassas Gap Railroad line, Longstreet encountered a sizable Federal detachment occupying Gainesville.[24] The Federals sent a force west to the gaps in the Bull Run Mountains to contest Longstreet's linking up with Jackson while the rest of the Federal forces concentrated in the area opposite to Jackson's position. Pope believed he would be able to defeat the separate Confederate corps in detail. However, Longstreet wasn't long in turning the Federal flank covering the Bull Run Mountain gaps after which he broke through along the railroad and affected a junction with Jackson's corps.[25] With the preliminary maneuvering over, the main battle was about to be begin.

On August the 29th Pope was unaware of Longstreet's imminent arrival; he still believed he could envelope and annihilate Jackson command before turning against the remainder of Lee's army.[26] Pope began his attacks from the east upon Jackson's left flank along the Bull Run axis. Jackson had chosen his position wisely and defended it with vigour, Longstreet's corps sat inactive on Jackson's right flank and although Lee had ordered him to advance he was reluctant to do so and he only very meekly reconnoitered his front for a place to attack the next day.[27] After meeting with some resistance, Longstreet's reconnaissance force returned to their lines without having achieved anything meaningful.

For some unexplainable reason,* Pope now believed that the Confederates would be in headlong retreat come the next day, he couldn't have been more wrong. Lee had no intention of retreating, but rather was contemplating another wide ranging flanking

* Probably due to a complete failure of intelligence gathering.

maneuver with his left. On the 30th Pope ordered another attack on Jackson's position only to be repulsed once again. Longstreet now made an attack on Pope's left flank.[28] Pope shifted troops from his right to help stem the tide of Longstreet's advance against his left. With Jackson's left flank now relieved of pressure, Jackson went on the offensive in support of Longstreet's attack. The Federals were forced to retire to Henry House Hill, the location where Jackson had first acquired the name of 'Stonewall'. Disillusioned and demoralized, Pope began to plan for his withdrawal across the Bull Run to Centreville, which he subsequently undertook on the evening of the 30th.[29]

The next morning, Lee set Jackson in motion on a flanking maneuver to the north and then east with the intention of cutting off Pope from Washington by occupying Centerville or Chantilly. Longstreet was left in position so as to confuse Pope before Longstreet was ordered to follow Jackson's route the following day. Jackson's men were exhausted after having marched and fought for the past seven days, when they met up with Federal troops around Chantilly their attacks did not succeed in taking the enemy positions.[30] The Federal troops and their commander were also exhausted. When Longstreet's corps linked up with Jackson, the Federals retreated to Fairfax Courthouse before they were given permission by the Secretary of War to further retreat upon the fortifications of Washington.

The campaign of Second Manassas had destroyed the second threat that had menaced Virginia upon Lee's assumption of command. It was a great victory where Lee had maneuvered and out commanded the federal general, but victory had come at a cost to the Confederates who suffered some 9,500 causalities to the 14,500 Federal causalities.[31] With the Federals holed up in Washington, Lee looked north for his and the Confederacy's first invasion of Federal territory.

♦ ♦ ♦

After the Union army retreated into Washington D.C. following

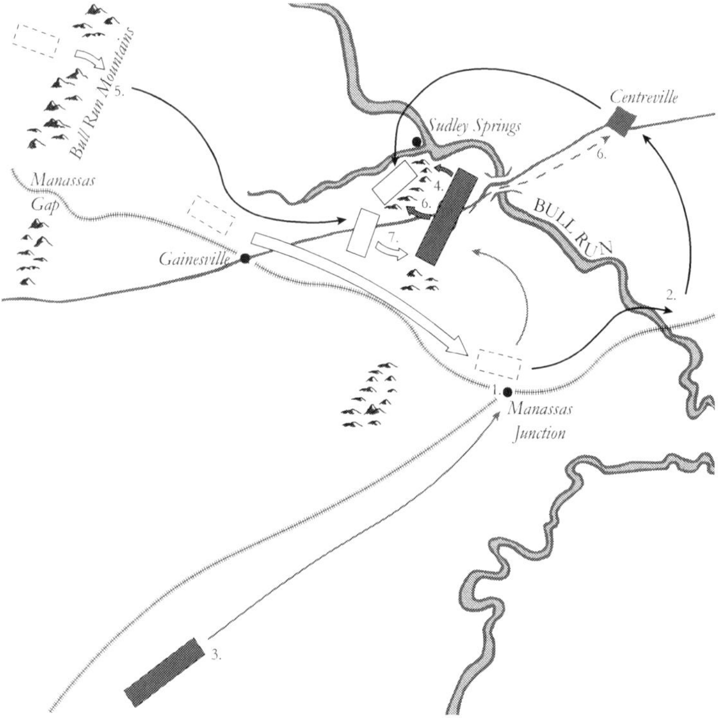

Second Battle of Manassas

1. Jackson captures Federal supplies at Manassas. 2. Jackson evacuates Manassas, and occupies stony ridge. 3. Pope's Federals return from the South. 4. Pope attacks Jackson's defensive line, and is repulsed. 5. Longstreet breaks through the Bull Run Mountains, reinforcing Jackson. 6. Pope attacks Jackson, and is repulsed. 7. Longstreet surprises Pope with his counter-attack.

the Second Battle of Manassas, Lee's plan was to cut off the capital from the northern states by liberating the neutral southern state of Maryland. McClelland, returned from the peninsula was the ranking officer on the scene and was tasked with foiling Lee's invasion. The element of surprise was lost when a Union soldier had found Lee's plans for invasion wrapped around three cigars, and so, the Federals were alerted to Lee's intention.[32] However, this was somewhat counteracted when Lee became aware of this unfortunate information from a Confederate spy.* Lee began by sending his cavalry, under the command of J.E.B. Stuart, by the most direct route to Washington to screen his advance up the Potomac River.

The main force of the Confederate army went north from Manassas and crossed the Potomac to the east of Harpers Ferry, once across the Potomac they went northeast to the town of Fredrick. Lee's crossing the Potomac had alerted and aroused the Federal government into action, McClelland was dispatched from D.C to find and destroy the Army of Northern Virginia. Meanwhile, Lee sent Jackson to capture Harpers Ferry at the confluence of the Potomac and Shenandoah Rivers for the purpose of securing the Federal provisions there and to have an excellent place for crossing the Potomac back into Virginia when the time came. Longstreet was sent north in the direction of Hagerstown to impede the advance of the Pennsylvania militia or other reinforcements.

By the time McClelland had left Washington, Lee's army was dispersed over a large area – it was now time for them to concentrate. The place Lee had chosen to concentrate his forces was the town of Sharpsburg in between the Potomac and Antietam Creek; he took up defensive positions behind the

* Washington DC, Maryland, and the northern states were crawling with Confederate spies and sympathizers, the same was true in much of the Confederacy. This, coupled with the fact that newspapers published with an incredible lack of descretion, made strategic intellegence unreasonably easy for either side to obtain.

Antietam creek and waited for McClelland to attack him there. McClelland obliged Lee with battle, as he was being pressured by Lincoln and the administration to attack; the battle began in earnest on the 17th of September – after Jackson and most of the Confederates were allowed to unite with the main body of Lee's army.[343']The morning of the 17th McClelland ordered an attack on Lee's left flank, commanded by Jackson. The attack was pressed hard, the Confederate's gave ground but the lines did not break.[34] McClelland continued his attack on another sector by committing his centre and left, which made progress against Lee, making it to the outskirts of Sharpsburg. McClelland's left flank was so focused on advancing towards Sharpsburg that they didn't notice a group of Confederates coming up from Boteler's Ford to the south.[35] The Confederate force, commanded by General A.P. Hill, advanced upon the unexpecting Federal left and halted their advance on Sharpsburg in its tracks.

On the 18th Lee remained in his positions around Sharpsburg even though he had only one route of retreat across the Potomac, at Boteler's Ford, which could be easily cut off if McClelland had the intelligence or resolve.[36] However, McClelland, who consistently overestimated Lee, was overly cautious and instead of attacking he waited for reinforcements to come from D.C. On the night of the 18th Lee withdrew the Army of Northern Virginia across the Potomac to safety.

The Battle of Sharpsburg was a draw, even though it could have been much worse for Lee if the Federals were commanded by a more competent general. The battle was a draw, but Lee's invasion campaign was a failure. McClelland believed he had performed an incredible feat at Sharpsburg, and so, he did not pursue Lee's battered army. Instead he argued with the Lincoln administration over how best to proceed.

McClelland proceeded slowly as was his norm, while Lee proceeded to split his army into two commands. Jackson was sent to the Shenandoah Valley in case the Federals decided to advance via that route, while Lee and Longstreet fell back along the most direct route in front of McClelland's advance towards Richmond. In November 1862 after too many disagreements with his commanding general, Lincoln decided to relieve McClelland of his command and replace him with the reluctant General Ambrose Burnside.[37] Burnside's strategy was by no means imaginative, his plan was to march on the Confederate capital by the Richmond-Fredericksburg and Potomac Railroad.

♦ ♦ ♦

Burnside was another timid commander; his strategy would become incoherent as President Lincoln interfered with his plans in an attempt to infuse a certain degree of aggressiveness into Burnside's operations. While Lincoln demanded aggressive action, Burnside was cautious and had no aptitude, or desire, for dividing his force to take advantage of momentary Confederate weaknesses. Once Burnside arrived opposite Fredericksburg at Falmouth in December 1862, he decided to wait for his pontoon bridges to arrive so that his entire army could cross the Rappahannock River as a whole.[38]

This delay allowed Lee to recall Jackson from the Valley and to form up his troops into strong defensive positions to the west of Fredericksburg. Lee placed Longstreet's corps on his left, with its far left hinged on the Rappahannock upstream from Fredericksburg. Longstreet's center was located on Marye's Heights which was further strengthened by a stone retaining wall on the crest of the heights and a canal and a drainage ditch to their front at the bottom of the slope. Longstreet's right wing linked up with Jackson's left wing. Jackson's line stretched to the south and east along the bluffs and was hinged on the Rappahannock to the south of Fredericksburg.[39] On the east side of the river, Burnside had amassed his artillery on Stafford Heights,* which made it impossible for Lee to contest the crossing at the river with any substantial force in Fredericksburg. However, Lee

* Close to George Washington's childhood home.

intended to make him pay for every street block of Fredericksburg before the Federals got the chance to attack his main lines west of the city.

By the tenth of December, Burnside's pontoon bridges were in place and he began crossing his troops; the crossing wasn't completed until the twelfth.[40] Burnside's orders for the attack on the thirteenth were woefully insufficient in strength, unimaginative and "…made sense only if Burnside still believed that only a part of Lee's army was confronting him."[41] The attacks were repulsed; Burnsides next idea was to continue the frontal assaults in both Jacksons and Longstreet's sectors but with greater numbers. These attacks were also repulsed and that largely ended the fighting for the day. Both sides remained in their positions during the 14th, on the 15th before the federal army retreated across the Rappahannock taking with them all their accoutrements.

Lincoln was furious at the failure of Burnside to destroy Lee at Fredericksburg and in January of 1863 Lincoln relieved him of his command, he was replaced by General Joseph Hooker.[42] In the meantime the Union army remained in its position opposite Fredericksburg. By the time spring came around Hooker had adapted a new plan (it was developed by Burnside) for crossing the Rappahannock upstream to turn Lee's line before marching on Richmond.

The Battle of Chancellorsville was largely an extension of the Battle of Fredericksburg when the campaigning season began again in the spring of 1863. Hooker began by maneuvering the main body of his army upstream while leaving around forty thousand troops opposite Fredericksburg. Upon learning that Federal troops had been embarked on ships at Washington, Lee sent Longstreet south with much of his corps to guard against that seaborne threat.[43] When Hooker began to move his army Lee was at a decided numerical disadvantage of almost two to one. However, Lee had the advantage of interior lines and an

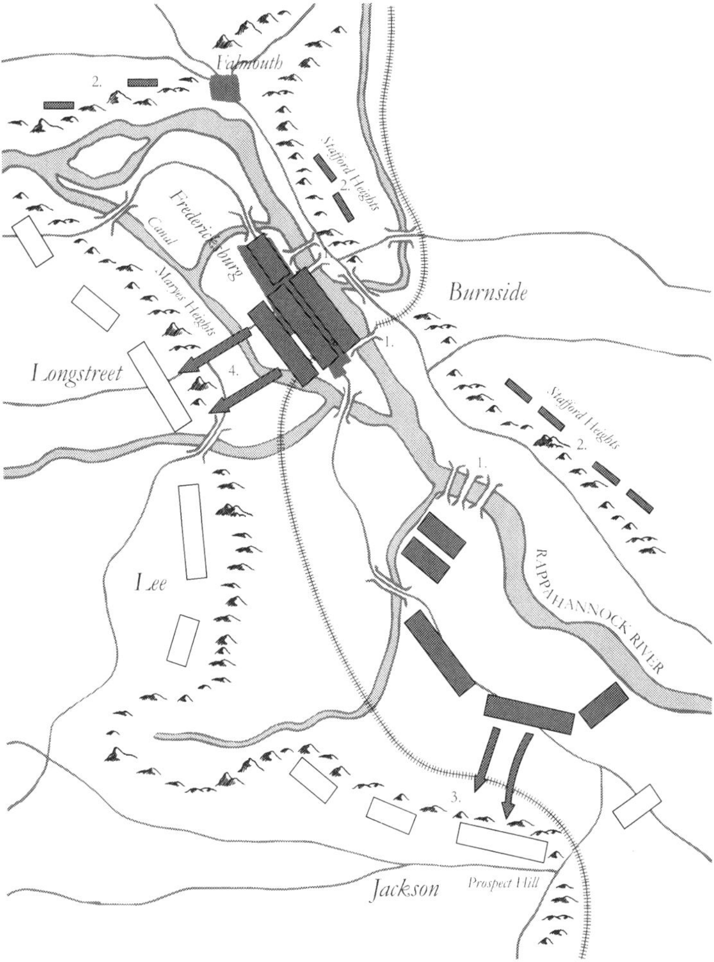

Battle of Fredericksburg

1. Pontoons constructed across the Rappahannock. 2. Federal artillery on Stafford Heights. 3. Attack on Prospect Hill. 4. Attack against Marye's Heights.

undivided army (minus Longstreet).

The desperation of the situation would not allow Lee to keep his army unified for long. Lee had fortified the fords from Bank's Ford upstream of Fredericksburg to Port Royal below the city to the south. However, Lee could not cover the entire river without dangerously over stretching his forces, and so, Hooker was able to maneuver further upstream and cross the Rappahannock using the U.S. Ford, Kelly's Ford, Germanna Ford, and Ely's Ford.[44] Hooker's plan was to keep Lee occupied in front of Fredericksburg while maneuvering with the main body of his army into the rear of Lee's army. Lee had no intention of making it that easy.

Once Lee realized Hooker had crossed the Rappahannock, he moved his army west while leaving a screening force of ten thousand men in their fortifications west of Fredericksburg to guard against the forty thousand Federal men opposite Fredericksburg. Hooker occupied Chancellorsville shortly after crossing U.S. Ford in late April 1863 and halted his advance on Lee there to take up a defensive position. It was May when Lee began to take the fight to his static enemy. J.E.B. Stuart, commander of the Confederate cavalry, reconnoitered the Federal right and discovered that it was not dug into position and therefore was vulnerable to a flank attack.[45]

Lee now adopted a most audacious plan and further divided his force into three separate parts.* Jackson was ordered to lead his corps on a wide ranging flanking maneuver into the unprepared Federal right flank, while Lee made demonstrations in front of Hooker to keep his attention fixed upon that sector.[46] When Jackson's corps was in place and ready for the attack, the three separate parts of Lee's army were so detached from each other as to make it impossible for them to support each other if they were attacked in detail, this plan was bold. Jackson was in position the evening of May the 2nd and he launched his attack

* Four if you count Longstreet's corps, that had already been sent south.

with only two hours of day light left.[47]

Jacksons maneuver succeeded in rolling up the Federal right, while Lee's frontal attack kept Hooker's attention away from his right flank. Unfortunately for Lee, and for the cause of the Confederates, Jackson was shot and injured that night by his own pickets while out reconnoitering for another route by which to out flank the Federals. Jackson's corps was taken over by the cavalryman J.E.B. Stuart.[48]

While Jackson's flank attack had been underway the Federals across from Fredericksburg began to cross but not with the full forty thousand men who were posted there. Instead some seventeen thousand men were marched over to U.S. Ford to reinforce the main army under Hooker. Only twenty-three thousand men made the crossing at Fredericksburg.[49] On May the 3rd Stuart and Lee's corps were reunited, while Hooker decided to secure his right wing by withdrawing it to the Rapidan River. His lines were in the shape of a 'U' with another 'U' shaped salient around the town of Chancellorsville. Hooker's main offensive had been blunted, and he began to withdraw his army back across the Rappahannock.

Lee now turned his attention back to the Federals who were occupying Fredericksburg, and shifted some ten thousand men back to that sector while leaving Stuart to make sure that Hooker's retreat was the genuine article.[50] General John Sedgwick's Federal detachment, which had advanced from Fredericksburg, was isolated and was forced to retreat across the Rappahannock via Scott's Ford. Once again the two armies stood opposite each other with the Rappahannock in between them, but now the initiative had shifted back to General Lee's Confederates.

♦ ♦ ♦

With the initiative back in his hands, Lee began his second invasion of the North. He began by moving his army northwest on another strategic flanking maneuver. He advanced up the Shenandoah and Cumberland valleys into Pennsylvania with the

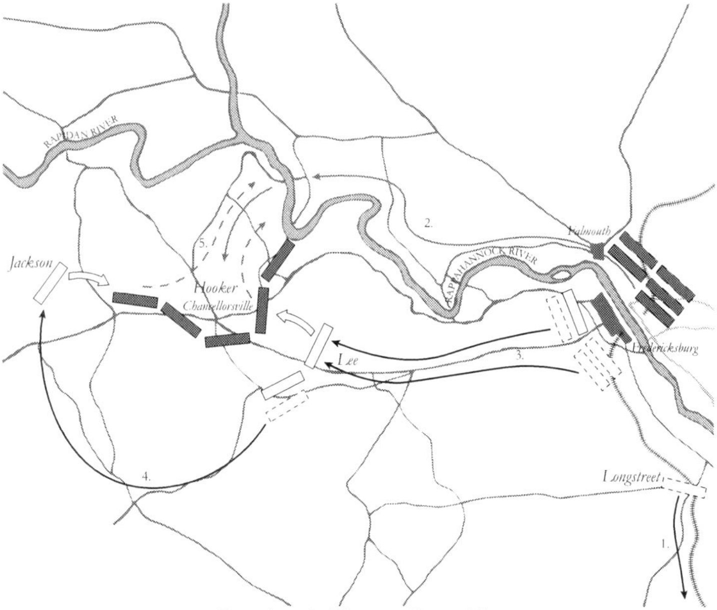

Battle of Chancellorsville

1. Longstreet, and his Corps is dispatched south to protect the Confederate seaboard. 2. Hooker manuevers his army up the Rappahannock River, occupies Chancellorsville. 3. Lee responds to Hooker's manuever. 4. Jackon manuevers into and attacks Hooker's open right flank. 5. Hooker retreats over the Rappahannock.

object of capturing Washington DC after drawing out and destroying the Federal army. Lee's invasion had the secondary objective of relieving the Virginia countryside from the desolation of war by bringing the fighting to the countryside of the North.

Hooker, who was still in command wanted to recross the Rappahannock and move onto Richmond. Lincoln wouldn't allow Washington to be left undefended and vetoed Hookers plan, instead ordering him to concentrate on defeating Lee's army. The eyes of Lee's army (Stuart's cavalry) had been out of touch with the Army of Northern Virginia since they crossed into Union territory.[51] Therefore Lee had no way of really knowing where the Union forces were, until the 28th of June when one of Longstreet's scouts reported the Federals converging at Fredrick, Maryland and marching north towards Gettysburg and the Army of Northern Virginia. It was also gleaned that Hooker and been relieved of command by Lincoln and superseded by General Meade.[52] The Army of Northern Virginia was stretched across the south of Pennsylvania, but with the intelligence begotten from the scout, Lee sent out the orders to assemble the army at Cashtown, Pennsylvania. On the 29th of June Lee, still without Stuart, began to push southeast from Cashtown with minor skirmishes around Gettysburg beginning on the 30th.[53] As reinforcements began to pour in the two armies started to gravitate towards each other around the town.

Gettysburg was first occupied by Union cavalry, who were able to withstand the Confederate skirmishers until they were reinforced by infantry. The Confederate advance guard once reinforced was able to push the Federal cavalry out of town. After being pushed out of the village, Union forces began to take up defensive positions on the ridges and hills to the southeast of Gettysburg. The Union positions took the shape of a fishhook running from Little Round Top in the south to Cemetery Ridge and Culp's Hill in the north and northeast.[54] Lee's lines mirrored this shape opposite the Union lines, which meant that

Lee would be giving up the advantage of interior lines. The lines had become largely static by July 2nd when Stuart and the cavalry rejoined the army.

Lee had concocted an extremely bold plan to be executed the next day; the plan consisted of three parts which were to be implemented simultaneously. The first part was to produce diversionary attacks upon the Federal left flank at Little Round Top and on the Union right flank at Culp's Hill.[55] The second part of the plan was to have Stuart and the cavalry ride on a flanking maneuver to the north around the Federal lines and into the rear of the fish hook.[56] The third part of Lee's plan involved a massive assault of infantry, led by General Pickett, upon the centre of the Federal lines at Cemetery Ridge to be coordinated with Stuart's assault upon the rear.[57]

Lee's plan was audacious, and because it relied on impeccably precise timing, it was perhaps too audacious and slowly but surely the plan began to fall apart. The diversionary attacks upon the left and right flanks of the Union lines failed to draw any considerable amount of Federal reserves in either direction. Next Stuart's cavalry was held up by Union cavalry, under the command of Gen. George Custer (of later infamy) and could not make it into position in time to coordinate their attack with the Confederate assault upon the Federal centre.[58] Last but not least the assault on the centre, which came to be known as 'Pickett's Charge', was cut to pieces as they had a large open field to cross and went unsupported by Stuart's cavalry.

After the survivors of Pickett's charge returned to the Confederate lines, Lee greeted them with sorrow and immediately accepted responsibility for the failure to achieve victory exclaiming "…all this has been my fault – it is I that have lost this fight…"[59] The Army of Northern Virginia was able to withdraw itself intact across the Potomac as Meade did not vigorously pursue Lee. Back in Virginia, Lee offered President Davis his resignation, Davis refused to accept it and thus Lee continued in command of the Army of Northern Virginia.[60] Once again the initiative switched back to the Federal army, Lee would remain on the strategic defensive for the remainder of the war never again to regain the offensive. Meade belatedly pursued Lee into Virginia and the rest of 1863 was spent maneuvering and jockeying for position. By the end of 1863 the Rapidan and Rappahannock were once again the two rivers that separated the opposing forces.

The spring of 1864 witnessed another change of generals in the Union army, this time it would be permanent. General Ulysses S. Grant, the hero of Fort Henry, Fort Donnelson, Shiloh and Vicksburg, was promoted by President Lincoln to the rank of Lieutenant General, in charge of the overall Union strategy for the direction of the war as commander-in-chief.[61] Grant would accompany the Army of the Potomac, still commanded directly by General Meade, while Grant's old second in command, General Sherman, would become commander in the trans-Allegheny theatre.

♦ ♦ ♦

General Grant had been widely successful in the Trans-Allegheny theatre where he had started the war. The successful culmination of his campaign against Vicksburg had severed the Confederacy in two along the Mississippi River Valley. With Grants transfer to the Eastern theatre came grumblings from within the Army of the Potomac that while Grant might have been met with success in the west, he had also never gone up against Lee. Notwithstanding the Union's victory at Gettysburg, 'Lee-phobia' had crept into the Army of the Potomac, morale was bad on both sides, and both sides had to resort to the use of firing squads in order to stem the tide of desertions.[62] Grant was resolved to not be overcome with 'Lee-phobia', even though he found himself in almost the same predicament as Burnside, Hooker and Meade.

From now on the Federals would consistently enjoy a two-

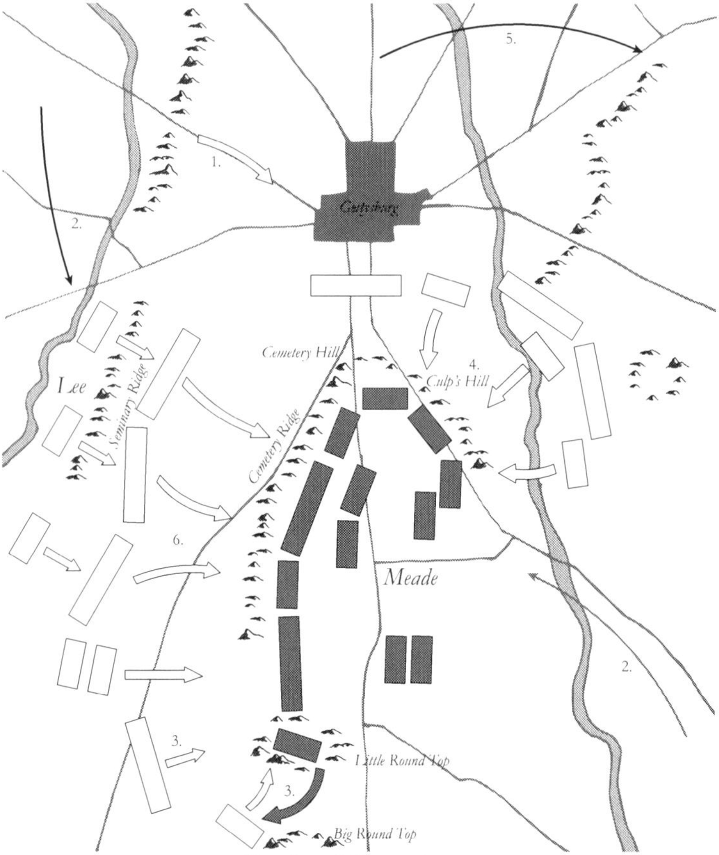

Battle of Gettysburg

1. Confederate vanguard captures Gettysburg (July 1st) 2. Direction of Reinforcements. 3. Confederate attack on the Peach Orchard, Wheatfield, Devils Den, and the Round Tops (July 2nd). 4. Assault on Culp's Hill (July 2nd & 3rd). 5. Stuart's cavalry engages Custer's cavalry to the east (July 3rd). 6. Pickett's charge (July 3rd).

to-one manpower advantage over Lee's army and Grant was determined to make good use of it. In other relevant areas such as agriculture/industrial output, the Union far outpaced their Confederate counterparts, sometimes at a ratio of four to one.[63] No particularly brilliant strategy was devised by Grant to achieve victory in the east. Characterized by the term attrition, Grant knew he could grind Lee's army into submission if only he and the country had the resolve.

Grants strategy could be summarized into three points. First, he endeavoured to make no glaring mistakes that Lee could take advantage of. Second, he made sure to keep his lines of communication with Washington open. And third, to use his numerical superiority to try to turn Lee's flank and thus force him to withdraw if he could not overcome Lee's defensive lines via the most obvious, direct route.[64] At the Battles of the Wilderness, Spotsylvania Courthouse and Cold Harbour, Grant turned Lee's right flank – but Lee escaped in time to avoid a flank attack and kept his lines of communications open with Richmond. After inflicting considerable casualties on Grant at the Battle of Cold Harbour, Lee was at last pushed into the fortifications surrounding Richmond and Petersburg and both sides settled in for a siege.

Grant's unimaginative tactics and strategy in the east resulted in terrifyingly high causalities and almost ruined the Lincoln administration's prospects for re-election in 1864. Morale throughout the North was reaching new lows with anti-war riots and demonstrations occurring in New York and elsewhere. A peace candidate running for the Democrats emerged to challenge the Lincoln administration, the failed General McClelland.[65] Grant's right hand man, General William Tecumseh Sherman, (who succeeded Grant to independent command in the Trans-Allegheny theatre), came at the right time to save Lincoln and Grant. Sherman captured Atlanta in September of 1864, just a few months before Northern voters went to the polls. Atlanta was one of the most strategically important cities of the Confederacy, it produced much of their arms and the most important railways ran through Atlanta travelling in every direction. The wars end now appeared to be in view, the capture of Atlanta gave heart to the Northern cause and the franchised public voted Lincoln back into office for another term.

In the dark winter months of 1865, with little hope for salvation Lee was promoted in responsibility and, as General-in-Chief, given the authority to direct the entire strategic war policy of the Southern Confederacy.[66] Grant stuck to his strategy and continued to press Lee's lines even without any glorious breakthrough victory. The spring of 1865 saw the Army of Northern Virginia, it was coming to be known as 'Lee's Miserables', worn down and depressed.[67] The Confederacy had been cut up and divided by successful Federal campaigns and the Union's overwhelming sea power.

Lee's last hope was to abandon Virginia and head west to combine with the forces under the command of J.E. Johnston, but this was not to happen. The Army of Northern Virginia left the defences of Richmond and Petersburg on the 3rd of April 1865, by the 9th Grants army had caught up with Lee and put an end to his westward movement. At the Court House of Appomattox Lee surrendered his army to Grant and the war that had raged for four long years was over in the Eastern theatre. Soon afterwards the other Confederate armies would follow Lee's example and lay down their arms. In his farewell letter to his soldiers, Lee thanked the men of the Army of Northern Virginia for their service throughout the war.[68]

♦ ♦ ♦

General Robert E. Lee was and is a primary example of a gentleman. He was a patriot who loved his country and attached his fate to his native state of Virginia. He was a patriarch who loved his wife and children, and freed his slaves, whom he had inherited from his father in law, even before the emancipation proclamation had been added as a war policy by President Lincoln. The responsibility of high command and Lee's ultimate failure to defend his country's liberty and independence left Lee broken hearted, poor and without a home, as Arlington House, was stolen from him by the Federal government and turned into a cemetery for Union war dead.[69] A vindictive Union Quartermaster-General made sure the old mansion would be rendered unlivable by interning the war dead in close proximity to the living quarters.*

After Appomattox Lee had hoped to retire from public life to somewhere in the country. Instead he was offered the position of President at Washington College in Lexington, Virginia. Lee accepted. Under his stewardship the small college blossomed into a major institution for the south, it has since been renamed Washington and Lee University. Although Lee was barred from state and federal office by the fourteenth amendment and ineligible for the first round of presidential pardons. Lee used his position at the college to promote the federal reconstruction efforts in the south and encouraged northern students to attend college in Lexington. While Lee was never arrested for treason, as he technically could have been from 1865-68 he was eventually pardoned during the second round in 1868, however his citizenship was never restored.

Lee's Christian faith helped to resign him to his bitter fate and he used his celebrity and gravitas to convince his fellow Southerners to not hold a grudge against their foe of yesterday but rather to work in good faith with the Northerners to rebuild the United States of America. He would be heard saying or writing, "I believe it to be the duty of everyone to unite in the restoration of the country" & "Go home…and help to build up the shattered fortunes of our old state." Lee's character was so near flawless that he became a hero in both the North and

* Lee's son would later regain ownership after a court battle, only to sell it back to the US government.

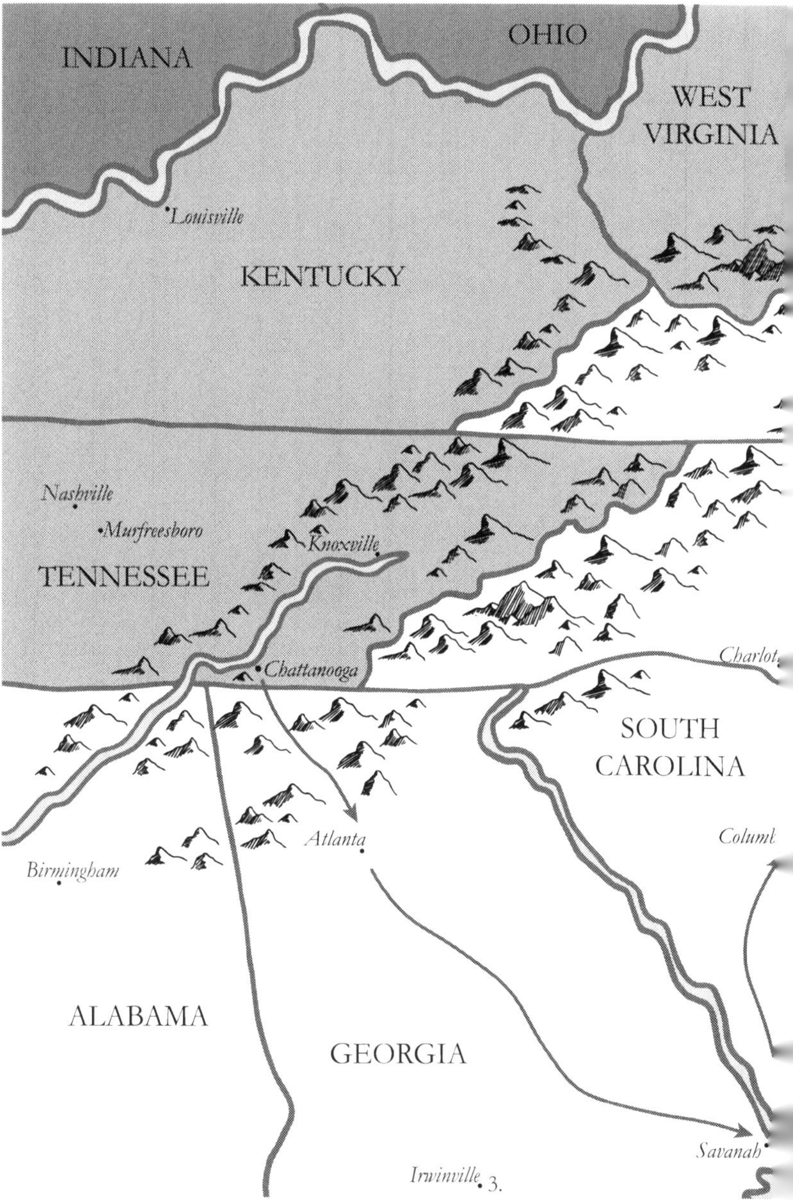
INDIANA
OHIO
WEST VIRGINIA
Louisville
KENTUCKY
Nashville
Murfreesboro
Knoxville
TENNESSEE
Chattanooga
Charlot
SOUTH CAROLINA
Atlanta
Columb
Birmingham
ALABAMA
GEORGIA
Savanah
Irwinville
3.

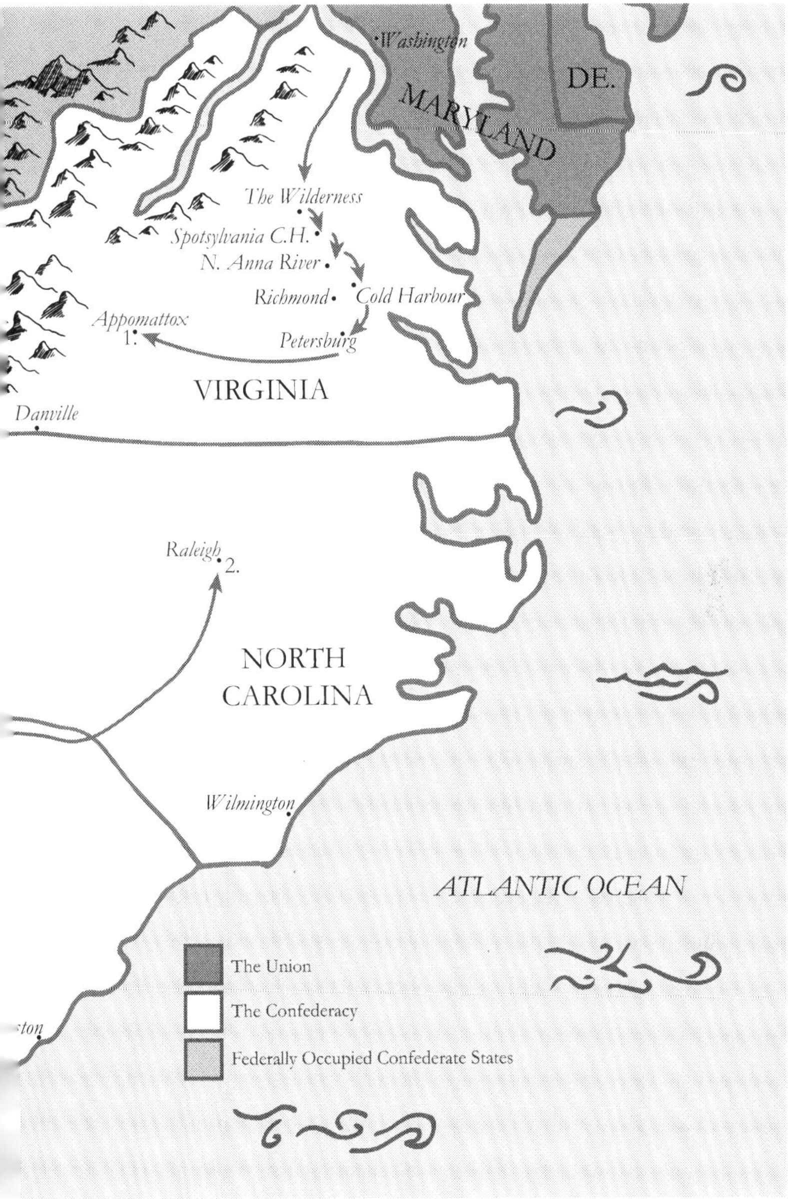

Unconditional Surrender

1. Lee surrenders at Appomattox. 2. Johnston surrenders at Raleigh. 3. President Davis is captured at Irwinville.

South. It wasn't for nothing that Lee was dubbed the 'Marble Man', comparable only to George Washington.

The audacity of Lee's campaigns and battles continue to be studied the world over, and his example of loyalty and devotion to family, country and liberty continue to inspire and influence his countrymen to this day.

Modernity

"We shall defend out island, whatever the cost may be, we shall fight on the beaches, we shall fight on the landing grounds, we shall fight in the fields and in the streets, we shall fight in the hills; we shall never surrender."

-Winston S. Churchill, British Statesman

The Modern Age

After the Quadruple Alliance's victory over Napoleon, the four powers who comprised the alliance, Russia, Prussia, Austria and the United Kingdom came together to form the Concert of Europe. The concert was a loosely organized, non-binding venue for the powers to discuss the security problems of the continent before events spiraled out of control. While France was initially not allowed to participate, it wasn't long before the restored monarchy of France was permitted back at the table of great powers.[1] At first the stated purpose of the concert was to foster peace amongst the great powers and to avert the kind of catastrophe that the French Revolution and Napoleon had plunged Europe into. With this in mind the more conservative monarchies attempted to use the concert to shore up their autocratic regimes by agreeing to assist in the suppression of any further societal upheavals. While the United Kingdom had been a key founding member, it generally, and consistently in accordance with its historical strategy, declined to partake in continental politics where its vital interests were not at stake. The most noticeable product of British involvement in the concert was with the 'Treaty of London (1839)' in which the powers officially recognized the neutrality of Belgium to be an immutable fact of international relations.[2]

With time, the fabric of the Concert would erode as jealousies and competition amongst the leading powers would lead to war in the latter half of the 19th Century. The wars that did erupt during this period were largely contained to small areas and after the fighting was over the Concert allowed the belligerents to sit down and work out their differences in peace.* The relative peace that Europe enjoyed after Waterloo was also helped along the way because the major European powers fixed their attention upon their near-abroad and the far flung reaches of the world in their quest to expand the size and scope of their imperial systems.

Between the American Revolution and the Napoleonic Wars, the pace of expansion for the European empires had drastically declined, some of the earliest of the empires ceased to exist as they either ran out of impetus or were subsumed into the larger more efficient systems. The French Revolution and Napoleons regime forced the governments of Europe to focus their attention almost entirely upon the French threat to Europe. With the exceptions of Napoleon's expedition in Egypt, French agitations on the Indian subcontinent and minor actions in the Caribbean Sea, the twenty years of war were completely confined to the European continent.

♦ ♦ ♦

After the fall of Napoleon, France, the United Kingdom, Russia and to a lesser extent Portugal, Spain, Belgium and the Netherlands, resumed their search for lands to annex. At this point in time the only land left available was in Africa, the Far East and the Pacific Islands. In the east, Russia continued to advance across the Eurasian steppes until it reached all the way to the Pacific. After the American Civil War, the Americans completed their 'manifest destiny' by conquering the tract of land between the Mississippi River and the Pacific Ocean.

The empires of China, Persia and the Ottomans were in decline and their provinces were becoming attractive targets for the burgeoning powers of Europe. Japan was the only non-European entity that was unified, strong and rapidly westernizing its military and economy. Before long the coastal areas of China

* See the Crimean War, Austro-Prussian War, & Franco-Prussian War.

had been divided amongst the major powers, next was the continent of Africa and the Pacific Islands. The Persian, Ottoman, Abyssinian (Ethiopian) Empires and Afghanistan were the only non-European entities left that had a loose grip (but none-the-less a grip) over their territory. From the year 1815 to 1900 the European powers had come to dominate 85 percent of the world's landmass, all this was possible because of the relative peace within Europe and the technological advancements which would become known as the Industrial Revolution.

Commerce, industry and empire worked together in a complex symbiotic relationship to progress and reinforce themselves. The industrial revolution was kick-started in the United Kingdom as the British were on the cutting edge of the new technologies and were by far the best positioned to exploit them. British society was by far the most liberal and intellectually dynamic of all the European nations (challenged only by France in these spheres). Its geographical position as an island and its strong naval tradition coupled with its vibrant and economically diverse empire further allowed the British to exploit opportunities that were not available to other states.

The first invention that started the ball rolling was the development of the steam engine. Prior to the exploitation of steam, the human race had relied solely upon muscle power (be it human or animal) to get things built or to get around on land. The harnessing of steam replaced muscle power allowing goods to be manufactured on an industrial scale, its application to engines further revolutionized transportation of goods and people by steamship (at sea) or train (overland). Manufactured goods (be they cloth, cookware or weapons) could now be mass produced and transported almost anywhere around the globe cheaper and more efficiently than ever before in human history. The revolution that began with steam quickly spread to revolutionize other aspects of human society and industry.

Before long the way humans communicated with one another was also vastly improved by the invention of the telegraph and later the radio and telephone. Prior to the telegraph a letter could only travel as fast as a horse or ship could take it. The telegraph, using a sort of electronic code, could transmit messages through cables across the globe near instantaneously. Radio and telephone later made it possible to transmit voices through either landlines (telephone) or the atmosphere (radio). The last breakthrough that shall be briefly examined here is the harnessing of electricity.

Prior to electricity, humans had relied on simple combustibles (i.e. wood, coal, oils) to light and heat their homes. Electricity could be used to generate both heat and light. More in the near future could be expected to be derived out of electricity as it would one day surpass steam as a means of powering various other devices. While these three innovations were of vital importance to the progress of human society, there were literally hundreds if not thousands of offshoots that were made possible by the discovery and harnessing of these various phenomena.

The day of the all-powerful commanders-in-chief, directing strategic policy and commanding tactical dispositions from a prominent position on the battlefield was over. Industrialization, mass conscription and improved communications made it possible for the nation-states to field and equip armies on a scale never before thought possible. Improvements to the reload rate, range and destructive firepower of personal arms and artillery forced commanders to disperse their soldiers over increasingly large areas as it became too dangerous to amass large amounts of men into small spaces as new weaponry could easily desolate an entire army in ways unthinkable prior to the twentieth century. Likewise, a rifleman with a breach loading carbine rifle could easily hold as much ground as five or more of his muzzle loading predecessors.

Generals would still be present in the vicinity of danger, but the highest levels of command and authority were usually found in relative safety to the rear. The lower ranking officers were usually found at the sharp end of the spear, in the thick of the fighting. The responsibility of the junior officers, in terms of square miles had grown proportionally with the area of responsibility of the army as a whole.

But the more things changed, the more they stayed the same. As new technologies allowed armies to do more with less, the battlefield grew from a couple of square miles to the point where they could span entire countries, and almost entire continents. Before the average distance between the left and right wings of an army would have been a couple of miles at most, but now it could be as much as a hundred miles or more. With the expansion of the battlefield also came the blurring of the continuum between the realms of tactics, strategy and grand strategy. Broken down to its simplest denominators war is essentially a question of troop numbers, troop movements, logistics and leadership. In the way that the modern age grew the battlefield and caused the realm of tactics to overlap that of strategy, it also proportionately grew the realm of strategy to overlap that of grand strategy and therefore expanded the sphere of grand strategy to the point where it encompassed nearly every inch of the globe. In short, the modern age witnessed the exponential expansion of society and with society also with war.

One of the most noticeable, if not the most important, changes to warfare (and society) was the introduction of flight into the equation. While flight was a spectacular innovation it has often had its importance exaggerated. Airplanes unlocked a third dimension on the battlefield that had never been exploited, but the plane was essentially another vehicle and it tended to assume roles that were as old as war itself; supply, transport, reconnaissance and bombardment. Staying power on the ground was and is still essential for success in war, but the addition of airpower could greatly enhance a side's efficiency if co-ordinated properly with ground forces.[3]

Perhaps though, the greatest change ushered in by the modern age wasn't the blurred continuum of tactics, strategy and grand strategy but rather the subsequent re-calibration. Out of necessity came the creation of an administrative level of command – generally known as the 'chiefs of staff' or the 'general staff'. The 'staffs' were tasked with creating the war plans that would largely concern itself with the logistics of supply and troop movements on the level of grand strategy and strategy. Such planning became increasingly necessary as it alleviated the various grades of general officers from the responsibilities of strategic policy. In the modern age it would no longer be possible or desirable to have, for example, a John Churchill directing the entirety of the United Kingdom's strategic policy while at the same time tactically commanding the army to his front in pitched battle. This development had been a long time coming but sometime around the turn of the twentieth century all the pieces were in place.

The era that had been ushered in by the Concert of Europe and the harnessing of steam brought with it a new hope of peace, prosperity and progress for the people of Europe and the world. But a dark sickness had been festering in the heart of Europe that threatened to destroy all the progress mankind had made since the fall of Napoleon.

♦ ♦ ♦

Prussia had been created in the Thirteenth and Fourteenth century by an order of Teutonic knights crusading against the heathen Slavs of the southern Baltic region. The knights were a military order sanctioned by the Catholic Church to colonize and Christianize the north eastern plain of Europe that had (and has) been used as a highway for invasions into western and southern Europe.[4] This area was on the path taken by the great barbarian peoples who had overthrown the later Roman Empire. During the feudal-medieval period Prussia had been divided into two sections, Prussia and Brandenburg; they were never truly independent but rather vassal fiefdoms to more powerful kingdoms. By 1701 Prussia had become an independent kingdom in its own right, uniting Brandenburg and Prussia by annexing the land in-between.[5]

Without any easily defendable borders and the fact that they were descendants of a military order, the Prussians were by nature and necessity a military people. Much like the Spartans of old, the Prussian youth began training at an early age and employed stern drill and discipline to ensure that the soldiers they fielded were the most tactically superior units in Europe. Unlike the major powers of the west, Prussia was relatively poor when it came to arable land and too focused on its contiguous land rivals to be able to develop a serious maritime capability.

When France was the dominant power of Europe, Prussia was a natural ally for the United Kingdom and was an integral part of British strategy; Prussia would supply the soldiers, the United Kingdom would supply the finance.[6] This formula had been employed in the wars against Louis XIV, the Seven Years War and the Revolutionary/Napoleonic Wars.

During the Seven Years War, Prussia had been surrounded by enemies on all sides only to be saved from certain destruction by its general-king, Fredrick the Great. With the victory over Napoleon, Prussia had expanded its clout westward over the German principalities towards the Rhine River and the coal rich region of the Ruhr. The acquisition of this new valuable resource[*] allowed for the exponential growth of Prussian power through industry. Before long, Prussia and Austria were at odds over who would hold hegemony over the old (Germanic) Holy Roman Empire, now called the German Confederation.

Troubles emerged between the two German powers after the German Confederation, under the leadership of Prussia and Austria, successfully annexed the southern portion of the Danish peninsula, known as Schleswig-Holstein, from the Kingdom

* Coal was an instrumental ingredient in the production of steam.

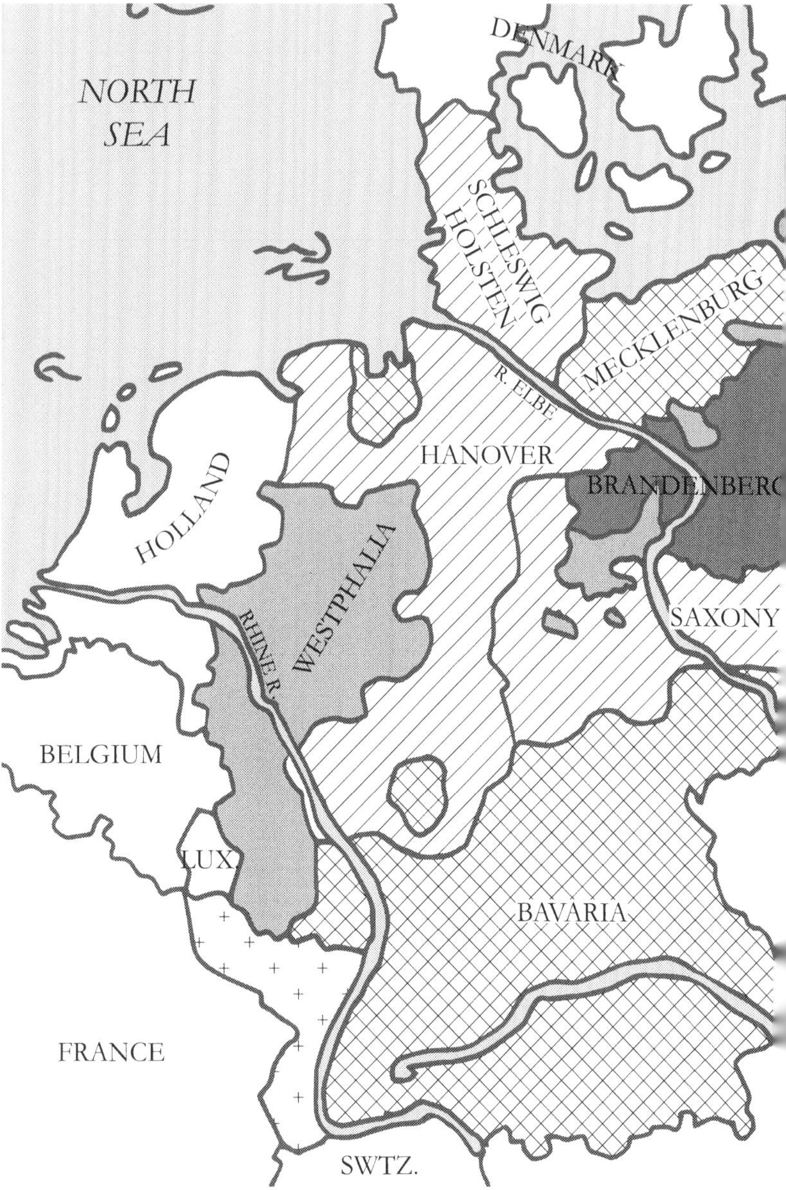
DENMARK
NORTH SEA
SCHLESWIG HOLSTEN
MECKLENBURG
R. ELBE
HANOVER
HOLLAND
BRANDENBERG
WESTPHALIA
RHINE R.
SAXONY
BELGIUM
LUX.
BAVARIA
FRANCE
SWTZ.

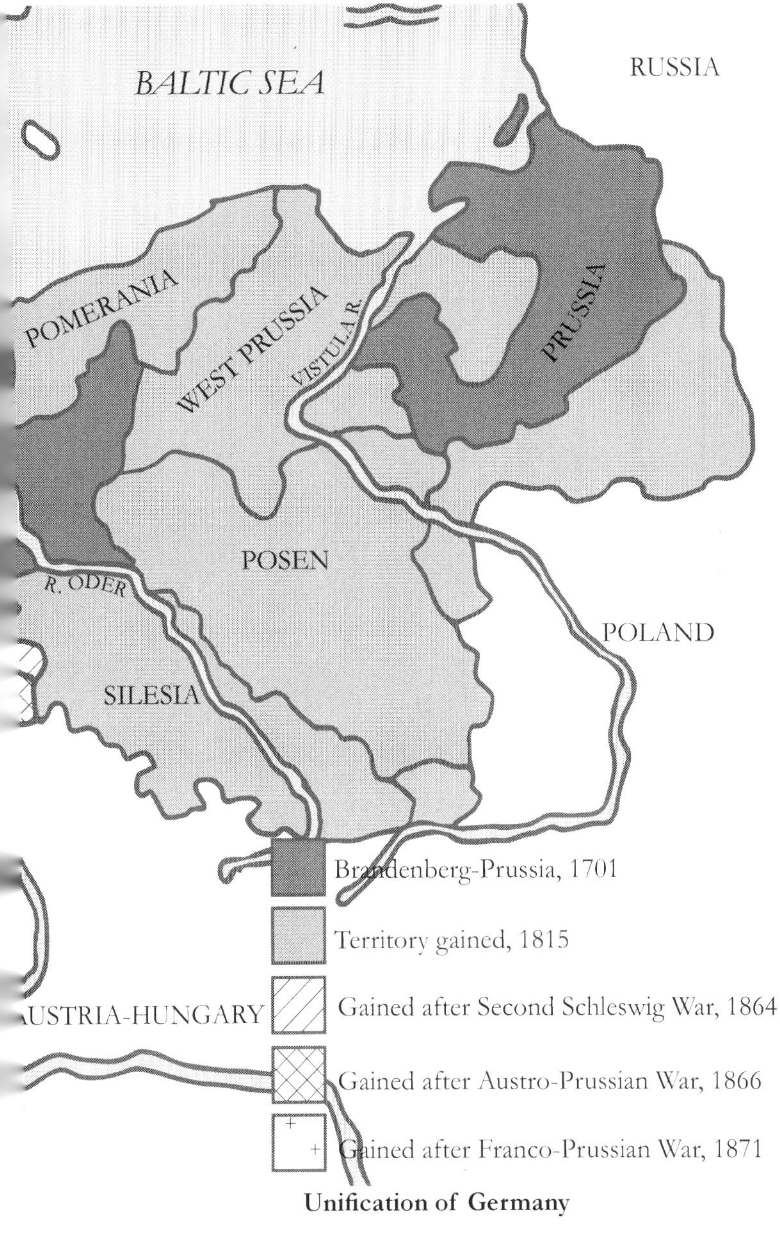

Unification of Germany

of Denmark in 1864. War was declared between Prussia and Austria in 1866 with Prussia emerging victorious; Prussia had very effectively incorporated the new developments of railroads and breach loading rifles into its strategy and won a decisive victory.[7] With Prussia's position of leadership within the German Confederation, The Prussian Chancellor, Otto von Bismarck, was confident enough to instigate a war against Prussia's traditional enemy, France and her Emperor Napoleon III.*

The immediate cause belli were the perceived insult picked up by the French contained within the 'Ems dispatch'.[8] Both sides were wary of each other's potential future threat, but both had confidence that victory would be decisive if they were to act swiftly. Once again the Prussian forces better utilized the new developments and were quick to bring the war onto French territory. At the Battle of Sedan the Prussians captured the main French field army including Napoleon III in 1870.

Without a leader, the citizens of Paris created a provisional government for national defence, styled the 'Second Republic', and opted to continue the war by raising additional armies.[9] The new French recruits were no match for the professional, battle hardened Prussians who quickly laid siege to Paris itself. After the capitulation of Paris and the fall of the Republic, King Wilhelm of Prussia went a step further to humiliate the French people by having himself crowned as Emperor of the new German Empire in Louis XIV's palace at Versailles. The peace treaty required France to pay war reparations as well as to acquiesce in the German annexation of the coal producing-industrial regions of Alsace-Lorraine.[10]

The German Empire now stood astride the centre of Europe, but for all that was gained on the continent the Germans had nothing to show for itself outside of Europe. By the time the German Empire was inaugurated in 1871 all the prime

* A nephew of Napoleon Bonaparte, through Napoleon's younger brother Louis.

real estate throughout the world had been snatched up; there were still pickings to be had on the fringes, but those territories weren't particularly endowed with natural resources or strategic value. In 1884-5 the great powers of Europe met in Berlin to finalize the details of their division of the world (Africa in particular);[11] only Afghanistan, Ethiopia, the landlocked portion of China and the Middle Eastern Ottoman Empire remained outside of European hands. The colonies that Germany had been able to secure were almost economically useless except as coaling stations for warships. They did bring some prestige with them but left much to be wanted by the greedy hearts in Berlin.

♦ ♦ ♦

The rise of Germany and their humiliation at Versailles left France seeking revenge for their lost territory and searching for allies to help fulfill its security objectives. That alliance came about in 1890 when France and Russia signed a secret mutual defence treaty.[12] Under the reign of a new Emperor, Kaiser Wilhelm II, and the leadership of a new chancellor, Germany was becoming (and felt) increasingly isolated within Europe. Wilhelm II attempted to reach out to the various powers (with the exception of France) for an alliance, but his own pet policies, regarding increased naval construction and financial isolation, only worsened German relations with Great Britain and Russia.[13] At the end of the day, Germany and Austria were able to mend fences and crafted a defensive alliance that would come to be known as the Central Powers.

Great Britain was now the only power left in isolation, it had traditionally sought to stay aloof from continental relations only abandoning its policy of isolation in favour of brief wartime coalitions against whomever was threatening to become a hegemon. Kaiser Wilhelm's initiation of the naval construction race between Germany and the United Kingdom made it clear to the British government that Germany had ambitions to disrupt the status quo on the waves, in Europe, and beyond. In 1904 the United Kingdom and France signed the 'Entente Cordiale' which essentially settled colonial boundaries between the two states and established promises of mutual defence.[14] Before long the UK would join with Russia and France in their defensive alliance making up the Triple Entente. With the powers of Europe now divided into two camps the prospect for another century of peace was bleak to say the least; all that was needed was a spark to set the continent ablaze.

The spark that ignited the conflict came when Archduke Franz Ferdinand (heir apparent of the Austrian Empire) was assassinated while touring Sarajevo. The man responsible for the murder was a member of the Serbian nationalist terror group, the 'Black Hand', which was bent on keeping Serbia from being absorbed into the Austrian Empire. The Austrians were quick to declare war and mobilize their forces against Serbia; the Russians, who had a treaty with the Serbs and shared a common ethnicity, mobilized against the Austrians.[15] In support of their Austrian partners, the German Empire pre-emptively attacked France by invading through the neutral country of Belgium, thus forcing the United Kingdom and France into the war.

Part of the overall German strategy was to hold the Russians in the east with a reduced force while attempting to overwhelm French resistance in the west. After initial success against the French, the German advance* became bogged down and both sides began to dig themselves into field entrenchments that would become permanent structures over the next few years. In the east, the Russians planned to use their numerical superiority to overwhelm the Germans. However, the western advance of the Russians would push their supply line to the breaking point.

Although the Germans and Austrians were outnumbered by the Russians in the east, the Russians were forced by the Priprat Marshes to split their forces allowing the numerically weak Central Powers to defeat the Russians in detail at the Battles of

* Known as the Schlieffen Plan.

Tannenberg and the Masurian Lakes.[16] While the war in the east petered out, ending with the eventual collapse of the Russian government under the weight of military incompetence, internal, and foreign subversion and the threat of further German success, the war in the west intensified to the point of absurdity.

When Britain entered the war it immediately resorted to its ancient naval strategy and quickly bottled the German Navy up in its ports. To counter the British blockade, the Germans resorted to using the relatively new war machine, the submarine in an attempt to cut off the British Isles from importing supplies.[17] As the war in the west ground into a contest of attrition, in 1915 the British (and to a lesser extent the French) decided to open a second front on the Central Powers southern border. By this time the Ottoman Empire had joined with Germany and Austria, and were attempting to control the Suez Canal, threatening to disrupt allied shipping and reinforcements from India and Australia. In 1915, the Lord of the Admiralty, Sir Winston Churchill,* put a plan in motion to attack the Dardanelles and carve up the Ottoman Empire. The attack at Gallipoli was poorly commanded and failed to properly seize the initiative and surprise. What could have potentially forced the Ottomans out of the war became bogged down into trench warfare and the British were forced to withdraw from the peninsula.

Even with these setbacks the British still had options to bring the war to the Ottomans. Using Egypt as a base of operations the 'Egyptian Expeditionary Forces' took the fight north into the Palestine/Trans Jordan region and successfully pushed the Ottomans back towards the Anatolian Plateau.[18] Along the way, the British were aided in their advance by the Arabic tribesmen who could and did operate with ruthless efficiency throughout the stretch of desert west of the Euphrates and east of the Mediterranean coast. The war in the Middle East kept the Otto-

* Descendent of John Churchill, Duke of Marlborough and future Prime Minister.

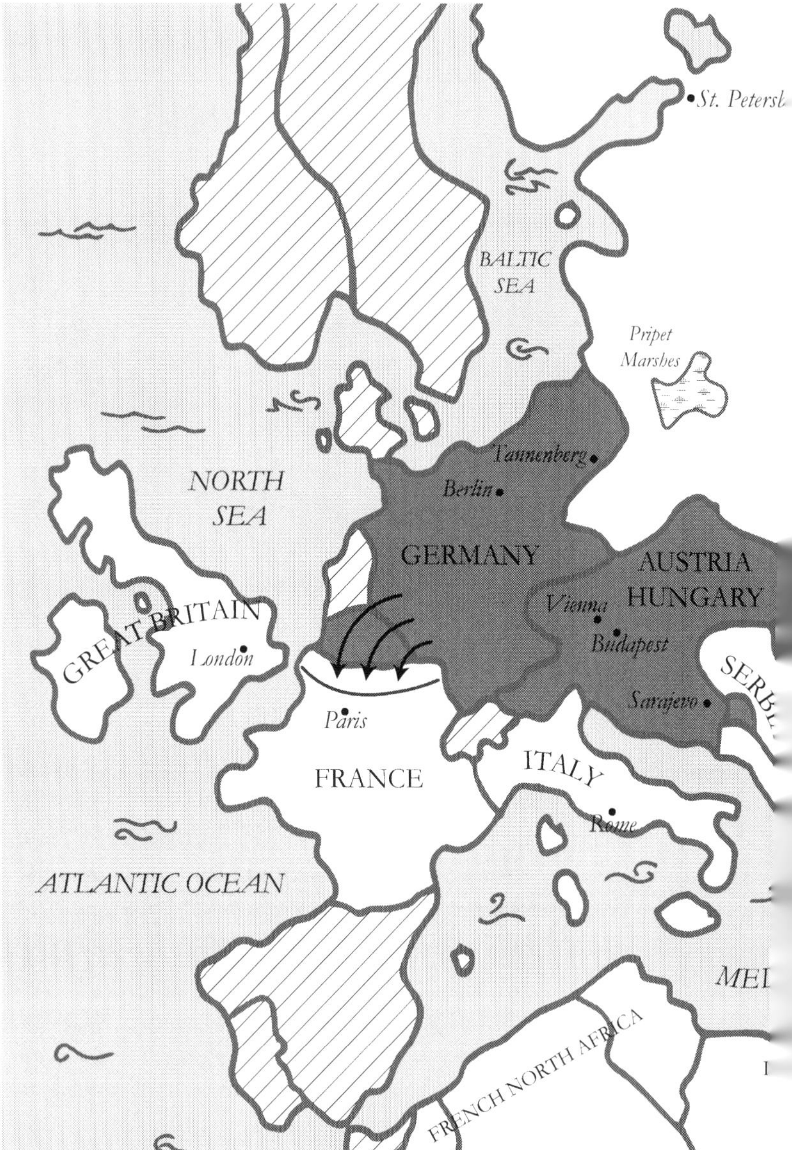
St. Petersb
BALTIC
SEA
Pripet
Marshes
Tannenberg
Berlin
NORTH
SEA
GERMANY
AUSTRIA
HUNGARY
Vienna
Budapest
GREAT BRITAIN
London
SERB
Paris
Sarajevo
ITALY
FRANCE
Rome
ATLANTIC OCEAN
MED
FRENCH NORTH AFRICA

First World War

mans attention fixated upon that sector and even drew some of Germany's resources into that theatre and away from Northern France.

After the capitulation of the Russian government in 1917, the Germans were able to recall their soldiers from the east and redeploy them in the west. But with the bad news for the allies also came some good, in the form of the United States entering the war on the side of France and the United Kingdom. In the Germans attempt to strangle the British Isle's they had instituted a policy of unlimited submarine warfare which meant they would attack any ship (regardless of nationality or neutrality) that was destined for British ports. In 1915, the unrestricted submarine war policy directly led to the deaths of 139 Americans.[19] Still President Woodrow Wilson kept America out of the war as the German government promised to abandon their policy.

As the war dragged on, and the German economy buckled under the British blockade, the Germans felt it necessary to reinstitute the unrestricted submarine policy - declaring all waters surrounding the British Isles as a war zone. The policy incensed the American public, but what really pushed them into the allied camp was the publication of the Zimmerman telegram; a captured communication between the German and Mexican governments, promising aid from Germany if the Mexicans were to initiate a war with their neighbours to the north.[20] Even though Mexico declined Germany's offer, the Telegram proved Germany's less than friendly intentions towards the United States. While American military aid would take a while before it materialized in Europe, the United States entry into the war revitalized the morale of the allies.

The Germans, who had miscalculated with their submarine policy and their attempts to woo the Mexicans with diplomacy, now gambled with a major spring offensive in the west to end the war in 1918 before the full weight of the United States could be brought to bare against Germany. The offensive was stalled soon after it began and was thrown back while the British made limited yet important breakthroughs with their deployments of the newly developed tank and the new tactic of the creeping barrage.* By the fall of 1918 the German trench system was broken and the army in retreat. Furthermore, the economy was in shambles and the Kaiser's regime operating under the threat of revolution. An armistice was signed on November 11, 1918 putting an end to the killing that had inaugurated the modern age.

* Coordinating infantry attacks with artillery bombardments, each moving forward together.[21]

Dwight D. Eisenhower

Dwight David Eisenhower was born October 14, 1890 in Denison, Texas to his parents Ida and David; he was the third of seven boys. The family name, Eisenhower, came from Dutch-German ancestors who had immigrated to the British American colonies prior to the American Revolution.[1] Shortly after Dwight's birth the family moved from Texas to Abilene, Kansas in 1892. Dwight came to consider Abilene his hometown and it was there that he broadened his appreciation for the outdoors under the apprenticeship of a kindly older man.

His parents raised him in a religious manner, with daily Bible readings, as well Dwight was to become an avid reader of history, especially military history. Although his mother was an ardent pacifist, the family had a collection of history books that Dwight devoured with alacrity. In his early teens Dwight was diagnosed with a leg infection that was believed to be life threatening by the local doctor; but luckily for mankind Dwight recovered to his healthy, pre-infection self.

The Eisenhower family was unable to afford sending all their children to college, so Dwight and his brother, Edgar, made a pact together, one would work for a year while the other studied.[2] Every year the two would alternate positions until they were both finished. Dwight was to go second and when his year at work was up, he was persuaded by his brother to wait and continue working for another year. In the meantime, one of Dwight's friends brought to his attention that he could apply to either Annapolis (the navy college) or West Point (the army college) as neither school required tuition, only the promise of subsequent service. After requesting his case to be examined by the U.S. Senator of Kansas (Joseph L. Barlow), Dwight won an entrance exam contest which granted him acceptance into West Point in 1911.[3]

By 1915, Dwight graduated amongst one of histories most celebrated classes, later known as the 'class the stars fell on' for the high percentage of generals it would one day produce.[4] Dwight did not graduate at the top of the class, but it is reported that he was fond of his studies and that he enjoyed the bonds of friendship created there. Once graduated, Dwight served in the infantry while being sent around the country from camp to camp. While stationed in Texas, Dwight was married to Mamie Geneva Doud in 1916; they would produce two sons although the first would die at the age of three.[5]

When the United States entered the Great War against the Central Powers, Germany and Austria-Hungary, Dwight was denied his request to be sent over to France with a combat commission. Instead Dwight was assigned to Fort Leavenworth, Texas before being transferred to Maryland then Gettysburg, Pennsylvania where he was tasked with training the new 'tank corps'.[6] Although Dwight never saw action in the actions of the Great War, he was noted for his organization capabilities working with the tank corps and his ability to assign his subordinates in positions within the organization to maximize its efficiency.

After the conclusion of peace in 1918, Dwight served as staff under the command of various generals. In the immediate aftermath he had been promoted to major and assigned as an observer to the cross country march designed to showcase the new mobility of the mechanized forces. The march from Washington D.C. to San Francisco averaged five miles a day,[7] a worse average than non-mechanized units from days gone by; a sad display for the new organization and the state of the American transportation infrastructure, but these were lessons that could be learned from. Soon after the march, Dwight was reassigned to the tank corps before being sent to the Panama Canal Zone where he served as executive officer to General Fox Conner.

From Panama, Dwight was returned to the United States and was enrolled at the Command and General Staff College where he graduated first in class.[8] In 1935 Dwight was transferred to the Philippines to advise the local government on the creation of their army; in this role he was subordinate to General Douglas MacArthur (of later Pacific fame). Once returned to the United States, Dwight was promoted to Brigadier General after having successfully performed in the Louisiana Maneuvers* in 1939.[9] After the completion of the maneuvers in Louisiana, Dwight was transferred to the War Plans Division were he would serve until the US became actively involved in the world war.

♦ ♦ ♦

The peace treaty that was signed at Versailles in 1919 officially ended the war that had seen the deaths of countless millions of Europeans and others from around the globe. Unlike after the war with Napoleon the peace that followed this war did not bring stability back to the people of Europe or the world. The Treaty of Versailles was responsible for the creation of numerous smaller nation-states in Europe as the larger empires of Russia, Austria and the Ottoman, had been broken up during the course of the war.[10] Economic prosperity was also short lived, the early twenties saw an economic boom throughout the west, but by the end of the decade the steam had run out. In 1929 the stock market crashed on Wall Street bringing an end to the prosperity of the post-war period.

The ideology of communism (as espoused by Marx and Engels) had been expanding its influence throughout Europe for over half a century. When the Russian imperial family was overthrown by the communist, Vladimir Lenin, it was the first time in history the ideology was given a home within a state. Russia

* A large scale army maneuver involving some four hundred thousand men.

was renamed the United Soviet Socialist Republics. The main tenet of communist ideology was that no individual should be allowed to own private property, all profits/produce would be owned collectively by the centralized government.[11] While the Soviet government claimed its legitimacy from the people, the democracy the state purported to represent was practically non-existent (there was only one party to vote for). The government was run by an authoritarian party with a dictator at the helm. Theoretically all powerful, the state had the power to redistribute wealth across the board and was invested with the ownership of all production, be it industrial or agricultural.

On an economic level, communism is the polar opposite of capitalism and almost as soon as the war was over, the liberal, capitalist democracies of the west intervened in what was then a Russian civil war between monarchists and communists. In an attempt to restore the Imperial family and capitalism to the Russian state the west gave assistance to the monarchists known as the 'White Russians'. After the communists emerged victorious from the civil war, the government launched a series of five year plans aimed at modernizing the Russian economy and entrenching the Communist Party in power. These plans were directly responsible for the starvation and deaths of millions of Soviet subjects, especially those subjects living to the west of Russia proper in the Ukraine and eastern Poland.[12] By the time the Great Depression came about in (1929) the USSR was largely unaffected by the worldwide economic crisis because their recent economic policies had already brought about an even worse calamity; things simply couldn't get any worse for the average Soviet citizen.

In contrast to the Soviet economy (which was beginning a recovery), the liberal democracies and the capitalist economies of the west were dramatically affected by the stock market crash of 1929. Unemployment skyrocketed as governments around the world ineffectively attempted to alleviate their populations' sufferings by enacting policy that increased the states responsibility for its citizen's welfare. The ideology of socialism was quickly becoming legitimate in the countries experiencing the worst effects of the failing free market.

Socialism is/was basically a mix between capitalism and communism, in that there is still individual ownership of property and profits, but the state generally controls the means of production (usually that of industry) and employs progressive taxation (i.e. high taxes) as a way to mitigate the gulf between the rich and poor. Most governments and societies in the west (especially the English speaking world) were still uneasy about the state owning industry, but found it acceptable to adopt progressive tax policies in order to fund back-to-work infrastructure projects. The new economic policies had mixed results when it came to reducing unemployment and growing the economy, but were reasonably successful when it came to restoring confidence in the stock market.

In Italy a strongman, Benito Mussolini, had risen in the image of a reincarnated Roman Emperor. Mussolini combined a populist, state centric form of socialism with a heavy dose of police state authoritarianism.[13] That mixture would soon become infamous under the name of fascism.

Germany was perhaps the country hardest hit by the depression, not only did it have a capitalist economy, but it had also lost its industrial heartland along the Rhine River and was on the line for war reparations to be paid out to the victors of the Great War. Unemployment and inflation became so bad that the German currency became worthless; extreme measures from the government would need to be taken.[14] On top of the near perfect storm of the economic crisis, the Germans did not have a strong tradition of constitutional parliamentary government, and so, when push came to shove the German people accepted a radical demagogue to lead them as their Fuhrer.

Much like the fascists in Italy the National-Socialist Party (or

Nazi Party) mixed a very strong form of socialist economics with police state authoritarianism and topped it all off with a virile racism/ethnic superiority complex that has rarely been equaled before or since. Adolph Hitler, the leader of the Nazi Party is now considered the personification of evil, but at the time people from around the world, and all over the political spectrum admired him for various reasons. Once Hitler seized power in a coup in 1933, he proceeded to direct the economy towards the improvement of German infrastructure and the reconstruction of the German military as a way to drastically reduce unemployment and to improve the economy.[15] Hitler had managed to put Germany back to work, but by reconstructing the military, Hitler had broken treaties and put Germany on a collision course with Europe and the rest of the world. This time though the Germans would have a strong ally outside of Europe, Imperial Japan.

The Japanese had been allied with Great Britain and the Entente powers during the First World War, but had become alienated after Versailles as they believed they were not being treated as equals amongst the major European powers.[16] In the mid-Nineteenth century the Japanese had begun the process of modernization and had since then sought to learn as much from the Europeans as possible. They built their army on the model of the Prussians and their navy on that of the British.

The main Japanese islands were not particularly endowed with resources, so once the military was deemed ready the government sought to carve out an empire for itself on the Asian mainland. At first encountering the Russian Empire in nearby Manchuria, the Japanese embarrassed the Russians on land and sea during the Russo-Japanese war in 1905. After the First World War the Japanese government (now heavily influenced by their military) grew weary of western self-righteousness, regarding national self-determination, and began to increase the pace of their conquest in East Asia. While Japan began to bite off large chunks of China, it was also busy casting its greedy eyes on the various European colonial interests in the region and waited for their opportunity to strike.

♦ ♦ ♦

At the heart of its ideology, the Nazi regime in Germany did not accept the Treaty of Versailles' status quo. The regime depended on expanding its borders (at the expense of its neighbours) to placate its population and to supplement its economic base. The first provocation employed by Hitler was to occupy and remilitarize the Ruhr region in March of 1936 something that was strictly prohibited by the Versailles treaty. This act incurred no wrath upon the Nazi regime. The next territory that was seized was the newly created nation-state of Austria* in 1938 . Through the device of a rigged election the Nazi Party of Austria invited the German state to merge the two states into one; this event would later become known as the Anschluss, which is German for connection or union.[17] The Anschluss between the two countries created pressure on Czechoslovakia, whose western territory, was heavily populated by German nationals,† and was now wedged in-between the new German Reich.

Hitler began to agitate for the annexation of the Sudetenland which caused the major powers of Europe to hold a conference at Munich to attempt a peaceful settlement. Ominously, the Czechs were not invited to observe or participate.[18] The Munich Agreement was largely a success for Hitler as he achieved his goal of annexing the Sudetenland without sparking a general war with France and the United Kingdom (as those two powers had a military alliance with the Czechs. Believing that the Germans would cease in their efforts of expansion, the Munich

* The non-German provinces of the Austrian Empire had been separated from Germanic Austria, in the aftermath of the First World War..

† The Sudetenland, as it was called, was highly industrialized, and was home to the Skoda arms manufacturing industrial complex. At that point Skoda was one of the most advanced, and productive arms manufacturing concern in the world.

Agreement was also claimed as a success in the eyes of the war weary western politicians and public who were fearful of reliving the carnage of the First World War. When he returned to London, British Prime Minister Neville Chamberlain infamously proclaimed there would be 'peace in our time'.[19] In Hitler's eyes the appeasement engaged in by the French and British politicians proved that they were weak and in no position to engage Germany in another war.

And so, believing he could gain more territory without going to war in the west, Hitler reached out to the Soviet dictator, Joseph Stalin, and negotiated the 'Non-Aggression Pact' between the two states creating an agreement by which the two dictators agreed not to attack each other and carve up and divide Poland amongst themselves. On September 1st, 1939 the German and Soviet armies converged upon Poland from the east and west and were able to crush Polish resistance within a matter of weeks. Poland was a red line in the sand for the British and French,* after which war was officially declared against Germany.[20]

When the Germans invaded Poland in 1939, they had left their western frontier largely undefended under the assumption that the French and British wouldn't act with sufficient speed or resolve even if they did declare war. Hitler's gamble proved correct, a defensive strategic doctrine had taken deep root in France, where the belief was prevalent that the next war would be fought much like the last war, the First World War. The French had spent the interwar period building a massive fortification complex called the 'Maginot Line' along their eastern frontier with Germany.[21] The British, who would need to cross the English Channel before coming to grips with the Germans, had wasted much of their technological advantages (in the realm of tanks and fighter aircraft) through budget cuts to the military during the interwar period. The British would spend much of

* There was another defensive alliance between the UK, France, and Poland.

the remainder of 1939 and the spring of 1940 transporting their army over the channel into Belgium and France.

Once the Germans had secured their border with the USSR in Poland, they began to shift their soldiers back to their western frontier in anticipation for the spring offensive in 1940. This intervening period of military inactivity, known as the 'Phony War' would be suddenly disrupted by the new German strategic doctrine of lightening warfare, or in German, 'Blitzkrieg'.

In contrast to the armies of Great Britain and France, who had barely changed since the Great War, the new German army had highly developed the new technologies of tanks, trucks and airplanes to new levels. Most importantly the Germans had stressed the integration of their new war machines into their tactical doctrines. Generally speaking, the armoured units would be used to punch holes through an enemy's lines, overrunning the enemy as they retreated instead of turning back to deal with the pockets of resistance that remained. The German infantry would then be used to follow up the armour and clear out the left over defences. All the while the fighter and bomber aircraft would coordinate (via radio) with the ground units to break up any hardened resistance.

With the initiative given over to the Germans, Hitler and his generals seized the opportunity and attacked France without remorse. Through the use of mobility, firepower and the coordination of the various arms, the Germans pushed the French through the Ardennes hills and the south of Belgium.[22] The German blitz resembled the strategic maneuver of the Schlieffen Plan of 1914, only this time it worked. The French center and left wing was routed in the Ardennes and Belgium while their right wing in the Maginot Line was cut off and forced to surrender.

Almost as soon as the British disembarked in France they were forced to withdraw in the face of the German onslaught.*

* The Germans neglected to pursue the British as they felt that capturing

The evacuation of some three hundred thousand British (and some French) military personnel at Dunkirk was nothing short of a miracle that went a long way towards salvaging the morale of the British public.[23]

In under two months the new German army had been able to achieve what was impossible in the west only twenty-five years earlier; the complete destruction of the French ability to conventionally resist. With France under German occupation and a puppet regime in Vichy, the only government remaining in open resistance to the Nazi horde was that of the United Kingdom. The summer months of 1940 would be the darkest days the British Isle would face in almost a thousand years of its history as the war would now be brought directly to the seas and skies around and overtop the proud, defiant nation.

Seeing as the British Navy made it impossible for the Germans to invade the Isles with land forces, they were now forced to assault the British by other means. In an attempt to quickly knock the British out of the war, the Germans resorted to their old strategy of blockade by submarine while putting their recently created air force to the test. At first the German air force's (or Luftwaffe) strategy was to attack the Royal Air Force bases throughout southern England. The 'Battle of Britain' initially was going in favour of the Germans as they attacked the RAF's airfields and production facilities, but suddenly in the fall of 1940 Hitler directed his Luftwaffe general to switch targets away from British air capabilities to British civilian centers in an effort to terrorize the public into submission.[24] The new British Prime Minister, Winston Churchill, was supremely capable at rallying the British people, steeling their resolve to continue the war against the Nazis, alone if need be. When Hitler decided to shift focus towards the cities he gave the RAF a reprieve and allowed them to rebuild their air force.

Having largely failed to destroy the British ability to resist

Paris was a higher priority.

with the air campaign, Hitler looked to the south in order to shore up his Italian allies as they tried to conquer the British holdings in North Africa and the Middle East. Come the early spring of 1941, the British and American governments signed the 'Lend Lease' agreement, which sold fifty destroyers to the UK and guaranteed that munitions and food stuffs would be supplied to the British in exchange for access to the global network of British bases.[25] While the United States was not actively involved in the war, it had set itself up as the 'arsenal of democracy' and provided a lifeline to the only belligerent power left in resistance to the ascendant Axis powers.

After having been thwarted by the RAF in 1940-41, Hitler set in motion his most ambitious plan to date; the invasion and occupation of Soviet Russia. Operation Barbarossa broke the treaty of non-aggression between the two dictators and expanded the war on an enormous scale. The United Kingdom and the USSR had multiple reasons to distrust each other, but now neither state would go it alone against their common Nazi foe. Before long an alliance between the two was brokered.

The Japanese had signed a non-aggression treaty in the spring of 1941 with the Soviets in the far east and now, in collusion with their Nazi allies, shifted their attention south towards the British and western European colonial holdings. With incredible rapidity the Japanese occupied the coast of China and went on to invade French Indochina. The opportunistic Japanese aggression provoked economic sanctions on key war materials* from the United States.[26] With these new sanctions imposed upon them, the Japanese understood that further conquest would be necessary for them to acquire the materials necessary to wage war and maintain their positions.

The Japanese believed that sooner or later the United States would enter the war on the side of the British and to that undesirable end, they planned to pre-emptively attack the American

* Such as rubber and oil.

Pacific fleet hoping to buy enough time for them to consolidate their empire before the Americans could enter the war decisively.[27] On December 7, 1941 the Japanese launched their surprise attack on the US naval base at Pearl Harbour, Hawaii while simultaneously continuing their advances into Thailand, Burma, Malaysia, the Philippines and the New Guinean Islands.

A few weeks after the Japanese brought the Americans into the war against them, Hitler decided to act in concert with his Asian ally and declared war on the United States. Come the new year of 1942, the British were on the defensive and under threat of invasion in their colonial strongholds of India and Australia, but luckily for the Allied cause the United States had now officially entered the war and pledged to fight it out on both the Pacific and European fronts.

♦ ♦ ♦

With Hitler's declaration of war against the American Republic amidst his invasion of Soviet Russia, it became of the utmost importance for the United States to extend a lifeline of manufactured goods and raw materials to the Soviet Union. Of equal importance to the allied war effort was the insertion of American troops into direct combat against the forces of Nazism. The Soviet dictator, Joseph Stalin, had lobbied the British and American governments to open up a second front with an invasion of France. While sympathetic to the Soviet plight, the American President, Franklin Delano Roosevelt, was persuaded by the more experienced and practical Winston Churchill that an invasion of France was impractical at the moment. mainly due to logistical considerations.[28] Instead of France, the British and Americans agreed upon a plan for the invasion and expulsion of German forces from North Africa. In the meantime, the United States began to transport men and material to the British Isle's in preparation for a move against the Germans.

When the United States initially entered into the war Eisenhower was serving under General George Marshall on the gen-

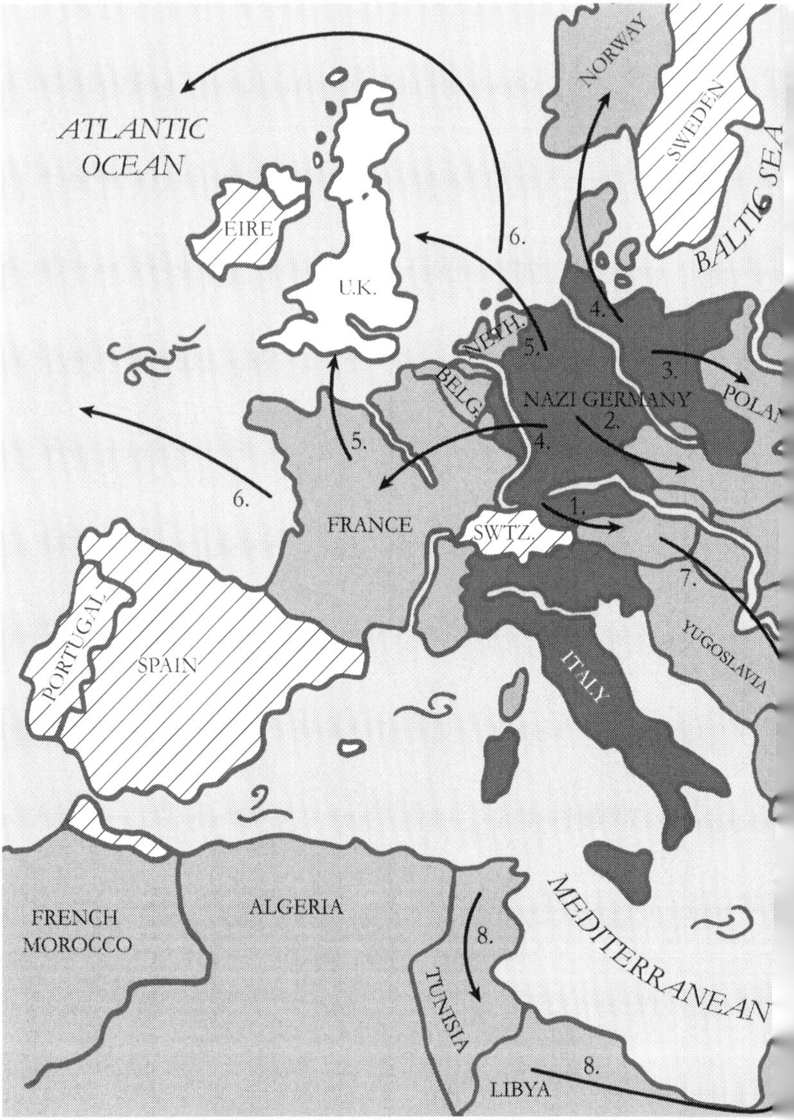

Nazi Germany's Advances

1. Anschluss between Germany & Austria. 2. Nazi annexation of the Czech Sudetenland. 3. Germany & the USSR divide Poland. 4. Blitz-kreig against Holland, Belgium, France, Denmark, and Norway. 5. The

Battle of Britain. 6. Main thrusts of U-Boat attacks. 7. Nazi invasion of the Balkan states, and Crete. 8. Reinforcement of Italian North Africa, to the Second Battle of el-Alamein. 9. Nazi invasion of the USSR.

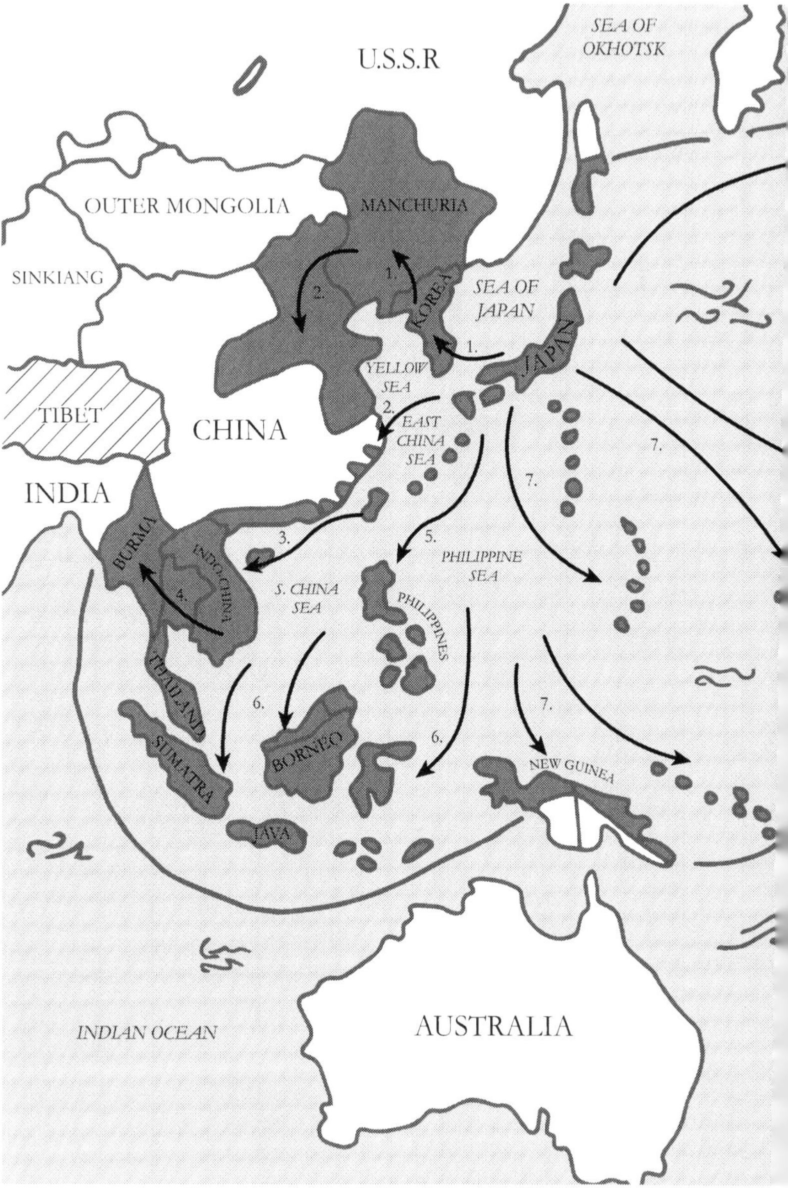

Imperial Japenese Advances

1. Annexation of Korea, and Manchuria, 1910-35. 2. Conquest of northern and coastal China, 1932-45. 3. Invasion of French Indo-China. 4. Invasion of Thailand,

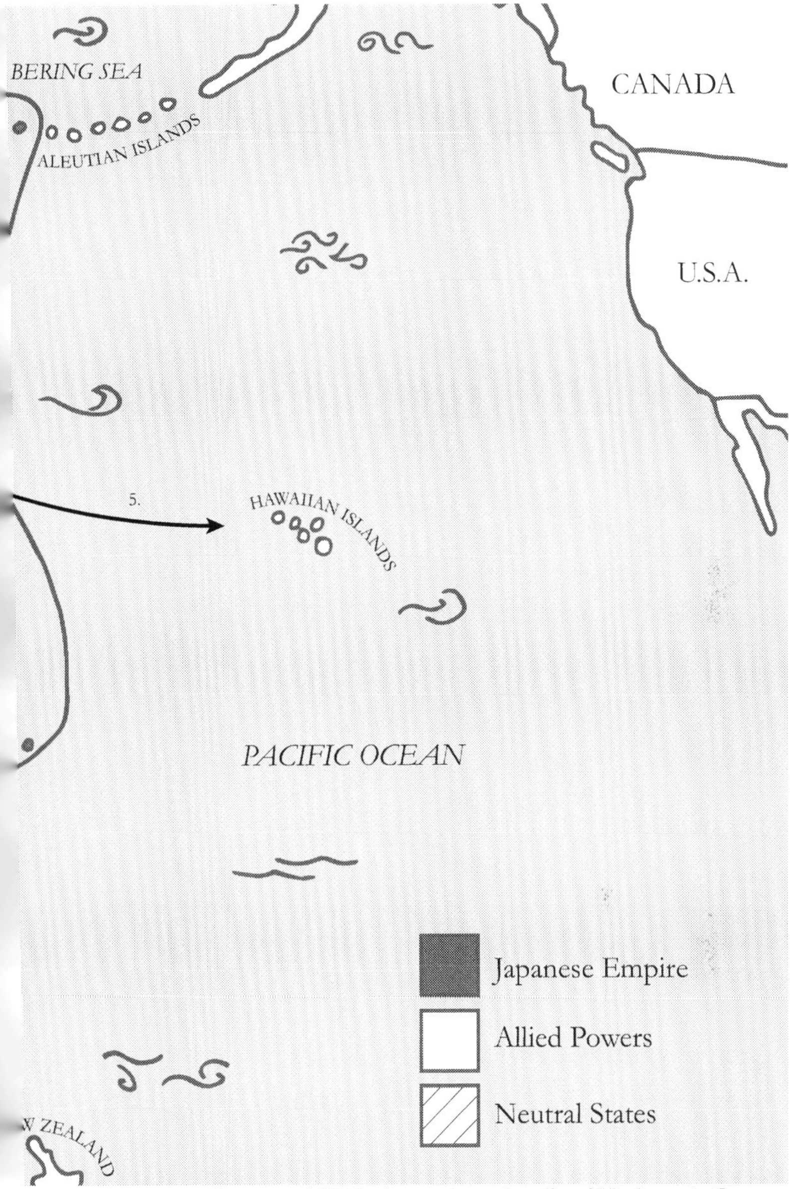

and Burma. 5. Invasion of Philippines and attack on Pearl Harbour. 6. Conquest of the Dutch East Indies. 7. Invasion of Papua New Guinea, and the Pacific Islands.

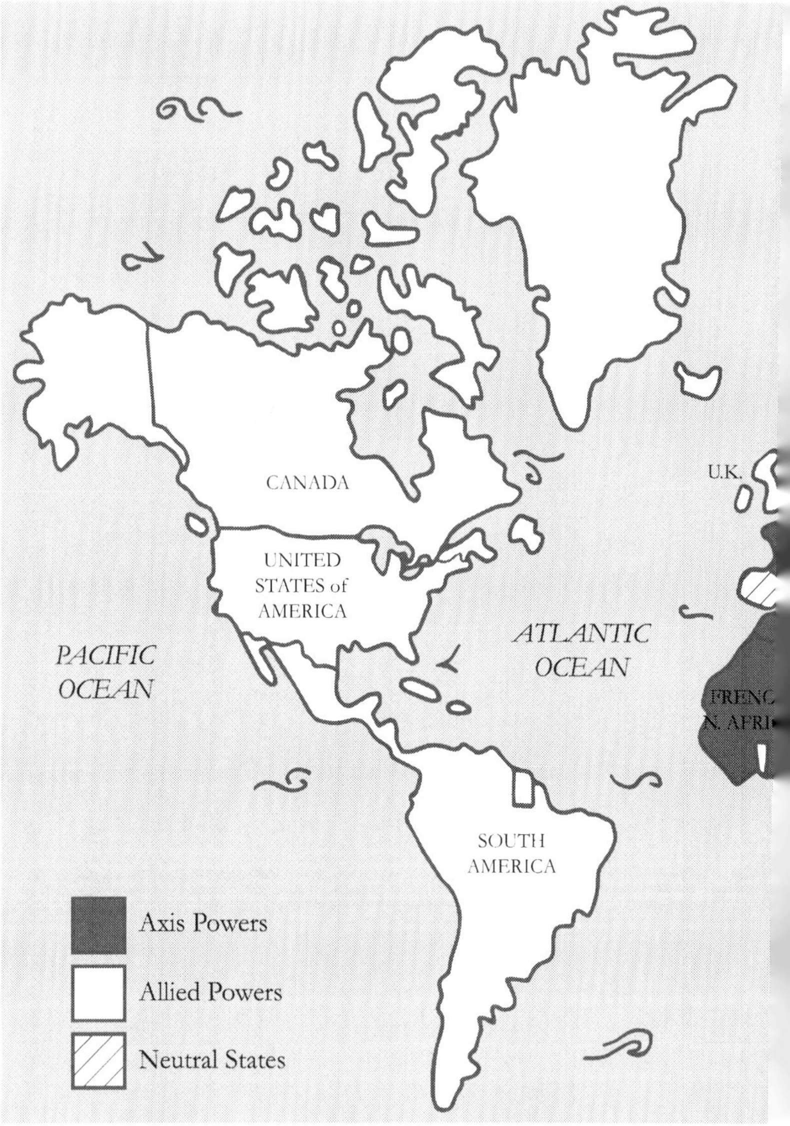
CANADA
UNITED STATES of AMERICA
PACIFIC OCEAN
ATLANTIC OCEAN
SOUTH AMERICA
U.K.
Axis Powers
Allied Powers
Neutral States

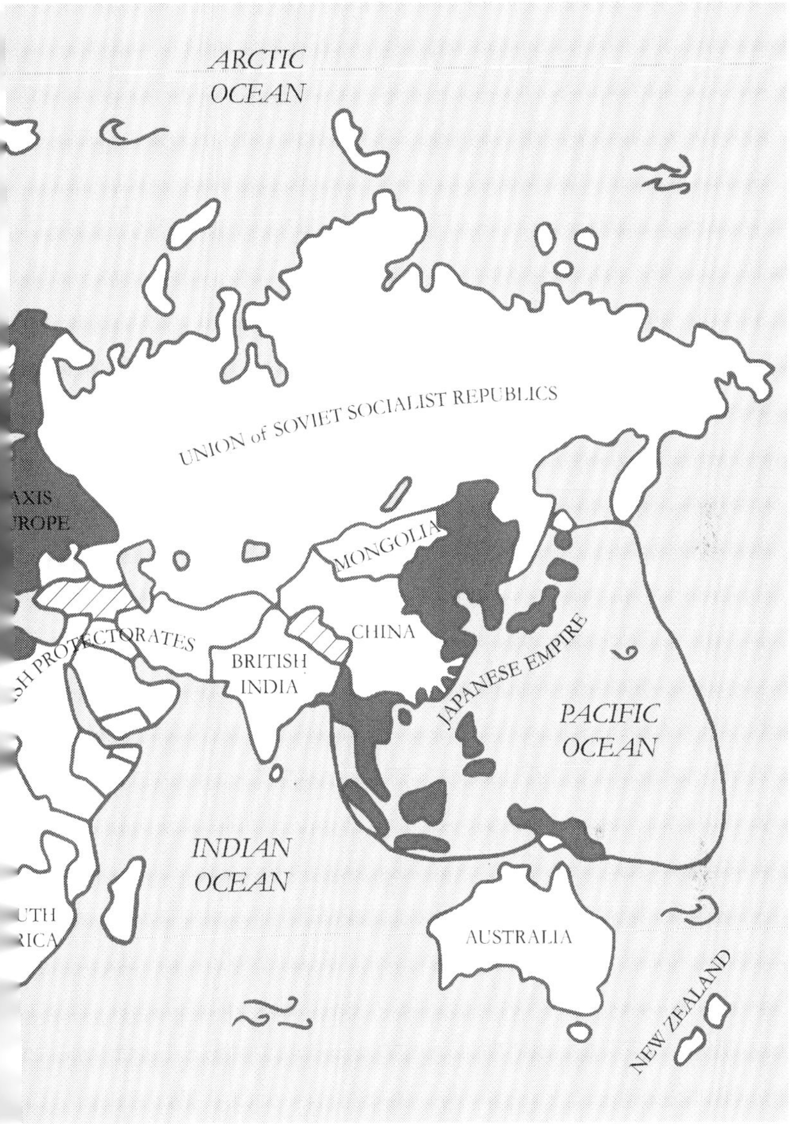

Global Situation in 1942

eral staff in the War Plans Division, before long he was Chief of the War Plans Division and was directly responsible for drafting the strategy for defeating Nazi Germany and Imperial Japan. While working on the general staff General George Marshall became impressed with Eisenhower's aptitude for leadership and organization. Marshall kept a close eye on Eisenhower as he was grooming his protégé for higher command.[29]

In the spring of 1942 Eisenhower was sent to Great Britain to report back to Marshall on the state of the American forces garrisoned there. When Eisenhower's report came back to Washington it was negative in its tone regarding the commanding American officer, General James Chaney. Marshall sent Eisenhower back to Great Britain to replace Chaney and promoted him to Commander of the European Theatre for the United States.[30] Almost as soon as he assumed command in the United Kingdom, Eisenhower was put in charge of coordinating the allied effort for the invasion of North Africa.

Operation Torch as it would come to be codenamed would see American and British combat units' land along the north western coast of Africa. The Allied landings would take place in coordination with the westward drive of the British Eighth Army from Egypt after their victory over General Rommel's 'Afrika Corps' at the Second Battle of el-Alamein. El-Alamein proved to be a tipping point for the British as it saved Egypt, the Suez Canal and the oilfields of the Middle East from falling into German hands. Now as General Montgomery was successfully driving the Germans out of Egypt, Libya and into Tunisia, In November of 1942 Operation Torch landed allied forces into French held Morocco and Algiers capturing the three key cities of Casablanca, Oran and Algiers.

The landings were a success and went largely unopposed as the French authority in the colony had been persuaded to side with the allies. However due to petty political infighting amongst the French and logistical difficulties hindered the rapid advance of the Allies from capturing their final objective, the Axis stronghold of Tunisia. As the allied advance became bogged down the Germans were able to reinforce their army in Tunisia and prepare strong defensive positions, amidst the mountainous Tunisian terrain for when the Allies arrived. In comparison to the British and German counterparts, the Americans were extremely inexperienced when they first landed in North Africa, most importantly, generals at the division and battalion levels had rarely been tried in their newfound positions of leadership. This inexperience would cost the Americans dearly when the Germans sprung their ambush and counter attacked the Americans as they advanced through the Kesserine Pass.

The ambush caught the Americans off guard as they were advancing in a leisurely fashion, some of the commanding officer reacted poorly and became demoralized at the shock of the German attack. The 'Marshall system' (which was rigorously practiced by Eisenhower) called for the replacement of officers who could not produce results or were unable to work with others as a member of a team.[31] The generals who failed to maintain operational efficiency under stressful situations were either recalled to Washington or shuffled to another post (often times the officers would be given another chance elsewhere). Eisenhower cared little for rank or seniority, only results; if an officer failed to achieve success within the realm of the possible he would be relieved and replaced by someone who could.

The Battle of Kesserine Pass was the first major battle for Eisenhower to hold authority over. After a few incompetent men were relieved of command, the American juggernaut was once again on the move towards Tunisia and the ancient city of Carthage. In the early spring of 1943 the American forces and the British under Montgomery linked up and were able to isolate the Germans in Tunisia. Regardless of their success at the Battle of Kesserine Pass, defeat was all but inevitable for the Germans. General Rommel, the German commander, requested permission from the German high command to withdraw his forces to Sicily and the Italian mainland; Hitler refused his request. There would be no retreat, but Hitler permitted him to be evacuated back to the continent.[32]

As the Allies advanced the Americans took the city of Bizerte (ancient Utica) while the British seized the capital, Tunis (ancient Carthage). When all was said and done, the Allies were able to capture some two hundred thirty thousand German troops and gained a strategic stepping stone for further conquest into the Axis held 'fortress Europe'. With the Germans now expelled from North Africa the initiative had swung into the allied camp; it was now theirs to lose.

♦ ♦ ♦

Around the same time as the Second Battle of el-Alamein, the Russians had emerged victorious from the colossal Battle/Siege of Stalingrad. The Soviets were finally able to turn the tide against the Nazi and slowly but steadly begin to take back much of their lost territory.

With North Africa now in Allied hands and the Soviets taking the brunt of the violence, Stalin continued to pressure the British and Americans into invading France. Churchill was still hesitant about a cross channel invasion in 1943 and continued to lobby FDR for the Anglo Allies to attack the 'soft underbelly' of Nazi occupied Europe, either in Greece or Italy. At this point FDR had become the arbitrator between Churchill and Stalin and with the weight of American resources, industry and manpower behind his opinion, FDR was more or less able to call the shots on what strategic policy would be pursued. In the immediate aftermath of the Tunisian campaign FDR and Churchill agreed that it was unwise to venture a cross channel invasion, but FDR was still unable to countenance an invasion of Greece (which was advocated by Churchill), as he believed it would have become a quagmire at best, a disaster at worst. Instead of Greece or France, the Anglo Allies were agreed to the invasion of Sicily as a prelude to the invasion of mainland Italy.

The island of Sicily remained as strategically important to the conquest of Italy as it had been in the days of Scipio and Hannibal. Operation Husky would also be the first time in which the British and Americans would be forced to operate as a team in close quarters. Eisenhower was once again put in overall command of the operation with the British commander, Gen. Sir Harold Alexander acting as his deputy and ground commander.[33]

The plan of invasion had three parts. The British army was to make its landing along the southeast coast, including an assault on Syracuse, while two American armies landed along the southern coast to the west of the British. Prior to the amphibious landings of the regular army units, the plan included dropping highly trained parachute divisions further inland to create confusion amongst German communications and seize important bridges in advance of the regular army. As was to become common to airborne operations, the paratroops became scattered once they landed, but were none-the-less able to seize and hold some of their objectives and create sufficient havoc amongst the Axis defenders to be considered a general success.

The seaborne landings were largely successful and the allies were able to expand their beachheads without much trouble. But as soon as their armies began to venture inland the Germans counterattacked and were able to stall the centre (US) and right wing (UK) of the Allied advance. The left wing of the combined allied forces, commanded by General George Patton, was largely left unopposed. Under the initiative of Patton, the left wing was as able to drive towards the northwest with a wide flanking maneuver and capture the important city of Palermo.[34]

Outflanked by Patton's maneuver, the Axis forces withdrew to defensive positions southwest of Mount Etna.* With steady pressure applied against the 'Etna Lines', the allies broke through

* On the north east corner of Sicily.

along the two coastal roads. Unlike the campaign in Tunisia, the German and Italian forces were able to retreat across the Straits of Messina in relative safety and good order. On August the 17th the Allied forces captured Messina which marked the complete liberation of Sicily in under two short months.[35]

Cracks had begun to appear within the commanding ranks of the Allied structures; most notably between Gen. Patton and Gen. Montgomery. Patton was criticizing others for not being aggressive enough, while Montgomery complained that Patton wasn't being a good team player. Eisenhower had been able to successfully manage the important personalities under his command thus averting sore feelings amongst the British and American public. The campaign in Sicily had been a success and with the allies now in undisputed control of the major Mediterranean shipping lanes, it was now possible to begin operations to knock Fascist Italy out of the Axis camp.

Even before the allies could land a single soldier in Italy the fascist dictatorship of Mussolini collapsed as he fled north out of fear of the invasion that was to come. Hitler was irate when he heard of his ally's abdication and sent German reinforcements into Italy to prop up Mussolini's regime in the north and to stiffen Italian resistance.[36] Even with German reinforcements, the Axis forces defending Italy had no idea where the Allied landings would take place and were therefore forced to disperse their units.

Operation Avalanche planned on having three separate landings that were fairly well spread apart. The right wing of the Allied force landed at Taranto on the boot heel of Italy, while the center of the force landed across the Straits of Messina at Reggio di Calabria. The third prong of the assault landed further north (than the other two) along the western coast of Italy at the city of Salerno. After the initial landings in September 1943 the allies were able to consolidate their beachheads and after a heavy German counter-attack had been rebuffed, they began to advance up the peninsula. As soon as the Axis forces gave up on the Allied beachheads they were able to reorganize their defensive lines across the peninsula from the Adriatic to the Mediterranean.

The German high command had come to the conclusion (with which Hitler agreed) that it would be much too costly to defend the peninsula south of Rome. So while they took action to retain the ancient city for as long as possible, their main efforts would be concentrated further north. In the immediate aftermath of the Allied landings and the failed Axis counter attacks, the Germans set up the 'Gustav Lines' of defence to the south of Rome.[37] Fighting, over what would come to be known as the 'Winter Lines' in 1943, resembled the static warfare of the First World War with heavy fighting occurring over the central road into Rome that was dominated by the Monte Casino monastery.

The Italian peninsula was ideal for creating defensive positions with its relatively skinny girth from coast to coast and the Apennines Mountains running the length down the center of the peninsula. The one geographic advantage the Allies could avail themselves of was the long, relatively indefensible western coastline. As long as the Allies retained air superiority and their numbers of landing craft in the theatre they would be able to leap frog past the German lines into the rear. This is exactly what the Allies did in an attempt to break German resistance by landing at Anzio just to the south of Rome in the new year of 1944. The Anzio landing (code named Operation Shingle) caught the Germans unprepared and Rome practically undefended. But the American commander, General John Lucas, threw away his advantage of surprise and decided on consolidating his beachhead at Anzio instead of rapidly advancing on Rome.[38]

The German commander in Italy, General Albert Kesselring, had foreseen the possibility of such an amphibious operation and had planned for such contingencies by creating highly mo-

FRANCE
PORTUGAL
SPAIN
EASTERN TASK FORCE U
1.
Algiers
CENTRAL TASK FORCE U.K.
Gibraltar
1.
Oran
WESTERN TASK FORCE U.S.
1.
Rabat
Casablanaa
ALG
MOROCCO
San

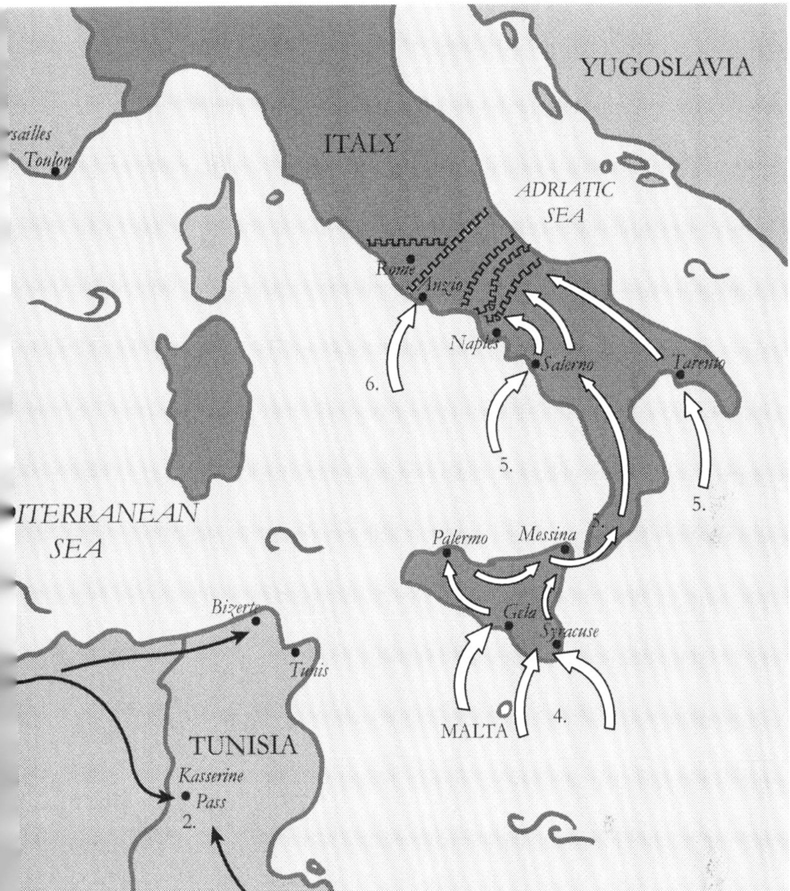

Allied Operations in the Mediterranean

1. Operation Torch. 2. Battle of Kasserine Pass. 3. Gen. Montgomery's 8th British Army links up in Tunisia. 4. Operation Husky. 5. Operation Avalanche. 6. Anzio Landings.

bile units, held in reserve, to be deployed in a rush anywhere they were needed.[39] While the Americans reinforced themselves at Anzio, the Germans dug into defensive positions around the beachhead. After tough fighting, the Allies were able to break through the Winter Lines and relieve pressure on the surrounded beachhead. The Germans were forced to retreat further north while the Allies walked into Rome unopposed on the fourth of June, 1944.* With Rome in allied hands fighting in Italy would be contained to the northern region where Allied air superiority would become increasingly less pronounced. Furthermore, events elsewhere in Europe, the Pacific and Southeast Asia required the use of the Allies landing craft. So out of geostrategic necessity the Italian theatre would be relegated to the backburner of Allied military policy.

♦ ♦ ♦

While the Allied forces had been invading Italy, Eisenhower had been transferred back to England to oversee the necessary staff work in preparation for the major Allied invasion into continental France.[40] Ever since the Americans and British had entered into their partnership with the Soviets, the Anglo powers had come to the conclusion (and agreement) that the main action against Germany would have to take place via France. To that end, the British Isle's had become one massive supply depot of supplies and men.

Operations in Northern Africa and the Mediterranean had been necessary to satiate the American public's and Soviet demands for active engagement of the common enemy. But wartime planners at the highest levels had known from the outset that the final outcome must be decided on the northern plain of Europe.

The western coast of France would have been difficult to make a landing on the scale that was required, it was heavily de-

* The Germans had previously agreed to not invest in the defence of Rome in an effort (on both sides) to save the ancient capital from destruction.

fended by U-Boats and furthermore, the Atlantic Ocean created weather and waves that were not favourable to an amphibious landing.[41] The one area of coastal France where the Allies could nullify the German submarines was within the English Channel, it also had the advantage of relatively calm waters. Once it had been decided that the operation would take place within the channel it was still necessary to decide the exact location of the landing.

The shortest distance across the channel was at its eastern extremity, the Pas de Calais. A landing at Calais was the most logical, there was a good port and it was fairly close to the Rhine and Germany. Calais was also the most obvious to military planners on both sides and the Germans promptly reinforced their defences in the area. Eisenhower had no intention of being that obvious with the eventual invasion of France and furthermore the Allies had learned the dangers of assaulting a well-defended port facility with the botched raid on Dieppe in 1942.[42] The landings into France were planned (as it was decided) to take place on the beaches of Normandy in between the Cotentin Peninsula and the Seine River estuary.

As the cross-channel invasion was intended to be the knockout blow against the Nazi regime, the numbers involved in the Normandy landings would make it the largest amphibious assault since Xerxes attempted to subdue the Greeks two and a half thousand years before. The scale and magnitude of the invasion created logistical problems without precedent in history, and were extenuated by the fact that the assault waves would be landing on beaches instead of capturing port facilities. Therefore, the plan called for the quick capture of the port city of Cherbourg. But for the purpose of immediately supplying the beachheads, the Allies constructed floating harbours, called Mulberrys that could be sailed to the beaches and sunk in place creating functioning harbours.[43]

In conjunction with the initial amphibious landings and to

facilitate the capture of Cherbourg, Eisenhower planned to have two American airborne divisions dropped further inland from the beaches at the base of the Cotentin Peninsula. In addition, there was to be a British airborne division dropped further inland in support of the British and Canadian armies in their mission to capture the village of Caen.[44] With the plan set and the staff work complete the last detail to confirm was the date and that depended as much as anything on the weather and the moon. The day that was finally chosen for the assault was June 6th, 1945.

The assault was largely successful even though heavy resistance was encountered on the beaches and the airborne landings became scattered over a large area. Surprise and concentrated mass (made possible by air superiority) allowed the allies to create a beachhead and hold out against the Germans as they threw in reinforcements in a piecemeal fashion. The Allies were further aided by Hitler's intervention into Germany strategy. Convinced that the Normandy landings were a diversion for what he believed to be the main invasion across the Pas de Calais Hitler refused to authorize the use of a Panzer army, garrisoning the Calais sector.

In the immediate aftermath of the beach landings the Americans would be tasked with capturing the port city of Cherbourg while the British were given the objective of capturing the city of Caen. Once Cherbourg was captured the Allies were able to bring over sufficient men, equipment and supplies to begin to contemplate breaking out of their beachheads. The breakout began along the base of the Cotentin Peninsula in the American sector. To the east in the British sector, the Germans were offering a stout defence as Caen was dangerously close to their supply lines with Germany.[45]

While progress at the beachhead expansion had gone slower than expected, the breakout phase of the operation met with so much success that the forces involved quickly outpaced their logistical capabilities. Luckily for the Allies, the breakout provided numerous opportunities for opening up new supply lines. One such opportunity was to drive west towards France's western coast to open up her Atlantic ports for allied use. This operation had the added benefit of denying German submarines usage of a base of operations (thus further securing trans-Atlantic shipping), but they also carried the risk of heavy casualties as the Germans had invested these ports with fanatical Nazi SS troopers.[46]

In addition to the westward drive was the opportunity to pursue an advance up the Rhone valley in the south of France. Operation Anvil-Dragoon had originally been planned to coincide with the landings at Normandy, but had been forced into postponement as the requirements for landing craft became too acute. The operation involved the obvious risks, but at the same time the rewards were too great, and in fact essential to overall success from a logistics standpoint, to be ignored. Prime Minister Churchill continued to advocate that the resources earmarked for southern France be deployed into Greece and the Balkans instead. Eisenhower protested saying that invading the Balkans would be of no practical use for the main force in Normandy and that the Germans could easily halt an invasion from that direction by occupying important mountain passes. While Eisenhower's plan was logical for the tactical-strategic necessities of the invasion of France, Churchill's proposition made sense in the realm of longterm strategic policy. Either way Eisenhower's plan for the invasion of southern France won out in the end.

Unlike the drive to Brest and the Atlantic ports, Anvil-Dragoon would require another amphibious assault. At this point the Allies could afford to transfer landing craft into the Mediterranean theatre and so the operation was considered feasible. Difficulties notwithstanding, the advantages to be accrued (if successful) were almost too good to be true. For one, opening up the southern ports would relieve the much congested ports

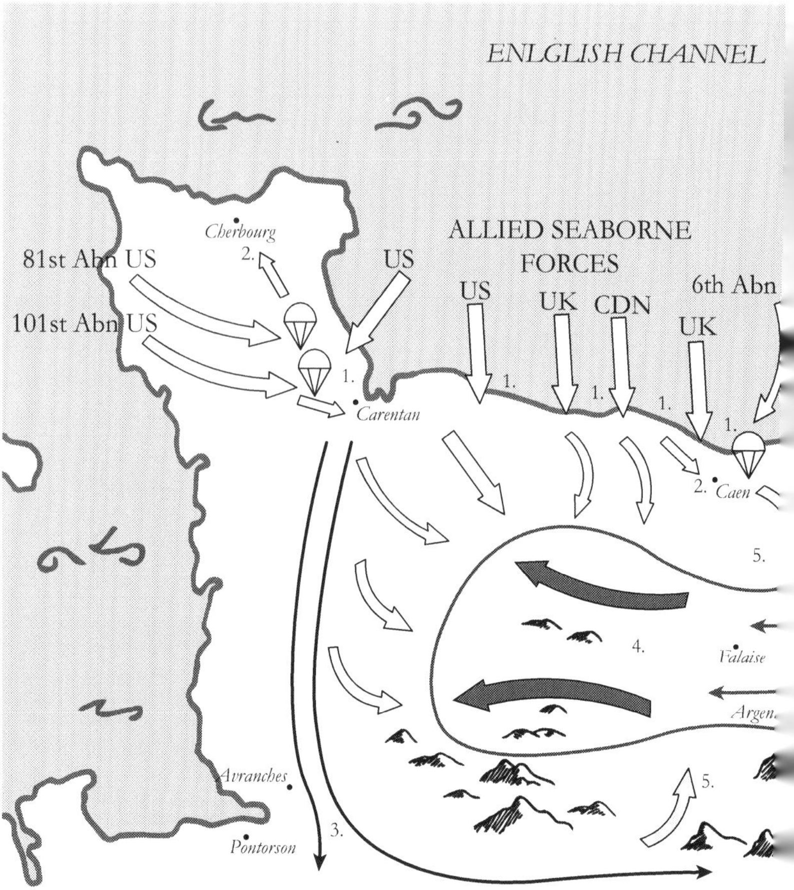

ENLGLISH CHANNEL
ALLIED SEABORNE FORCES
Cherbourg
81st Abn US
101st Abn US
US
US
UK
CDN
UK
6th Abn
1.
2.
Carentan
Caen
3.
4.
5.
Falaise
Argen
Avranches
Pontorson

Normandy Campaign

1. Operation Overlond. 2. Capture of Cherbourg and Caen. 3. Breakout along the Cotentin Peninsula. 4. German offensive operations to retake the Contentin Peninsula. 5. Encirclement of the German Forces.

in the north, while also increasing the volume of supplies the Allies could introduce into the continent. Secondly and perhaps as important, a swift advance up the Rhone valley would effectively cut off and trap a great number of German troops in the west of France before they could extricate themselves back to Germany. After extensive staff work the amphibious operation was executed according to plan and was able to make good progress on its advance up the Rhone.

With the writing on the wall for the German army in France, the German High Command now attempted to pull its forces back to the eastern bank of the Seine River where they believed they could reform for a counter attack. Countermanding the wishes of the German High Command, Hitler ordered the Panzer Army out of Calais to attack the western base of the Cotenin Peninsula where the Americans had recently broken out of their beachheads.[47] The ensuing advance and withdrawal would become famous as the Battle of the Falaise Gap. With a brutal efficiency the Allied air forces struck at the advancing panzer armies and paralysed their movements towards the Atlantic coast. Before long there was no choice but for the Germans to order a retreat. As the American armies, commanded by Bradley and Patton, wheeled around to encircle the German army the British and Canadians under Gen. Montgomery were tasked with pushing south out of the Caen sector in order to sever the German from his only route of escape.

The German army, knowing what was in store for his army were Montgomery to succeed, put up a fanatical defence in the Caen sector and was able to keep the route open for many a German soldier to pass through. But it was only a matter of time before the encirclement was complete in the south and a great many Germans were forced to lay down their arms in surrender (some two hundred thousand soldiers).[48] More Axis troops capitulated after Falaise than had been captured by the Allies in Tunisia.

And so, with the immediate crisis of the beachhead and breakout over, Eisenhower's attention was turned towards the complete destruction of the German's capability to further resist.

Two short days before the Normandy landings commenced, the Allied armies in Italy, commanded by Gen. Mark Clarke marched their way through Rome unopposed by the Germans. The German High Command saw little strategic value in defending the city, and so, withdrew their armies further north closer to Germany to more easily defendable lines.[49] While the capture of Rome gave a boost to the morale of the Allied cause, the German people were not told of the bad news. The magnitude of the Normandy campaign quickly dwarfed the triumphal procession through Rome, but soon enough there would be another triumph through a world class capital city.

After the Battle of Falaise Gap, the Germans practically abandoned Paris. Much like Rome, Paris was not easily defended and had little strategic value other than for propaganda. On August 19, 1944, four years, one month and twenty-seven days after it had been crushed under the boot heel of Nazi tyranny, the Allies, led by the Free French army, marched in triumph through that great city. With Paris now under Allied control, the only, natural barrier left for the defence of Germany was the Rhine River – made stronger by the construction of the 'Siegfried Lines', a system of fortified emplacements on the west bank of the Rhine. Defying conventional strategic wisdom (by not concentrating all forces on the eastern bank), the Germans had no intention of simply giving up the western bank without a fight. The Germans continued to occupy significant portions of eastern France, Belgium and the Netherlands.

As the Allies continued their drive towards the Rhine they began to run into the same problems as before; they were quickly out stripping their ability to supply themselves, especially in the crucial ingredient of modern war – gasoline and diesel. The

London
UNITED
KINGDOM
Dunkirk
Antwer
Cherbourg
Dieppe
La Harve
Carentan
Caen
Paris
Brest
Lorient
St. Nazaire
MASS SURRENDER
OF GERMAN
OCCUPATION
FORCES IN FRANCE
La Rochelle
Bordeaux
Toulouse
SPAIN

Operation Dragoon & the Breakout

problem of supply would always be a pressing concern for Eisenhower. The assault and capture of the southern coast of France had added valuable port facilities into the supply chain, but France's Atlantic ports were too well guarded and or damaged (by sabotage) to be of immediate usefulness to the Allies. Brest was captured in Sept 1944, but Lorient and St. Nazaire were held by the Germans until the final surrender.[50] In an attempt to meet some of the demand for fuel the Allies had built an underwater pipeline connecting southern England to Normandy so as to pump the resource to where it was needed without involving ships.

In light of the fuel shortages, it became necessary for Eisenhower to prioritize what operation and army would receive the required supplies to fulfill its objectives. Each one of Eisenhower's army group commanders (Montgomery, Bradley, Patton and Devers) pleaded for enough supplies to have a go at crossing the Rhine in 1944 before winter set in. The plan that was decided upon, Montgomery's, was by far the most rational on a strategic level, but it was also the most ambitious. Some of Eisenhower's American contemporaries criticized him in the aftermath for pandering exclusively to the British when it came to green lighting the operation to cross the Rhine. Hindsight has nearly all but proven that Eisenhower's decision was not only objective and strategically sound, but was instrumental in bringing the war to an end, even if the operation failed to meet its primary objectives.

♦ ♦ ♦

Montgomery's plan called for the capturing of the Belgian and Dutch ports along the North Sea coast, most important of which being Antwerp, then the best port of Europe.[51] The primary objective of the operation was to seize bridgeheads across the River Maas, Waal and the lower Rhine as well as the main roads along the Eindhoven, Nijmegen and Arnhem axis. The secondary objective was to establish lines sufficiently advanced from Antwerp to assure a timely capture and exploitation of the port facilities there.[52]

Tasked with seizing the roads and bridges were the famous airborne divisions of the Normandy invasion; the 101st and 82nd Americans and the 1st British Airborne. In conjunction with the airborne drops, elements of the First Canadian Army, the Second British Army and the Ninth US army would support the landings and enlarge the bridgeheads once captured. Resistance was expected to be light as intelligence reports suggested that the German soldiers occupying Holland were still refitting from their losses in Normandy.[53]

When the operation was launched in mid-September the airborne divisions met with initial success as they achieved near total surprise and as their landings took place in midday allowing them to quickly and easily concentrate on their designated rally points and capture the bridgeheads allotted to them. Events quickly began to turn against the British at Arnhem as bad weather set in, making it difficult for the regular army to relieve airborne divisions in a timely manner. After fighting "…one of the most gallant actions of the war…"[54] the First British Airborne was forced to retire from their advanced position on the eastern bank of the Rhine. Of the ten thousand men deployed, only twenty-two hundred would make it back alive.[597] While Market Garden failed to affect a permanent crossing of the Rhine or the capture of Amsterdam, it did succeed in putting Antwerp securely within Allied lines (which would further assist with allied logistic problems).

With Market Garden a mixture of success and failure, Eisenhower was required to continue operations against the Germans who remained on the western side of the Rhine, to the south of Montgomery's army group sector. In an attempt to strengthen the French forces in the Strasbourg – Vosage mountain region in the south and the Americans in the portion of the Rhine opposite the Ruhr industrial region, Eisenhower weakened his cen-

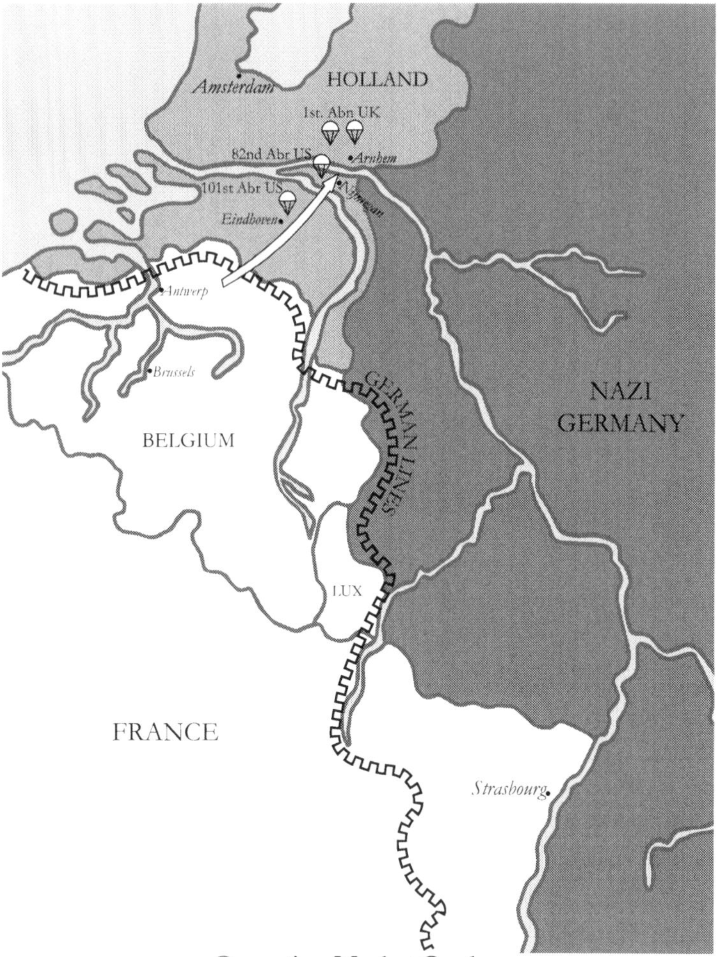

Operation Market Garden

ter in the Ardennes sector where Bradley's army group linked up with Patton's army group.[56] As winter began to settle in, it was believed that the Germans had no more power for a renewed offensive against the allied lines. And so, it was thought that the Ardennes, thus weakened, would be safe from a German counter attack.

Much to the wonderment of Eisenhower and the Allied command the German offensive came in mid-December. Tactically, the German achieved surprise against the local corps and army commanders, but on a strategic level it was less shocking as the Ardennes region was the only location where the Germans could amass overwhelming strength.[57] Having achieved tactical surprise, the Germans continued to exploit its success by driving west. As the direction of their advance became definite, Eisenhower and the Allies made plans to attack the German salient on both of its flanks.

But in the meantime something would be required to blunt the spearhead of the German advance; the 101st airborne, fresh off the line from Market Garden, was brought down from northern Belgium to the village of Bastogne.

Almost directly in the middle of the Ardennes massif, Bastogne lay at the center of an extensive transportation network; fourteen roads led in, fourteen roads led out. Bastogne and the road network were of vital importance to the German plan, which as far as Eisenhower and the intelligence agencies were concerned, was to capture the massive Allied fuel depot to the west of the Meuse (Maas) River. It is entirely possible that the German High Command intended on recapturing Antwerp as a means to separate the Allied army groups and destroy them in detail.[58] In any case the capture of Antwerp was completely unrealistic. None-the-less the German advance posed a serious threat to allied plans and needed to be reversed before the Allied lines could be moved to the Rhine in strength.

As Bradley and Patton prepared to divert resources into the

Ardennes, the 101st settled into defensive positions around Bastogne and prepared for a drawn out siege. While the German advance progressed westward, Eisenhower made preparations to remove or destroy the stores of fuel on the Meuse should the German advance continue. At this point the denial of Bastogne to the enemy took on a supreme importance as the road networks around Bastogne effectively cut the German salient in two and forced the German to take a wide berth should they attempt to transfer forces from one sector to another.

The 101st were pressed hard as the German army assaulted their positions from every direction. Bad weather prevented their resupply and as they had been rushed into Bastogne without sufficient ammunition or winter clothing their position around Bastogne was desperate to say the least.[59] Relief by air was, for a time, the only option to keep the 101st in a fighting capacity. However, poor winter conditions made resupply next to impossible and even at times counter productive as the supplies would, more often than not, land behind German lines for collection at their convenience.

Patton, and to be fair everyone in the Allied command, sensed the urgency of the situation and did everything in his power to relieve the 101st in Bastogne. His Third Army drove hard and fast to the north and were able to open up a line of communication (albeit a tenuous one) with the besieged troops by the 26th of December.[60] Seeing the utmost importance of controlling Bastogne, the Germans diverted manpower from this westward advance for an all-out attack on the village. In addition, the Germans opened up new offensives in the southern sector (near the Swiss border) as a diversion to assist their Ardennes offensive. The diversions in the south were insignificant except for the fact that Allied resources had been diverted from that sector to take part in the Battle of the Bulge. Sensing that they were simply diversions, Eisenhower ordered General Devers to closely watch as the German attacks developed but offered no addition resources.

While the German offensive halted to deal with the Bastogne redoubt, Eisenhower ordered his counterattack to begin in earnest. On January 1st, 1945 Montgomery was tasked with advancing south towards Patton's force, but due to bad winter weather, Montgomery's advance didn't begin until the 3rd.[61] In the meantime, the Germans came to see the futility of their advance and began to withdraw their forces before the allies could complete their encirclement. Although numerous Germans were allowed to escape the encirclement, they were forced to do so at the loss of nearly all their heavy equipment.[62]

It would take nearly to the end of January before the Allies could reduce the salient to the position from which the Germans first launched their assault. Once the Ardennes campaign had been halted and reversed the German capacity for offensive operations ceased to exist; there would no longer exist any hope for a negotiated peace on terms favourable to the preservation of Nazism. The last beacon of hope for Hitler was to stand on the defensive and make the allies pay for every inch of German territory in the bloodiest manner possible.

At this point the sustained aerial bombardment campaign that the Allies had been waging continuously against Germany began to pay huge dividends as German industrial production and oil refinement came screeching to a halt.[63] The destruction of Germany's industry and transportation infrastructure brought morale to all-time lows, but still Hitler and the Nazi's were unwilling to surrender; better for all of Germany to burn than to surrender, went their line of thinking. With the Ardennes salient crushed, Eisenhower was able to refocus his energy on eliminating German resistance west of the Rhine in preparation for a spring offensive into Germany itself.

♦ ♦ ♦

Along the Rhine frontier there were two areas of tantamount importance for the Axis and Allies alike, the Saar and Ruhr in-

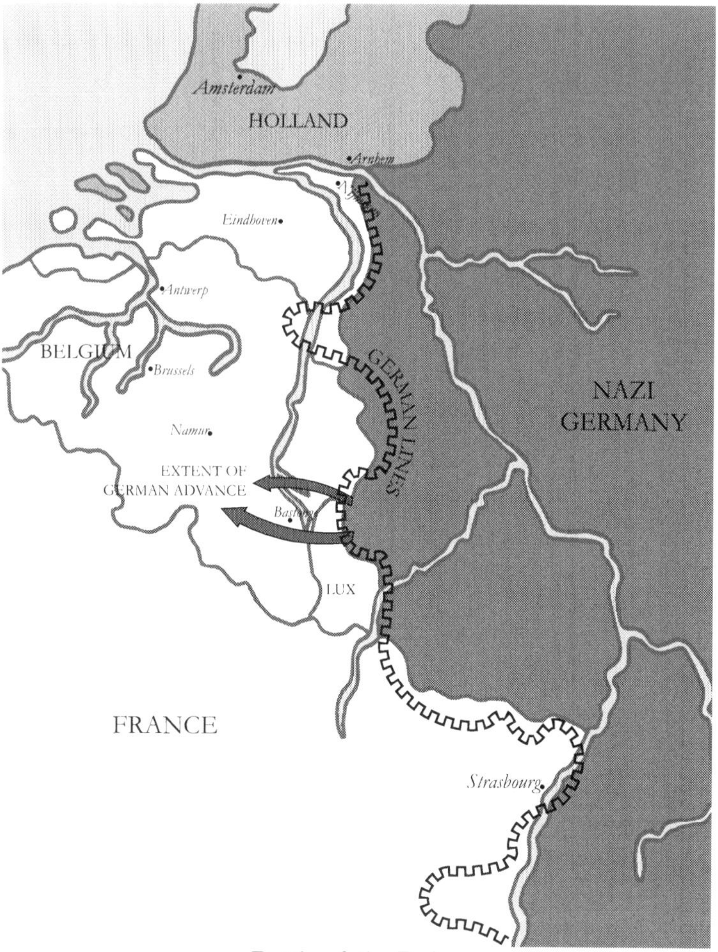

Battle of the Bulge

dustrial regions. Both areas were heavily invested with German troops, but the Saar, being on the western bank of the river, was considerably more accessible for the Allies as compared to the Ruhr. Being so, the Saar garrison would necessarily need to be reduced before the Allies could cross the Rhine in force. In the late winter/early spring of 1945, Eisenhower continued to push the Allies right up to the Rhine, overrunning the German territory to the west of the river; only the 'Saar-Palatinate triangle' remained under German control until the late days of March.

The Rhine River, as Eisenhower put it, was an obstacle that practically required an amphibious operation on the scale of the Normandy landings.

> "… [the Rhine] was a formidable military obstacle, … It was not only wide but treacherous, and even the level of the river and the speed of its currents were subject to variation because the enemy could open dams along the great rivers eastern tributaries…the crossing resembled an assault against a beach, except that the troops, instead of attacking from ship to shore, were carried from shore to shore."[64]

However, this time the operation would occur on a seven army front compared to the relatively small five division assault on Normandy. While the vastly increased scope of the Rhine crossing meant that the allies had a preponderance of strength in aircraft, artillery, tanks and infantry, these advantages by no means ensured that the Allied efforts would succeed.

Stretching from the Swiss border in the south to the Netherlands in the north, the Rhine could boast some twenty-seven major bridges spanning its wide berth.[65] Every single one of those bridges had been set with demolitions should Eisenhower's forces make a direct attempt on the crossing. Part of the orders that had been given to the various generals as they marched to the Rhine was to, if practicable, seize one of these bridges if any opportunity arose. Almost by sheer good luck one of those bridges was taken intact in the area of Remagen on March 7th.[66] General Pattor struck immediately and secured the bridge at Remagen. Once across, Eisenhower immediately ordered in reinforcements and a bridge-head was established with the help of quickly constructed temporary bridges. While the crossing at Remagen came as a welcome shock, it was also the first time, since Napoleon (over a century earlier), a hostile army entered into the German lands east of the Rhine. Conveniently located to the south of the Ruhr and north of the Saar, the Remagen bridgehead forced the German to reposition his forces along the Sieg River which formed the southern boundary of the Ruhr.

Almost immediately after the creation of the Remagen bridgehead, the Third Army (American) began its assault on the Saar industrial region, which rapidly met with success and was able to affect its own crossing of the Rhine further south by the 24th of March. In the northern sector, Montgomery had been severely hindered by the Germans flooding the Low Countries as the British made their way to the river's edge. The night/day of March 23/24th witnessed the launching of Montgomery's grand operation to cross the Rhine.

The tactical plan made some innovations on what had now become allied 'triphibious' doctrine. Instead of airborne operations preceding the main assault the night before, this time the main assault would take place under cover of darkness with the airdrops occurring the following day just out of range of friendly artillery (as opposed to further in the rear).[67] Stiff resistance was expected to be met in Montgomery's front, but almost everywhere the soldiers met with success. By the end of March, the Rhine was in the rear of every army sectors, the Ruhr complex was still in German hands, but the German was defeated; it was no longer a matter of if the German would surrender but when.

In light of the political arrangements concerning the division of German territory between the eastern and western allies, there were essentially three objectives left for the western allies to achieve at this point. (From north to south) the first was to capture the more important of the Baltic Sea ports and the remaining French Atlantic ports. The capture of the Baltic ports would be the responsibility of Montgomery.[68] The Second objective was the reduction of the Ruhr garrison, the denial of its further usefulness towards the German cause, and a subsequent advance through central Germany linking up with the Soviet army around the Elbe River; this was to be the responsibility of Bradley.[69] The third and final objective, given to General Devers, was to rapidly advance along the southern front into the Austrian Alps. It was believed that the Nazi political leadership along with fanatical elements of the SS and German army were planning on occupying the southern mountains in an attempt to wage a guerilla campaign once the conventional fighting proved hopeless.[70]

By April 1st, the Ruhr had been completely surrounded and the process of starvation quickly began to set in. Not wanting to unnecessarily inflict casualties, Eisenhower urged the German people to give up the fight, but alas, Hitler's grip on the German people and leadership was as formidable as ever. Operations against the Ruhr were completed by April 18, which allowed for the continued drive east to be given the go ahead.[71]

It was also in the month of April that concrete proof of German atrocities against the Jewish people and other such 'undesirables' was brought to the attention of Eisenhower. In an attempt to preserve the historical record for posterity and to dispel the (foreseeable) accusation that the Jewish holocaust were lies concocted by the Allies as a propaganda justification for the war against Nazi Germany, Eisenhower requested that members of the Allied press tour around the liberated death camps so they could see it for themselves.[72]

By the time the Nazi regime was annihilated, the Germans had managed to murder roughly six million Jews and roughly another six million undesirables' that Hitler had deemed unfit to live side by side with the German race. In addition to the discovery of the concentration camps, the month of April had also witnessed the death of US. President Roosevelt. The death of Roosevelt weighed heavily on the Allied population, but the rules of succession were based in long recognized constitutional traditions, so that the event had no practical effect on US or Allied policy

Eisenhower's advances to the Elbe River continued as planned and in accordance with Soviet advances from the east. On April 25th the first link up was achieved between Soviet ground forces and those of the western allies to the south of Berlin.[73] The forces of the allied powers were quickly arriving at their pre-arranged points along the demarcation lines; the Nazi had precious little territory left under its control. Still, Hitler continued to hold out from his bunker in Berlin and some German troops had been able to occupy portions of the Austrian Alps before the French and Americans could arrive. However, with the Soviet army laying siege to Berlin, Hitler was finally forced to admit defeat to himself and leave the pieces to be picked up by others. On April 30th, 1945 Hitler shot himself in the head, his close associates burned his remains, never to be found.

Responsibility now devolved upon Admiral Karl Doenitz. All remaining German forces, and a considerable number of civilians, began moving west in an attempt to surrender themselves to the Western Allies.[74] It now became an objective for nearly every German soldier to attempt to get in behind the advancing western lines so as to shield themselves from Soviet reprisals. Eisenhower, sensing that this could become a source of embarrassment for the western governments, immediately acted to put an end to this German obfuscation by demanding Admiral Doenitz sign onto the unconditional surrender treaty or else the Americans would begin shooting anyone caught crossing the Allied lines. The document of surrender was signed on May the 7th and officially came into effect at midnight of the 8th.[75]

The war that had been waged by Hitler and the Nazi regime was over after a ghastly six years. With most of continental Europe in shambles, the Empire of Japan still occupied vast tracts of conquered territory. Although Japan was on the defensive, hard fighting was still in the forecast. With Eisenhower's immediate problems over in Europe his thoughts and time was now taken up by the necessity of transferring soldiers from the European theatre to that of East Asia and the Pacific.

♦ ♦ ♦

With the convergence of the western and Soviet allies in the middle of Germany, celebrations shortly ensued amongst the victorious powers and in much of the world. But underneath the euphoria, deep seated political differences and distrust threatened to cause a falling out amongst the eastern and western allies. Not long after the German surrender, the Soviets would find any excuse to raise objections over trivial issues regarding the occupation of Germany.[76] The petty differences only became more exasperated after the two nuclear bombs dropped on Japan forced the Japanese Emperor to agree to an unconditional surrender in the Asian and Pacific theatres. It wasn't long before the petty grievances turned into open (but not active) hostilities; the classic rivalry between a landlocked superpower and its maritime rival had returned with a renewed intensity.

In order to put an end to Hitler's Nazi regime the western Allies were forced, out of necessity, to make a deal with a devil as evil as Hitler's Germany, Joseph Stalin's communist empire. Now that the Nazi regime was in ashes, the Soviet colossus, now occupying much of the Eurasian landmass, was becoming as threatening to the liberty of the human race as Hitler's regime ever was.

While the Russian communists had seemingly inexhaustible

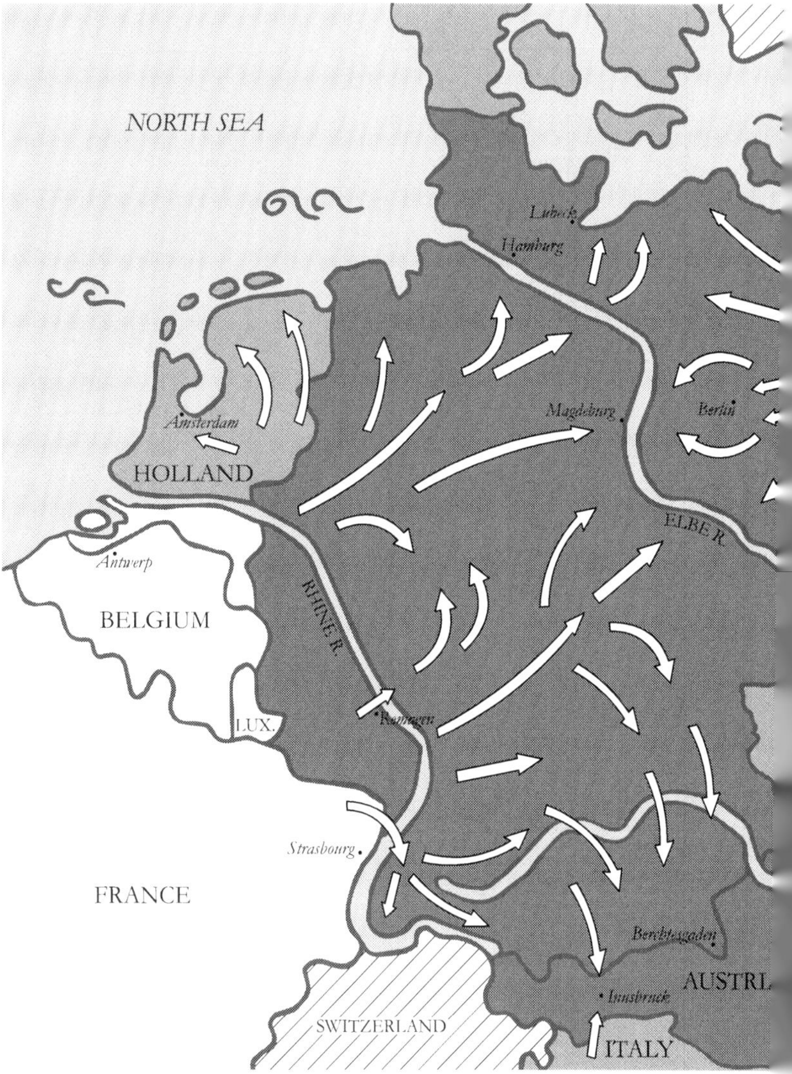
NORTH SEA
Lubeck
Hamburg
Amsterdam
HOLLAND
Magdeburg
Berlin
ELBE R.
Antwerp
BELGIUM
RHINE R.
LUX.
Remagen
Strasbourg
FRANCE
Berchtesgaden
AUSTRI
Innsbruck
SWITZERLAND
ITALY

The Thousand Year Reich

sources of manpower and landmass, the west was not without its own strengths. The western allies could effectively count upon every single naval vessel then in existence, the vast industrial capacity of the North American continent and lastly the wonder/terror of the nuclear bomb. The post war era witnessed the irresistible expansion of American influence and leadership on the world stage, and with it the only real hope of countering the aggressive potential of United Socialist tyranny.

While the euphoria still lasted amongst the allies, Eisenhower was invited to Moscow to meet with Dictator Stalin and Marshal Zhukov and to tour that great capital. After Moscow, Eisenhower was brought back to Germany where he served as the military governor of the US portion of occupied Germany. In this capacity, Eisenhower attempted to alleviate the plight of the average German by distributing army rations and medical supplies and worked to minimize the disruptions amongst the allies. At this point though, the problems amongst the allies had ceased to be the business of generals or military governors; they had entered into the realm of politicians. After Eisenhower's short stint as military governor he was brought back to the United States to replace General Marshall as the Chief of Staff for the American military.[77] As chief of staff Eisenhower was responsible for demobilizing and transporting back to the US the millions of soldiers that had been sent overseas since the hostilities began.

Eisenhower's views on nuclear weapons and American relations with the Soviets were considerably more liberal than President Truman and his State Department. Perhaps influenced by his close coordination with his Russian counterparts and the comradeship developed amongst old soldiers, Eisenhower believed that the Russians could still be partners. Furthermore, Eisenhower voiced his opinion that nuclear weapons should come under the purview of a United Nations mandate.[78] However, by the end of Eisenhower's posting as chief of staff and after continued Soviet obfuscation, his views on these two subjects had matured to the point of hawkishness.

In 1948, Eisenhower was chosen by a committee at Columbia University to take up the office of university President. Eisenhower's time at Columbia has often been referred to as his transition period from soldier to politician. It was during this period that Eisenhower was able to complete work on his war time memoirs titled 'Crusade in Europe'. Much of the staff at the school came to resent Eisenhower's position of leadership as he was largely absent from the institution in his (sequential) roles as advisor to the US Secretary of Defense, than later (informal) Chairman of the Joint Chiefs of Staff and finally as Supreme Commander of the North Atlantic Treaty Organization.[79] Upon his assumption of responsibility at the NATO command, Eisenhower had offered to resign his position at Columbia to which the university trustee's refused to accept. Eisenhower would continue in that role until his inauguration as the President of the United States.

Back in 1945, after President Roosevelt's death, Eisenhower had been visited by President Truman, where Truman guaranteed his support for Eisenhower should the general want to run for President (US) in 1948. Truman's offer came with the obvious caveat that Eisenhower would run on the Democratic Party ticket.[80] Earlier in the European campaign, Eisenhower had made it known that he had no intention to run for any political office. But later his stance on this would gradually evolve to the point that he would consider seeking higher office should there be a clear mandate from the general public for him to perform such a duty.

Once again in 1951, President Truman lobbied Eisenhower to run for the Democrats, but this time Eisenhower openly declared himself as a Republican and was convinced by that party to campaign as their nominee. Eisenhower won the Republican Party's early primaries and was practically acclaimed as their man for the White House. During the subsequent presidential campaign of 1952, Eisenhower refused, against the advice of his campaign team, to concentrate his efforts solely on the Republican stronghold in the Northern states and took his campaign into the Democratic bastion in the South. His strategy paid off, Eisenhower won by a landslide taking the electoral college seats in Virginia, Tennessee, Florida, and Texas, all considered Democrat strongholds.[81] It was the first time in over twenty years that a Republican was in the White House and also won bare majorities in the House of Representatives and the Senate.

Eisenhower's presidency was marked by colossal changes at home and important events abroad. On the domestic front, Eisenhower fought an uphill battle first with the desegregation of the armed forces then with the desegregation of public schools. Opposition amongst white Democrats in the South was so fierce that at one point Eisenhower had to send in the illustrious 101st airborne to escort nine black students into a white school.[82]

Since his days at Columbia, Eisenhower had understood that education was practically a matter of national security. In the later part of Eisenhower's second term his position on education was vindicated when the Soviet Union astonished the world by successfully launching the first satellite into orbit in 1957. The Americans immediately took steps to remedy the situation, one of which was the creation of the National Aeronautics and Space Agency (NASA). Before long the Americans were leaps and bounds ahead of anyone in the space race.*

While Eisenhower's administration had kept the majority of Roosevelt's 'New Deal' social welfare agencies in operation, he put an end to the price and wage control structures that the great depression and world war had ushered in. Eisenhower effectively restored the free, capitalist market back to the US economy by ending price and wage fixing.[83] As well his administration was

* This was further helped along by Eisenhower's policy of assisting Nazi super weapon scientists immigrate to the United States.

dedicated to the goal of producing balanced budgets, something that hadn't been attempted since the Democrats had begun their occupation of the White House during the Great Depression.[84]

Perhaps the most important and long lasting initiative Eisenhower's administration produced was the creation of the highway interstate system,* connecting all the major American cities with fifty thousand plus people together. The new highway system was designed to facilitate the evacuation of the civilian populations in the event of nuclear exchanges between the super powers. The road network had the added benefit of improving the Unites States ability to move troops around the country, while the road system doubled as usable landing fields for aircraft. In addition, the improved state of the road network stimulated the economy and massively expanded the volume of continental commerce by making cross country travel practicable for business and the average family.[85]

In the realm of defence policy and international affairs, Eisenhower's term in office spanned a rapid escalation of the American-Russian conflict known as the 'Cold War'. Initially in his presidency, Eisenhower took a hardline on the threat of communist tyranny, by supporting the policy of liberation for Eastern Europe (through peaceful means) before he came around to supporting the policy of containment. Although he had opposed the use of the atom bomb against the Japanese, Eisenhower came to use nuclear weapons as an integral part of American defence policy and as a means by which it could become possible to draw back the conventional forces and balance the budget.

Eisenhower had campaigned against the Democrats as the man who could put an end to the Korean War. Upon visiting the theatre Eisenhower felt compelled to scale back his support for 'liberation' and accepted the policy of containment. After Eisenhower threatened to use nuclear weapons against commu-

* And to a lesser extent construction of the St. Lawrence Seaway.

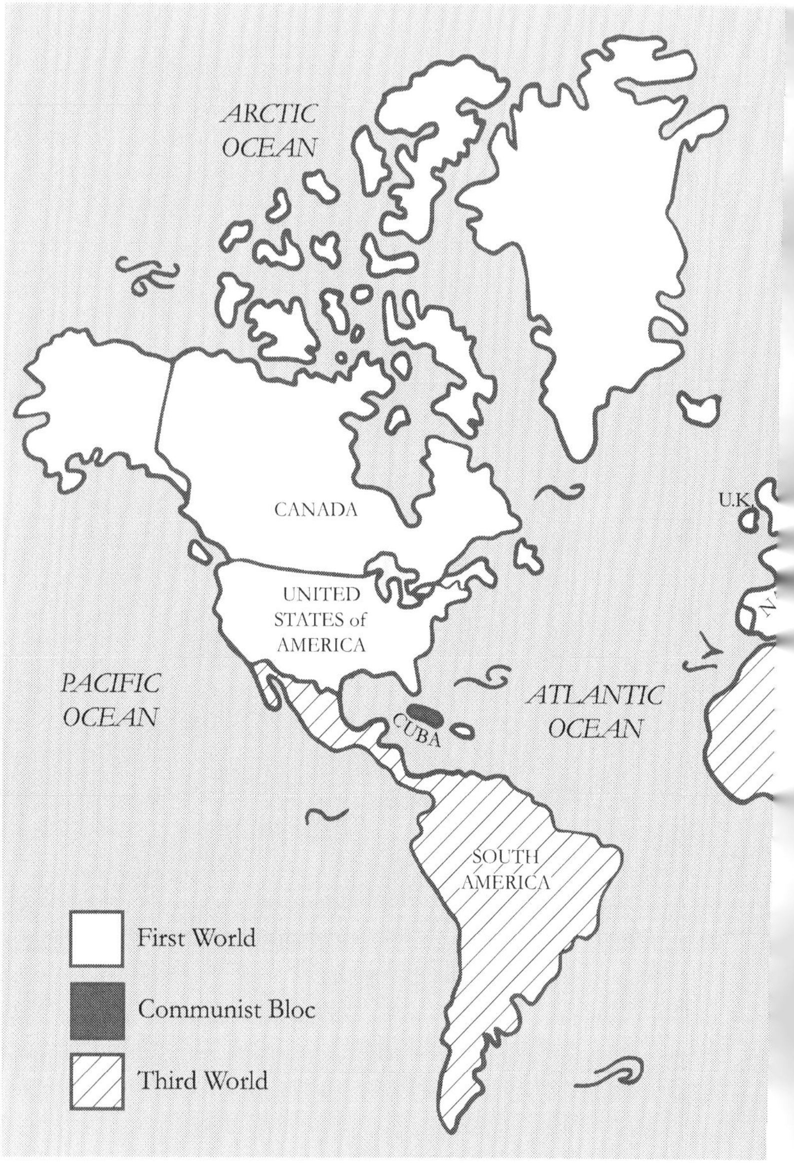
ARCTIC OCEAN
CANADA
U.K.
UNITED STATES of AMERICA
PACIFIC OCEAN
ATLANTIC OCEAN
CUBA
SOUTH AMERICA
First World
Communist Bloc
Third World

The Cold War

1. Korean War. 2. Vietnam War. 3. Afghan War.

nist China, coupled with the death of Stalin and the subsequent loss of support from Russia, China and North Korea felt compelled to sign an armistice with South Korea and the United States. This armistice, although frequently breeched, is still in effect today.

In keeping with Eisenhower's policy of producing balanced budgets, his tenure in office witnessed the expansion of America's intelligence agencies (especially the CIA) and an increase of clandestine operations as a way to cheaply subvert the spread of global communism.[86] The movement of decolonization that swept across the various western European overseas possessions* created a vacuum for the spread of communism via the use of subversive activity led by the USSR and its intelligence agencies. The battlefields of the Cold War stretched to the farthest and darkest corners of the earth, but was largely played out amongst the shadows. Luckily for the human race the conflict was confined to those dark recesses.

Eisenhower succeeded in avoiding entangling the US in another large scale conventional war in Asia, Europe or elsewhere. This was achieved largely through the use of nuclear threats and clandestine intelligence activities. Furthermore, the government he ran succeeded in producing three balanced budgets. Avoiding another war, balancing the budget and restoring the free market to the American economy should be remembered as astounding achievements in their own right and should be counted against any scandal or mistake that occurred under Eisenhower's watch.

Raised in a small Kansas town, Eisenhower grew up to be a world class leader of men, first as a general then as a president. Eisenhower's military career saw him responsible for not only the success of the American forces in Europe but also the success of the western Allies. He was the first American ever to hold a position of authority over a British soldier. First with the rank of Supreme Allied Commander (UN) then Five Star Gen-

* Largley in Africa, and South East Asia.

eral (US) then as Supreme Commander (NATO) Eisenhower was perhaps the most recognizable name produced out of the war against Nazi Germany.

Eisenhower's personality enabled him, better than anyone else, to successfully manage the politicians above him and the fighting generals subordinate to him; no one else could have done this job and still have met with the same success. Once President, these same personality traits helped Eisenhower to successfully deal with both enemies and allies alike.

The campaign across Northern Africa and through Europe was one of the most incredibly successful combined military operations in history. The great leap into Africa and the landings in Normandy were (and are) without precedent and are barely comparable with any other recorded human endeavor. The Battle of Falaise Gap and the chase to the Rhine are an almost theoretically perfect example of a battle of annihilation and pursuit. Eisenhower's able leadership and steady hand was directly responsible for the timely and cost effective destruction of National Socialism in Germany and the staunch defence of liberty against later communist expansion and the tyranny of Russia's United Socialist empire.

Had Eisenhower not fought against Hitler, the Nazi might well have made a negotiated peace. Had Eisenhower not won the presidency, the USSR sphere of influence might have been expanded over the entire Eurasian landmass and conquered the world. Eisenhower's efforts in life had destroyed one brutal tyranny as well as keeping another confined within reasonable boundaries so that one day it would collapse upon itself. When his term in office was over, Eisenhower and his wife retired to a farm in Pennsylvania where he lived out the remainder of his life.* After his death in 1969, Eisenhower's mortal coil was given its honours in Washington DC before being buried beside his

* The farm was located close to the battlefield of Gettysburg.

son* in Abilene, Kansas.[87] No one could say that he hadn't done his duty to the utmost limit of diligence. It wasn't without justification that the man could be eulogized as the "first citizen of the world".[88]

* Who had died at three years of age.

Ariel 'Arik' Sharon

Ariel Sharon was born as Ariel Scheinerman* on February 26, 1928 to his parents Shmuel and Vera. His parents had immigrated to the British Palestinian Mandate in 1922 from the Russian Empire.† They had met each other while studying at the university in Tbilisi, Georgia.[1] Originally Shmuel and Vera settled in Kfar Malal, an agricultural commune governed by socialist principles, where they gave birth to a daughter, Yehudit, in 1926 and two years later a son, Ariel.

Ten years after their settlement within the Mandate, the Scheinerman's were ostracized and expelled from access to the commune because of their disapproval of the Bolshevik's sense of justice and mob supported reprisals.[2] Bolshevism wasn't the only thing the Scheinerman's had to worry about as the denizens of Kfar Malal lived under a constant threat of marauding Arab horsemen. Ariel would later recall his mother sleeping with a rifle under her pillow after being traumatized by the threat of Muslim gangs.[3]

At the tender age of fourteen, Ariel joined the local youth militia and was active in night patrols guarding the village. Tensions were high amongst the Jews and Muslim Arabs as the contest between the British and Germans was reaching a climax in the western desert of Egypt. As the Islamic clerics of Palestine were openly supportive of Hitler and Nazi Germany, a German victory at the Second Battle of el-Alamein would have had dras-

* The last name 'Sharon' would come later as an honour and to make it sound more Hebrew.

† Ukraine and Belarus respectively.

tic consequences for the Jewish populations living in British Palestine. But the eventual Allied victory would not come without ramifications for the Jews. From the local militia, Ariel made his way into the 'Haganah' which was the underground precursor to the Israeli Defense Forces.* From his early days in the militia, Ariel's destiny must have seemed to be set in stone. A military career it would be.

♦ ♦ ♦

In the aftermath of the First World War and the subsequent dissolution of the Ottoman Empire, the French and British governments proceeded to carve out spheres of influence from the non-Turkish (Arab) lands of the Middle East. The lines that were eventually agreed upon gave the mandate for governing much of modern day Syria to the French. The British were given the responsibility for governing the stretch of land bridging the Eastern Mediterranean to the Persian Gulf, and the coastline of southern Syria to the Suez Canal.

While this division of territory has since been criticized as western imperialism at its worst, at the time it was met with little local resistance and was ratified by the League of Nations and even the new Ottoman-Turkish government.[4] The reality on the ground was that there was a massive vacuum of ungoverned territory. After four hundred years of uninspired, corrupt Ottoman governance and economic underdevelopment, the most logical choices to run the Mandate territories were France and Great Britain – two of the most highly developed and best governed states in the world.

Problems arose in the aftermath of the League of Nations Mandate as, in the pursuit of victory, the British government had made two separate and conflicting promises to the inhabitants of the region. One, was a promise to the Arab tribesmen that active support against the Turk would be rewarded with an

* The IDF was created when the state of Israel was formally recognized as a nation-state in 1948.

independent Arab state.[5] The second was an identical promise of statehood made to the Jews located along the eastern Mediterranean shoreline that had historically been the kingdom of Israel and Judea; the promised land of the Jews.

Theoretically there was plenty of land for both sides. However, cultural and religious differences made an agreement between the Arabs and Jews difficult to reach. This was further exasperated over who would control Jerusalem, the third holiest site in Islam and the capital of the ancient Jewish state of Israel. The two sides lived in relative peace amongst themselves, neither side feeling existentially threatened even as European Jews came trickling in, creating settlements. This movement would become known as Zionism – meaning the right of the Jews to return to their ancient homeland to create a state. While the early tensions within the Mandate resembled the age old conflict between agriculture (Jews) and herding (Arabs), events elsewhere in the world threatened to escalate the problems. A great evil, emanating from the heart of Europe threatened to disrupt the tentative balance amongst the Jews and Arabs.

♦ ♦ ♦

The Jewish state of Israel has a long and varied history that stretches back to the ancient Middle East. Much of that history is related to us from the Old Testament of the Bible. After escaping from slavery under the boot heel of the Egyptian Pharos, the Jewish tribes ventured north and east through the Sinai desert into the land of Canaan; the territory promised to them by God. Settling in this land the tribes of Jews came together to form the kingdom of Israel to be ruled by a monarch. The state was destroyed and the people once again enslaved when the Assyrian Empire sprung out of Mesopotamia and conquered their way towards Egypt around 600 BC.[6]

After the Assyrian conquest the peoples of Israel would be conquered by the Egyptians and Babylonians* in turn before

* The Babylonians depopulated Jerusalem, and exiled the elites to Babylon.

the Persian King, Cyrus the Great, conquered the Assyrians and Babylonians. The Jews were set free and given Persian funds to return to their homeland to rebuild their great temple in Jerusalem.[7] The home coming was relatively short lived.

When Alexander the Great was conquering his way through the area, the Jews submitted to his rule, and were largely left alone. However, when Alexander died, Israel was located inbetween two successor kingdoms, the Ptolemies in Egypt, and the Seleucid Empire in Syria and Iraq.

By the time Rome imposed its hegemony on the Mediterranean world, the kingdom of Israel had split into two separate dynasties. For a period, the states remained nominally independent by paying a tribute to Rome. The average Jew chaffed under Roman rule partially because they were the sole practitioners of a monotheistic religion and partly because there existed a radical segment of the population dedicated to restoring Israel as a united, independent state. Numerous rebellions and plots were initiated, none of which achieved lasting success, culminating with the Maccabee rebellion of 56-66 AD which earned the Jews the complete wrath of the Roman Empire.[8]

The Romans, at this point now governed by a monarchy, had never shied away from using mass deportation and genocide as a way to solve a problem in international relations. The policy implemented as the solution for the Jewish rebels was the utter destruction of their military capabilities and the complete dispersion of the Jewish people from their promised land. Had the Jewish rebels learned nothing from Carthage or Corinth? After the Jewish expulsion from Israel the landscape slowly crept back towards desert status, the inhabitants that migrated there were mostly nomadic herders, the Jews had been scattered into the wind.

While the Roman genocide was a colossal set back, the Jewish people migrated throughout the Roman Empire, but refused to assimilate with their host cultures. Their sense of identity could not be destroyed, they were Jews and the land of Israel was their promised land. Dormant they would lay, carving out communities in foreign lands waiting for the day they would be safe to return and reunite the wandering tribes into another Jewish state.

The territory of Israel would change hands frequently. The Romans, Greek Byzantines, Arab Muslims, European Crusaders, Egyptian Saracens, the Mongolian hordes, Ottoman Turks and finally the United Kingdom of Great Britain would each take control of the area before finally the area was given back to its rightful occupants. Before that could actually happen the Jewish people would have to undergo another ordeal by fire, worse than the Roman desolation, before a sufficient impetus would be given for the Jews of Europe to leave their adopted homes and return to their native land en masse.

The cataclysm that truly awakened the Jewish race into action was the Nazi Holocaust. Anti-Semitism had existed almost as early as the first creation of Israel as a state. It had become most pronounced in Europe as that was where the vast majority of Jews had fled after the Roman expulsion. While the Jews were generally disliked everywhere they congregated, the ruling elites found them to be indispensable as the Jewish religion allowed, or at least did not forbid, Jews from lending currency and charging a rate of interest. The European monarchs found this especially useful when it came to financing their dynastic wars or massive public works projects.

As the process of industrialization sped up and as international banking and finance became more complicated, the Jews became even more influential within European governments. This newfound level of importance did nothing to endear them to the general public as the Jews, with their 'foreign doings', came to be scapegoats for the failings and misfortunes of a nation. Anti-Semitism was everywhere, but it took on its ultimate form in Nazi Germany where Hitler's 'national socialist' regime initiated their 'Final Solution' to eradicate the Jews from Europe by any means necessary. The Soviet Union also actively targeted Jews, but this was largely confined to an ideological basis, as opposed to racial. It was still possible to be a Soviet Jew as long as the Jewish identity came second.

With the Nazi regime relegated to the dustbin of history and the Jews liberated from the death camps in 1945 there was a gradual surge of sympathy towards European Jewry. And suddenly, as if acting on command by a single brain, the Jews of Europe began to walk towards the sea, find any ship that would take them and complete the voyage to their promised land. The British, who largely controlled the Mediterranean waters attempted, in vain, to halt and reverse the flow of human traffic.[9] Their main concern was to keep the peace between Arab and Jew within the Mandate territory, but the influx of thousands of Europe's terrorized Jews would make it damn near impossible to keep that balance.

After what the Jews experienced at Hitler's hands, only the evilest devil would want to stop the Jews from congregating in Israel. The Nazi Holocaust had proven (or should have proven) to the Jews and to the world that a Jewish state had become necessary to ensure the continued survival of their race.

Only a devil could begrudge the Jews of their liberty and security, but that devil certainly did exist. Second only to Hitler and the Nazis, the 'Palestinian' Arab and his surrounding Arab neighbours hated the Jews and the Zionist movement more than they enjoyed fighting amongst themselves. In 1947 the United Nations drafted a resolution calling for the creation of two separate states within the British Mandate; one Arab and one Jewish. Eager to receive international recognition, the Jewish delegation accepted the territory the resolution allotted them.[10] Implacable and irate that the UN became involved and that the Arab had not received all the land, the 'Palestinian' Arab refused to recognize the legitimacy of the resolution. Instead of relying on diplomacy, the dastardly Arab resorted to the power of the sword.

♦ ♦ ♦

To be honest, anyone with a brain could see that the 1947 UN partition plan would do more to start a war than it would to foster a peaceful solution. It called for the two states to be separated into three practically unattached sections. The city of Jerusalem was to be governed by the UN, although there would be two separate municipalities, one Jewish, one Arab.[11] These three sections would be attached to each other by extraterritorial roads that in the event of hostilities, could be easily cut off from one another. At the time of partition, the Jews amounted to roughly thirty-three percent of the region's population, but were granted roughly fifty-five percent of the land, much of which was the Negev Desert.[12]

While the Jews were badly outnumbered by the 'Palestinian' Arabs, they made up for that weakness by being better organized, financed and relatively well equipped. When hostilities first began in 1947 the Jews quickly and with relative ease repulsed the Arab attacks, then began taking the fight into the 'Palestinian' territory.

In light of the disaster that was about to befall their Arab brothers, the surrounding Arab states (also recently created out of the British Mandate) banded together to form the 'Arab League' in an attempt to coordinate their military policy towards the common goal of driving the Jews into the sea. Egypt, Yemen, Somalia, Saudi Arabia, Jordan, Syria and Lebanon intervened to assist the 'Palestinians' promising to rid the area of its Jews.[13] The new Israeli government prepared for the worst as it had no intelligence service capable of gauging the Arab Leagues true strength (or weakness).

In hindsight, the new state of Israel was stronger than it believed itself to be. Israel could count on a unified command (except for two minor autonomous militia units) with the Haganah, interior lines of communication, excellent access to European financial institutions and also the credit to purchase weaponry of all kinds from the best manufactures in Europe and America.[14]

In comparison the members of the Arab League were not without their own advantages. They clearly surpassed the Jews in manpower reserves, surrounded the state of Israel on all sides except the Mediterranean and most league members already had existing (although primitive) air forces.[15]

As the Israeli's were fighting to hold onto what settlements they possessed, or had conquered from the 'Palestinian' Arab the war would largely be confined to the Mandate territory which was familiar to the Israelis. Whereas the various members of the Arab League would be forced to take the fight into Israeli territory. Attacking from every direction, but without coordination or common objectives, the advances of the Arab armies faltered and were dealt with in turn as the IDF was able to easily transfer units to which ever sector seemed most in danger. In the face of the seemingly invincible Israeli forces, the 'Palestinian' Arabs were eager to flee from their Mandate territory, either at the behest of the various Arab monarchs or out of fear for their personal safety.

Besides the fighting in the three Jewish sectors a battle developed in and around Jerusalem for control of the holy city. With the Jewish sector initially under siege, as it was effectively cut-off from supplies, it became of paramount importance for the IDF to lift the siege and relieve the Jewish population. A twenty-year-old Ariel Sharon, recently promoted to platoon commander* due to success in obstructing the advance of Iraqi forces into northern Israel, was engaged in the assaults on the Latrun redoubt, a fortified position overlooking the Tel Aviv-Jerusalem highway. The assault was unsuccessful and Sharon was wounded in the action, but his reputation for competence and bravery got him noticed by his superior and put him on the fast track for

* Roughly equivalent to 2nd or 1st Lieutenant or Captain.

promotion.[16] The IDF would go on to construct a make shift road* that sidestepped the main highway from Tel Aviv into Jerusalem and were thus able to supply their forces under siege.

Seeing the conflict spiraling out of control, the United Nations attempted to impose a ceasefire in June 1948. Both sides would flagrantly break the ceasefire, but as a British observer put it, the truce "...would be exploited by the Jews to continue military training and reorganizing while the Arabs would waste [the time] feuding over the future division of the spoils."[17]

This is exactly what happened. The Israeli's continued their conscription efforts almost doubling the size of the IDF and brought in more small, medium and heavy arms, while the various Arab League members were barely able to bolster their numbers within the theatre. Once again the UN attempted to introduce a new agreement in order to secure a peace. Without getting into the details, the proposal was so ludicrous that neither side (nor reality) could agree to any of its amendments and soon after the ceasefire expired fighting quickly resumed.

This time Israel would largely go on the offensive invading southern Lebanon and capturing the territory wedged in between Galilee and the Mediterranean. Further territory was seized that linked western (Jewish) Jerusalem to the Tel Aviv-Mediterranean corridor. After two more UN imposed ceasefires (which achieved nothing – other than underscore the ineffectiveness and irrelevancy of the UN) the final phase of the war was fought largely in the south as the Israelis attempted to consolidate their sovereignty over the Negev Desert. In this phase Ariel had recovered and was returned to platoon command. After his recuperation Ariel participated in the capture of Iraq-El-Manshia. Ariel's leadership in the assaults garnered him the attention of the Israeli Prime Minister David Ben-Gurion who honoured him with the name 'Sharon'.† After IDF forces

* Named the Burma Road. Some of the Israeli's had served with Field Marshall Slim against the Japanese in Burma.

† Meaning fertile land-plain or fair-good, Sharon also refers to a place in

planted the Israeli flag at the southernmost tip of the Negev the fighting was over.

The new and much enlarged state of Israel now encompassed all the Jewish territory of the UN Mandate and had conquered/annexed roughly fifty percent of the Arab partition. In comparison to the Mandate territories, the three Israeli sectors were now connected by wide births of land and not so easily isolated from each other. Although hard bargaining at the negotiation tables lay ahead, the Arab League states, whose forces were either destroyed or humiliated, were eager to sign ceasefires and peace treaties with the state of Israel as they realized there was no longer hope for victory.[19] Israel had achieved what, at the time, seemed impossible; it had repelled the advance of every major hostile Arab neighbour, and expanded its sovereignty to nearly eighty percent of the original Mandate territory.[20]

♦ ♦ ♦

As any observer would venture to assume, Israel's victory in 1948 did nothing to engender them to any of their Arab neighbours. Events in Egypt and within the context of the Cold War created new enemies and staunch allies outside of the Middle East. Before events would come together for another war, the Israeli's would be forced to reckon with the Arab 'Fedayeen'* guerilla inspired attacks. In response, the Israeli government called upon Sharon to train and command a crack company of 'offensive guerillas' whose mission was to take the fight to the Fedayeen and extract vengeance for their raids into Israeli settlements. This unit would become known as 'Unit 101'.[21]

In the immediate aftermath of the War of Independence, Sharon was promoted to company commander of a reconnaissance unit before moving to a position as an intelligence officer for IDF Central Command. After these postings Sharon took a period of leave to attend university in Jerusalem. Once recalled

Israel, the Plain of Sharon.[18]

* Fedayeen were islamic terrorist militias unassociated with any particular state.

into the service, Sharon was ideal to oversee the creation of Unit 101 as he had previously demonstrated an aptitude for aggressive tactics and forward thinking leadership. Unit 101 would take part in numerous reprisal operations earning a reputation for viciousness that would on occasion tread beyond the scope of morality. For example, Unit 101 was responsible for the 'massacre' of Arab civilians at the town of Qibya after they blew up a school building without knowing it was full of old men, women and children.[22]

As Unit 101 was detached from the regular army, the Israeli government could claim with some legitimacy that it was not responsible for the accidental civilian deaths at Qibya. In fairness, both the Arabs and Jews routinely indulged in such raid and reprisal tactics, making it difficult if not irrelevant to pinpoint who started the ball rolling. Although in all likelihood it was probably the 'Palestinian' Arabs.

In the years following the 1948 War, Egypt had drifted towards the Soviet sphere of influence and began to consider nationalizing the Suez Canal so as to deny its traffic to the western Europeans. Egypt was already using its position on the Sinai Peninsula to block Israeli seaborne trade through the Red Sea-Indian Ocean route. These two provocations created enemies out of the French, British and Israeli governments. The three countries had made plans for the eventual Egyptian nationalization (of the Canal) and decided to implement their military plans when Egyptian 'president' Gamal Abdel Nasser announced he would seize control in 1956.

♦ ♦ ♦

While the three partners shared a common enemy in Egypt, the French and British differed from the Israelis in their objectives. For the European duo the main objective was control over the Canal and a change of regime for the Nasser led Egyptian government. For the Israelis the objectives were to reopen maritime trade through the Red Sea, the neutralization of Egyptian forces

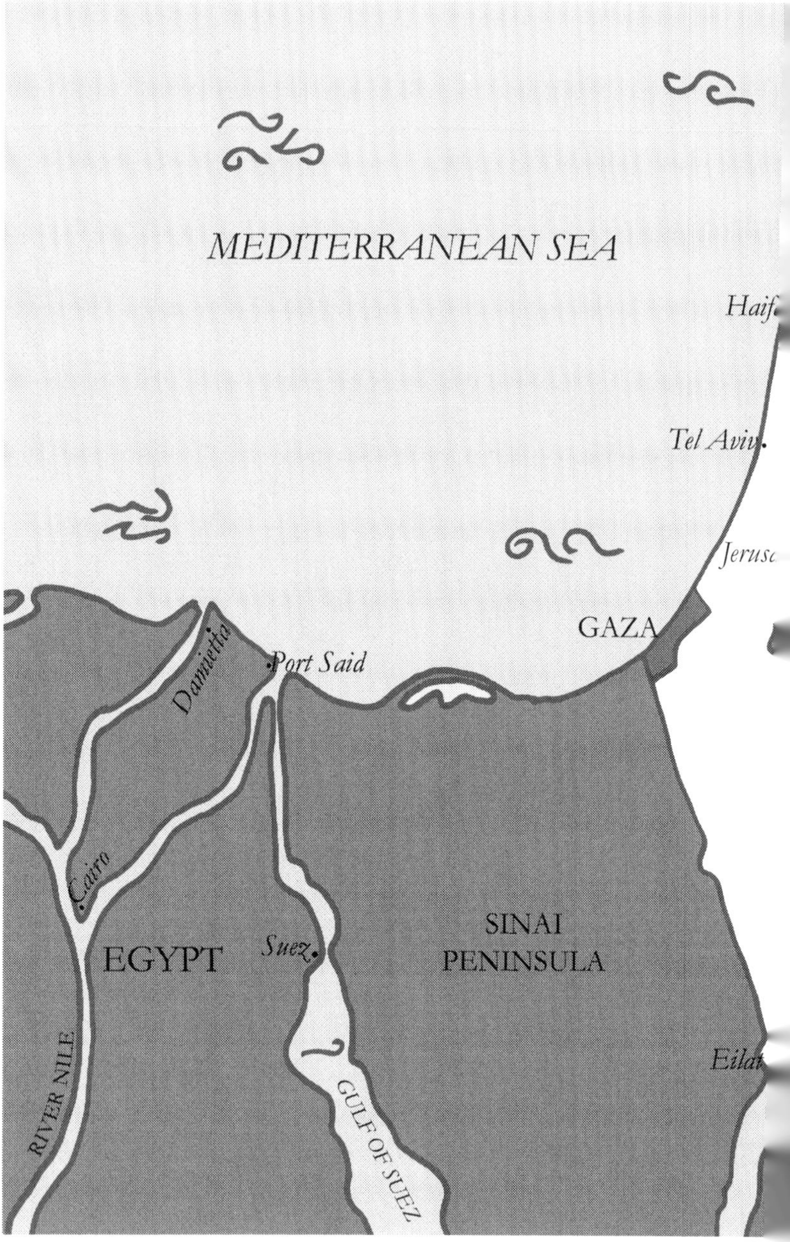
MEDITERRANEAN SEA
Haif
Tel Aviv
Jerus
GAZA
Damietta
Port Said
Cairo
EGYPT
Suez
SINAI
PENINSULA
RIVER NILE
GULF OF SUEZ
Eilat

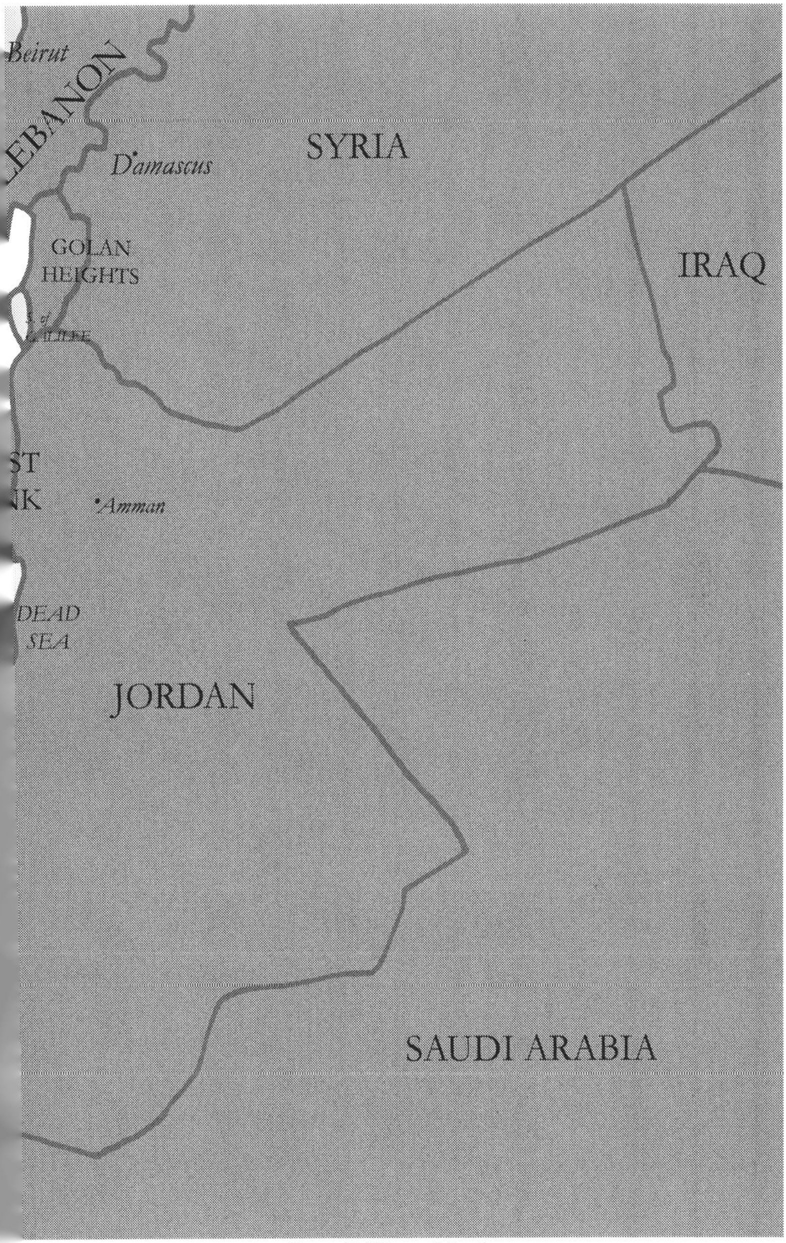

Israeli War of Indepence

in the Sinai and removal of the Fedayeen training camps in the Gaza Strip.[23]

Sharon's Unit 101 was combined with the 890th Paratrooper Battalion to form the 202nd Parachute Brigade, to which Sharon was put in command with the rank of Colonel.[24] As a means to protect the flanks of the Israeli forces operating to the north and south, the war plans allotted to Sharon and the 202nd the seizing and occupying of the strategic Mitla Pass, located in the central western Sinai. The 890th Paratroopers were dropped to the east of the pass, while Sharon and the remainder of the brigade were to follow on the ground from the Israeli border.[25] The four-hundred-man drop went off as planned with the troopers quickly digging into position to the east of the Pass. The remainder of Sharon's brigade overran the town of Themed on the morning of the 30th of October. They were able to link up with the Paratroopers late that evening after his column was strafed by Egyptian Mig fighters near the town of Nakla.[26]

Once arrived at the Mitla Pass, Sharon was presented with a dilemma. His orders from High Command were to hold the pass and advance no further. However, Egyptian infantry still occupied the western extremity of the pass and it was reported that a few brigades of Egyptian armour had been detached from their division at the Gidi Pass (to the north) with the intention of retaking the Mitla Pass.[27] If the Egyptian armour arrived in force the 202nd Brigade would be out-flanked and annihilated unless Sharon could seize the high ground from the Egyptian infantry at the eastern entrance of the pass.

The IDF high Command refused to give Sharon permission to attack Jebel el Heitan, but allowed him to send a reconnaissance party to ascertain the Egyptian strength.[28] Sharon decided upon a more aggressive course and sent two companies of the 890th paratroopers to reconnoiter-in-force the Egyptian positions. The infantry attack, aided by a handful of light tanks and mortars, met stiff resistance against the dug in Egyptians and were forced to take refuge in a defile. By the time Sharon learned what had befallen his initial assault he sent forth a relief party. In the second action that ensued during the dark hours of night the Israelis emerged victorious clearing out the cave defenses and, routing the Egyptians as they fled. When the dust settled the Israelis under Sharon's command suffered some thirty eight deaths compared to the two hundred sixty deaths exacted upon the Egyptians.[29] Upon receiving news that the Egyptians were advancing from the north, threatening to turn Sharon's flank, Sharon was forced to abandon the captured positions and re-form his lines to the east of the track junction, however, the Egyptian armour was ordered back towards the Gidi Pass and from there the Egyptians were sent back to the western bank of the canal.

In the aftermath of the attack Sharon was criticized for what was considered by some to be an unnecessary shedding of Israeli blood. Critics believed that his brigade wasn't actually in serious danger as the IAF controlled the skies and that Sharon had purposely went looking for a fight. However, his actions were largely vindicated by the IDF's chief of staff, General Moshe Dayan, who was forgiving of Sharon's actions in hindsight.[30] Dayan confirmed that Sharon did not know that air superiority had been achieved by the IAF, so that under the circumstances of the moment, Sharon's unauthorized action was tactically understandable. None-the-less, Sharon's reputation for tactical aggressiveness combined with independent action would begin to be considered a liability in the coming years.

In the wider context of the conflict, the IDF was successful in achieving its main military objectives as set out by the Israeli government. In the north the IDF had isolated Gaza City (and later occupied it) and had driven the Egyptians back to the Suez Canal via the coastal road. After the Mitla Pass was secure the IDF also advanced towards Sharm el-Sheik on the southern tip of the Sinai. In addition to the main force advancing south

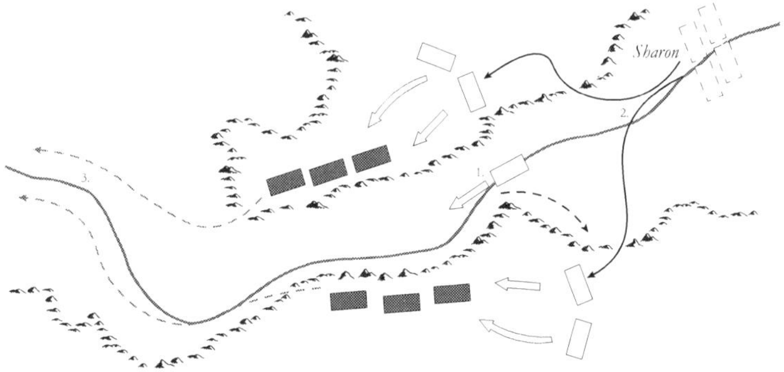

Battle of Mitla Pass

1. Sharon's reconnasance in force. 2. Night time operations against the Egyptian positions. 3. Egyptians retreat.

along the eastern coast of Sinai, two companies were detached from the 202nd and air dropped along the western coast to assist with the capture of Sharm el-Sheikh, which fell on the 7th of November. Israel could now boast to having achieved its objective in reopening its Red Sea trade routes. With the Egyptians expelled from the Sinai and the Israeli's holding positions ten miles east of the Suez Canal fighting in the Sinai largely halted. International diplomacy now intervened as both the Soviets and Americans took an increased interest in the happenings surrounding the Canal.

Even though President Eisenhower had signalled that Egyptian nationalization (of the Canal) would be unacceptable, Eisenhower's administration was furious with France, Great Britain and Israel as they had kept the Americans in the dark. The Soviets, who were wooing the Egyptians (and other Arab states) were increasingly concerned that their position in the Middle East would be endangered if the three allies succeeded in changing the regime in Cairo, and therefore began threatening to destabilize Europe and elsewhere should events in the Sinai not be brought to a conclusion.[31]

With the world's two superpowers demanding things return to the previous status quo, the British and French were forced to abandon their plan for regime change. The UN now became involved and established the Sinai Peninsula as a de-militarized zone with a UN emergency force creating a buffer zone between Israel and Egypt.[32] The UN intervention (supported by the US and the USSR) was an embarrassment for the French and British governments, but for Israel it had the benefit of securing its border with Egypt and guaranteeing access to the Red Sea and beyond.

♦ ♦ ♦

In the immediate aftermath of the Suez Crisis, Sharon was cashiered out of the 202nd as the officers practically mutinied after the Battle of Mitla Pass. Although Sharon wasn't fired from the

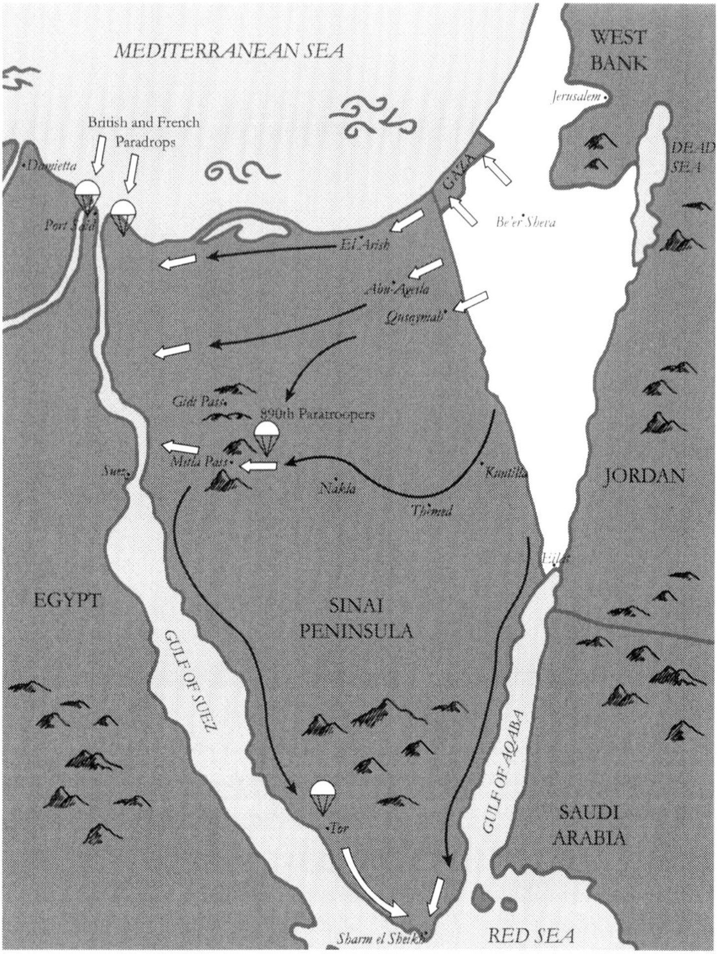
MEDITERRANEAN SEA
WEST BANK
Jerusalem
DEAD SEA
British and French Paradrops
Port Said
GAZA
Be'er Sheva
El Arish
Abu Ageila
Qusaymah
Gidi Pass
890th Paratroopers
Mitla Pass
Suez
Kuntilla
Nakla
Themed
JORDAN
Eilat
EGYPT
SINAI PENINSULA
GULF OF SUEZ
GULF OF AQABA
SAUDI ARABIA
Tor
Sharm el Sheikh
RED SEA

Suez War

service, he was sent to London to attend a school for middle ranking officers. After his time in the UK he returned to Israel, but Sharon's period of exile was still not over. Frustrated that his military career wasn't advancing as quickly as he had planned, Sharon decided to attend law school in Tel Aviv where he received his degree in 1966.[33]

Sharon's career in the military was far from being overtaken by him practicing the law. After acquiring his law degree, Sharon underwent tank training beginning with the basics of firing, maneuver, and communications: working his way up to the science/art of deploying a brigade of tanks onto a battlefield or into a theatre.

During his period of mechanized training Sharon became known for applying his unorthodox commando/paratrooper infantry doctrines towards developing new and unique Israeli armoured tactics. The use of armour was rapidly becoming dominant within Israeli strategic doctrine; Sharon was on the cutting edge of that development. However, Sharon was still stuck in a career rut until in 1962 he was offered command over a reserve mechanized brigade; he declined the opportunity preferring to hold out for command of an armoured brigade instead.[34] Even when he received command over an armoured brigade his ambitions were insatiable, he wanted to rise quickly.

Sharon's real break came in 1964 when Yitzhak Rabin was appointed the new chief of staff of the IDF, Yitzhak Rabin, was appointed to the position. Rabin had been politically pressured to assist Sharon in his career advancement, but he had also been impressed with the young man's work in the training and organization of the reserve brigade.[35] However, there was still much displeasure, amongst some politicians and some in the high command, with Sharon who was perceived to be insubordinate, overly ambitious and had a penchant for stretching the truth to suit his needs. Sharon was essentially given an ultimatum, he would be promoted to deputy commander of Northern Command for one year, at the end of which his behaviour would be evaluated and based upon that Sharon would either be promoted to Brigadier General or be dismissed from the service.[36]

As it turned out, Sharon passed the test "without a shadow of doubt"[37] and was shortly thereafter moved from Northern Command to the position of director of military training, and given the command of a reserve division (in Southern Command) with the rank of Major General. As director of military training, Sharon sought to infuse his commando mentality throughout the entirety of the IDF. Sharon's efforts in training vastly increased the IDF's level of preparedness when war would once again breakout amongst Israel and its Arab neighbours.

♦ ♦ ♦

So long as the Arab states could muster military strength they could never accept the existence of the Jewish state of Israel. While the leaders of the Arab states understood that active engagement with Israeli forces would result in the certain destruction of their forces, at times a little sabre rattling was necessary to divert attention away from their regimes corrupt and inefficient methods of governance. But the Jews were sensitive to the threats of a second holocaust that were being issued by the Arab governments.

By this time the two world superpowers were increasing their involvement in the region by taking sides and solidifying their military support. Israel was generally (although not fully or enthusiastically) supported by the US. Egypt, Lebanon, Syria and Jordan were becoming client states of the USSR, eager to receive advanced weaponry in exchange for access to markets and resources.[38] Egypt was of special importance to the Soviets as its geographic location allowed for further penetration of communist influence into southern Africa and the potential for disruption of global commerce through control of the Suez Canal.

As the Arabs were largely concerned over local matters, the

Soviets were mainly interested in humiliating the Americans and gaining influence throughout the region. Acting out of its own self-interest, the Soviets began whispering to the Egyptians and Syrians that the Israelis were massing their forces along the Syrian-Israeli border. This was of course untrue, but the Syrians and Egyptians took it seriously and began to mobilize their forces accordingly.[39] In support of their Syrian allies, the Egyptians sent two divisions into the Sinai and ordered the UN peacekeeping forces to evacuate the border area. Events quickly began to spiral out of control as all sides rapidly prepared themselves for war. A short while after Egypt moved into the Sinai, they announced the closure of the Gulf of Aqaba to Israeli commerce - knowing full well that this was part of what triggered war back in 1956.[40]

While Israel was preparing for a war on all fronts, its politicians and diplomats were frantically pursuing a peaceful solution. With the closure of the Gulf of Aqaba it was no longer possible to step back from the precipice. Regardless of the hesitation of their political masters, the IDF was confident, eager and well prepared in its mission to defend the state of Israel. The same advantages that Israel held in the War of Independence continued to be applied in the conflict of 1967. Interior lines, unified command and precious little territory to exchange for time. Likewise, the Arab states could count on the same advantages as before, overwhelming numbers, surrounding the Israeli borders and also the technological support of their superpower patron, the USSR. While the Arabs converged upon Israel's frontiers they waited for the right opportunity to declare war and strike at the Jews. For their part, the Israeli's were not about to wait patiently for the Arabs to make their move.

On the morning on June 5th, the IDF struck with a boldness that would put the German blitzkrieg to shame.[41] The first stroke came from the sky. The early morning witnessed almost the entirety of the IAF attacking, immobilizing or destroying the majority of the Egyptian air forces capabilities.[42] In conjunction with the air surprise the IDF launched its ground forces (comprised of three divisions on the Sinai front, of which Sharon commanded the division in the centre) along the northern and central Sinai routes.

♦ ♦ ♦

Sharon's division (comprised of roughly 14,000 men and 150 tanks) was tasked with the capture of the strategic town of Abu Agheila which the Egyptians were using as a rally point to build up their forces for an attack into southern Israel. Abu Agheila and the immediate area was well defended by an Egyptian infantry division (consisting of roughly 16,000 men and 90 tanks), drawn up in three lines of concrete bunkers and trenches with artillery and armoured elements to the rear.[43] The defensive complex was to be assaulted on the evening of the 5th and if all went according to plan would be reduced by the morning of the 6th. Time was of the essence; aggressive action was required.

Sharon's assault was audacious calling for the complete envelopment and isolation of the garrison. In order to affect this, Sharon deployed the majority of his infantry for an assault upon the Egyptian front while sending his armour around both flanks. The final envelopment would occur when the paratroopers were ferried (via helicopter) into the rear along the Egyptian lines of communication.[44] Before the beginning of the entire operation, Sharon prepared a massive shelling of the Egyptian defences by his artillery.

The artillery bombardment and the ensuing frontal infantry assault kept the Egyptian attention focused upon that sector. The Egyptians were so distracted that they did not observe the flanking maneuvers of the Israeli armour or paratroopers. Around midnight the trap was set, the Egyptians were attacked from every side and were unable to give each other support. By the morning the Egyptian division had either surrendered, escaped or lay dead; they ceased to exist as a fighting formation.[45]

Abu Agheila was now in Israeli hands (at the cost of some forty Israeli dead, one hundred fifty wounded) which opened up the central Sinai and threatened the Egyptians further to the east and south. With the loss of Abu Agheila, all Egyptian forces were ordered back towards the canal so as to not become isolated. Sharon's division was now given the task of capturing and holding Nakla while another force was detached (from Sharon's) and sent on to occupy the Mitla Pass cutting off the remnants of the retreating Egyptians.[46]

The capture of the Mitla and Gidi Passes largely ended Sharon's active involvement in the fighting. But there was still much to be accomplished by the IDF elsewhere. One division in the north of the Sinai theatre was tasked with the conquest of el-Arish and the Gaza Strip on the Mediterranean road towards Kantara on the Suez Canal. The third division (to the south of Sharon's) was given the responsibility of capturing the crossroads at Kuntilla thus threatening the Egyptians located at Themed after which they would link up with Sharon in order to hold the Gidi and Mitla passes.[47]

Even further to the south the Israeli Navy was to conduct an operation against Sharm el-Sheik and thus end the Egyptian blockade of the Gulf of Aqaba. By the time the assault on Sharm el-Sheik began the Egyptians had already begun their retreat out of Sinai but had left a paltry force for the defence of the coastal town. Within a day the town was captured and the straits were once again opened to Israeli traffic.[48] With that, actions in the Sinai largely died down, Israel controlled the eastern length of the canal and was now prepared to focus its attention on the Jordanians and Syrians along the West Bank of the Jordan River and Golan Heights.

The Jordanians now posed the most immediate threat to the Jewish state as its army was well equipped, professional and at some points was a mere ten miles from the Mediterranean from which they could sever Israel into separate parts. The main Jor-

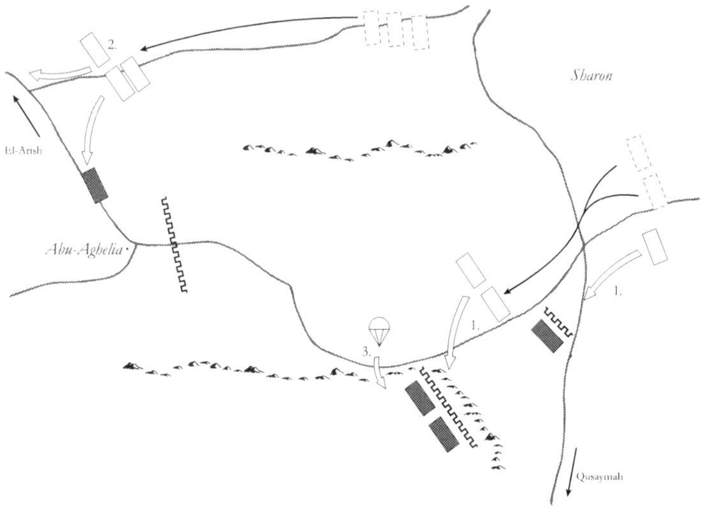

Battle of Abu Aghelia

1. Infantry pins down main Egptian defences. 2. Armour manuevers into Egyptian rear. 3. Paratroopers clear Egpytian trenches from the flank.

danian weakness lay in its air force which consisted of roughly thirty fighters.[49] After the near total destruction of the Egyptian air force on the first day of war, the IAF was able to transfer much of their strength to deal with the threat emanating from Syria and Jordan.

Initially the Israeli strategy had been to stay on the defensive in its central and northern commands while focusing on the southern Sinai front. After the lightning victories in Sinai, the Israeli's were capable of launching major offensives into the West Bank. Once again the IAF launched a devastating sortie against the Jordanian air force, destroying it in its entirety as the Jordanians refueled and rearmed. The first ground operation was the capture of East Jerusalem which was affected by the evening of June 7th, Sharon took Nakla on the morning of the 8th.[50] The capture of Jerusalem buoyed the spirits of the Jewish nation. In the course of the next few days the IDF succeeded in pushing the Jordanians back to the eastern bank of the Jordan, capturing the major Biblical cities of the West Bank; Hebron, Ramallah, Bethlehem and Jericho.[51]

During the last two days of the war the fighting was mainly focused around the Golan Heights, which dominated the Syrian-Israeli border. Since the War of Independence, the Syrians had sporadically used their advantage of elevation to barrage the Israeli settlements below. With the success in Sinai and the West Bank, the Israeli settlers in the north increased their demands for the IDF to deal with the Golan Heights problem and were successful in persuading the High Command into an aggressive course of action. Soviet pressure for a ceasefire was now coming to a boil, but the Israeli Defence Minister gave the green light for operations to proceed in the Golan Heights giving the commanders a forty-eight-hour time frame.[52] Fighting was fierce, but once again the IAF was used to great tactical advantage, effectively neutralizing the Syrian advantage of elevation.

By the end of the six days Israel had effectively conquered

the entirety of the original Palestinian Mandate territory while also acquiring the Sinai Peninsula and Golan Heights. The Russians, who were instrumental in provoking the conflict now scrambled to get a ceasefire put in place. Israel had essentially satisfied its security requirements and was ready for the olive branch as a means to consolidate their recent gains. The various Arab armies, thoroughly humiliated once again, were forced to abandon their dream of perpetuating another holocaust and were eager to negotiate lest the Israeli gain any further advantage. A ceasefire was signed on the 11th in which the Israeli government signaled their willingness to barter the Sinai and Golan territories in exchange for peace treaties.[53] All this belonged to the future, for now a wave of euphoria swept over Israel as the people rejoiced in the triumph of their arms.

♦ ♦ ♦

In his position at the head of training Sharon was instrumental in developing Israeli settler policy as he was quick to recognize that, post-1967, all land the Jews could lay their hands on and improve would effectively become theirs. Sharon was able to relocate training facilities into the newly conquered territories effectively creating the nucleus for further municipal expansion.[54] As head of training, Sharon would become involved with controversy over the humane treatment of Bedouin tribesmen who were evicted from their traditional grazing/camp grounds in the Sinai during this time period. Criticism of Sharon's record during this time was largely muted in the press as it was kept within military circles.

To be fair to Sharon, he was largely just enforcing policy created by the government, even if he was doing so with an unexpectedly cruel efficiency. It must also be remembered that the people being expulsed from their lands had very recently been advocating for another Jewish holocaust.

Before long Sharon would become embroiled in another conflict with his superiors. The source of tension this time was over the direction of Israeli strategic defence policy in the Sinai. The concept that was being espoused by his superiors was the construction of a series of static fortified positions along the eastern side of the Suez Canal. Sharon was dead set against the idea of a static defence and instead lobbied for the creation of a light reconnaissance line with strong, mobile armoured units held in reserve that could be moved to where they were needed most.[55] Emotions ran high as both sides (of the argument) thought their opposition would be courting disaster. As Sharon's concept was not supported by anyone in a position of authority it lost out when it came to implementation. This disagreement coupled with Sharon's dramatic proclivity for insubordination (involving a slammed door) effectively blocked Sharon's chances for promotion.[56]

Shortly after the meeting that ended with Sharon slamming a door on his way out, he was informed that his contract would not be renewed with Southern Command. No one in High Command or within the political establishment wanted to, or felt compelled to, intervene on his behalf. Sharon was given a choice, he could accept his accumulated vacation time or he could get paid out in hard currency.[57] As news spread of Sharon's situation and disillusion with the Labor Party, other political figures emerged attempting to swoon the war hero into their ranks before the upcoming elections in 1969.

Up to that point in time, Israeli politics had been dominated by the Labor Party, it was only very recent that a coalition of smaller parties began to coalesce to present a viable alternative. Sharon was approached by two dominant figures in the opposition coalition who promised him a place in cabinet in exchange for his running on their ticket. After that meeting Sharon came to the realization that the coalition would attempt to control him and he somewhat embarrassingly backed out of the political agreement. Regardless, word leaked into the media about Sharon's meeting with the opposition, forcing the Labor government and High Command to find any excuse to retain Sharon's services in the army.[58]

Conveniently a position was created to keep Sharon in the army and also out of the country until after the election. The job of 'Lecturer for the IDF' sent Sharon on a tour of speaking engagements in the US, Mexico, Japan, Hong Kong and South Korea where he would meet with many world leaders within military, political and diplomatic circles. With the election over and the Labor Party safely returned to power, Sharon was welcomed back to Israel and shortly thereafter promoted to Commanding Officer of Southern Command.[59]

As part of his promotion Sharon had to agree to not abandon the policy of static defence that had been all but fully implemented with the construction of the 'Bar-Lev Lines'. However, Sharon did tinker with the policy opting for a compromise between the two schools of thought weakening the static defensives and increasing the mobile reserves. In addition, Sharon green lighted the construction of eleven massive underground complexes capable of housing armoured units and creating safe positions for Israeli artillery to fire from a safe distance away from the bank of the Suez Canal.

Even before the ceasefire that ended the fighting in 1967, the Soviet Union began to double down on their gamble with their Arab client states. Arms and advisors from the USSR began to flood into Egypt. Intermittently Egypt and Israel fired at each other from across the canal since the ceasefire of 1967 took effect. Tensions ran high but outright war was avoided after the Israeli's decided to scale back the tempo of their efforts in the running aerial dogfight over the Canal.

Largely due to their wild success in the Six Days War, the disease of overconfidence took root within the IDF; after the next war it would come to be known as 'the Concept'. This sense of martial superiority set the stage for the next phase of war between the Arab states and Israel.

♦ ♦ ♦

The Arab states were generally unaccepting of the results of the 1967 war and as soon as the dust settled they were busy making plans to regain what they had lost. Egypt and Syria were the two states most steadfast in their belligerence towards the state of Israel. On the other hand, Jordan, the erstwhile nemesis of Israel, was afraid to lose even more of its territory and had decided to stay out of the coming conflict, even going so far as to warn the Israelis of war plans being created by Egypt and Syria.[60]

As previously stated, the Egyptians and Syrians had been receiving military equipment and advice from the Soviet Union, but the Arabs had grown to distrust the motives of the communists in Russia. For their part the Soviets were not acting in good faith with their Arab clients as their main concern had shifted towards maintaining the unstable détente they had achieved with the Americans. However, the Soviets were all too obliging when it came to selling military hardware to their clients.

Since the time of independence the Israelis had been drifting towards the western camp who had come to be their main supplier for advanced military hardware. Some say, even though it is denied, the western powers assisted Israel develop its nuclear capability. By now, the Israelis had created their own military industries which had made considerable strides in production and technological prowess.[61] The battles that would ensue would resemble what it would be or look like if the NATO and Warsaw Pact powers were to engage in a conventional war.

After their humiliating defeats in the 1967 war, the Egyptians and Syrians had undergone serious tactical reforms putting an emphasis on anti-tank and anti-air capabilities.[62] Along the Suez Canal, the Egyptians had acquired Soviet made surface-to-air missile defence systems (SAMs). In comparison to the Arabs previously stated goals of 'driving the Jews into the sea', the two Arab belligerents had much less ambitious objectives. They merely wanted to seize limited amounts of territory in order to disrupt the Israeli reputation of invincibility and to use as bargaining chips in future negotiations.[63] Even if their specific war aims were more limited than in previous times, their rhetoric of 'kill the Jews' went unchanged in an effort to rally their populations for war.

In the spring of 1973 the Egyptians and Syrians put the Russian military advisors on notice signalling their intention to force them out of the country.[64] This act was seen by the Israelis as further proof that war would once again be averted. The logic of 'the Concept' had become so ingrained within the halls of power that every new development was contorted to further reinforce the belief that Israel would not be attacked. In reality the Egyptians and Syrians had acted out of the belief that the Russians were leaking information of the planned Arab attack to American and Israeli intelligence. Even with intelligence coming from the upper echelons of the Egyptian and Jordanian government (where the Mossad operated a mole) the Israelis continued to believe in peace.[65] The summer of 1973 would be the final calm before the storm of war.

As summer turned to fall the Israelis began preparations for their religious celebrations of Rosh Hashanah and Yom Kippur (Jewish New Year). At the same time the Egyptians and Syrians began mobilizing their forces under the guise of massive training exercises. Achieving near total surprise,* the Arabs launched simultaneous attacks on the 6th of October. On the Sinai front, the Egyptians mustered roughly two hundred thousand infantry, thirteen hundred tanks and two thousand pieces of artillery, organized into two armies comprised of five divisions.[66] The Egyptian forces were able to affect their crossing in numerous areas thus isolating the Israelis occupying the Bar-Lev fortifications. After their successful crossings, the Egyptians dug themselves into defensive positions and prepared themselves for the

* The Egyptian mole turned out to be playing both sides and had lulled Israeli leadership into a dangerous complacency.

inevitable Israeli counter attack.

On the Golan front the Syrians had concentrated roughly fifty thousand soldiers, eight thousand tanks and six hundred pieces of artillery. The Syrians, attacking in conjunction with the Egyptians also achieved the element of surprise and easily drove the Israelis (roughly twelve thousand infantry, one hundred eighty tanks)[67] from their advanced positions on the cease-fire line. As the Syrian advances were considered the greater immediate threat to the major metropolitan areas, the lion's share of Israel's mobilized reserves began pouring into the northern region.

Meanwhile events in the Sinai were beginning to take a turn for the worse. Israeli counterattacks against the Egyptian bridgeheads had proved fatal as the Egyptian infantry came armed with powerful shoulder fired rockets and were protected against air attacks with their SAM sites on the western bank of the Suez. With their bridgeheads sufficiently established, the Egyptians began concentrating their armour in the southern portion of the Canal area for an advance upon the Gidi and Mitla Passes.[68]

Sharon, who had been a vocal proponent of bringing the war into Egypt through a crossing of the Canal, was back in command of a division in the Sinai theatre. One of Sharon's recon brigades had succeeded in finding the hinge that separated the two Egyptian armies in the vicinity of the northern shore of the Great Bitter Lake. Sharon practically begged Southern Command to be allowed to exploit this joint and immediately cross the Canal with his entire division. For various reasons Sharon's request was denied. On October 14th the Egyptian armoured elements ventured east outside of their SAM defence radius.[69] It was now time for an Israel counterstroke.

The two Egyptian columns that were headed for the two passes were counter attacked on both their flanks and all but annihilated. Sharon's division was now given permission to split the Egyptian and to establish a bridgehead on the west side of

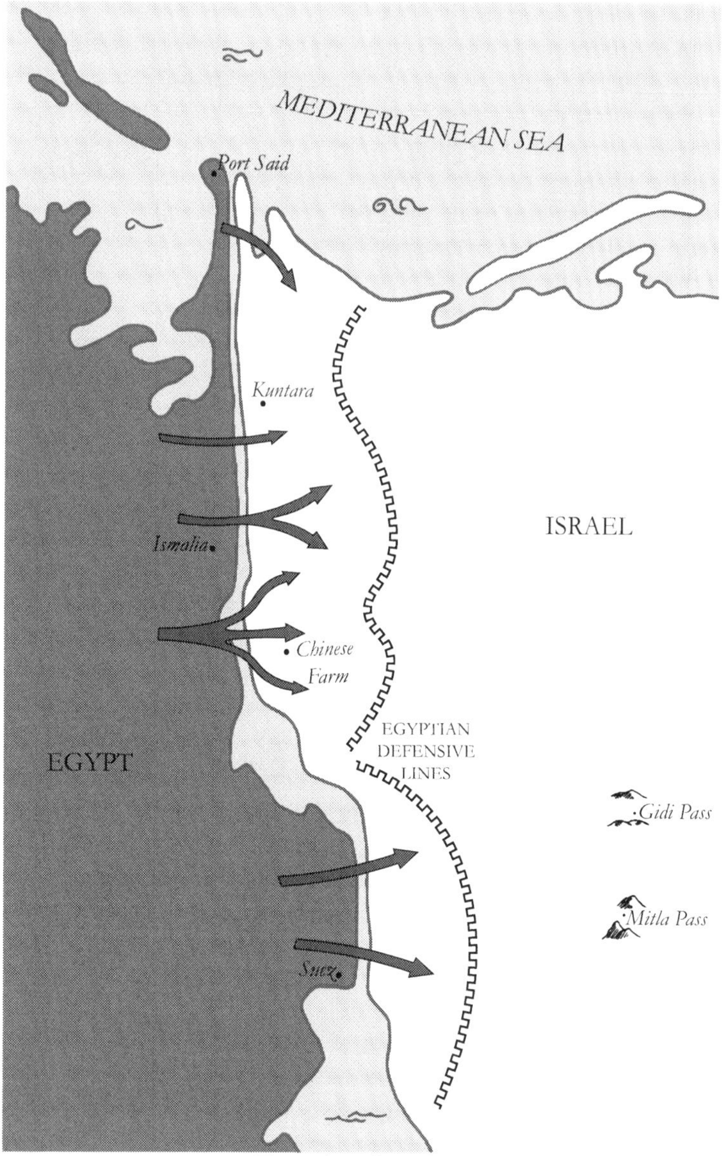

Egyptian Crossing

the Suez. On the night of the 15th a brigade of Sharon's paratroopers crossed the canal on rubber boats and set about attacking military targets especially the SAM sites. Following up the paratroopers came a small detachment of tanks and armoured personal carriers ferried over on small rafts. With a bridgehead established, but without permanent bridges, Sharon lobbied for permission to cross with his entire division.[70] Once again Sharon's request was refused, High Command was concerned that Sharon's division would become trapped as long as there were Egyptians on the eastern bank.

Sharon was correct in his reading of the situation, the quickest, most economical method for removing the Egyptians from the east bank was to cross over into Egypt itself. Instead of crossing, Sharon was ordered to assault the Egyptian positions located at the 'Chinese Farm' and 'Missouri' compounds.[71] Living up to his reputation for independent action, Sharon decided to follow his orders to the letter but not the intent. Sharon moved against the compounds with a detached brigade, the rest of his division slipped across the canal under the cover of darkness.

With the strength of the division behind him, Sharon was able to enlarge the bridgehead created by the paratroopers before he began to push his division north towards the city of Ismailia. Prior to Sharon's crossing, High Command had authorized Major General Adan's division to make the crossing as well.[72] It was understood that Adan would make the first crossing in force, as Sharon would be busy clearing the Chinese Farm and Missouri positions. Sharon, ever the hot head, refused to be second over the canal and was able to beat Adan to the punch.

In the wake of Sharon's crossing and advance north towards Ismailia, Adan's division swept in a southern direction and managed to encircle the city of Suez, cutting off the Egyptian Third Army on the eastern bank. With the majority of the Egyptian combat units isolated from each other and cut-off from their capital, Sharon's aggressive maneuver across the Canal effectively paralysed the Second and Third Egyptian armies. The Egyptian reserves on the west bank of the Canal attempted to re-establish contact with the Second and Third armies but were repulsed by the three Israeli divisions who had made the crossing (Adan had been followed up by Major General Kalman Magen's division).[73] Furthermore, Sharon's and Adan's divisions had been aggressively attacking the Egyptian SAM sites in conjunction with the IAF which effectively gave Israel control of the skies over the Canal and put the Second and Third armies in an increasingly perilous situation. Sharon and the Israelis were now within forty miles of Cairo, with barely anything capable of resistance in between.

It was now that the two superpowers, after having almost intervened in the conflict themselves, understood the urgency of the situation and attempted to broker a ceasefire. Operations in the northern Golan sector were also beginning to de-escalate. The IDF barely held back the initial Syrian assault, but after reinforcements had arrived the IDF was able to advance to within thirty miles of Damascus.[74] From these forward positions within Syria, the IDF held out against a combined assault by the Syrians, Iraqis and Jordanians.

The Russians and Americans both wanted a ceasefire between the belligerents but for different reasons. For the Russians, the reason was to prop up their influence in the region. The Americans wanted to stop the potential for the conflict to spiral out of control and saw an opportunity to replace the influence of the USSR with their own.

Much to the credit and hard work of the US diplomat, Henry Kissinger, the UN Security Council adopted a resolution calling for a ceasefire and the means by which to enforce it. The ceasefire gradually took effect with minimal disruption along both the Suez and Golan fronts. The road towards peace was a long

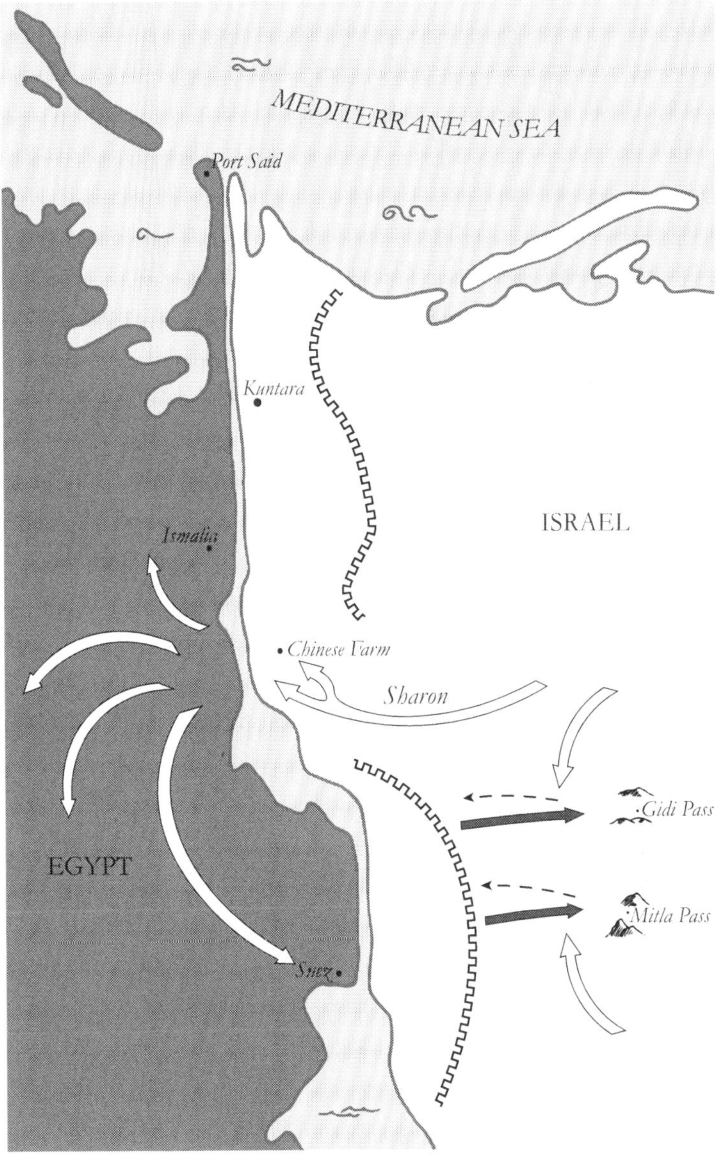

Sharon's Counter Attack

and arduous one, and in some instances was not achieved.* The United Nations was responsible for the creation and occupation of buffer zones between the various belligerents.

♦ ♦ ♦

The conclusion of fighting in late October of 1973 radically altered the geopolitical landscape of the Middle East. The Egyptians had satisfied their honour, after their humiliating defeat in 1967, through their initial cross canal invasion. This now allowed the Egyptians to enter into peace negotiations while being able to save face throughout the Arab world. The direct diplomacy between Israel and Egypt had the added benefit of gradually turning Egypt into an American client state (Egypt had been drifting towards the west since they had expelled the Soviet advisors in 1972).[75] The Kingdom of Jordan would also enter into peace negotiations with Israel, eventually opting to join the western camp. In contrast to Egypt and Jordan, Syria remained within the Communist-Russian camp, but they had finally come to realize the futility of conventional action against Israel. For the Arab peoples who continued on in hostility with Israel their only hope of victory over the Jewish state came in the form of harassing terrorist tactics, which at their worst was a deadly annoyance for the average Israel.

With the end of open hostilities and the resumption of (relatively) normal civilian life, Sharon's penchant for independent initiative and growing disaffection with the governing Labor Party led to his dismissal from military service in early 1974.[76] Prior to his return to command in 1973 his civilian-political career was interrupted by the war and had to be postponed out of necessity. When the election campaign resumed, Sharon won a seat in the Knesset (Israeli parliament). Disaffection over the Labor Party's (perceived) mishandling of the war did not sweep the Labor Party out of office immediately, but the population was eager for new Labor leadership.[77]

* Syria and Israel are still technically at war.

After a year in the Knesset Sharon vacated his seat in Parliament,* but remained as a special advisor to the new Labor Prime Minister, Yitzhak Rabin. In the elections scheduled for 1977, Sharon planned to make his return to the Likud Party but intended to make a bid for party leader. Upon failure to win the leadership, Sharon shopped around with the other parties but was rejected everywhere. Sharon settled on creating his own party† which he merged with Likud upon their victory in the general election. In exchange for the merger Sharon was given the portfolio of Minister of Agriculture.

In his position as Minister of Agriculture, Sharon once again took up the flag of the settler's cause. Sharon began encouraging the Jewish people to buy and develop as much land as was possible as a means of establishing their sovereignty over the conquered territory. After the 1981 elections in which Likud was narrowly returned to power, Sharon was appointed to the position of Minister of Defense.[78]

Shortly after the assumption of his new position, Sharon was responsible for the direction of military policy as Israel became a belligerent in the 1982 Lebanese War. The war was sparked in Lebanon after the Palestinian Liberation Organization (PLO) assassinated the Israeli Ambassador to the United Kingdom. The PLO is a terrorist organization dedicated to the destruction of the state of Israel, based out of Palestinian refugee camps in Lebanon with the tacit approval of the Arab-Muslim government of Lebanon. After the assassination, Sharon and the Israeli government were resolved to uproot the PLO from Lebanon and install a friendly Christian government to power in Lebanon.

Initially the IDF enjoyed success in overrunning the country and in the capture of Beirut, but the tide of international opinion relentlessly turned against Israel. Although much of world

* He sat for the Liberal Party of Israel at this time.

† Sharon created the Shlomtzion Party (Peace-Zion) in 1976, it was a right-wing party.

opinion had historically been prejudiced against Israel, the massacre of Muslim Palestinians at Sabra and Shatilla by Christian Lebanese forces destroyed any remaining international support Israel had.[79] Sharon, as defense minister, was held responsible by the world andmore importantly the Israeli population. The Israeli people had come to expect civilized behaviour even when operating amongst the barbaric Arabs who applied no such moral considerations when fighting the Jews.

Effectively forced to resign his position as the clamour of opposition arose, Sharon continued to be a part of the Likud cabinet except now without a portfolio.[80] Eventually Sharon would re-emerge as a challenger for the leadership of the Likud Party. In the year 1999 the Likud government fell and was replaced by the Labor Party. After which Likud underwent a leadership race in which Sharon was selected to lead the party.

Around this time the Palestinians political-terror leadership were planning to wage another guerilla war of terror against the state of Israel. The event that the Palestinians claimed propelled them into action was when Sharon paid a visit to the western wall of Jerusalem.[*81] PLO leader Yasser Arafat declared a new terror war, calling on the Palestinians of the West Bank to attack the 'occupation forces' of Israel (by which he meant civilians) by any means necessary, including the now common place suicide bomber. In the election of 2001, after the fall of the short lived Labor government, Sharon and the Likud Party were given a mandate to form the next government and to take a hardline with the Palestinian terrorists.[82] Sharon was quick to understand that in Israel's war on terror, it would be wise to create a unity government coalition that included the Labor Party.

The major development of Sharon's term as Prime Minister was the unexpected move towards 'unilateral disengagement' from the Gaza Strip and West Bank. This move came as a major

* This is preposterous in that operations of any sort are never initiated spontaneously.

shock to the world and the Israeli populace as Sharon had previously been seen as the patron saint of the settlement movement. In 2005 Sharon ordered the IDF to forcibly remove settlers and destroy the settlements angering the far right members of his political coalition.[83] The reaction was extreme from some segments of the populations with a group of Rabbis evoking an ancient curse condemning Sharon to death. However, the move was generally popular amongst the mainstream Israeli populace. In conjunction with pulling out from the conquered territories, the Israelis constructed border fences around the Gaza Strip and across the West Bank.

Disengagement was unpopular amongst the right of centre Likud Party which forced Sharon to fight for the leadership of the Party in 2005. After barely winning the leadership race against his longtime rival, Benjamin Netanyahu, Sharon decided to step down from Likud to form a more centrist party, Kadima. In the spring election of 2006 Kadima was elected to government on the first centrist platform in the modern history of the Israeli state, by this time Sharon was no longer capable of leadership.[84]

Unfortunately for the nation and state, the new year of 2006 witnessed Sharon incapacitated by a stroke and put into a coma by his doctors. The coma effectively ended Sharon's political career as he stayed unconscious until his life expired in early January 2014. Shortly after Sharon's incapacitation the Palestinians, with the aid of a new terror axis, Iran, Syria and their terror proxy Hezbollah (based in Lebanon), began to wage another terror campaign by indiscriminately lobbing surface-to-surface missiles into Israeli cities. The campaign of murder by missiles forced the Israeli government to once again invade Lebanon, the West Bank and Gaza to root out the terrorists from their enclaves; thus disrupting the path towards peace, unstable as it was.

Ariel Sharon's life was inexplicitly intertwined with the desti-

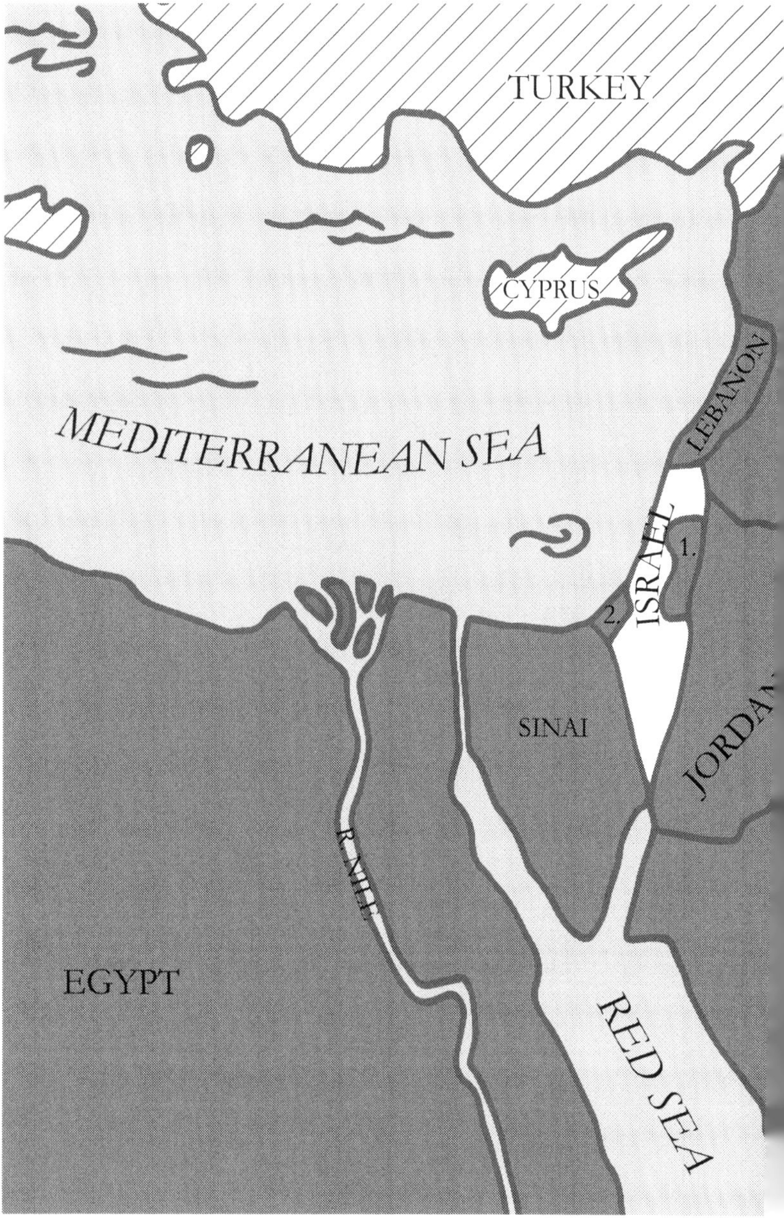
TURKEY
CYPRUS
LEBANON
MEDITERRANEAN SEA
ISRAEL
1.
2.
SINAI
JORDAN
R. NILE
EGYPT
RED SEA

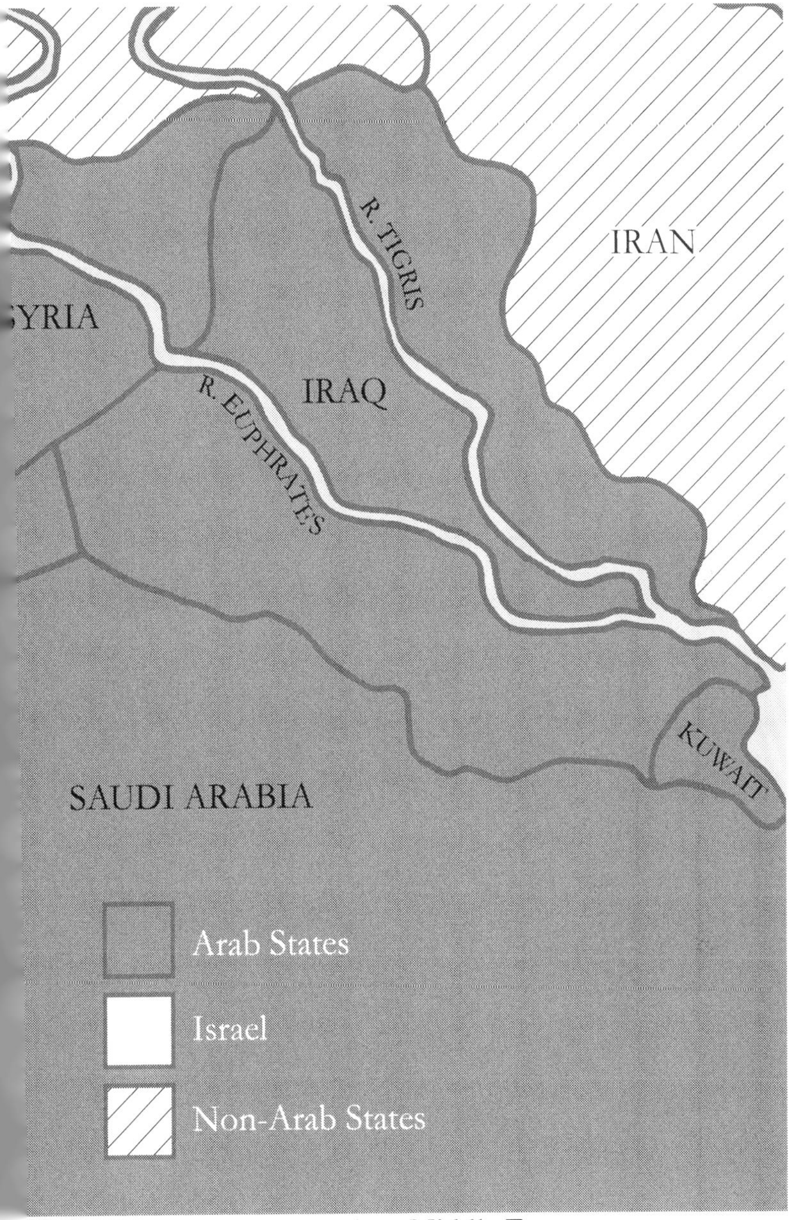

Modern Middle East

1. West Bank. 2. Gaza Strip.

ny of the state of Israel and the Jewish nation. Brought up in a violent and hostile region, Sharon rose to the challenge that was issued to his people. His experience in the village militias started him on a career path that would become all too familiar with his Israeli contemporaries. Audacious, aggressive and unconventional, Sharon's training and command with the commando's and paratroopers instilled these three characteristics into his methods once he assumed higher command. These three characteristics would work wonders for Sharon when applied to the field of battle, but when it came to 'office-politics' they severely hindered his advancement. Luckily for Sharon and Israel the top echelon of the Israeli halls of power would occasionally intervene to save Sharon from the petty infighting he would get himself into. The straw that broke the camel's back was Sharon's decisive maneuver across the Suez during the Yom Kippur War. While the crossing effectively won the War against Egypt and was based on fundamentally sound military principles, it was seen as an act of disobedience by his military superiors.

After the 1973 war, Sharon was viewed as the quintessential Israeli war hero,* but Sharon's military career was as good as over. Sharon would never reach the top command of the IDF military hierarchy largely because of his predisposition towards independent action. However, he would circumvent the military hierarchy through his civilian political career when he was appointed 'Minister of Defense', the civilian head of the IDF. With the defence portfolio, Sharon was responsible for waging Israel's first major campaign against the Palestinian guerillas in Lebanon and elsewhere, setting the stage (and policy) for what would be the next phase of Israel's struggle for survival.

Ever resourceful and full of surprises, the old warrior would make his final mark by radically transforming the political paradigm away from the extremities into the center and also through

* The numerous pictures of Sharon with the head bandage was great for this.

his policy of unilateral disengagement from the West Bank and Gaza Strip. While Sharon was not around long enough to see the results of his policy come to fruition, it was a tragic if not predictable, turn of history that Sharon's policy of unilateral disengagement did not produce a lasting peace settlement. However, Sharon's move did force the Palestinians hand proving that they were (and are) not interested in a lasting peace or even able to recognize Israel's right to exist. The Jewish people of Israel have demonstrated, time and again, that they want to live in peace and liberty within safe and secure borders. On the other hand, the Palestinian Arabs have proven themselves to be irreconcilable to peace or the existence of a Jewish state in Israel. Sharon's actions and leadership in the realms of tactics, strategy and politics earned him a position as not only one of Israel's greatest men, but also as one of liberty's greatest lieutenants.

Epilogue

"Freedom is never more than one generation away from extinction. We didn't pass it to our children in the bloodstream. It must be fought for, protected and handed on for them to do the same."

-Ronald Reagan, American President and statesman

A World Safe for Liberty?

Shortly after the beginning of political hostilities between the western and eastern blocks the military situation settled into an uneasy, yet inactive peace. Neither the Americans nor the Russians were particularly eager to continue fighting on the scale that had been required to subdue the Germans. So while the threat of a renewed conflict constantly hung over the people of Europe, political differences never materialized into kinetic, conventional warfare. The status quo of détente was further reinforced by the introduction of the nuclear weapons into the strategic calculus.

The destructive capabilities of the nuclear, and later hydrogen bombs forced militaries and governments to rethink how they approached warfare and politics on the global stage. The 'big game' was forced away from the traditional center of power in Europe only to re-emerge along the peripheries in Asia, Africa and later Central and South America. Instead of confronting each other directly, the two superpowers would supply proxy armies with arms and advisors to fight on their behalf. Some major conflicts would occasionally emerge to speed up the tempo of the otherwise static warfare in Europe. The Korean War, the Arab-Israeli Wars, the Vietnam War, and Soviet-Afghan War are the most dramatic examples of when one superpower intervened militarily to combat the spreading influence of the other. However, the two powers would never directly come into conflict with the other, and thus they were able to avoid igniting a conventional war or nuclear exchange.

While the two sides had reached an equilibrium, they were by no means equal. Generally speaking, the ground forces of either side were of equal quality, but in Europe the Eastern Bloc held the advantage of numbers, contiguous territory and interior lines. The Soviets had a preponderance of conventional forces located in Eastern Europe that, without the American nuclear umbrella, could have easily steamrolled over the nations of Western Europe. The Western nations, led on by the United States, went practically unchallenged on the high seas and were consistently one step ahead on the air force tech tree. Furthermore, the west generally held the advantage of numbers when it came to the battlegrounds in the periphery. It was easier for the Americans to supply their military in Vietnam, half way around the world, than it was for the Russians to supply their forces in Afghanistan next door.

While the respective militaries were roughly equal, when it came to the realm of economics the West reigned supreme. In the long run the capitalistic system of the west rapidly outpaced the socialist economy of the Eastern Bloc. After the destruction that was reaped in Europe during the Second World War, the only industrialized economy that didn't need to be rebuilt was the United States. The United States economy was ascendant and greatly benefited from the reconstruction of Europe. The Marshall Plan that was implemented in the late 1940's loaned an enormous amount of money to the western nations that had been liberated by the British and Americans, which effectively saved their economies and opened up their markets for American trade.[1] The loan offer was extended to the Soviets and the eastern nations, but were rejected out of hand. The Russians were bent on controlling their conquered territories and refused to allow the allure of capitalism to seep into their new empire.[2]

The Soviet economy, while socialistic in nature, essentially depended on the subjugation of its denizens and the conquest and ransacking of neighbouring countries. It was more focused on the redistribution of wealth than on its creation. Predictably the Soviet economy faltered when it ran out of countries to pilfer. However, the enormity of the socialist empire, its vast resource wealth and the totalitarian nature of the government artificially propped up the Soviet state. The enormous structure of the government created a top heavy architecture that would eventually crumble unless more territory could be added to its foundation.

As the Cold War dragged on through the decades, it began to appear as if it would take on a life of permanence. But beneath the façade of permanence the Soviet Union was buckling under the weight and cost of its military and government. The containment strategy that had been implemented by successive US governments was beginning to pay off. By aiming to limit the spread of communism, the west succeeded in depriving the Russians of new lands to loot. Time was on the side of the west.

Then came along President Reagan and his plan to accelerate the collapse of the evil socialist empire. With the Soviets already finding it difficult to keep up with the military spending of the US, Reagan further increased American spending forcing the Russians to break their back in an attempt to keep pace.[3] With the western economies miles ahead of the communist bloc the Americans could drastically increase their military spending as a percentage of their GDP without drastic damage being done to their economy. The Russians were already spending a greater percentage of their GDP on their military and would find it impossible to maintain the status quo in conventional forces.

The Central European nations were the first to break away. There had been rebellious tendencies within the conquered nations of Central and Eastern Europe, but any revolt had been easily put down as long as the Soviet Russians still maintained their economic and military supremacy within their sphere of influence. Yearning to breathe free, the East German Republic was the first to break away. The world watched with fixation to see what the power brokers in Moscow would do. The Communist leaders in Moscow did nothing to stop the people of East Germany from uniting with their brothers to the west. The Berlin Wall, the physical embodiment of the Cold War, came down and with it the impression of Cold War permanence. Shortly thereafter the remaining 'Soviet republics' that had once been proud nation-states were free to liberate themselves without fear of reprisal from the gangsters in Russia. The Cold War was over, the West had won through the power of their economies and the idea that all people should be free.

♦ ♦ ♦

Jubilation swept through the world as the footage of the Berlin Wall being torn down was broadcast on television. This would be a new era of peace and prosperity; it was being heralded by some as the end of history. It was true that there were still state centrist holdouts in communist China and North Korea, but it was believed that the power of democracy and capitalism would sooner or later sweep away the failed ideology that was socialism. However, the ruling elites in China and North Korea had no intention of relinquishing their hold on power, or to admit that their experiments at governance had been a failure. Even if the old socialist states agreed with the principle of opening up their economies to allow for some capitalism, their elites could never countenance the thought of accepting democracy, or liberty as the guiding principle of the state.

The end of history was further interrupted by the petty squabbling amongst the small states of Europe, Africa and the Middle East. As the US stood preeminent astride the world stage, it took it upon itself to police the trouble areas of the globe. These conflicts were largely based along ethnic and religious fault lines. Although they were relatively small in scale, more often than not they degenerated into the realm of genocide.*

* See the conflicts in Rwanda, Iraq and the Balkans.

The US, usually backed by the UN and its western allies in NATO would generally intervene in these conflicts, attempting to restore a semblance of law and order or to return the area to its previous status quo. So when Saddam Hussein's Iraq invaded neighbouring (oil rich) Kuwait, the US intervened, liberating Kuwait of its Iraqi conquerors and restoring the previous borders. Later in the Balkans Crisis, the US and NATO intervened, setting up buffer zones to save the Muslim Bosnians from the Slavic Serbians. Although some questioned the motivation of the US, its military prowess was generally used as a tool for good. Without precedent in history the US would go on to outspend the next ten states combined in military spending.[4]

The perception of invincibility cast its deceptive shroud over American hegemony. A state, whose territory had not been violated by foreign aggression since the Japanese attack at Pearl Harbour, deluded itself into thinking that nothing of that magnitude could ever happen again.

Then on Tuesday September 11, 2001 two passenger airplanes slammed into the World Trade Center in downtown New York City. Two more planes had been hijacked by Islamic terrorists, one was flown into the Pentagon in Washington DC, while the other was rescued by its passengers and crash landed into a Pennsylvania field. The world watched anxiously as the world trade center and the stability of the 1990s came burning to the ground.

The American public came together in their desire to revenge their three thousand fellow citizens who had perished in the burning towers. It wasn't long before the culprits were located. Al-Qaeda, an Islamic terror group led on by Osama Bin Laden, and their sponsor government in Afghanistan, the Taliban, were the ones who were responsible for the 911 atrocity. Eager to get back at the murders in Afghanistan, US President, George W. Bush, declared the 'War on Terror' and began planning for the invasion of Afghanistan. The immediate goals in Afghanistan were to remove the Taliban from its seat of power, install a friendly regime that wouldn't give Al-Qaeda sanctuary and to eject Al-Qaeda from their mountain training facilities.[5]

Meeting with initial tactical success in ejecting Al-Qaeda and removing the Taliban from government, the Americans found that rebuilding the country along western lines would be next to impossible. Before long the US became distracted by another dictatorial regime that was threatening to construct weapons of mass destruction.

Saddam Hussein had been left in power in Iraq after the First Gulf War and since then had been experimenting with chemical weapons and was thought to be developing a nuclear program. The American public, no longer asleep, were becoming extremely sensitive to the damage that a chemical, biological or small nuclear weapon could potentially do to a major American city. With this in mind, President Bush supported by much of Congress and the population, was not about to tolerate Hussein's continued provocations.

Although there was no direct links to Iraq and the 911 attacks, there were plenty of reason for the world community to get behind the plan for disposing of Hussein. In fact, there were something like sixteen different UN resolutions that Hussein had violated since the First Gulf War.[6] The most alarming of which was his supposed development of WMD. While Hussein pretended to cooperate with the UN agencies who were sent to inspect his weapons facilities, only an idiot could actually believe in his sincerity. It was a known fact that Hussein had stockpiles of weapons grade chemicals, but it was somewhat debatable as to wither or not he was developing nuclear capabilities. Almost unanimous were the intelligence agencies of the West (including Russia) in saying Hussein was developing nuclear weapons, this, compiled with Hussein's obfuscation with the UN created an atmosphere of mistrust that eventually led the US, at the head of the 'coalition of the willing', into a war with the Iraqi dictator.

In the fall of 2003 the coalition forces sprang into action from their bases in Kuwait. Driving north into Iraq, conventional Iraqi resistance withered away in the face of the coalition blitzkrieg. Once again the West met with quick tactical success, but once again the situation degenerated as soon as the Americans attempted to reconstruct the Iraqi state along western lines. The Iraqi population had previously been kept in order by the brutality of the Hussein regime, but now with Hussein gone the country erupted into civil war and fractured along religious and ethnic lines. The Kurds* in the north did their best to stay out of the fighting that was raging on to the south between the Sunni and Shite religious factions. Within the two main religious factions there were numerous local militias/terrorist organizations that joined in the fighting.

The Americans were now caught up in an increasingly dangerous situation that threatened to spiral out of control. Part of the problem was caused by the American strategic doctrine that had given them such success in the early battles. Speed, maneuverability, firepower and the economy of force† were not particularly well suited towards the occupation and pacification of a volatile region. Traditional American military doctrine had no workable solution to the problem, so it became a political necessity for a solution to be found. Even one from outside the box if necessary.

And then General David Petraeus came along with his unorthodox counter-insurgency plan. The prevailing methodology within US military circles had been to find and eliminate the terrorist insurgents. Petraeus's plan essentially called for a switch away from the offensive towards securing the Iraqi population from the insurgents.[7] While the new strategy was novel within the modern American context, similar strategies had deep theoretical roots and had been implemented in different regions

* Probable descendants of Xenophon's Carduchians.

† Economy of force is a euphemism for low troop numbers.

throughout history.

A similar strategy had proven successful after the American Civil War during the reconstruction era, when a shadow government organized under the aegis of the Ku Klux Klan threatened to destabilize the Southern States and reverse the social progress made. In response to the intimidation and terror tactics used by the KKK, the Federal government garrisoned troubled areas with soldiers. With time the strategy worked, the KKK was rooted out of local governments and beaten back into the shadows away from major population centers.

The main reasons for success against the KKK was that the federal government had the advantages of time, numbers and public opinion. In contrast to this, Gen. Petraeus held none of these advantages. Time was running out for the Americans. Public opinion was swinging decisively against the Bush administration, and the war, and furthermore the initial coalition troop numbers were spread too thin to be of any use against the hordes of insurgents in Iraq. By the year 2006 the political left in America were dead set against continuing the War in Iraq let alone authorizing more troops to be sent. After a vigorous debate Petraeus was given authority, numbers, time and some confidence from the public to turn the situation around in Iraq.[8]

It didn't take long for Petraeus's strategy to produce results. The troop surge that Petraeus had asked for and that Bush had authorized, initially increased the rate of causalities amongst coalition forces. Those increased casualties had been predicted, and quickly began to die down once the insurgents' understood that the Americans had mustered their resolve and came equipped with staying power. Regardless of the success that Petraeus achieved in Iraq, the American (and international) leftist, progressive movement had made up their minds on the War on Terror, and had declared American hegemony and the values for which the US stood to be the preeminent evil operating in the world.

♦ ♦ ♦

In 2008 a war-weary American public elected a president who promised (amongst many other things) to end the wars in Afghanistan and Iraq. Barrack Hussein Obama was the first black man elected to the office of President, he was also the most radical left wing progressive to occupy the White House. While Obama had been one of the most vocal anti-war, anti-surge Democrats in congress, it could be said that once he assumed office he suddenly found that wielding American power was a bit more nuanced than the simple campaign slogans his election team had sold the American public.

Starting off with what critics called 'the apology tour' Obama travelled to the major European and Middle Eastern cities and apologized for what he believed to be Americas sins. While this might have played well with Americas traditional western allies, the villains of the world soon realized that American foreign policy was about to get a lot softer. The next flight of fancy for Obama was to unilaterally declare a reset in relations with the Russian dictator Putin. The Bush administration had taken a hard line with Putin and had signed agreements with Poland and the Czech Republic to build up missile defence capabilities in Central and Eastern Europe. President Obama scrapped those plans, and received nothing in return from the tyrants in Russia.[9]

Eager to live up to his commitment of getting out of Iraq, Obama openly declared to the world the timetable for US withdrawals. With the situation in Iraq improving by the day, the war in Afghanistan was beginning to deteriorate at a rapid pace. Forced into action, Obama reluctantly (and begrudgingly) commissioned Gen. Petraeus to apply his counter-insurgency strategy with the accompanying troop surge required. Almost as soon as the second troop surge was authorized Obama again openly declared to the world the time-tables for US withdrawal from Afghanistan.[10] The troop surges and counter insurgency strategy worked well initially in the two warzones, but Obama's willingness to broadcast America's lack of resolve to the enemy would ultimately undermine the strategy's effectiveness.

Instead of the boots on the ground approach, Obama preferred to deploy armed drones by the thousands as a means to curb the growth and spread of terrorism throughout the Middle East. After the capture and execution of Osama Bin Laden, the 911 Al-Qaeda mastermind, Obama declared the 'War on Terror'* over and won. During their re-election campaign Vice President Joe Biden would infamously exclaim, "Osama Bin Laden is dead, GM† is alive."[11]

It became evident early on that Obama was all but completely disengaged from foreign policy and instead wanted to focus his attention on 'fundamentally transforming' the nature of the American republic. While Obama was busy imposing socialised medicine, progressive ideology and getting himself re-elected the villains of the world took notice and made plans to take advantage of America's distraction.

♦ ♦ ♦

The 'Arab Spring' which began as a protest movement against the corrupt dictatorships of the Middle East quickly fractured from what seemed to be a 'pro-democracy' movement into two camps. One camp was relatively modern and stayed true to western ideals of democracy and liberty, while the other camp represented a more traditional Islamic strain, calling for the imposition of Sharia Law and the creation of an Islamic caliphate. The Obama administration initially supported the Arab Spring movement and worked actively against former American allies (and dictatorships) like Mubarak in Egypt and Qaddafi in Libya.‡ However, the democracies that were set up, were quickly hijacked by the most radical Islamists bent on imposing Sharia Law upon their populations. Civil wars ensued. Egypt has been

* Obama actually stopped using the term 'War on Terror'.

† General Motors, a car company 'saved' by Obamas stimulus-deficit spending.

‡ Qaddafi was bombed by US and NATO planes.

able to overthrow the Islamist regime and return to a semblance of order, but only after a lengthy protest and a military coup. Libya, to this day, remains in a practical state of anarchy where the former state has fractured into numerous local fiefdoms.

Syria is another country where the Arab Spring came close to overthrowing a brutal and corrupt dictatorship. This time the movement in Syria was almost completely void of any pro-democracy factions and was mostly made up of Al-Qaeda and other Sunni terrorist organizations. The US was on the verge of intervening in the civil war after the Assad regime was implicated with using chemical weapons on the rebel population. The situation in Syria was infinitely more complex than the one in Libya or Egypt, with Russia and Iran acting as the backers of the Assad regime and the rebels being overwhelming made up of Islamic terrorist types.

As it turned out the Syrian rebels have ambitions outside of Syria. One of the main branches of the rebel movement fighting the Assad regime, known as ISIS, has turned its gaze to the east and conquered large portions of northern and western Iraq. ISIS, which stands for 'the Islamic State of Iraq and Syria' was rejected by the top echelon of Al-Qaeda leadership for being too extreme in their methods and strategy. Now a weakened Iraqi state, with only the minimal backing from US and western advisors is slowly retaking its lost territory from ISIS. Should their fortunes reverse and Baghdad fall to ISIS, it is highly likely that the Islamic Republic of Iran, a longtime enemy of the US and the west, would step into the eastern portion of Iraq in an effort to protect the Shite population from the ravages of the Sunni Islamic State.

The regime in Iran is currently another complication for the stability of the Middle East and the progress of liberty. One of the biggest state sponsors of terrorism, extremely anti-Semitic/anti-western in its rhetoric and openly developing their nuclear capabilities, Iran has the potential to destabilize the region and throw the Middle East and southern Asian into a nuclear arms race. The Islamic revolution that took power in the late 1970's hoisted a strict adaptation of Sharia Law upon the Iranian population and has been working with Shite terror groups to spread their version of Islam into the states of Syria and Lebanon amongst other areas.

♦ ♦ ♦

Once the most powerful empire on earth, the nation of China is once again on the rise. After its liberation from Imperial Japan, China underwent a civil war between communists and nationalists. The communists won and went on to impose their 'cultural revolution' and economic ideology onto the country, with all its catastrophic loss of life and wasted economic potential. During the 1970s US President Nixon had been able to fracture the unity of the international communist movement when he convinced the Chinese communists to break away from the grip of Russian influence. However, even with the Chinese nominally on side with the Americans the Communist Party's grip on power was not loosened. Even after the collapse of the USSR and the gradual introduction of capitalism into the Chinese economy, the Party's dictatorial control over the state and population has not wavered.

The introduction of capitalism has greatly benefited the Chinese economy as it now moves ever closer towards its destiny of surpassing the US as the single largest economy on the globe. With this newfound prosperity has also come newfound ambitions. Traditionally China has been geographically confined to the eastern portion of the Asian continent, and without a navy worthy of the name, it has had few opportunities to expand its influence. Now China is rapidly building up its maritime capabilities, with a particular emphasis on submarines and aircraft carriers. This is partially paid for by interest payments from financing the US government's debt.

Wanting to flex their muscles a bit, the Chinese are now staking claims against territory traditionally under the jurisdiction of their maritime neighbours, who are generally allies of the US. Australia, Indonesia, the Philippines, and Japan all have mutual defence treaties (with the US) that are aimed at containing a burgeoning China. Even if China can be militarily contained in the short term, the state centric approach to government and the seemingly positive economic results* emanating from China provide much of the world's population with a seemingly attractive alternative to capitalism and individual liberty.

To the north of the China and the Middle East further trouble is brewing for the cause of liberty. In the early months of 2014 the Ukrainian people ousted their corrupt pro-Russian government, in favour of setting up a pro-Western government. In response Russian dictator, Vladimir Putin, moved troops into the Crimean Peninsula, a strategic province of the state of Ukraine. All the while massing troops along Ukraine's eastern border, Putin arranged a succession referendum to take place in the Crimea while stating that much of Eastern Ukraine would logically want to rejoin mother Russia.

The Putin regime has been taking steps to reconstruct the former Soviet Union (or Czarist empire) by expanding its influence into Russia's 'near abroad' either through overt military action or the diplomatic strengthening of ties such as was seen in the recent inauguration of the 'Eurasian Economic Union, between the states of Belarus, Russia and Kazakhstan.[12] The ideology behind Putin's EEC is essentially totalitarian, socially conservative to an extreme, and economically state centrist, an imitation of the now defunct USSR. Free speech, open markets, individual rights have no place in Putin's neo-Russian empire. This revanchist Russian attitude is taking place within the context of Obama scrapping the missile defence plans in Central Europe, and his 'pivot to the Pacific' which

* The Chinese have averaged eight percent economic growth annually, although it is a mirage, largely caused by their currency manipulation.

GREENLAND
U.S.A.
CANADA
UNITED STATES
OF AMERICA
PACIFIC
OCEAN
ATLANTIC
OCEAN
5.
1.
3.
Free Countries
Totalitarian Countries
Other Countries

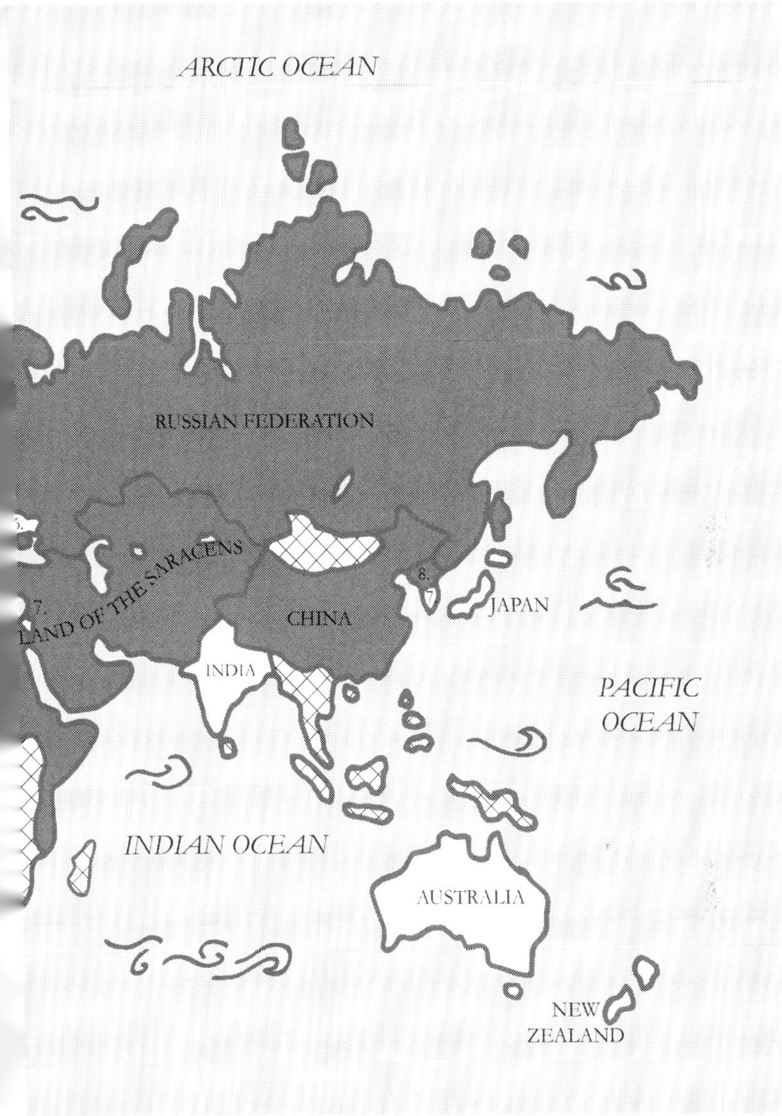

Global Situation 2017

1. United Kingdom. 2. Switzerland. 3. The European Union. 4. Norway. 5. Iceland. 6. Ukraine. 7. Israel 7. South Korea 8. North Korea called for the transfer of much of US naval capabilities from the Mediterranean Sea to the Pacific Ocean.

The European Union is another serious threat to liberty. What was setup in the aftermath of the Second World War to facilitate economic growth between the countries of Europe (especially France and Germany), has turned into a de facto united states of Europe ruled out of the Reichstag in Berlin.

While the respective states of the EU are democratic in nature, the executive branch is anything but. Chosen in complete secrecy, the President and executive branch comes up with legislation while the bureaucracy is charged with following it out. The elected officials from the member states are merely charged with rubber stamping whatever legislation the executive comes up with. The EU has effectively accomplished for Germany what the Kaiser and Hitler couldn't; a European empire.

Perhaps the single most dangerous policy the EU has put in place is the policy of completely open internal borders. Coupled with an extremely porous external border and Germany's call to allow anyone in the world residence in Germany, and you have an explosive mix.

Predictably, migrants, especially from the Middle East, have flooded into Europe on their way to Germany, causing massive disruptions to civil society. The scale of this movement of people makes it nothing short of an invasion. The Islamic way of life is incompatible with secular, western society. With almost weekly Islamic terrorist attacks within the EU, it is threatening to become even more authoritarian than it already is, further eroding the liberties of the peoples of Europe.

The progressive movement has all but completely embraced the failed ideology of a top-down, state centric economy. Furthermore, the 'progressive has deemed all tradition values as backwards and neanderthal. The values of hard work, family, patriotism, duty, charity and everything else that made America and the West the premier world power are considered passé and not worthy of pursuit. Much like the last generation of the Roman republic and the denizens of the empire, the adherents of the progressive movement are more concerned with 'bread and circuses' then they are with the preservation of their constitution and republic. In short, a large portion of the American public is more worried about getting free stuff, than they are concerned with internal and external threats to their liberty.

Some blame can be placed on politicians for legitimizing and pandering to this progressive ideology, but much of the blame rests squarely on the shoulders of the individuals who take their liberties for granted and are ignorant of, or hold a distorted view of world history, thus dooming themselves to repeat it. The struggle is far from over, and as we have seen in this epilogue much of the world still lives under the darkness of tyranny and oppression. Further efforts and great deeds will yet have to be made to keep western civilization and the rest of the world from entering a new dark ages.

♦ ♦ ♦

With all the darkness currently threatening liberty around the world, there are also some reasons to have hope. 2016 was a particularly good year for the cause.

First came the victory for Brexit in the UK referendum in June. The majority of the British people voted to leave the European Union and take back control of their country's sovereignty. Once again the British Isles are the sole hope for the downtrodden peoples of Europe yearning to throw off the yoke of the German Reich.*

The second ray of hope came in the extremely unexpected election of Donald Trump to the Presidency of the United States. Trump is an outrageous businessman who seems bent on destroying the status quo and reversing the tide of corruption engulfing the United States and global politics. It is yet to be seen whether Trump is up to the colossal task set before him, but so far his actions are promising. Securing the southern border, introducing extreme vetting for immigration from Islamic countries, and reintroducing a strong, principled foreign policy abroad are all steps in the right direction.

* The French came close to electing an Anti EU president in 2017. Branded as a fascist and a racist by the authoritarian pro EU progressive crowd, Marie Le Pen ultimately lost the election. Had she been successful, her victory would have spelt the death of the EU.

Words and symbolism mean a lot with the Presidency, and in comparison to Obama, Trump is an unapologetic advocate for western civilization and its cornerstone, liberty. So we will leave off with a quote from what will undoubtedly become a much celebrated speech in years to come.

> "The fundamental question of our time is whether the West has the will to survive. Do we have the confidence in our values to defend them at any cost? Do we have enough respect for our citizens to protect our borders? Do we have the desire and the courage to preserve our civilization in the face of those who would subvert and destroy it? We can have the largest economies and the most lethal weapons anywhere on earth, but if we do not have strong families and strong values, then we will be weak and we will not survive."

Hopefully by the end of this work the reader shall have gained some perspective on the historic struggles that made men free and are grateful of the sacrifices made by others who have enabled the flame of liberty to continue to burn.

Notes

Why Liberty

1. www.merriam-webster.com/dictionary/liberty
2. Pg. 8. Locke, John.
3. Pg. 49. Vincent, Nicholas.
4. Pg. 76. Hobbes, Thomas. (Chapter XIII, 9)

Xenophon of Athens

1. www.iep.utm.edu/xenophon
2. Pg. 10. Morris, Ian & Barry B. Powell.
3. Pg. 338. Strassler, Robert B.
4. Pg. 27. Hart, Liddell.
5. Pg. 28. Ibid.
6. Pg. 252. Morris, Ian & Barry B. Powell
7. Pg. 252. Ibis.
8. Pg. 25. Hanson, Victor Davis. (The Savior Generals)
9. Pg. 554. Strassler, Robert B. (Herodotus)
10. Pg. 555. Ibid.
11. Pg. 31. Hanson, Victor Davis. (The Savior Generals)
12. Pg. 57. Strassler, Robert B. (Thucydides)
13. Pg. 97 Ibid.
14. Pg. 118. Ibid.
15. Pg. 341. Pomeroy, Burstein, Donlan & Roberts.
16. Pg. 257. Keegan, John. (1994)
17. Pg. 347. Pomeroy, Burstein, Donlan & Roberts.
18. Pg. 347. Ibid.
19. Pg. 352. Ibid.
20. Pg. 40. Field Marshall Viscount Montgomery of Alamein
21. Pg. 7. Taylor, Michael. (Ancient Warfare)
22. Pg. 321. Xenophon (Anabasis, I. VIII. 27)
23. Pg. 373. Ibid. (Anabasis, II. III. 25-28)
24. Pg. 397. Ibid. (Anabasis, II. V. 31-34)
25. Pg. 437. Ibid. (Anabasis, III. II. 1-3)
26. Pg. 471. Ibid. (Anabasis, III. IV. 14-15)
27. Pg. 473. Ibid. (Anabasis, III. IV. 21-23)

28. Pg. 485. Ibid. (Anabasis, III. IV. 47-49)
29. Pg. 491. Ibid. (Anabasis, III. V. 16)
30. Pg. 5. Ibid. (Anabasis, IV. I. 10-11)
31. Pg. 11. Ibid. (Anabasis, IV. I. 27-28)
32. Pg. 13. Ibid. (Anabasis, IV. II. 1-2)
33. Pg. 19. Ibid. (Anabasis, IV. 16-18)
34. Pg. 29. Ibid. (Anabasis, IV. III. 10-12)
35. Pg. 31-37. Ibid. (Anabasis, IV. III 16-34)
36. Pg. 41. Ibid. (Anabasis, IV. II)
37. Pg. 69. Ibid. (Anabasis, IV. VII. 3-4)
38. Pg. 73. Ibid. (Anabasis, IV. VII. 13)
39. Pg. 75. Ibid. (Anabasis, IV. VII. 20)
40. Pg. 77. Ibid. (Anabasis, IV. VII. 26)
41. Pg. 81. Ibid. (Anabasis, IV. VIII. 7)
42. Pg. 83. Ibid. (Anabasis, IV. VIII. 10-19)
43. Pg. 87. Ibid. (Anabasis, IV. VIII. 22)
44. Pg. 89. Ibid. (Anabasis, IV. VIII. 25-26)
45. Pg. 353. Pomeroy, Burstein, Donlan & Roberts.

Epaminondas of Thebes

1. Pg. 376. Cornelius Nepos.
2. Pg. 377. Ibid.
3. Pg. 378. Ibid.
4. Pg. 5. Plutarch (Lives II, gutenberg.org).
5. Pg. 369. Pomeroy, Burstein, Donlan & Roberts.
6. Pg. 7. Plutarch. (Lives II, Gutenberg.org)
7. Pg. 369. Pomeroy, Burstein, Donlan & Roberts.
8. Pg. 12. Plutarch. (www.gutenberg.org)
9. Pg. 96. Hanson (editor). Makers of Ancient Strategy.
10. Pg. 37. Pomeroy, Burstein, Donlan & Roberts.
11. Pg. 17. Plutarch (www.gutenberg.org)
12. Pg. 18. Ibid.
13. Pg. 343. Thucydides, 5.71.
14. Pg. 34. Hart, Liddell B.
15. Pg. 372. Pomeroy, Burstein, Donlan & Roberts.
16. Pg. 97. Hanson (editor) Makers of Ancient Strategy.
17. Pg. 372. Pomeroy, Burstein, Donlan & Roberts.
18. Pg. 97. Hanson (editor) Makers of Ancient Strategy.
19. Pg. 104. Hanson (editor) Makers of Ancient Strategy.
20. Pg. 382. Cornelius Nepos.
21. Pg. 125. Xenophon (Hellenica, VII. I. 15)

22. Pg. 129-131. Ibid. (Hellenica, VII. I.22)
23. Pg. 26. Plutarch. (Lives II, Gutenberg.org)
24. Pg. 139. Xenophon (Hellenica, VII. I. 33-38)
25. Pg. 147. Ibid (Hellenica, VII. I. 41-42)
26. Pg. 149. Ibid (Hellenica, VII. I. 44)
27. Pg. 174. Beck, Hans.
28. Pg. 36. Hart, Liddle B.
29. Pg. 219. Xenophon (Hellenica, VII. V. 18)
30. Pg. 221. Ibid (Hellenica, VII. V. 21-22)
31. Pg. 36. Hart, Liddle B.
32. Pg. 225. Xenophon (Hellenica, VII. V. 24-25)
33. Pg. 225. Ibid (Hellenica, VII. V. 26-27)

Publius Cornelius Scipio Africanus

1. Akinde, Michael. (2006) www.akinde.dk/history/index.php?title=publius_cornelius_scipio_africanus
2. Pg. 96. Mackay, Christopher.
3. Pg. 10. Hart, Liddell B. (Scipio Africanus)
4. Probably a fabrication of later historians as it is almost the exact same as the pledge Hannibal made to his father before the two embarked to Iberia.
5. Pg. 119-120. Miles, Richmond.
6. Pg. 73. Ibid.
7. Pg. 74. Ibid.
8. Pg. 112-113. Ibid.
9. Pg. 271. Keegan, John. (A History of Warfare)
10. Pg. 6. Jones & Sidwell.
11. Pg. 17. Mackay, Christopher.
12. Pg. 21. Ibid.
13. Pg. 54. Ibid.
14. Pg. 48. Ibid.
15. Pg. 204. Plutarch (Lives II, Gutenberg.org)
16. Pg. 49. Mackay, Christopher.
17. Pg. 171-173. Miles, Richard.
18. Pg. 179. Ibid.
19. Pg. 63. Mackay, Christopher.
20. Pg. 65. Ibid.
21. Pg. 173. Polybius. (The Histories, Book I: 63)
22. Pg. 178. Miles, Richard.
23. Pg. 181. Ibid.
24. Pg. 182. Ibid.
25. Pg. 198. Ibid.

26. Pg. 187. Ibid.
27. Pg. 189. Ibid.
28. Pg. 64-65. Mackay.
29. Pg. 196. Miles, Richard.
30. Pg. 224. Ibid.
31. Pg. 203. Ibid.
32. Pg. 212. Ibid.
33. Pg. 218-219. Miles, Richard.
34. Pg. 23. Livy (The War with Hannibal Book XXI)
35. Pg. 25. Ibid
36. Pg. 25-26. Ibid.
37. Pg. 225. Miles, Richard.
38. Pg. 31. Livy (The War with Hannibal, Book XXI)
39. Pg. 42. Ibid.
40. Pg. 220-221. Miles, Richard.
41. Pg. 45. Hart, Liddell B.
42. Pg. 271. Keegan, John (A History of Warfare)
43. Pg. 268. Miles, Richard.
44. Pg. 72. Livy (The War with Hannibal)
45. Pg. 77. Ibid.(The War With Hannibal)
46. Pg. 79-80. Ibid. (The War With Hannibal, Book XXI)
47. Pg. 45. Hart, Liddell B.
48. Pg. 45. Ibid.
49. Pg. 98. Livy (The War With Hannibal)
50. Pg. 100. Ibid.
51. Pg. 47. Hart, Liddell B.
52. Pg. 47. Ibid.
53. Pg. 48. Ibid.
54. Pg. 48-49. Ibid.
55. Pg. 55. Field Marshall Viscount Montgomery of Alam ein.
56. Pg. 49. Hart, Liddell B.
57. Pg. 341. Livy (The War With Hannibal, Book XXVI)
58. Pg. 379. Ibid (The War With Hannibal, Book XXVI)
59. Pg. 412-417. Ibid. (The War With Hannibal, Book XXVI)
60. Pg. 420. Ibid. (The War With Hannibal, Book XXVI)
61. Pg. 453-454. Livy (The War With Hannibal, Book XXVII)
62. Pg. 454. Ibid. (The War With Hannibal)
63. Pg. 515. Ibid. (The War With Hannibal, Book XXVIII)
64. Pg. 515. Ibid.
65. Pg. 516. Ibid.
66. Pg. 519. Ibid.
67. Pg. 521, 543-544. Ibid.

68. Pg. 50. Hart, Liddell B.
69. Pg. 565-566. Livy (The War With Hannibal, Book XXIX)
70. Pg. 595. Ibid.
71. Pg. 597. Ibid.
72. Pg. 51. Hart, Liddell B.
73. Pg. 627. Livy (The War With Hannibal, Book XXX)
74. Pg. 644. Ibid.
75. Pg. 220-221. Lazenby, J.F. (Hannibal's War)
76. Pg. 57. Montgomery of Alamein.
77. Pg. 57. Ibid.
78. Pg. 58. Ibid. Pg. 53. Hart, Liddell B.
79. Pg. 58. Montgomery of Alamein.
80. Pg. 675. Livy (The War With Hannibal, Book XXX)
81. Livy (From the Founding of the City, Book XXXVII, 1)
72. Ibid. (Book XXXVII, 45)
83. Ibid. (Book XXXVIII, 53)
84. Ibid. (Book XXXVIII, 53)

Marcus Junius Brutus

1. Pg. 572. Plutarch. (Lives II)
2. Pg. 572. Ibid.
3. Pg. 298. Holland, Tom.
4. Pg. 572. Plutarch. (Lives II)
5. Pg. 572. Ibid.
6. Pg. 576. Ibid.
7. Pg. 154. Goodman & Soni.
8. Pg. 574. Plutarch (Lives II)
9. Pg. Pg. 340-341. Miles, Richard.
10. Pg. 74. Mackay, Christopher.
11. Pg. 347. Miles, Richard.
12. Pg. 77-80. Abbott, Frank F.
13. Pg. 18-109. Mackay, Christopher.
14. Pg. 109 & 114. Ibid.
15. Pg. 33. Jones & Sidwell.
16. Pg. 125. Mackay.
17. Pg. 126. Ibid.
18. Pr. 129. Ibid.
19. Pg. 104. Holland, Tom.
20. Pg. 133. Mackay.
21. Pg. 134. Ibid.
22. Pg. 135. Ibid.

23. Pg. 141. Ibid.
24. Pg. 42. Jones & Sidwell.
25. Pg. 42. Ibid.
26. Pg. 10. Suetonius.
27. Pg. 30-31. Caesar (The Conquest of Gaul)
28. Pg. 236. Holland, Tom.
29. Pg. 237. Ibid.
30. Pg. 270. Ibid.
31. Pg. 270. Ibid.
32. Pg. 273. Keegan, John (A History of Warfare)
33. Pg. 148. Mackay, Christopher.
34. Pg. 148-149. Ibid.
35. Pg. 150. Ibid.
36. Pg. 260. Holland, Tom.
37. Pg. 220-221. Goodman & Soni.
38. P. 53-54. Hart, Liddell B.
39. Pg. 309. Holland, Tom.
40. Pg. 576. Plutarch (Lives II)
41. Pg. 610. Ibid.
42. Pg. 584-585. Ibid.
43. Pg. 178. Shakespeare (Julius Caesar, III. II)
44. Pg. 345. Holland, Tom.
45. Pg. 591. Plutarch (Lives II)
46. Pg. 590. Ibid.
47. Appian. (Roman Civil Wars. Book IV. 108)
48. Pg. 601. Ibid.
49. Pg. 604. Ibid.
50. Pg. 604-605. Ibid.
51. Pg. 605-606. Ibid.
52. Appian. (Roman Civil Wars. Book IV, 124)
53. Pg. 608. Ibid.
54. Pg. 164. Mackay, Christopher.
55. Pg. 166-167. Ibid. & Pg. 358. Holland, Tom.
56. Pg. 363. Holland, Tom.
57. Pg. 602. Plutarch (Lives II)

Magna Carta

1. Pg. 242. Churchill, Winston S. (The Birth of Britain)
2. Pg. 6, 44 & 47. Vincent, Nicholas.
3. Pg. 22. Ibid.
4. Pg. 56-57. Ibid.

5. Pg. 57. Ibid.
6. Pg. 44. Alderman, Clifford Lindsey.
7. Pg. 57. Vincent, Nicholas.
Pg. 107. Alderman, Clifford Lindsey.
8. Pg. 252. Churchill, Winston S. (Birth of Britain)
9. Pg. 257. Ibid.
10. Pg. 75. Vincent, Nicholas.
11. Pg. 257. Churchill, Winston S. (Birth of Britain)

William Wallace

1. Pg. 41. Murison, A.F.
Pg. 13. Mackay, James.
2. Pg. 36. Mackay, James. (William was a squire to his father)
3. Pg. 60. Ibid.
4. Pg. 28. Goring, Rosemary.
5. Pg. 1. Fisher, Andrew.
6. Pg. 25. Murison, A.F.
7. Pg. 79. Mackay, James.
8. Pg. 119-120. Mackay.
9. Pg. 57, 73. Murison, A.F.
10. Pg. 138. Mackay, James.
11. Pg. 147. Ibid.
12. Pg. 147-148. Ibid.
13. Pg. 105-106. Fisher, Andrew.
14. Pg. 18. Ross, David R.
15. Pg. 157. Mackay, James.
16. Pg. 169. Ibid.
17. Pg. 158. Ibid.
18. Pg. 363. Keay & Keay. (Says Scots were half the number of English, but gives no number).
Pg. 103. Murison, A.F. (contemporary & post contemporary English chroniclers give the number of the Scots at three hundred thousand)
Pg. 138, 150. Fisher, Andrew. (Schiltrons would likely not have exceeded two thousand men. Puts number at twenty-six thousand infantry, sourced from Pg. 117. Prestwich, Armies and Warfare.)
19. Pg. 101-102. Murison, A.F. & Pg. 189. Mackay, James.
20. Pg. 363. Keay & Keay.
21. Pg. 151-152. Fisher, Andrew. & Pg. 104. Murison, A.F. (On Welsh contingent's refusal to attack).
22. Pg. 164. Fisher, Andrew.
23. Pg. 105. Murison, A.F.

24. Pg. 105. Ibid.
25. Pg. 965. Keay & Keay.
26. Pg. 965. Ibid.
Pg. 207-208. Mackay, James.
27. Pg. 208. Mackay, James.
28. Pg. 592. Keay & Keay.
Pg. 194. Fisher, Andrew.
29. Pg. 209. Mackay, James (sourced from Ronald McNair-Scott. Robert Bruce, King of Scots. (1982) Pg. 241)
30. Pg. 33-34. Goring, Rosemary.
31. Pg. 185. Keay & Keay.
32. Pg. 815. Ibid.
33. Pg. 815. Ibid.
34. Pg. 9. Houston, Rab.

John Churchill: Duke of Marlborough

1. Pg. Hussey, John (date of birth)
Pg. 39. Holmes, Richard (names of parents)
2. Pg. 46. Holmes, Richard.
3. Pg. 48 Ibid.
4. Pg. 22. Hussey, John (regarding the commission)
Pg. 91. Spencer, Charles (regarding the conversation) (British Military Greats)
5. Pg. 22. Hussey, John.
6. Pg. 23. Ibid.
7. Pg. 23. Ibid.
8. Pg. 192-193. Ricker, Saywell, Strong & Vallery.
9. Pg. 44. Holmes, Richard.
10. Pg. 138-140. Holmes, Richard. & Pg. 153. Ricker, Saywell, Strong & Vallery.
11. Pg. 156. Ibid.
12. Pg. 33. Hussey, John.
13. Pg. 27-30. Churchill, Winston S. (The Age of Revolution)
14. Pg. 53. Hussey, John (Queen Anne reassures parliament of her intentions to continue the war)
15. Pg. 25-26. Hussey, John.
16. Pg. 29. Ibid.
17. Pg. 32-33. Ibid.
18. Pg. 36-37. Ibid.
19. Pg. 195. Holmes, Richard.
Pg. 41. Churchill, Winston S. (The Age of Revolution)
20. Pg. 55-56. Hussey, John
21. Pg. 91. Ibid.

22. Pg. 99-100. Ibid.
23. Pg. 113. Ibid.
24. Pg. 50. Churchill, Winston S. (The Age of Revolution)
25. Pg. 50. Ibid.
26. Pg. 50. Ibid.
27. Pg. 135. Hussey, John.
28. Pg. 135-137. Ibid.
29. Pg. 140-141. Ibid.
30. Pg. 93-94. Hussey, John (on intelligence funds being used to pay cartographers to make maps)
Pg. 128. Ibid (regarding infiltration of enemies headquarters)
Pg. 143. Ibid (regarding reconnoitering from the hilltop)
31. Pg. 143. Ibid.
32. Pg. 100. Hart, Liddell B.
33. Pg. 152. Hussey, John.
34. Pg. 52. Churchill, Winston S. (The Age of Revolutions)
35. Pg. 53. Ibid.
36. Pg. 157. Hussey, John.
37. Pg. 155. Ibid.
38. Pg. 157. Ibid.
39. Pg. 233. Holmes, Richard.
40. Pg. 57. Hussey, John.
41. Pg. 53. Churchill, Winston S. (The Age of Revolutions)
42. Pg. 333. Holmes, Richard.
43. Pg. 58. Churchill, Winston S. (The Age of Revolution)
44. Pg. 340. Holmes, Richard.
45. Pg. 60. Churchill, Winston S. (The Age of Revolution)
46. Pg. 169. Hussey, John (regarding Godolphin)
Pg. 165. Ibid (regarding Sarah)
47. Pg. 166-167. Ibid.
48. Pg. 167-168. Ibid.
49. Pg. 177. Ibid.
50. Pg. 181. Ibid. (see map)
51. Pg. 200. Ibid.
52. Pg. 88-89. Churchill, Winston S. (The Age of Revolution)
53. Pg. 90. Ibid.
54. Pg. 211. Hussey, John.
55. Pg. 90. Churchill, Winston S. (The Age of Revolution)
56. Pg. 216-217. Hussey, John.
57. Pg. 90. Churchill, Winston S. (The Age of Revolution)
58. Pg. 90-91. Ibid.
59. Pg. 91. Ibid.

60. Pg. 94. Spencer, Charles. (British Military Greats)

George Washington

1. Pg. 6-7. Chernow, Ron.
2. Pg. 26. Ibid.
3. Pg. 14. Ibid.
4. Pg. 22. Ibid.
5. Pg. 26. Ibid.
6. Pg. 27. Ibid.
7. Pg. 153. Churchill, Winston S. (regarding the massacre in New England) (The Age of Revolution)
Pg. 153. Boot, Max. (regarding Indians aptitude for Guerilla warfare)
Pg. 133-134. Ibid. (regarding massacre in Virginia)
Pg. 42-43. Chernow, Ron (regarding Indians attacking prisoners)
8. Pg. 151-152. Ibid.
9. Pg. 31-32. Chernow, Ron.
10. Pg. 36-37. Ibid.
11. Pg. 38. Ibid.
12. Pg. 48. Chernow, Ron (During the parley after the Battle of Fort Necessity, the French commander stated the assault had been in retaliation for the 'assassination of Jumonville.)
13. Pg. 45. Ibid. (Sir. Horace Walpole would exclaim 'the volley fired by a young Virginian in the backwoods of America set the world on fire.)
14. Pg. 194. Ricker, Saywell, Strong & Vallery.
15. Pg. 14 Boyer, Paul S.
16. Pg. 89-90. Hine, Robert V. & John Mack Faracher.
17. Pg. 16. Boyer, Paul S.
Pg. 201 Ricker, Saywell, Strong & Vallery.
18. Pg. 144. Chernow, Ron.
19. Pg. 16. Boyer, Paul S.
20. Pg. 16. Ibid.
21. Pg. 16. Ibid.
22. Pg. 18. Ibid.
23. Pg. 18. Ibid.
24. Pg. 302. Middlekauff, Robert.
25. Pg. 309. Ibid.
26. Pg. 314. Ibid.
27. Pg. 224. Chernow, Ron.
28. Pg. 225. Ibid.
29. Pg. 229. Ibid.
30. Pg. 189-190. Churchill, Winston S. (The Age of Revolution)

31. Pg. 367. Middlekauff, Robert.
32. Pg. 367. Ibid.
33. Pg. 369. Ibid.
34. Pg. 369. Ibid.
35. Pg. 391. Ibid.
36. Pg. 302. Chernow, Ron.
37. Pg. 304. Ibid.
38. Pg. 21. Fleming, Thomas.
39. Pg. 419. Middlekauff, Robert.
40. Pg. 316-317. Chernow, Ron.
41. Pg. 422. Middlekauff, Robert.
42. Pg. 423-424. Ibid.
43. Pg. 339-340. Chernow, Ron.
44. Pg. 342. Ibid.
45. Pg. 7. Esposito, Colonel Vincent J. (Map 7)
46. Pg. 371. Chernow, Ron.
47. Pg. 462-463. Middlekauff, Robert.
48. Pg. 72. Boot, Max.
49. Pg. 72. Ibid.
50. Pg. 580-581. Middlekauff, Robert.
51. Pg. 583. Ibid.
52. Pg. 590. Ibid.
53. Pg. 590. Ibid.
54. Pg. 591-592. Ibid. (regarding ties to Spain and France)
Pg. 593-594. Ibid. (regarding US-UK bilateral treaty)
55. Pg. 240-241. Churchill, Winston S. (The Age of Revolution)
56. Pg. 433-435. Chernow, Ron.

Arthur Wellesley: Duke of Wellington

1. Pg. 16. Longford, Elizabeth.
2. Pg. 32. Glover, Michael.
3. Pg. 25. Longford, Elizabeth.
4. Pg. 27. Ibid.
5. Pg. 16. Kafker & Laux.
Pg. 303. Schama, Simon. (The Dauphin had died on June 4th so it is plausible that the family was still in morning in mid to late June)
6. Pg. 275. Churchill, Winston S. (The Age of Revolution)
7. Pg. 278-282. Ibid.
8. Pg. 282-283. Ibid.
9. Pg. 124. Paret, Peter.
10. Pg. 112. Spencer, Robert.

11. Pg. 170. Padfield, Peter.
12. Pg. 109. Spencer, Robert.
13. Pg. 505. Webster, Wesley & Daniher.
14. Pg. 29. Longford, Elizabeth.
15. Pg. 35. Glover, Michael.
16. Pg. 37. Longford, Elizabeth.
17. Pg. 39. Ibid.
18. Pg. 36. Glover, Michael.
19. Pg. 37. Ibid.
20. Pg. 38. Ibid.
21. Pg. 60. Longford, Elizabeth.
22. Pg. 60. Ibid.
23. Pg. 60. Ibid.
24. Pg. 41. Glover, Michael.
25. Pg. 41-42. Ibid.
26. Pg. 130-131. Bryant.
27. Pg. 80-81. Longford, Elizabeth.
28. Pg. 51. Glover, Michael.
29. Pg. 315. Churchill, Winston S. (The Age of Revolution)
30. Pg. 91. Longford, Elizabeth.
31. Pg. 95. Ibid.
32. Pg. 62. Glover, Michael.
33. Pg. 63. Ibid.
34. Pg. 64. Ibid.
35. Pg. 326-327. Churchill, Winston S. (The Age of Revolution)
36. Pg. Arnold, James R. "A Reappraisal of Column Versus Line in the Peninsula War" (View wiki. 'Column Formation')
37. Ibid.
38. Pg. 134. Longford, Elizabeth.
39. Pg. 133. Hart, Liddell B.
40. Pg. 171. Longford.
41. Pg. 134. Hart, Liddell B.
42. Pg. 95. Glover.
43. Pg. 87. Boot, Max.
44. Pg. 135. Hart, Liddell B.
45. Pg. 335. Churchill, Winston S. (The Age of Revolution)
46. Pg. 337. Ibid.
47. Pg. 337. Ibid.
48. Pg. 107. Glover, Michael (regarding the number of British in arms)
Pg. 108. Ibid. (regarding the Iberian contingents)
49. Pg. 111. Ibid.
50. Pg. 219. Longford, Elizabeth.

51. Pg. 139. Hart, Liddell B.
52. Pg. 114. Glover, Michael.
53. Pg. 231. Longford, Elizabeth.
54. Pg. 254-255. Ibid.
55. Pg. 371. Ibid.
56. Pg. 371. Ibid.
57. Pg. 274. Longford, Elizabeth.
58. Pg. 123. Keegan, John (Face of Battle)
59. Pg. 189-190. Glover, Michael.
60. Pg. 189. Ibid.
61. Pg. 126. Keegan, John (Face of Battle) (11am)
Pg. 309. Longford, Elizabeth (11.25am)
Pg. 377. Churchill, Winston S. (The Age of Revolution) ('late in the afternoon')
62. Pg. 313-314. Longford, Elizabeth.
63. Pg. 126. Keegan, John (Face of Battle)
64. Pg. 320. Longford, Elizabeth.
65. Pg. 326. Ibid.
66. Pg. 127. Keegan, John (Face of Battle)
67. Pg. 382. Churchill, Winston S. (Age of Revolution) 'six years of life in exile lay before him.'
Pg. 364. Longford, Elizabeth.
68. Pg. 181. Wellesley, Jane (British Military Greats)

Robert E. Lee

1. Pg. 12. Blount Jr, Roy.
2. Pg. 19. Ibid.
3. Pg. 18. Lattimore, Ralston B.
4. Pg. 64. Blount Jr, Roy.
5. Pg. 98. Simkins, Francis Butler.
6. Pg. 219. Hine, Robert V. & John Mack Faragher.
7. Pg. 205. Simkins, Francis Butler.
8. Pg. 206-207. Ibid.
9. Pg. 7. Stephenson, Nathaniel W.
10. Pg. 11. Ibid.
11. Pg. 10. Ibid.
12. Pg. 215. Simkins, Francis Butler.
13. Pg. 217. Ibid.
14. Pg. 75. Blount Jr, Roy.
15. Pg. 13. Davis, Burke.
16. Pg. 22. Lattimore, Ralston B.
17. Pg. 19. Ibid.

18. Pg. 34. Lattimore, Ralston B.
19. Pg. 144. Freeman, Douglas S.
20. Pg. 44. Esposito, Colonel Vincent J.
21. Pg. 282. Freeman, Douglas S.
22. Pg. 282. Ibid.
23. Pg. 58. Esposito, Colonel Vincent J.
24. Pg. 60. Ibid.
25. Pg. 62. Ibid.
26. Pg. 62. Ibid.
27. Pg. 62. Ibid.
28. Pg. 63. Ibid.
29. Pg. 63. Ibid.
30. Pg. 64. Ibid.
31. Pg. 64. Ibid. (see map)
32. Pg. 107. McPherson, James M.
33. Pg. 67. Esposito, Colonel Vincent J.
34. Pg. 67. Ibid.
35. Pg. 69. Ibid.
36. Pg. 69. Ibid.
37. Pg. 111. Canton, Bruce.
38. Pg. 399. Freeman, Douglas S.
39. Pg. 72. Esposito, Colonel Vincent J. (see map)
40. Pg. 72. Ibid.
41. Pg. 72. Ibid. (see map)
42. Pg. 73. Ibid.
43. Pg. 180. Davis, Burke.
44. Pg. 84. Esposito, Colonel Vincent J. (see map)
45. Pg. 472. Freeman, Douglas S.
46. Pg. 475. Ibid.
47. Pg. 86. Esposito, Colonel Vincent J.
48. Pg. 450. Henderson, Lieutenant Colonel G.F.R.
49. Pg. 87. Esposito, Colonel Vincent J. (Map)
50. Pg. 89. Esposito, Colonel Vincent J. (Map)
51. Pg. 221. Davis, Burke.
52. Pg. 220. Ibid.
53. Pg. 221. Ibid.
54. Pg. 155. Carhart, Tom.
55. Pg. 155. Ibid.
56. Pg. 159. Ibid.
57. Pg. 98. Esposito, Colonel Vincent J.
58. Pg. 265. Carhart, Tom.
59. Pg. 215. Fremantle, Lieutenant Colonel James

60. Pg. 257-258. Davis, Burke.
61. Pg. 244. Walsh, George.
62. Pg. 164. Davis, William C.
63. Pg. 221. Simkins, Francis B.
64. Pg. 251. Churchill, Winston S. (The Great Democracies)
65. Pg. 100-101. Hanson, Victor Davis. (The Savior Generals)
66. Pg. 768. Freeman, Douglas S.
67. Pg. 763. Ibid.
68. Pg. Lattimore, Ralston B.
69. Pg. 85. Hanna, Jennifer. (Wikipedia source for 'Arlington House')

The Modern Age

1. Pg. 82. Kissinger. (Diplomacy)
2. Pg. 162. Spencer, Robert. (GB & France guarantee Belgian neutrality)
3. Pg. 29. Eisenhower. (on the need of airpower for victory)
4. Pg. 253-254. Cambridge Medieval History VII. Decline of Empire & Papacy
5. Pg. 40. Spencer, Robert.
6. Pg. 192-193. Ricker, Saywell, Strong & Vallery.
7. Pg. 830. McKay, Hill & Buckler.
8. Pg. 81-83. Medlicott, W.N.
9. Pg. 832. McKay, Hill & Buckler.
10. Pg. 832. Ibid.
11. Pg. 239. Pakenham, Thomas.
12. Pg. 158-159 & 161. MacMillan, Margaret. (alliance formalized in 1894)
13. Pg. 141. Ibid.
14. Pg. 891. McKay, Hill & Buckler
15. Pg. 893. Ibid.
16. Pg. 128, 181-182. Gilbert, Felix & David Clay Large.
17. Pg. 899. McKay, Hill & Buckley.
18. Pg. 896-897. Ibid.
19. Pg. 899. Ibid.
20. Pg. 72. Dulles, Allen.
21. Pg. 305. Montgomery of Alamein.

Dwight D. Eisenhower

1. Pg. 3. Smith, Jean Edward.
2. Pg. 37. Ambrose, Stephen
3. Pg. 18. Smith, Edward Jean.
4. Pg. 27. Ibid.
5. Pg. 59. Ibid.

6. Pg. 42. Ibid.
7. Pg. 69. Ambrose, Stephen. (1983)
8. Pg. 72-73. Smith, Jean Edward.
9. Pg. 11. Eisenhower, Dwight D.
10. Pg. 157. Gilbert, Felix & David Clay Large.
11. Merriam-Webster dictionary online.
12. Pg. 960-961. McKay, Hill & Buckler.
13. Pg. 964. Ibid.
14. Pg. 159. Passant, E.J., W.O. Henderson, C.J. Child & D.C. Watt.
15. Pg. 970. McKay, Hill & Buckler.
16. Pg. 247. Gilbert, Felix & David Clay Large.
17. Pg. 200-201. Passant, E.J.
18. Pg. 314. Kissinger, Henry. (Diplomacy)
19. Pg. 316. Ibid.
20. Pg. 204. Passant, E.J.
21. Pg. 49. Beevor, Antony.
22. Pg. 232-233. Hart, Liddell B.
23. Pg. 80-81. Keegan, John. (The Second World War)
24. Pg. 137. Beevor, Antony.
25. Pg. 319. Gilbert, Felix & David Clay Large.
26. Pg. 219-220. Beevor, Antony.
27. Pg. 248. Ibid.
28. Pg. Pg. 315. Churchill, Winston S. (The Hinge of Fate) (Memorandum from FDR to Churchill carried by Harry Hopkins and General Marshall) (Invasion impractical until at least April 1st)
Pg. 325. Ibid. (regarding final plan approved and supported)
29. Pg. 41-42. Ricks, Thomas E.
30. Pg. 199. Smith, Jean Edward.
31. Pg. 53-58. Ricks, Thomas E.
32. Pg. 156. Eisenhower, Dwight D.
Pg. 343. Keegan, John (Second World War).
33. Pg. 160. Eisenhower, Dwight D.
34. Pg. 495. Beevor, Antony.
35. Pg. 499. Ibid.
36. Pg. 349-351. Keegan, John. (Second World War)
37. Pg. 353. Ibid.
38. Pg. 68-69. Ricks, Thomas E.
39. Pg. 353, 358. Keegan, John (Second World War)
40. Pg. 220. Eisenhower, Dwight D.
41. Pg. 79. Ibid. (same conditions applied to the Torch landings)
42. Pg. 198-199. Ibid.
43. Pg. 376. Keegan, John. (Second World War)

44. Pg. 377. Ibid.
45. Pg. 258. Eisenhower, David D.
46. Pg. 280. Ibid.
47. Pg. 612. Beevor, Antony.
48. Pg. 410. Keegan, John. (Second World War)
49. Pg. 614-615. Beevor, Antony.
50. Pg. 280. Eisenhower, Dwight D. (regarding Brest)
Pg. 398. Ibid. (regarding St. Nazaire & Lorient)
51. Pg. 226. Eisenhower, Dwight D.
52. Pg. 306-307. Ibid.
53. Pg. 131. Ambrose, Stephen E.
54. Pg. 312. Eisenhower, Dwight D.
55. Pg. 438. Keegan, John. (Second World War)
56. Pg. 337-338. Eisenhower, Dwight D.
57. Pg. 338. Ibid.
58. Pg. 654 Beevor, Antony.
59. Pg. 662. Ibid.
60. Pg. 159. Patton, George S. Junior.
61. Pg. 666. Beevor, Antony.
62. Pg. 365. Eisenhower, Dwight D.
63. Pg. 368, 404. Ibid.
64. Pg. 338. Ibid.
65. Pg. 336. Ibid. (see map)
66. Pg. 724 Beevor, Antony.
67. Pg. 387-388. Eisenhower, Dwight D.
68. Pg. 398. Ibid.
69. Pg. 398. Ibid.
70. Pg. 397-398. Ibid.
71. Pg. 406. Ibid.
72. Pg. 408-409. Ibid.
73. Pg. 410. Eisenhower, Dwight D.
74. Pg. 532. Keegan, John. (Second World War)
75. Pg. 759. Beevor, John.
76. Pg. 444-445. Eisenhower.
77. Pg. 445-446. Ibid.
78. Pg. 688. Rhodes, Richard.
79. Pg. 485. Smith, Jean Edward. (regarding chairmanship of the JCS)
Pg. 493. Ibid. (regarding NATO command)
80. Pg. 444. Eisenhower, Dwight D.
81. Pg. 526. Smith, Jean Edward.
82. Pg. 723. Ibid.
83. Pg. 560. Ibid.

84. Pg. 654. Ibid.
85. Pg. 652-653. Ibid.
86. Pg. 120. Lind, Michael.
87. Pg. 765. Smith, Jean Edward.
88. "1969 Year in Review: Eisenhower, Judy Garland die" www.upi.com/archives

Ariel 'Arik' Sharon

1. Pg. 4. Landau, David.
2. Honig, Sarah (Feb 15, 2001) "Another Tack: Yoni & the Scheinermans." (The Jerusalem Post)
3. Pg. 7. Landau, David.
4. Pg. 6-7. Owen, Roger.
5. Pg. 914. McKay, Hill & Buckler.
6. Pg. 267-274. Bright, John. (A History of Israel)
7. Pg. 361-362. Ibid.
8. Pg. 4. Boot, Max.
9. Pg. 124-125. Gilbert, Martin. (Israel: A History)
10. Pg. 149. Ibid.
11. Pg. 153. Ibid.
12. Pg. 32. Bregman, Ahron. (regarding percentage of Mandate territory given to the Jews)
Pg. 36. Gilbert, Martin. (Atlas)
Pg. 149. Gilbert, Martin. (Israel). (500,000 Jews to 1.3 million Arabs)
13. Pg. 159. Ibid.
14. Pg. 78. Crevald, Martin Van.
15. Pg. 205. Morris, Benny.
Pg. 398. Ibid.
16. Pg. 14. Landau, David.
17. Pg. 269-271. Morris, Benny.
18. Pg. 22. Freedland, Jonathan. Ariel Sharon's Final Mission Might Well Have Been Peace. (Friday 3, 2014). The Guardian.
19. Pg. 33. Bregman, Ahron.
20. Pg. 32. Ibid.
21. Pg. 173. Dayan, Moshe.
22. Pg. 26. Landau, David.
23. Pg. 57-58. Bregman, Ahrin.
24. Pg. 148. Dupuy, Trevor N.
25. Pg. 148. Ibid.
26. Pg. 170. Ibid.
27. Pg. 171. Ibid.

28. Pg. 171-172. Ibid.
29. Pg. 174. Ibid.
30. Pg. 243. Dayan, Moshe.
31. Pg. 217. Dupuy, Trevor N.
32. Pg. 217-218. Ibid.
33. Pg. 50. Landau, David.
34. Pg. 51. Ibid.
35. Pg. 52-53. Ibid.
36. Pg. 53. Ibid.
37. Pg. 55. Ibid.
38. Pg. 41. Barker, A.J.
Pg. 225. Dupuy, Trevor N.
39. Pg. 227. Dupuy, Trevor N.
40. Pg. 70-71. Bregman, Ahron.
41. Pg. 84. Ibid.
42. Pg. 84-85. Ibid.
43. Pg. 257-58. Dupuy, Trevor N.
44. Pg. 289. Ibid.
45. Pg. 261. Ibid.
46. Pg. 261. Ibid.
47. Pg. 264. Ibid.
48. Pg. 275. Ibid.
49. Pg. 52. Barker, A.J.
50. Pg. 303-304. Dupuy, Trevor N.
51. Pg. 94. Bregman, Ahron (see map)
52. Pg. 373, 380. Dayan, Moshe.
53. Pg. 325-326. Dupuy, Trevor N.
54. Pg. 70. Landau, David.
55. Pg. 98. Bregman, Ahron.
56. Pg. 74-75. Landau, David.
57. Pg. 75. Ibid.
58. Pg. 76-77. Ibid.
59. Pg. 77. Ibid.
60. Pg. 119-120. Bregman, Ahron.
61. Pg. 115. Barker, A.J.
62. Pg. 124. Bregman, Ahron.
63. Pg. 124-125. Ibid.
64. Pg. 427. Gilbert, Martin. (Israel: A History)
65. Pg. 113-114. Bergman, Ahron.
66. Pg. 403. Dupuy, Trevor N.
67. Pg. 128. Bregman, Ahron.
Pg. 444. Dupuy, Trevor N.

68. Pg. 470. Dupuy, Trevor N.
69. Pg. 485-486. Ibid.
70. Pg. 118-119. Landau, David.
71. Pg. 393. Rabinovich, Abraham.
72. Pg. 118. Pollack, Kenneth.
73. Pg. 118-120. Ibid. (regarding Magen's crossing)
74. Pg. 454. Gilbert, Martin.
75. Pg. 739. Kissinger, Henry.
76. Pg. 139. Landau, David.
77. Pg. 141. Ibid.
78. Pg. 170. Ibid.
79. Pg. 509. Gilbert, Martin.
80. Pg. 210. Landau, David.
81. Pg. 621. Gilbert, Martin.
82. Pg. 622-623. Ibid.
83. Pg. 632, 635. Ibid.
84. Pg. 524. Landau, David.

Epilogue

1. Pg. 94. Judt, Tony.
2. Pg. 91-92. Ibid.
3. Pg. 225. Gaddis, John Lewis. (regarding increased US military spending)
4. Books.sipri.org/product_info?c_product_id=476 (April 2014) SIPRI (Stockholm International Peace Research Institute)
5. Pg. 47. Burke, Jason.
6. Georgewbush_whitehouse.archives.gov/infocus/iraw/decade/sect2.htm
7. Pg. 540. Boot, Max.
8. Pg. 243. Kaplan, Fred.
9. Pg. 25-26. Hanson, Victor Davis. (2009) Encounter Broadside no. 5
10. Cnn.com/2011/politics/06/22/Afghanistan.troops.drawdown/
11. Cbsnews.com/news/biden-we-are-better-off-bin-laden-is-dead-and-general-motors-is-alive/
12. Pg. Tasch, Barbara (May 29, 2014) time.com/135520/Russia-kazakhstan-belarus-treaty/

Bibliography

Books

Abbott, Frank F. A History and Description of Roman Political Institutions. (1901) Ginn & Company. Cambridge.
Alderman, Clifford Lindsey. That Men Shall be Free: The Story of the Magna Carta. (1962) Julian Messner, Inc. New York.
Ambrose, Stephen. Eisenhower: (Volume 1) Soldier, General of the Army, President-Elect (1893-1952). (1983) Simon & Schuster. New York.
Appian. The Civil Wars. (1913) Loeb Classical Library. London.
Barker, A.J. Arab-Israeli Wars. (1980) Hippocrene Books, Inc. New York.
Beck, Hans. Central Greece and the Politics of Power in the Fourth Century BC. (2008) Cambridge University Press. Cambridge.
Beevor, Antony. The Second World War. (2003) Back Bay Books. New York.
Blount, Roy Jr. Robert E Lee. (2003) Penguin. New York.
Boot, Max. Invisible Armies. (2013) Liveright Publishing Corporation. New York.
Boyer, Paul S. American History. A Very Short Introduction. (2012) Oxford University Press. Oxford.
Bregman, Ahron. Israel's Wars. A History Since 1947. (2010) Routledge, London.
Bright, John. A History of Israel. (Second Edition). (1974) The Westminster Press. Philadelphia.
Bryant, Arthur. Nelson. (1970) Collins. London.
Burke, Jason. The 9/11 Wars. (2011) Penguin Books. New York.
Caesar, Julius. The Conquest of Gaul. (1982) Penguin Books. London.
Canton, Bruce. The Civil War. (2004) Houghton Mifflin Company. New York.
Carhart, Tom. Lost Triumph. (2005) G.P. Putnam's Sons. New York.
Chernow, Ron. Washington. (2010) The Penguin Press. New York.
Churchill, Winston S. A History of the English Speaking Peoples: The Age of Revolution. (1957) Dodd, Mead & Company. New York.
Churchill, Winston S. A History of the English Speaking Peoples: The Birth of Britain. (1956) McClelland & Steward Limited. Toronto.
Churchill, Winston S. The Hinge of Fate. (1950) Houghton Mifflin

Company. Cambridge.
Crevald, Martin Van. Sword and the Olive: A Critical History of the Israeli Defense Force. (1998) Public Affairs. New York.
Davis, Burke. Gray Fox. (1956) The Fairfax Press. New York.
Dayan, Moshe. Story of my Life. (1976) William Morrow and Company. Inc. New York.
Donnachie, Ian & George Hewitt. The Birlinn Companion to Scottish History. (2007) Birlinn Limited. Edinburgh.
Dulles, Allen. The Craft of Intellegence. (2006) Rowman & Littlefield. Washington DC.
Dupuy, Trevor N. Elusive Victory. The Arab-Israeli Wars. 1947-1974. (1978) Harper & Row, Publishers. New York.
Eisenhower, Dwight D. Crusade in Europe. (1948) Doubleday & Company, Inc. Garden City. New York.
Esposito, Colonel Vincent J, editor. The West Point Atlas of the Civil War. (1962) Frederick A. Praeger. New York.
Fisher, Andrew. William Wallace. (2002) Birlinn Limited. Edinburgh.
Fleming, Thomas. Washington's Secret War. (2005) Harper Collins Publishers. New York.
Freeman, Douglas S. Lee's Lieutenants. (2001) Simon & Schuster. New York.
Freemantle, James. The Freemantle Diary. (1954) Burford Books. New Jersey.
Furnas, J.C. The Americans. A Social History of the United States 1586-1914. (1969) G.P. Putnam & Sons. New York.
Gaddis, John Lewis. The Cold War. A New History. (2007) Penguin Books. New York.
Gilbert, Felix., & David Clay Large. The End of the European Era. 1890 to Present (Fifth Edition). W.W. Norton & Company. New York.
Gilbert, Martin. Israeli: A History (Revised and Updated Edition). (2008) Harper Perennial. New York.
Gilbert, Martin. The Routledge Atlas of the Arab-Israeli Conflict (Tenth Edition). (2012). Routledge. New York.
Glover, Michael. Wellington as Military Commander. (1968) Penguin Books. New York.
Goodman, Rob & Jimmy Soni. Rome's Last Citizen. The Life and Legacy of Cato, Mortal Enemy of Caesar. (2012) Thomas Dunne Books. New York.
Goring, Rosemary. (editor) Scotland the Autobiography. (2007) Penguin Books. London.
Hanson, Victor Davis. How the Obama Administration Threatens our National Security. (2009) Encounter Books. New York.
Hanson, Victor Davis (editor). Makers of Ancient Strategy: From the Persian Wars to the Fall of Rome. (2010) Princeton University Press. Princeton.
Hanson, Victor Davis. The Savior Generals: How Five Great Commanders

Saved Wars That Were Lost – From Greece to Iraq. 2013) Bloomsbury Press. New York.

Hart, Liddell B.H. Strategy. (1986) Frederick A. Praeger, Publishers. New York.

Hart, Liddell B.H. Scipio Africanus: Greater than Napoleon (1926) Da Capo Press. Cambridge. Massachusetts.

Henderson, Lieutenant Colonel. G.F.R. Stonewall Jackson and the American Civil War. (1911) Longmans, Green, and Company. New York.

Hine, Robert V. & John Mack Faracher. The American West. A New Interpretive History. (2000) Yale University Press. New Haven.

Hobbes, Thomas. Leviathan. (1994) Hackett Publishing Company. Indianapolis.

Holland, Tom. Rubicon. The Last Years of the Republic. (2003) Anchor Books. New York.

Holmes, Richard. Marlborough. Britain's Greatest General. (2008) Harper Perennial. London.

Houston, Rab. Scotland. A Very Short Introduction. (2008) Oxford University Press. Oxford.

Hussey, John. Marlborough: Hero of Blenheim. (2004) Weidenfeld & Nicolson. London.

Jones, Peter & Keith Sidwell. The World of Rome: An Introduction to Roman Culture. (1997) Cambridge University Press. Cambridge.

Judt, Tony. Post War. A History of Europe Since 1945. (2005) William Morrow. New York.

Kafker, Frank A., & James M. Laux. The French Revolution: Conflicting Interpretations (Second Edition). (1976) Random House. New York.

Kaplan, Fred. The Insurgents. David Petraeus and the Plot to Change the American Way of War. (2013) Simon & Schuster Paperbacks. New York.

Keay, John & Julia Keay. (editors) Collins Encyclopaedia of Scotland. (1994) Harper Collins Publishers. London.

Keegan, John. A History of Warfare. (1994) Vintage Books. New York.

Keegan, John. The Face of Battle. (2004) Pimlico. London.

Keegan, John. The Second World War. (1990) Penguin Books. New York.

Kissinger, Henry. Diplomacy. (1994) Simon & Schuster Paperbacks. New York.

Landau, David. Arik. (2014) Alfred A. Knopf. New York.

Lattimore, Ralston B. Lee. (1964) Colortone Press. Washington, D.C.

Lazenby, J.F. Hannibal's War. (1998) University of Oklahoma Press. Oklahoma City.

Lind, Michael. The American Way of Strategy. (2006) Oxford University Press. Oxford.

Livy, Titus. The War With Hannibal; Books XXI-XXX of the History of Rome from its Foundation. (1972) Penguin Classics. London.

Locke, John. Second Treatise of Government. (1980) Hackett Publishing Company, Inc. Indianapolis.
Longford, Elizabeth. Wellington. (1992) Abacus. London.
Mackay, Christopher. Ancient Rome. A Military and Political History. (2004) Cambridge University Press. Cambridge, United Kingdom.
Mackay, James. William Wallace. Braveheart. (1995) Mainstream Publishing. London.
MacMillan, Margaret. The War that Ender Peace. (2013) Allen Lane. Toronto.
McKay, John P., Bennett D. Hill & John Buckler. A History of Western Society. Volume C. From the Revolutionary Era to the Present. (2006) Houghton Mifflin Company. Boston.
McPherson, James M. Crossroads of Freedom: Antietam. (2002) Oxford University Press. New York.
Middlekauff, Robert. The Glorious Cause. (1982) Oxford University Press. Oxford.
Miles, Richard. Carthage Must Be Destroyed: The Rise and Fall of an Ancient Civilization. (2010) Penguin Books. London.
Montgomery, Viscount. A Concise History of Warfare. (1972) William Collins, Sons & Company, Ltd. London.
Morris, Benny. 1948: The First Arab-Israeli War. (2008) Yale University Press. New Haven.
Morris, Ian & Barry B. Powell (editors). The Greeks (2006) Pearson Prentice Hall. Upper Saddle River, New Jersey.
Murison, A.F. William Wallace. Guardian of Scotland. (2003) Dover Publications, Inc. Mineola, New York.
Owen, Roger. State, Power and Politics in the Making of the Modern Middle East. (3rd Edition). (2006) Routledge. New York.
Padfield, Peter. Maritime Power: and the Struggle for Freedom. Naval Campaigns that Shaped the Modern Worlds 1788-1851. (2003) The Overlook Press. New York.
Pakenham, Thomas. The Scramble for Africa. White Man's Conquest of the Dark Continent from 1876 to 1912. (1991) Perennial. New York.
Paret, Peter (editor). Makers of Modern Strategy. From Machiavelli to the Nuclear Age. (1986) Princeton University Press. Princeton.
Passant, E.J. (W.O. Henderson, C.J. Child & D.C. Watts, contributors). A Short History of Germany 1815-1945. (1971) Cambridge University Press. New York.
Patton, George S. Junior. The War As I Knew It. (1975) Houghton Mifflin Company. Boston.
Plutarch. Plutarch's Lives; Volume II. (2001) The Modern Library. New York.
Pollack, Kenneth. Arabs at War: Military Effectiveness, 1948-1991. (2002) University of Nebraska Press. Lincoln, Nebraska.
Polybius. The Histories. (1922) Loeb Classical Library. London.

Biblography

Pomeroy, Sarah B., Stanley M. Burstein, Walter Donlam & Jennifer Tolbert Roberts (editors). Ancient Greece: A Political, Social and Cultural History. Second Edition. (2008) Oxford University Press, Inc. New York.
Prestwich, Michael. Armies and Warfare in the Middle Ages. (1996) Yale University Press. New Haven.
Rabinovich, Abraham. The Yom Kippur War: The Epic Encounter that Transformed the Middle East. (2005) Schocken Books. New York.
Ricker, John C., John T. Saywell, A. Earle Strong & Hugh J. Vallery. The British Epic. (1959) Clarke, Irwin & Company Limited. Toronto.
Ricks, Thomas E. The Generals. American Military Command from World War II to Today. (2012) Penguin Books. New York.
Rhodes, Richard. The Making of the Atomic Bomb. (1986). Simon & Schuster. New York.
Ross, David R. On the Trail of Robert the Bruce. (2000) Bell & Bain, Ltd. Glasgow.
Schama, Simon. Citizens: A Chronicle of the French Revolution. (2004) Penguin Books. New York.
Simkins, Francis Butler. A History of the South. (1963) Alfred A. Knopf. New York
Shakespeare, William. Julius Caesar. (2008) Oxford University Press. Oxford.
Smith, Jean Edward. Eisenhower. In War and Peace. (2012) Random House, Inc. New York.
Spencer, Charles. The Duke of Marlborough (British Military Greats). (2005) Cassell Illustrated. London.
Spencer, Robert. The West and the Wider World. (1966) Clarke, Irwin & Company Limited. Toronto.
Strassler, Robert B. (editor). The Landmark Herodotus: The Histories. (2007) Anchor Books. New York.
Strassler, Robert B. (editor). The Landmark Thucydides: A Comprehensive Guide to the Peloponnesian War. (1996) Free Press. New York.
Stephenson, Nathaniel W. The Day of the Confederacy. (1919) Yale University Press. New Haven.
Suetonius. The Twelve Caesars. (1979) Penguin Books. New York.
Vincent, Nicholas. Magna Carta: A Very Short Introduction. (2012) Oxford University Press. New York.
Walsh, George. Whip the Rebellion. Ulysses S. Grant's Rise to Command. (2005) A Forge Book. New York.
Webster, Wesley & Daniher. World Civilization. (1944) The Copp Clark Co. Limited. Toronto.
Wellesley, Jane. The Duke of Wellington (British Military Greats). (2005) Cassell Illustrated. London.
Xenophon. Anabasis; Books IV-VII, Symposium and Apology. The Loeb Classical Library. London.

Xenophon. Hellenica; Books V-VII, Anabasis; Books I-III. The Loeb Classical Library. London

Magazines

Taylor, Michael. The March of the Ten Thousand. Ancient Warfare. Volume VII, Issue 5. (2014) Karwansaray Publishers. Rotterdam.

Internet

Akinde, Michael. Scipio Africanus. (2006). www.akinde.dk/history/index.php?title=publius_cornelius_scipio_africanus (last visited 2014-10-30)

Arnold, James R. A Reappraisal of Column Versus Line in the Peninsular War. (2004) www.napoleon-series.org/military/organization/maida/c_maida.html (last visited 2014-10-30)

Freedland, Jonathan. Ariel Sharon's Final Mission Might Well Have Been Peace. (Friday 3, 2014). The Guardian. www.theguardian.com/commentisfree/2014/jan/03/ariel-sharon-final-mission-peace-israel (last visited 2014-10-30)

Hanna, Jennifer. Arlington House: The Robert E. Lee Memorial Cultural Landscape Reoirt, Volume 1. (2001)www.nps.gov/parkhistory/online_books/arho/clr.pdf (last visited 2014-10-30)

Livy, Titus. From the Founding of the City: Books I-XLVI.en.wikisource.org/wiki/From_the_Founding_of_the_City (last visited 2014-10-30)

Nepos, Cornelius. Lives of Eminent Commanders. www.tertullian.org/fathers/nepos.htm (last visited 2014-10-30)

Polybius. Lives. Volume II. http://www.gutenberg.org/files/14114/14114-h/14114-h.htm (last visited 2014-10-30)

Tasch, Barbara. Russia, Kazakhstan, Belarus Sign Treaty Creating Huge Economic Bloc. (2014). Time. www.time.com/135520/russia-kazakhstan-belarus-treaty/ (last visited 2014-10-30)

www.cnn.com/2011/POLITICS/06/22/afghanistan.troops.drawdown (last visited 2014-10-30)

www.cbs.com/news/biden-we-are-better-off-bin-laden-is-dead-and-general-motors-is-alive/ (last visited 2014-10-30)

www.merriam-webster.com/dictionary/liberty (last visited 2014-10-30)

www.georgewbush_whitehouse.archives.gov/infocus/iraw/decade/sect2.htm (last visited 2014-10-30)

www.upi.com/Archives/Audio/Events-of-1969/Eisenhower-Judy-Garland-Die/ (last visited 2014-10-30)

Index

Index

Index

89956383R00295

Made in the USA
Columbia, SC
05 March 2018